The distribution and redistribution of income

The distribution and redistribution of income

Third Edition

Peter J. Lambert

Manchester University Press

Manchester and New York

Distributed exclusively in the USA by Palgrave

Published by Manchester University Press
Oxford Road, Manchester M13 9NR, UK
and Room 400, 175 Fifth Avenue, New York, NY 10010, USA
www.manchesteruniversitypress.co.uk

Distributed exclusively in the USA by
Palgrave, 175 Fifth Avenue, New York NY 10010, USA

Distributed exclusively in Canada by
UBC Press, University of British Columbia, 2029 West Mall,
Vancouver, BC, Canada V6T 1Z2

British Library Cataloguing-in-Publication Data
A catalogue record for this book is available from the British Library

Library of Congress Cataloging-in-Publication Data
A catalog record for this book is available from the Library of Congress

ISBN 13: 978 0 7190 5732 8

First published 1989 by Manchester University Press
This (third) edition published 2001 by Manchester University Press
First digital paperback edition published 2008

Printed by Lightning Source

For Polly

Contents

Preface to the third edition

Great strides took place in theoretical research on distributional issues during the 1980s and 1990s. By late 1998 it had become obvious to me that a new edition of this book would be needed to take account of the developments that have occurred since 1992 when the second (1993) edition was prepared. For this new edition, I have reorganized material, introduced additional topics (in two entirely new chapters) and expanded upon some issues (by means of new sections in chapters and new exercises). Some material has also been dropped to make way for these innovations.

Expanded treatments are to be found, in particular, on making welfare comparisons between socially heterogeneous populations, both with and without the aid of equivalence scales (in chapter 3), and on inequality decomposition analysis and intermediate inequality (in chapter 5). An entirely new chapter deals with poverty analysis (chapter 6), and another with equity issues surrounding the design and the redistributive effects of an income tax system (chapter 10).

As the effects of the major economic changes in western countries of the 1980s and 1990s are evaluated, and set against the different fortunes of those in the developing world, poverty analysis has become more important and also topical. Poverty comparisons require important choices, on the part of the analyst, about the definition of income, the poverty line and how to aggregate across persons or households. Recent theoretical advances allow a diversity of judgements to be maintained about what the appropriate choices are whilst yielding unambiguous comparisons. Poverty was barely touched upon in the previous edition of the book. The substantial body of work which now exists is explained and assessed in the new chapter 6.

Another big change of the 1980s and 1990s has been the move towards income tax simplification. The high marginal rates of the 1970s have been abandoned, and the gap between comprehensive income and taxable income trimmed. The purpose has been to squeeze horizontal inequity out of the system, at the same time toning down the rate structure which had led in the first place to the selective tax reliefs, mainly for those at the top, which had been perceived as inequitable. There is a young and growing literature which provides measurement theory for the assessment and comparison of income tax equity characteristics. This work is the subject of another new chapter, chapter 10.

In order to make way for these two principal innovations, within a volume of roughly the same extent, I have dropped two chapters. The old chapter 8, on income tax revenue growth, and chapter 11, on the endogeneity of labour supply, were the obvious candidates for the chop. The former topic was all but played out, I felt, as an area for theoretical research by the mid-1980s, and in fact has only a tangential connection with the central theme of the book anyway. I could not add to this material now, and decided to let the 1993 chapter stand down. It can of course still be drawn upon; it forms a reasonably self-contained treatment of the way things stood. The old chapter 11, on endogenous labour supply, was out of character with the rest of the book, I felt, containing no implementable measurement theory and serving, in fact, to guide the reader conceptually *away from* the sort of measurement theory which is expounded in the main body of the book and *towards* the quite different topic of optimal income taxation – about which I had (and still have) very little to say. The book now concludes with the chapter on the net fiscal system, and this seems a natural stopping point. Everything in the second half of the book, that has been constructed for income tax systems (from material presented in the first half of the book), is 'opened out' to cover tax and benefit systems, and more generally the entire government operation, in this final chapter. Big and fundamental issues are raised by this extension; it seems fitting to end the book on such a note.

I am grateful to John Creedy, André Decoster, Yves Duclos, Udo Ebert, Diego Escobar, Björn Gustafsson, Stephen Jenkins, Farhad Nili, Essama Nssah, Guy Van Camp and Gerre Verbist for many comments and suggestions. I hope that some improvements can be detected as a result of their valued inputs. My particular thanks go to Stephen Jenkins for his always generous advice and especially for preparing figures 2.1 and 2.2 for me at a busy time. I also thank Akiko Akemine, Secretary of *The Developing Economies*, for granting permission to reproduce, as figure 6.2, a graph from the article 'The structure of Chinese poverty, 1988' by Björn Gustafsson and Li Shi which appeared in 1998 in volume 36 of *The Developing Economies* (pp. 387–406), and Blackwell Publishers for permitting me to reproduce as figure 5.1 a graph from the article 'Inequality decomposition analysis and the Gini coefficient revisited' by Richie Aronson and me which appeared in 1993 in volume 103 of *The Economic Journal* (pp. 1221–1227). The reshaping and consequent rewriting of large parts of the book were planned during a tumultuous period for me, and the work itself got delayed. In the last year of the twentieth century, everything settled beautifully. It is my great pleasure to add my beloved Polly to my children, Tom and Hugo, as dedicatee of this edition.

Peter J. Lambert
University of York

Preface to the second edition

The research effort into matters of income distribution and redistribution moves forward. There have been advances on many fronts since this book was conceived and written in 1988. Questions which were then open, or even unasked, have since been posed, clarified, and in some cases resolved. Thus, by 1993, it was time to revise *The Distribution and Redistribution of Income*, adding new material to all chapters. At the same time, the need for an affordable paperback edition had become apparent. I am pleased that, thanks to Francis Brooke, Publisher at Manchester University Press, these twin concerns of timely updating and paperbacking for a wider market have now been simultaneously addressed.

This expanded version of the book includes additional citations and relevant results from some fifty sources which were unavailable when I wrote the original. Some unfortunate omissions have also been rectified in revising, the most important of these being my failure to credit Serge Kolm and Johan Fellman for their parts in the developments described in chapters 3–4 and 6 respectively.

Many of the new additions come in chapter end-notes, but there are significant changes in the text as well. Thus in chapter 3, reservations recently expressed about the role of the principle of transfers in the equivalent income context are indicated, and progress with the differences-in-needs dominance approach is also noted. In chapter 5, a welfare rationale due to Muliere and Scarsini for a social evaluation function based on the generalized Gini coefficient is described, and also Mehran's class of linear inequality measures is introduced. The relationship of this class to Pfähler's class of progressivity indices is exposed in chapter 7. The inequality and welfare impacts of differentiated income taxes, barely appreciated in 1988, are discussed in some detail in chapter 6, and a clarification of the distinction between the reranking and horizontal inequity induced by such taxes is given at the end of chapter 7. In chapter 7 of the first edition, a lacuna was noted, to the effect that the impact of pre-tax distributional change on measured progressivity was 'a relatively unexplored area' which 'appears to have received little attention'. This lacuna is now filled in, as a sequence of exercises in the revised chapter 7 demonstrates. In chapter 9, on tax reform, some neat results of Buchholtz *et al.* and Yaari on equal sacrifice taxes are contrasted, and Yitzhaki and Slemrod's dominance test for detecting welfare-improving modifications in the balance of indirect taxes is described. These are the main additions, but there are also many smaller ones throughout.

Serge Kolm has a claim dating back to the middle 1960s to much of the material developed in chapters 3 and 4, including the Atkinson and Shorrocks theorems and even the Atkinson index. I was unaware of this at the time of writing, and have now made the appropriate attributions. Ultimately, however, one has to concede that it was Tony Atkinson who (in 1970) captured the attention of the profession and showed the possibilities for implementation of the new measurement techniques. In the subsequent literature, there has been at best a patchy recognition of Kolm's prior contribution, and I am sorry to have perpetuated this. In defence of the way things have emerged, one could point to Kolm's somewhat opaque terminology and his deductive style which, though penetrating and elegant, is also very condensed and difficult for economists to grasp. Johan Fellman has an irrefutable claim to theorem 6.1, which I described in the first edition as a Jakobsson–Kakwani theorem: his very simple proof of this theorem preceded that of Nanak Kakwani by one year and was even published in the same journal. I offer no excuse for this unfortunate oversight: the theorem is now called the Jakobsson–Fellman theorem.

I thank Ranjan Ray at The Delhi School of Economics, Shlomo Yitzhaki at The Hebrew University and John Creedy at The University of Melbourne for allowing me to subject their students to the first edition of this book, and the students themselves for humouring me. There are many others to whom I am also indebted, including some of my own students at York, for asking questions, suggesting improvements and pointing out typographical errors. Worthy of especial mention are Mr Geneuhc Kim and Ms Magda Mercader, whom I have not met but who assiduously subjected the entire book to close scrutiny and wrote me long letters about it from DELTA in Paris. My longest-standing debt is undoubtedly to my former mathematics teacher, Tom Jackman of Kirkham Grammar School, who laid the foundations some thirty years ago for the way I approach measurement issues. Francis Brooke is responsible for the re-emergence of the book in its new form, as I have said, and I thank him most warmly. I hope to hear in due course from the main beneficiaries, the readers of this edition, about things which could be improved still further.

Peter J. Lambert
University of York

Preface to the first edition

The purpose of this book is to bring together, in a single body, the many strands of formal analysis of income distribution and redistribution which have developed since the beginning of the 1970s. In order to lay down a self-contained and unified treatment, we have to draw on several distinct traditions within economics, principally those of social policy analysis, welfare theory and public finance. This is done by adopting a consistent mathematical approach, and working within a framework of analysis that is both elegant and economical.

The compulsion to write such a book arose from regularly giving a course of lectures on income distribution and redistribution to final-year undergraduate students at the University of York, without the backing of a suitable textbook. The course is attended by economics, econometrics/statistics and mathematics students. The material is well-suited to so mixed an audience: the economic, the mathematical and the statistical elements come together because the main focus is upon measurement.

The book can be used in many ways. For researchers, it will serve as a work of reference, spanning several active areas of endeavour which have not previously been drawn together. Teachers can use the book as a source from which to construct lecture courses. For postgraduate students wishing to specialize in theoretical or applied work in this area, the book will provide an entrée and the necessary formal background. Practitioners will find in it the mathematical underpinnings of measurement techniques that they have grown familiar with. It can also be seen as delineating a topic in applied mathematics.

The book owes much to a careful criticism of the original outline by Stephen Jenkins, whose copious scribbled notes of advice enabled me to give the written product a wider perspective than might have been. Wilhelm Pfähler, with whom I have written articles in this area (and who has himself written, but did not publish, what is known between us as The Bible on these matters), has advised me throughout. He has inflicted perceptive and hard-hitting criticism with good nature and charm, thereby greatly influencing my approach to researching and writing the book. Both Stephen and Wilhelm read the manuscript, and provided critical comments which have led to many improvements. However, they can in no way be held to account for the inadequacies which remain: I lay claim to those; they are of my making.

Massimo Marrelli at the University of Naples, and Essama Nssah at the University of Yaoundé helped the book along by inviting me to their universities to lecture on the material it contains. The time I spent in each place gave me the tranquility (if this can be believed of either city) in which to shape the later chapters, unencumbered by the usual pressures of family and job. Their interest in the material, and that of their students and colleagues, was a great encouragement.

It is a particular pleasure to acknowledge the input that is due to my co-writer of several joint papers, John Hutton. John guided me, successfully I think, from mathematics into economics; his well thought out and roundly considered views added quality to my own mathematical outpourings in those days. John Hey is also due a tiny bouquet for his sustained and enthusiastic advocacy of integration by parts over all the years I have known him. Daron Acemoglu, Valentino Dardanoni, Andreas Pfingsten, Ian Preston and Peter Simmons were generous with discussion and advice. Many others, in addition to some of those those already named, have helped the book along by giving me access to their unpublished work. Finally, I must thank my colleagues at the University of York, and especially Tony Culyer as Head of Department, for the provision of so conducive an atmosphere within which to work.

I dedicate the book to my children, for the happiness they have brought.

Peter J. Lambert
University of York

Notation

$a(x)$	average rate of tax on income x
b	overall average rate of benefit
$b(x)$	benefit received by income unit with income x
CE	cost effectiveness of income tax
C_F	per capita cost of inequality in distribution F
$C_K(p,q)$	Copula for joint distribution K
cov $\{x,y\}$	covariance between variates x and y
$D(F\|Z)$	poverty deficit for distribution F conditional on poverty line Z
e	constant inequality aversion parameter
$E(c)$	entropy measure with parameter c
$e^{Y,Z}$	elasticity of Y with respect to Z
$f(x)$, $g(x)$	frequency density functions for income
$F(x)$, $G(x)$	distribution functions for income
g	total tax ratio (overall average rate of tax)
$GL_F(p)$	generalized Lorenz curve for income distribution F
G_F	Gini coefficient for distribution F
$G_F(v)$	extended Gini coefficient for distribution F
G_F^p	Gini coefficient among poor in distribution F
H	index of horizontal inequity
$H(F\|Z)$	headcount index for distribution F conditional on poverty line Z
$I_F(e)$	Atkinson index for distribution F
$I(F\|Z)$	income gap ratio for distribution F conditional on poverty line Z
$K(x,y)$	joint distribution function for x and y
$L_B(p)$	concentration curve for benefits
$L^*(p)$	Lorenz curve for post-tax income
$L_F(p)$	Lorenz curve for income distribution F
$LP(x)$	liability progression at income x
$L(p)$	Lorenz curve
$L_T(p)$	concentration curve for tax liabilities

$L_{T-B}(p)$	concentration curve for net taxes
$L_X(p)$	Lorenz curve for pre-tax income
$L_{X+B}(p)$	concentration curve for income including benefits
$L_{X-T}(p)$	concentration curve for post-tax income
$L_{X-T+B}(p)$	concentration curve for final income
$m(x)$	marginal rate of tax on income x
M_F	Mehran index for distribution F
N	number of income units or population size
p	rank: as $p = F(y)$, rank of an income unit with income y
p_{iF}	proportion of population in group i in distribution F
$P(F|Z)$	poverty index for distribution F conditional on poverty line Z
Q	number of poor income units
$q_U(x)$	inequality aversion function for utility function $U(x)$
$R_T(q)$	relative concentration curve for taxes
$R_{X-T}(q)$	relative concentration curve for post-tax income
$RP(x)$	residual progression at income x
$RP^*(x)$	modified measure of residual progression: $RP^*(x) = 1/RP(x)$
$R_B(q)$	relative concentration curve for benefits
$R_{X+B}(q)$	relative concentration curve for income including benefits
S	Schutz coefficient
$t(x)$	tax liability of an income unit with income x
$T_{RN}(x)$	revenue-neutral replacement tax
$T_{WN}(x)$	welfare-neutral replacement tax
$TIP_F(p)$	three I's of poverty curve for distribution F
$U(x)$	utility-of-income function
$U_e(x)$	constant inequality aversion utility of income function
$U(x,F)$	utility functional defined over own income and distribution
v	distributional judgement parameter for extended Gini coefficient
$V(\mu,I)$	abbreviated social welfare function
x_1, x_N	lowest and highest incomes in an income distribution
$W; W_F$	welfare; welfare in a distribution F
z	income exceeding highest income in distribution(s) under consideration
$z_1, z_2, \ldots, z_n$	equivalence scale
$Z; \mathbf{Z}$	poverty line; vector of poverty lines
α	poverty aversion parameter in FGT index
$\Gamma_i, \Gamma(x)$	normalized poverty gap
$\theta(x|Z)$	poverty contribution (deprivation) function
ξ_F	equally distributed equivalent (EDE) income for distribution F
$\mu; \mu_F$	mean income; mean income of a distribution F
μ^p_F	mean income among poor in distribution F

Π	progressivity index (for tax schedule, net taxes, tax system)
ρ	regressivity index (for benefits)
σ_F^2	variance of an income distribution F
$>_R$	ordering by Rawlsian leximin, thus: $F >_R G$

1

Introduction and summary

1.1 Introduction

The last thirty years have seen considerable interest shown, both theoretical and empirical, in matters of income distribution and redistribution. How may we evaluate trends in income distribution through time, and differences between countries? Who is poor, and how much poverty does a country have? How far can and should a government go in redistributing money income? What constitutes an 'improvement' in an income tax, or in a tax and benefit system? Put baldly, who gets what, and who should get what?

The economist can provide a structure in which such questions may be made precise. Is the 'what' of 'who gets what' money income? Money income is what we observe and tax, but it is not a very good indicator of well-being. How does this perspective influence the measurement techniques which are appropriate? As for the 'should get', it is clear that not all income differences are inequitable. In particular, to what extent can differences in needs justify inequalities in money income? How should needs be taken into account in a tax and benefit system?

These questions are, of course, very old. They are being addressed analytically at the present time, in new work which takes as its point of departure the body of literature already existing. Thus, the structure within which the new theoretical refinements are being made is largely determined.

This book provides a synthesis of the many strands of distributional analysis that have grown up since the early 1970s. To bring this material together, it is necessary to draw on several different traditions within economics. For example, the description and empirical measurement of income distribution and identification of the poor is typically carried out in the field of social policy analysis. On the other hand, the evaluation of income distribution in terms of social welfare draws upon ethical and positive aspects of welfare economics. By contrast to all of this, questions of income tax progression and fiscal incidence have, largely, been addressed within the public finance literature.

The separate endeavours are thus dominated by different groups of researchers, whose paths do not cross as often as they should. By adopting a consistent mathematical approach, we aim to draw together these separate strands, to provide a coherent and unified treatment. By this, we hope to furnish analysts, and others interested in distribution and redistribution, with a wider perspective, both as a resource for future researches and also to foster communication.

Much of the work in the three areas, distribution, poverty and redistribution, described in this book, can in fact be seen as stemming from three papers, those of Atkinson (1970), Sen (1976) and Jakobsson (1976) respectively.

In his fundamental contribution, 'On the measurement of inequality', Atkinson established a normative basis for the measurement of income inequality. The much-celebrated *Atkinson theorem*, in fact derived some years before by Serge Kolm in a less well-appreciated study (see Kolm, 1969), enables prescriptive significance to be read into certain configurations of (the statistical/descriptive) Lorenz curves. A great deal has been done since, to add to our understanding of how to compare income distributions; and the Atkinson theorem itself has become widely employed.

Sen pioneered the axiomatic approach to the construction of poverty measures, in his 1976 paper 'Poverty: an ordinal approach to measurement'. This paper has been cited by researchers ever since. It suggests a number of possible axioms for the measurement of poverty. Although one particular subset of these yields a unique poverty measure, advocated by Sen, it is not for this particular measure that the paper became so important. Rather, the very fact that axioms were proferred and discussed is what had the profound effect. An industry of effort and revelation followed, some researchers introducing their own favoured axioms in an attempt to pin down a unique poverty measure, and others adopting a different focus, identifying dominance conditions for less poverty according to all indices adhering to the 'core axioms' (those felt to be incontrovertible), and for ranges of possible poverty lines.

Jakobsson's paper, 'On the measurement of the degree of progression', was supplemented by Kakwani's (1977a) independent, and more elegant, treatment of the same topic one year later. Their central results are known in this book as the *Jakobsson/Kakwani theorems*, and they expose the links between progressive income taxation and concentration curve properties of the distributions of tax and of post-tax income. From these has flowed a stream of other work, which has further increased our understanding of how progressive income taxation interacts with income distribution. A catalogue of widely-used indices of income tax progressivity has followed.

The book takes these three contributions to measurement, in the areas of distribution and redistribution, as starting points. It proceeds by a build-up of material, and the drawing in of many technical insights and additional strands of literature by means of interlinked and cross-referenced exercises. It aims to represent the literature as it stood at the end of the 1990s.

The book will serve not only as a work of reference for research economists and practitioners, but also as a text and source book for postgraduate students, lecturers devising courses and applied mathematicians.

1.2   How to use this book

It is intended that the book will be accessible to readers with backgrounds in mathematics/statistics and in economics. With only basic knowledge in one of these two areas, and rather more in the other, whichever it may be, a reader should be able to get the flavour, and much of the detail, of an active and lively area of economic research.

You could have a strong mathematical background and little or no economics. This would suffice to make the formal material in this book accessible. For such readers, the book can be seen as a treatise in applied mathematics. Through it, you can learn something of the wider concerns, in this case ethical, which direct attention when problems of distributional measurement are being addressed. Especially in this area of economics, one may pursue the mathematics to exhaustion, and still not have satisfied the thinking economist.

If you are an economist for whom the language of mathematics is quite natural, you should have little difficulty with the formal analysis in this book. The consistent mathematical approach will serve as a medium without getting in the way.

As an economist reader whose mathematics is more hesitant, you must first of all be pursuaded that a mathematical approach is needed for this book. The language of mathematics is there to give expression to ideas, and to facilitate approaches from which new insights flow; the literatures spanned by this book could not be described in any other way. Nevertheless, you can find a good deal of non-mathematical material here. Your interest will be in the problems of measurement, the statement of results, their qualifications and limitations, and the economic and philosophical concerns which remain unresolved. You will either have to work quite hard at the formal proofs in this book, or take them on trust.

There are many ways to dip into this book profitably, without engaging in a complete reading from one end to the other. Depending on the reader's interest, and on the extent of his or her mathematics, there are several limited forays which can be recommended.

Basic material is presented in chapter 2, and this should not be omitted. Its purpose is to bring readers from the various disciplines and backgrounds to a common point of departure. From there, all readers could comfortably move on to Lorenz curves and generalized Lorenz curves, as in chapter 3.

Consideration of social welfare foundations, as in chapter 4, sections 1 and 2, could follow. If mathematics is not your strong suit, you could scan the rest of chapter 4, on inequality aversion; if you are adept, you could immerse yourself more fully in this material. At this point, you could go one of two ways.

You could pass to indices of inequality and abbreviated social welfare functions, as in chapter 5, and follow this by a study of poverty, as in chapter 6. With more time at your disposal, you could continue with progressive income taxes and progressivity, as in chapters 7 and 8, concluding with net fiscal incidence, as in chapter 11. This would bring you up-to-date in issues of summary measurement, including normative implications.

Alternatively, you could go straight to progressive income taxes, as in chapters 7 and 8, follow this by the social welfare effects of single-crossing and double-crossing income tax reforms, as in chapter 9, sections 2 and 3, and read on, in chapter 10, about the new issues which arise, and techniques which must be adopted, to take non-income heterogeneity (differences in need) into account when analysing the tax system. By this route, you will also have reached a frontier point.

Either of these two approaches could form the basis of a short lecture course, which could be an interdisciplinary one, serving to give students an appreciation of both the fruitfulness and the limitations of what has been achieved in the relevant area. In the seminar programme, mathematics students could be directed to certain of the technical exercises, and economics students to essay-type ones – and occasionally the other way round – and they could present their findings to each other in class discussion.

Because of the emphasis on measurement in this book, for postgraduate students it will provide a ready source of MSc dissertation topics: chapters 3, 6, 8 and 10 are especially suited to empirical implementation. Students who are keen to use data from their own countries, to make comparisons, discern trends and produce policy angles, will find much to explore in this area of economics, and ample scope for bringing to bear their own insights and wider reading.

The practitioner user of this book will find in it, *inter alia*, a compendium of distributive progressivity indices for taxes and for the net fiscal system. These are collected from across the literature, and their foundations and properties can be understood by reading the book, especially chapters 2, 5, 8, 10 and 11.

A few remarks about the exercises are in order. They are there to fulfil a range of different purposes, and should be used accordingly. Some of the technical exercises give additional results, not essential to the main flow and placed so as not to distract. Others invite the reader to derivations which are closely related to ones that have gone before; the results in these exercises may be drawn upon later in the book. The essay-type exercises encourage the reader to consult papers on subsidiary topics, and occasionally to speculate on unresolved matters. A pertinent quotation from an article is frequently used to attract attention; the reader is invited to review or describe the whole argument. These exercises may be pursued if the curious reader wishes. Their main function is as a signal, to inform the user of the book that this-or-that economist has addressed this-or-that topic, in this-or-that journal.

1.3 Chapter summaries

These brief summaries, of the chapters that follow, are to help the intending user to find his/her way through the book.

Chapter 2 The size distribution of income

Chapter 2 is essential reading for all users. It contains 'something for everybody', serving to bring mathematician and economist readers to the same point of departure. By the same token, there are many changes of gear in this chapter. Thus, the discussion ranges from data presentation to mathematical specification; and then back to data again, for consideration of income inequality, and on to the mathematical representation of this (principally, through the Lorenz curve); and finally to a discussion of redistribution through income taxation. In particular, there is a careful discussion of frequency density functions; even the mathematically most accomplished of my own students are sometimes made uncomfortable by being asked to make the leap from familiar probability distribution to unfamiliar income distribution, as one of simple mathematical analogue. As the chapter proceeds, foretastes are given of many issues which will be dealt with in detail in later chapters. Hence this chapter is something of an appetizer.

Chapter 3 Lorenz curves and welfare comparisons

Chapter 3 begins with the Atkinson (1970) theorem, providing welfare approval, in the form of unanimous preference, for the Lorenz-dominating income distribution in comparisons of two income distributions having the same mean. Also given is the generalization by Shorrocks (1983a), which widens considerably the scope of the Atkinson result, enabling normative conclusions to be reached whenever two generalized Lorenz curves do not cross. Both theorems have become standard among researchers. There are complications when (generalized) Lorenz curves do cross, but, as we go on to show, information on variances can sometimes be adduced to provide a (weaker) welfare prescription in such cases. Generalized Lorenz curve analysis is intended for situations in which there are no differences in 'needs' between income units. Finally in this chapter, we report on the recent advances made by Ebert (1997) and Atkinson and Bourguignon (1987), who have shown that generalized Lorenz curves still provide the key to making welfare comparisons when there are systematic differences in need, if these can either be quantified by means of an equivalence scale or simply categorized.

Chapter 4   Social welfare and inequality aversion

In this mathematically more demanding chapter, parts of which could be omitted by non-mathematical readers, we do three things. First, we lay down some alternative rationales for measuring social welfare as the average across an income distribution of a concave utility-of-income function (as assumed in the bulk of the previous chapter). Then, we show how social welfare functions of a similar form, but allowing for differences in need, can arise. Finally, taking the erstwhile average-utility form as given, we develop a measure of inequality aversion with intuitively agreeable properties. In particular, its relationship with the extremely inequality-averse decision criterion for ranking income distributions, Rawlsian leximin, is established formally; and the restriction, in terms of measured inequality aversion, that is needed for unanimous preference results when unequal-mean income distributions have generalized Lorenz curves crossing an odd number of times, pointed out in the previous chapter, is examined.

Chapter 5   Abbreviated social welfare functions and inequality indices

By reducing the arguments of the social welfare function to *per capita* income and an index of inequality, we gain the ability to rank income distributions for which the generalized Lorenz configuration does not permit a robust (unanimous preference) welfare prescription. There are implications for the design of an inequality index, posed by the requirement that it appear as an argument in an abbreviated social welfare function – and others, even more stringent, by the requirement that it be capable of analysing sources of inequality by ranging across population subgroups. The Atkinson (1970) paper gave a lead in the first respect, by proposing an index of inequality whose primary input is a parameter quantifying the degree of inequality aversion assumed of the underlying social welfare function. Penetrating analyses by Bourguignon (1979), Cowell (1980) and Shorrocks (1980) have set the scene for inequality decomposition analysis. The Gini coefficient, much-loved by the practitioners and many theorists, has been extended to incorporate a distributional judgement parameter, rather like Atkinson's, by Yitzhaki (1983), and its decomposition properties have finally been understood. The Atkinson and extended Gini indices, very different in origins, are compared and contrasted. Whilst Atkinson's index derives from an individualistic, average utility-of-own-income social welfare function, for the Gini coefficient and its extension an additional argument must be included in the utility function being averaged, admitting envy or altruism effects into the social welfare function.

Chapter 6   Poverty

For the measurement of poverty using personal or household income distribution data, and for making poverty comparisons, we need to know who is poor and how poor. This requires important choices to be made about the definition of living standards, the appropriate cut-off or 'poverty line', the depth of poverty a person or household experiences and how to aggregate this across distributions. In the first part of the chapter, we discuss these issues and also set the scene by describing the pioneering contribution of Sen (1976). We go on to consider connections between the measurement procedures for the conceptually distinct but closely related phenomena of welfare, inequality and poverty. We then consider some widely-used classes of poverty indices, and their implied value judgements, turning finally to dominance and sequential dominance criteria which enable poverty comparisons to be made whilst allowing for a diversity of such judgements.

Chapter 7   The income tax

We begin this chapter by explaining the 'progressive principle', which underlies most income tax systems, and go on to consider what justifications are available for this principle. We then describe the main features of a typical income tax system. As we show, the concept of progression can only meaningfully be applied when restricted to income units enjoying the same tax treatment. This brings us to the twin commands in social justice of vertical and horizontal equity, which can be applied to the direct tax system. We see that the typical income tax contains horizontal inequity.

Chapter 8   A progressive income tax schedule

If tax liability is a function of income only, and there are no differences in need among taxpayers, then progression provides more welfare after tax than an equal-yield proportional ('flat') tax would, applied to the same incomes. This insight, stemming from the work of Fellman (1976) and Jakobsson (1976), leads to the identification of two normatively significant distributive consequences of a progressive tax schedule, disproportionality in the tax burden and redistributive effect upon incomes. Measures of the *degree* of progression of an income tax schedule are briefly considered. A similar lead to that given by Atkinson (1970) for inequality measurement was provided by the Jakobsson (1976) and Kakwani (1977b) papers for the measurement of income tax progressivity. Progressivity indices encapsulate the income tax schedule and pre-tax income distribution in a single number. Some Jakobsson/Kakwani theorems quantify the impacts on disproportionality and redistributive effect of changes in income tax progression, given the pre-tax income distribution, and this leads us to catalogues of well-defined progressivity indices. Finally in this chapter, we reproduce Pfähler's (1990) analysis, showing how, for a typical income tax schedule, many of these progressivity indices can be decomposed to show the contributions of the tax base and of the rate structure.

Chapter 9   Income tax reform and social welfare

This chapter concerns the welfare effects of income tax reforms, specifically, of adjustments to an income tax schedule. Popular analysis begins, and often ends, by identifying the pattern of gainers and losers when taxes are changed. Drawing on the material developed so far in the book, we go much further in some special cases. The first is where everyone gains or loses by the reform. That is, there is a tax cut or tax increase ('hike') for all. We report on some results of Pfähler (1984) for progression-neutral tax cuts/hikes for all. If the old and new tax schedules cross, they do so at break-even levels of income separating gainers from losers. Single-crossing reform involves redistribution from one end of the post-tax income distribution to the other, and double-crossing reform, redistribution from the middle to both ends or *vice versa*. For both types, support can be given in social welfare terms, even in some cases of an increased tax yield. Composite tax reforms, involving a progression-neutral tax cut/hike and redistribution from rich to poor, lead to new 'single-crossing properties', those of Hemming and Keen (1983), which are readily applicable and also throw new light on some theorems in chapter 8.

Chapter 10   Differences in income tax treatment

If the taxpaying population is homogeneous in all attributes but income, the horizontally and vertically equitable tax should be a function of money income only, a schedule whose degree of progression is a matter of societal taste. But if needs differ between taxpayers, non-income differences in tax treatment are required. In this chapter we focus on the distributive consequences of such differences, a topic that did not receive a great deal of research attention until the mid-1990s. The analysis is cast in terms of living standards rather than money incomes, thus factoring out the needs dimension – and the social policy analyst and taxman may not agree on how this should be done. Hence, even the best-designed multi-attribute income tax can be judged to have perverse effects. We examine the overall distributive effects, showing in particular how the vertical stance of the tax (its effective progression) can be summarized, and how to measure horizontal inequities. For this latter, we consider both some recent 'classical' approaches, according to which the unequal tax treatment of pre-tax equals reduces the redistributive capacity of the income tax system, and some alternative 'reranking' approaches, which are based upon disassociation between people's perceived pre- and post-tax living standards.

Chapter 11   The net fiscal system

In this final chapter, we widen the remit and consider the distributional impact of the net fiscal system, which includes non-income taxes and cash and other imputed benefits flowing from the government's expenditure programme. Attributing the benefits of government expenditures to income units is problematic: there is no uncontroversial and operational guiding principle. *Modulo* the practical difficulty of furnishing appropriate raw material for analysis, a sound approach to the measurement of net fiscal incidence progressivity can be given. Indices of benefit regressivity and net tax progressivity are obtained by minor extension of what was done for income taxes in chapter 8, and it turns out that net tax progressivity can be determined from the two separate inputs, tax progressivity and benefit regressivity. Horizontal inequities can also be located and tracked down to the tax and benefit components of the net fiscal system. An interesting and politically relevant interaction between taxes and benefits is revealed by all of this: under certain precise conditions, regressive (disequalizing) taxes can reinforce the equalizing effect of regressive benefits, and the horizontal inequities in the two systems can either be reinforcing or offsetting. But because of the aforementioned attribution problems, all results must be heavily qualified.

1.4   Prerequisites

Readers having basic calculus and a modicum of statistics at their disposal will find themselves technically accomplished enough to engage in the analytical argument in this book. It is helpful, too, to have some previous knowledge of economics. We describe the minimum requirements briefly here. In an Appendix, we expand upon these somewhat.

You should know what a continuous function is, and how to differentiate one that is differentiable. You should also know how to characterize increasing and strictly increasing functions, and concave and strictly concave ones, in terms of their derivatives. The concept of elasticity, of a function with respect to its argument, is a vital input. The intermediate value theorem for differentiation is used twice in the book. It helps to be passingly familiar with the concept of an infinitesimal number. You should know what open and closed intervals are. It will help enormously if you can appreciate that an integral $\int f(x)\,dx$ is akin to a sum $\Sigma f(x_i)\Delta x_i$, in case the variable x is continuous rather than discrete. Integration by parts is a technique used pervasively in the book. The intermediate value theorem for integration is used once. These topics are dealt with in all good mathematics for economists texts, for example in Hoy *et al.* (1996).

There are some prerequisites from basic probability and combinatorics. Thus, you should have come across random variables, expectation, mean and variance, and the normal probability distribution. Jensen's inequality is used several times. It is helpful, but not essential, to know what the support of a probability distribution is. At one or two points, permutations are used (to specify rearrangements of a vector of incomes). Many undergraduate texts in probability and statistics give adequate coverage of all these topics. For example, Hogg and Tanis (1988) does.

It is useful to know how economists structure the problem of individual choice. In particular, it helps to be familiar with the relations of strong and weak preference and indifference; to know about the utility representation of the preference relation; and to have encountered the constrained utility-maximization problem whose solution determines the individual's demands for the goods in question. Deaton and Muellbauer (1980) is good on all of this.

Appendix: Some basic analytical concepts and results

Here, we enlarge slightly upon some of the concepts referred to above, and also outline specific results which are drawn upon later in the book. By scanning here for the italicized keywords, the reader can pick out quickly what is at stake, and decide whether it might be advisable, perhaps at some later point, to consult one of the textbooks referred to.

The modulus function,

$$y = |x - x_0| \tag{1.1}$$

(where $|x - x_0| = x - x_0$ if $x \geq x_0$ and $x_0 - x$ if $x \leq x_0$) is *continuous* everywhere but not *differentiable* at the point $x = x_0$.

An *increasing function* has a non-negative first derivative, and a *strictly increasing* one has a positive first derivative 'almost everywhere'. For example, the function $y = x^3$ is strictly increasing, yet $dy/dx = 0$ at one point, $x = 0$. Similarly, a *concave function* has a non-positive second derivative, and a *strictly concave* one has a negative second derivative almost everywhere (consider the case of $y = -x^4$). The 'almost everwhere' *caveat* means, in mathematical parlance, 'except on a set of measure zero', or that we can effectively ignore the isolated exceptions: we do this in chapters 3 and 8, when defining strictly concave utility functions and strictly progressive income tax schedules respectively.

If $f(x)$ is continuous for $b \leq x \leq c$ (we write this $x \in [b, c]$, and call $[b, c]$ a *closed interval* in the rest of the book) and differentiable for $b < x < c$ (on the *open interval* $x \in (b, c)$), then the *intermediate value theorem for differentiation* says that there exists a number $d \in (b, c)$ such that

$$\frac{f(c) - f(b)}{c - b} = f'(d) \tag{1.2}$$

Elasticity is a measure of the response of a function to a change in its argument. It finds much favour among economists. Thus, let

$$e^{y,x} = e^{f(x),x} = \frac{xf'(x)}{f(x)} = \frac{x}{y}\frac{dy}{dx} \tag{1.3}$$

denote the elasticity of $y = f(x)$ with respect to x. Two useful results, used at various points in the text, are that

$$e^{A,B} = e^{A,C}e^{C,B} \tag{1.4}$$

and

$$e^{A+B,C} = \frac{A}{A+B}e^{A,C} + \frac{B}{A+B}e^{B,C} \tag{1.5}$$

where A, B, C are quantities all related to each other (so that movements of one against another can be measured by elasticity).

An *infinitesimal number* can be thought of as a number so small that it is neither finite and non-zero nor identically zero. The derivative dy/dx can be regarded as the ratio of two infinitesimal numbers, dy and dx, and the partial derivative $\partial y/\partial x_i$ (in the case that y is a function of several variables) as the ratio $dy \div dx_i$ when no other variable x_j, $j \neq i$, is allowed to undergo an infinitesimal change. For example, by approximating the infinitesimals in (1.3) by small finite changes, the elasticity $e^{f(x),x}$ can be interpreted, roughly, as the percentage change in $f(x)$ consequent upon a change of one per centage point in the argument x.

Integration by parts is a technique used to advantage at many points in the book. The rule is

$$\int_c^b f(x)g'(x)dx = -\int_c^b f'(x)g(x)dx + [f(x)g(x)]_a^b \tag{1.6}$$

When integrating a function that is a product, if you recognize part of the integrand as a derivative (in (1.6), the term $g'(x)$ is recognizably a derivative, within the integrand on the left), and so can integrate it (to give $g(x)$), then you can re-express the integral. Just integrate this recognizable part, and differentiate the rest; but do not forget to change the sign, and to add on the extra term evaluated between the limits of integration. The *intermediate value theorem for integration* says:

$$\int_b^c f(x)dx = (c-b)f(d) \text{ for some } d \in (b, c) \tag{1.7}$$

Jensen's inequality says that if $U(x)$ is strictly concave and X is a non-degenerate random variable, then

$$E[U(X)] < U(E[X]) \tag{1.8}$$

where E is the expectations operator.

The *support of a function*, for example, of a probability distribution, is a useful concept. Loosely, the support of $f(x)$ is that set of values of x on which $f(x)$ is non-zero. (Topologically, it is the complement of the union of all open sets on which $f(x)$ vanishes, equivalently, the closure of the set of points on which $f(x)$ is non-zero; but we shall not need to use these properties.)

A *permutation* σ *of N objects* is a function specifying a rearrangement of these objects. For example, in the case $N = 5$, three permutations are

$$\sigma_1 = (123)(45), \qquad \sigma_2 = (1)(24)(35) \quad \text{and} \quad \sigma_3 = (1453)(2) \qquad (1.9)$$

Applied to the ordered set of numbers $\{1,2,3,4,5\}$, these yield, respectively

$$\{2,3,1,5,4\}, \qquad \{1,4,5,2,3\} \quad \text{and} \quad \{4,2,1,5,3\} \qquad (1.10)$$

Thus, in plain English, $\sigma_1 = (123)(45)$ tells you that '1 goes to 2, 2 goes to 3, 3 goes (back) to 1, 4 goes to 5, 5 goes (back) to 4', etc. Both σ_2 and σ_3, as given in (1.9), have fixed elements in their cycle structure. We may denote by $\sigma(i)$ the permuted value of i (so that $\sigma_1(4) = 5$, $\sigma_3(2) = 2$, etc.). If $\mathbf{x} = (x_1, x_2, \ldots, x_N) = (x_i)_{1 \le i \le N}$ is a vector, then by $\mathbf{x}_\sigma$ we shall mean the rearranged vector $(x_{\sigma(i)})_{1 \le i \le N}$. There are $N! = N(N-1)(N-2)(N-3) \ldots 3.2.1$ different permutations of N objects. The number of ways of choosing r different objects from a set of N objects is $_NC_r = N!/\{r!(N-r)!\}$.

Suppose that an individual has *preferences* expressed over bundles of n goods. Under certain assumptions, a *utility representation* of the preference relation can be employed (see Beardon and Mehta 1994, on this). This is a function $U: R^n \to R$ with the property that $\mathbf{x}$ is strongly preferred to $\mathbf{y}$ if and only if $U(\mathbf{x}) > U(\mathbf{y})$, and x is indifferent to y if and only if $U(\mathbf{x}) = U(\mathbf{y})$.

An individual choosing how much to buy, of each of goods $1, 2, \ldots, n$ at prices p_i per unit $(1 \le i \le n)$, can be modelled as maximizing an appropriate $U(\mathbf{x})$ subject to the constraint $\Sigma p_i x_i = m$, where m is his income. The maximum value of $U(\mathbf{x})$ achieved in this *constrained utility-maximization problem* may be written as a function, $V(\mathbf{p}, m)$ say, in recognition that, mathematically, the problem changes if prices and income do – and so, therefore, does the most-preferred combination of goods and the utility derived. $V(\mathbf{p}, m)$ is known as the individual's *indirect utility function*. The optimal x_is are the *demands* for the goods $1, 2, \ldots, n$ and the *income elasticity of demand* and *price elasticity of demand* can be expressed in terms of the relevant partial derivatives.

Since the utility function $U(\mathbf{x})$ arises as a merely ordinal representation of preferences, it is unsafe, if tempting, to read significance into the level of value achieved. If $V(p, m)$ doubles when prices fall by so-much, is the person twice as happy? It is, arguably, less meaningful still to compare utility values between different individuals. Problems of *ordinality/cardinality* and *interpersonal comparability*, well-rehearsed in economics, arise in this book in chapters 3 and 4.

2

The size distribution of income

'Income and wealth are the two box scores in the record book on people's economic positions' (Okun 1975, p. 65). We are indeed interested in people's economic positions, more generally in the well-being of individuals, households and families; and since this book is about *income* and not about *wealth*, we had better make plain the distinction between these right away.

One crucial distinction is that income is a *flow* whilst wealth is a *stock*. Income is the flow of money to the individual/household, measured as so-much-per-week or so-much-per-year. There are many different income concepts and components of income, such as earnings and self-employment income, unearned income, transfer payments from government (cash benefits for the support of low-income families, state pensions, etc.); and also imputed items such as the value a household can be reckoned to derive from the ownership of its own home and from the existence of public-sector activities like education and defence. By contrast, wealth is the stock of assets owned by the individual/household, both financial (savings, stocks, shares, government securities) and physical (e.g. property and durable consumer goods).

Our interest is primarily in people's income: we shall assess economic position in terms of ability to sustain a flow of consumption, and thereby to enjoy a standard of living. But it would be a mistake to think that wealth did not come into the picture. Indeed, a nice but fraught economists' definition of income is, simply, 'that which can be spent whilst maintaining intact the value of a household's wealth'. This conceptual definition of 'true' income is very hard to adhere to when the statistician goes about measurement, but it does underline the fact that wealth ought to be (assumed to be) maintained – the house kept in good repair, and in times of rapid inflation savings not allowed to dwindle in real (purchasing-power) terms, and so on – if well-being is to be assessed purely in terms of income flow. The flow out of wealth that otherwise occurs, through the depreciation of assets, both physical and financial, would constitute a reduction in economic well-being that we fail to recognize.

It is important for the collection and interpretation of statistical data on income distribution, to get clear what the *time unit* is and what the *income unit* is, upon which measurement is to be based. A 'snapshot' of incomes in week 15 of a given financial year might give a gloomy view of economic well-being if that was the coldest, most inclement week of the year and many unskilled workers were laid-off; a 'moving picture' of the weekly income distribution as the weeks roll by would be harder to capture on paper, analyse and draw inferences from. Should we, perhaps, rather be concerned with the distribution across currently living individuals of their entire lifetime's income, in order truly to assess 'who gets what'?[1] This is the problem of the time unit; the issue of the income unit is just as vital. Should we care about, and therefore measure: income per family? per adult, neglecting children? per household, however many adults? per individual, attributing a share of parental income to each child? The question of how to treat households is a vexed one. What if we wish to compare economic well-being between two societies with different customs – one having extended family units and the other a preponderance of single-person households?

These are just some of the problems which face the compiler and interpreter of income distribution statistics. The problems we address in this book are those of interpretation, once the data have been arrived at. However, much real-world debate on income distribution and tax and benefit policy is really about the essential preliminaries themselves – about what should be the appropriate income unit, time period and definition of income. We shall not pursue such lines of enquiry in this book. Rather, we shall construct an analytical framework within which to formalize the issues that arise when evaluating features of income distribution; we shall do it on the presumption that essential preliminaries have been agreed; and also assuming that the empirical inputs, namely the data sets in question, are adequately described and can be rendered compatible with one another for comparative purposes.

2.1   Data and data manipulations

Summary income distribution tabulations, in which numbers of incomes and their values are classified by income ranges, are published by government statisticians in most countries. In contrast to this highly aggregated level of presentation, of what is known as *grouped data*, it has become feasible in recent times to store income distribution *microdata* (or 'unit record data') in computers, and to make subsets of this data available to the researcher.

Microdata are typically derived from household surveys. The official British income distribution data are derived from the *Family Resources Survey* (FRS), having previously been taken from the *Family Expenditure Survey* (FES). These are annual surveys compiled from a process of interview. They use the family or household as sampling unit, and record, at each interview, not only the many different forms of income the household may recently have received (see the list below taken from the FES documentation) but also household composition, the ages of the adult members, their occupations, geographic location, type of housing, outgoings for various categories of expenditure (everything from rent, mortgage interest and insurance premia to beer, books and electrical goods is detailed), and other attributes.

- earned income
- self-employment income
- employer's superannuation contributions
- employer's national insurance contributions
- property income
- imputed income from owner occupancy
- investment income
- occupational pensions
- taxable transfer payments (e.g. pensions, sick pay)
- untaxed transfer payments (e.g. child benefit)

A thriving industry of econometric effort has grown up around the availability of this type of data, focusing primarily on estimating behavioural relationships, such as household demand for consumption goods and for leisure.

Households Below Average Income (henceforth HBAI) is the principal publication in which the UK's official income distribution data are summarized, using the week as the time unit. HBAI draws upon the FRS and also upon data obtained from the Inland Revenue (the UK income tax authority) for very high incomes. Its close attention to lower incomes makes this a particularly valuable resource for poverty analysis (the topic of chapter 6 of this book).[2]

Household survey microdata typically do not reveal people's income tax liabilities or payments (these may differ, and in any case not all components of income are taxed on the same basis, some being taxed currently and others in arrears). The *Survey of Personal Incomes* (SPI) uses the tax year (beginning 6 April) as the time unit and the 'tax unit' (single person or married couple) as the income unit. The income values which are recorded do not include untaxed state benefits, interest on National Savings Certificates, employers' superannuation and National Insurance contributions or (currently) imputed income from owner occupancy. This data source also under-represents the lowest incomes in society, excluding, for example, all incomes which are below the basic annual tax allowance. Until 1990, the publication entitled *Survey of Personal Incomes* reported data derived from this survey in grouped form. From 1991 onwards, summary statistics for the SPI data have appeared in *Inland Revenue Statistics*. These data are supplemented with most state benefits, some of the lowest incomes and also some imputed items such as business 'perks' in the annual summary tabulation published in *Economic Trends* (ET).[3]

Household survey microdata need to be adjusted or manipulated by the analyst to make them tell about well-being. Obviously a single-person household with £500 per week has a very different living standard from a couple with two children and £500 per week. A widely accepted procedure is to assume income is shared equally within each household, and deflate the total or *per capita* amount using an *equivalence scale*, which converts incomes to a common base measuring purchasing power or living standard. HBAI uses the so-called McClements scale, a version of which is defined as follows. First, calculate the income household's conversion coefficient, as:

> 0.61 for the first adult (head)
> +0.39 for the spouse of the head (if any)
> +0.46 for a third adult
> +0.36 for subsequent adults
> +0.09 for each dependent aged 0–1 year
> +0.18 for each dependent aged 2–4 years
> +0.21 for each dependent aged 5–7 years
> +0.23 for each dependent aged 8–10 years
> +0.25 for each dependent aged 11–12 years
> +0.27 for each dependent aged 13–15 years
> +0.36 for each dependent aged 16 or over

and second, divide the household's income by this coefficient.[4] The resulting measure is known as *equivalized* (or *equivalent*) *household income*, and is evidently denominated in nominal terms (pounds) for a married couple with no children, and adjusted to yield comparable living standards for all other households. Note, however, that this particular scale neglects the differing needs and expenses of pensioner households, for example. An interesting survey of derivations of equivalence scales based on the econometric analysis of household demands is to be found in Deaton and Muellbauer (1980, chapter 8).

There is plenty of room for disagreement among analysts about what the appropriate equivalence scale should be for deflating household incomes. Atkinson *et al.* (1995) have suggested using a simple 'square root rule' for international comparisons. This involves deflating household incomes by the square root of the number of members. Buhmann *et al.* (1988) and Cutler and Katz (1992) have suggested parametrization as a way to take account of a range of possible judgements about the needs of families of different sizes. Cutler and Katz's deflator takes the form $(N_A + \varphi N_C)^\theta$, where N_A and N_C are the numbers of adults and children in the family and φ and θ are parameter values between 0 and 1 which tell the importance of children and economies of scale respectively in determining what is called the 'number of adult-equivalents' in the household. We return to the issue of adult-equivalents in some detail in the next chapter (see also exercise 2.1.1 below). For this particular scale, the reference group is that of single persons (whose money income is taken as a measure of their living standard), unlike the McClements. Clearly, if the analyst judges children to be irrelevant for the determination of living standards (see exercise 2.1.2), then $\varphi = 0$ should be selected. The values $\varphi = \theta = 1$ can be selected if per capita money income is held to be the measure of living standard; this would ignore the possibility of economies of scale in large households. Setting $\varphi = 1$ yields Buhmann *et al.*'s scale, and further setting $\theta = \frac{1}{2}$ yields the Atkinson *et al.* square root rule.

When incomes have been converted using an equivalence scale ('equivalized'), they can be pooled. The resultant overall distribution of equivalent income may be presented in tabular form, with numbers of incomes and amounts grouped by ranges, or portrayed visually by means of histograms. The histogram showing numbers of incomes (rather than amounts) is known as the *frequency density polygon*. Figure 2.1 shows the frequency density polygon for the HBAI dataset of 1997/8, using 50 equally-sized 'bins', and plotting vertically the number (or proportion) of individuals in each bin.[5] If variable bin widths are used – for example finer at the bottom and broader at the top in order to make the low-income profile clearer and give less attention to unimportant gradations among top income units – it is *numbers (or proportions) of incomes per unit of the bin-width*, or their *density*, which should be plotted vertically, in order that the areas of the vertical bars stay proportional to the numbers in the relevant ranges, and also so that the picture would improve in quality the finer the 'mesh' (and not shrink to nothing in the limit).[6]

Kernel density estimation, a comparatively new technique for smoothing the blips that can occur with sample microdata, permits the fitting of a continuous curve along the tops of the vertical bars in a frequency density polygon such as that in figure 2.1, by passing a 'moving window' along the data, ordered from poorest to richest, and estimating the frequency density as one goes (see exercise 2.1.4 below). Figure 2.2 shows a kernel smooth derived using the same HBAI data as for figure 2.1.[7] In the next section of this chapter, the starting point for the analysis will be a smooth *frequency density function*, in idealized form, but very much like that of figure 2.2.

We shall not formulate the mathematical analysis in this book to rest (explicitly) upon equivalent income as the relevant concept. Not least, this is because when we come to analyse taxation and distribution, it is the *money* income of households which the government taxes. One cannot operate a redistributive family policy, for example, directly in terms of equivalent income. Transfers of income from richer to poorer, and their effects, will be central in the analysis, but to transfer a unit of *equivalent* income from a rich single person to a poor couple with children, for example, would mean taking 61 pence from the single and giving more than £1 to the family in the case of the McClements scale cited above: where does the extra come from?

Money income after all taxes and all benefits is known as *final income*, and that before all taxes and benefits as *original income*. The former provides a more satisfactory basis for defining living standards than the latter. We defer consideration of the benefits attribution issue until chapter 11. For our

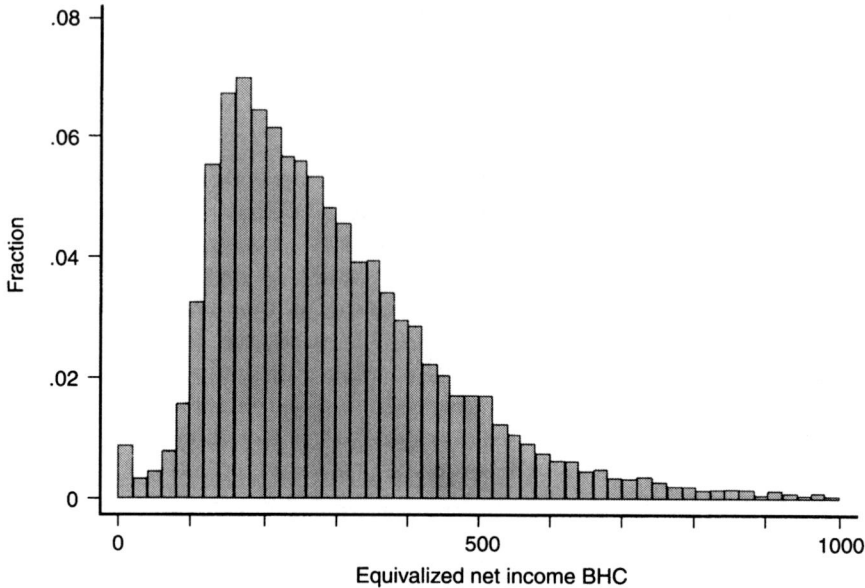

Figure 2.1   Frequency density polygon for HBAI data, 1997/8
Source: courtesy of Stephen Jenkins

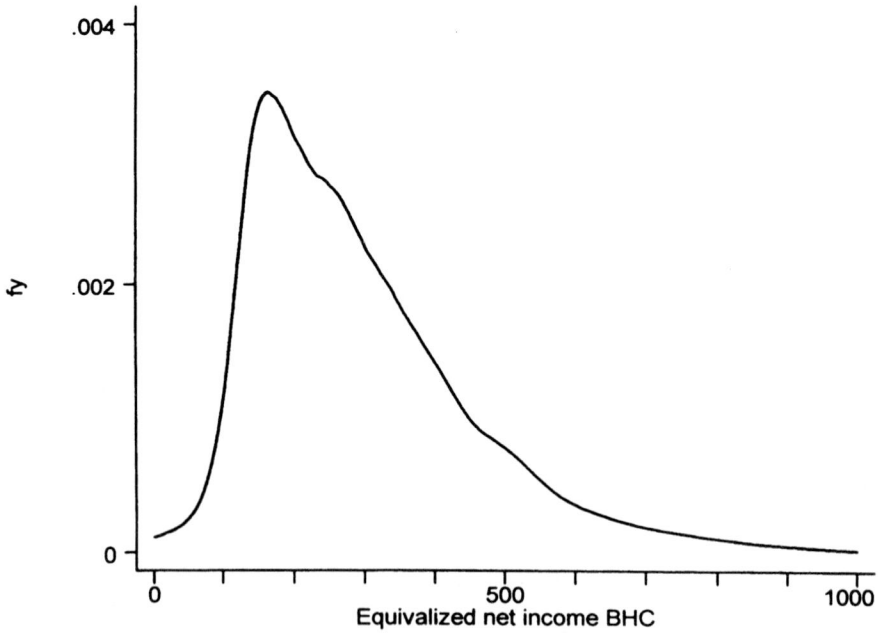

Figure 2.2   Kernel density estimate for HBAI date, 1997/8
Source: courtesy of Stephen Jenkins

mathematical structures, we had better keep the definition of income and the income unit deliberately vague, permitting analysis in terms of individuals as well as households, and of money income transfers (as in chapter 3), as well as of the effects of taxation policies on living standards (as in chapter 10). Analytically, we may simply begin with the words 'let x be the income of an income unit . . .' and vary the context as and when appropriate.

Exercises

2.1.1 Describe Cowell's (1984) discussion of different concepts of income and of income unit. Explain how an equivalence scale is used to turn family money income into PENNI.
2.1.2 What factors are involved in the calculation of equivalence scales? See chapter 5 in McClements (1978) and also Coulter *et al.* (1992a). How do Pollak and Wales (1979) distinguish the equivalence scale appropriate for demand analysis from the type required to make welfare comparisons? Illustrate with reference to their question 'What expenditure level would make a family with three children as well-off as it would be with two children and $12,000?' (p. 216).
2.1.3 What are the problems involved in deeming two consumers 'equally well-off'? Describe Fisher's (1987) view, using his milk–whisky example in illustration.
2.1.4 Describe the progression which is explained in Cowell *et al.* (1996) from histograms and bin sizes to the kernel density estimate, giving a brief overview of the kernel procedure itself.

2.2   Mathematical representation

One way to describe an income distribution in mathematical terms would be simply to list all of the incomes, for example from smallest to largest. Thus, if N is the number of income units, the incomes could be listed as $x_1, x_2, \ldots, x_N$ where $x_1 \leq x_2 \leq \ldots \leq x_N$. Although this starting point is convenient for some purposes, as we shall see, there are gains in both expositional clarity and analytical power to be had from adopting a different approach. The frequency density function provides an alternative beginning.

Envisage a very large population, and subdivision of income ranges, yielding ever-more-detailed information, proceeding to an infinitesimal limit. This requires us to imagine that income is *continuously distributed* along an interval, rather than *discretely*, as above. The gain is in the access to the mathematical calculus which this provides: the convenience and elegance of smooth functional forms.

A smooth function of x, which we shall call $f(x)$, can be used to represent the limiting shape of the 'top' of a frequency density polygon when subdivision is carried to this limit. This function indicates the density of the proportion of income units (in the whole, N) at each income x. For example, $f(x)$ may be unimodal, as in figure 2.2, with incomes densely clustered around a modal (most common) value, and with relatively fewer in the 'upper tail'. Formally, *for any income level x and infinitesimal dx, $f(x)$ dx is the proportion of income units whose incomes lie in the range [x, x + dx]*. Infinitesimal numbers are discussed briefly in the mathematical prerequisites section of chapter 1. Of course, $f(x)$ dx is also the area of the rectangle erected on the interval [x,x + dx]. If we sum this across all such infinitesimal sub-intervals along the horizontal axis, the mathematical process for this being *integration*, we obtain total proportion of all income units, namely unity:

$$1 = \int f(x) \mathrm{d}x \tag{2.1}$$

The limits of integration will be the lowest income x_1 and highest income x_N; N itself must, of course, be very large in order that our imagined device of *continuously* distributed income should not be too unrealistic.

In some modelling, an idealized frequency density function $f(x)$ is adopted which has support running all the way from $x = 0$ to $x = \infty$, rather than being contained within a finite interval [x_1, x_N] (see, for example, the lognormal distribution). Then (2.1) becomes $1 = \int_0^\infty f(x) \, \mathrm{d}x$. Nothing much is lost by this even if the support of $f(x)$ is in fact bounded, for $f(x)$ can always be defined to be identically zero outside of its support. However, to avoid the appearance of convergence problems at the top end, in such cases we may choose to write, instead

$$1 = \int_0^z f(x) \mathrm{d}x \tag{2.1a}$$

where z will be described as 'any income level in excess of the highest one actually occurring'. Occasionally we will just write

$$1 = \int f(x) \mathrm{d}x \tag{2.1b}$$

omitting the limits of integration altogether.

When the population size is N (assumed very large), for each x there are $Nf(x)$ dx income units whose incomes lie in the range [x, x + dx]. Each of these has an income differing from x only infinitesimally. Hence the total income of these people is only infinitesimally different from $Nxf(x)$ dx. Summing over all [x,x + dx], that is integrating, we arrive at total income overall, which can be written $N\mu$ where μ is mean income. Dividing by N, we find

$$\mu = \int_0^z xf(x) \mathrm{d}x \tag{2.2}$$

(with z as before), just as for the expected value of a random variable x whose probability density function is $f(x)$. The proportion of income units, and the total income accruing to those units, between two income levels $x = a$ and $x = b$, are

$$\int_a^b f(x)dx \quad \text{and} \quad N\int_a^b xf(x)dx$$

respectively. The first of these is the analogue of $P(a \le x \le b)$ for a random variable. Dividing the second expression by N, we see that $\int_a^b xf(x)dx$ expresses the income of this restricted group of income units *per capita of the overall population.*

We can exploit other connections with random variables and probability theory. For example, we may use statistical measures of dispersion, such as the variance σ^2:

$$\sigma^2 = \int_0^{\bar{z}} (x-\mu)^2 f(x)dx \tag{2.3}$$

to measure the spread, which has to do with the *inequality*, in an income distribution. In the next section of this chapter we discuss income inequality.

Another connection is in the context of *social choice*. If we are willing to attribute to an income x a level of *utility*, say $U(x)$, and to assert that this information alone quantifies that income unit's well-being (a vexed question, as we have noted), then we may evaluate average utility in society, as

$$W = \int_0^{\bar{z}} U(x)f(x)dx \tag{2.4}$$

and call it 'social welfare'; and go on to compare this between distributions we might be interested in. In furtherance of this, we may set up a little 'thought-experiment': imagine that an individual or family unit from outside our country would have an equal chance of occupying any existing rôle in society, and so of having any of the incomes now existing. Thus we generate a 'disinterested' view of income distribution, in which frequency density actually *becomes* probability density: the individual or family unit is more likely to occupy one of the relatively numerous rôles. The social welfare ranking of distributions becomes a matter of evaluating expected utility for an outsider over uncertain prospects. This 'veil of ignorance' approach to social choice will be considered in more detail in chapter 4.

Equivalent to the frequency density function $f(x)$ as a starting point for analysis is the *distribution function* $F(x)$, defined as

$$F(x) = \int_0^x f(t)dt \tag{2.5}$$

This measures the proportion of income units with incomes of at most x, and it typically has the sort of shape indicated in figure 2.3. The *median income* in a distribution – that income level, say x^*, which is exactly half-way up the distribution of income units when ranked from poorest to richest – is readily identified from the distribution function: it satisfies $F(x^*) = \frac{1}{2}$.

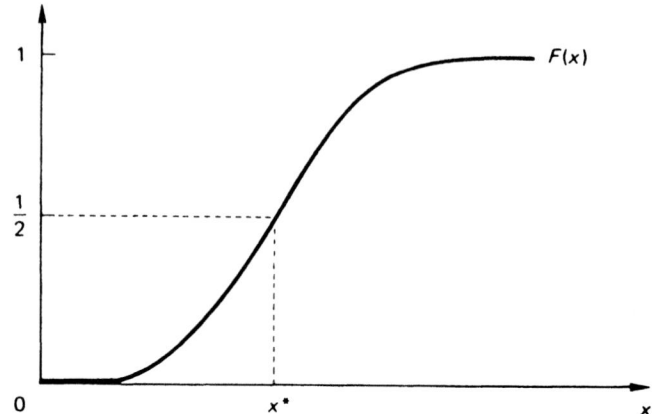

Figure 2.3   The distribution function $F(x)$

The equivalence of the frequency density function $f(x)$ and distribution function $F(x)$ in specifying an income distribution is clear from (2.5), and its converse

$$f(x) = F'(x) \tag{2.6}$$

which comes by differentiation in (2.5). Thus the information content in both functions is the same; knowing one tells you the other. We shall tend to use $f(x)$ and $F(x)$ interchangeably in what follows. For example, we may speak of ranking a pair of distributions $\{F, G\}$ or, equally, of ranking the pair $\{f, g\}$.

When choosing a mathematical specification for the frequency density function $f(x)$, or distribution function $F(x)$, we can resort to a well-documented catalogue of probability distributions. One of the simplest and best-understood is the lognormal, in which the logarithm of income is assumed normally distributed. Its parameters can be chosen to make it fit reasonably well to observed data, as can those of some other families (see exercises 2.2.3–2.2.5). However, most or all of the possible candidates from probability theory have unimodal frequency density functions, whereas, in very recent investigations using microdata, the kernel technique is beginning to reveal bimodality as the rule of the day (exercise 2.2.6).

Exercises

2.2.1 Use integration by parts to show that if $f(x)$ has bounded support, then the mean μ is given by $\mu = \int_0^z [1 - F(x)]\,dx$ for any finite z equal to or exceeding the highest income. Can you extend this result to the case of infinite support (is there a possible convergence problem)?

2.2.2 If a population of N income units has distribution function $F(x)$, and another population of M income units has distribution function $G(x)$, show that the distribution function $H(x)$ for the combined population of $N + M$ income units is given by $H(x) = \theta F(x) + (1 - \theta)G(x)$, where $\theta = N/(N + M)$. If $f(x)$ has support $[a_f, b_f]$ and $g(x)$ has support $[a_g, b_g]$, what is the support of $h(x)$?

2.2.3 '. . . Part of the "conventional wisdom" . . . is that earnings are approximately lognormal, but with an upper tail that is better described by the Pareto function' (Harrison, 1981, p. 621). How did Harrison examine this claim? Describe his conclusions.

2.2.4 'In many applications, the Singh-Maddala provides a better fit than the gamma which performs much better than the lognormal . . . the beta distribution . . . includes the gamma as a limiting case . . . the generalized gamma . . . includes the lognormal, Weibull, gamma, exponential, normal and Pareto distributions as special or limiting cases . . . two genaralized beta distribitions are considered . . . one of these includes the Singh-Maddala *and* the generalized gamma . . . the second includes the beta . . . and the generalized gamma' (McDonald, 1984, p. 647). Describe McDonald's synthesis of many previously considered models for the distribution of income.

2.2.5 '. . . a new optimizing model of firm behaviour . . . predicts the earnings distribution to follow the beta distribution of the second kind . . . the stronger theoretical foundations, superior empirical performance, and ease of use of this density suggest it as a replacement for the lognormal and Pareto densities in future modelling work' (Parker, 1999, p. 244). Describe Parker's model in detail.

2.2.6 'During the 1980s, the distinct clump in the concentration of people around middle-income levels began to break up and polarise towards high and low incomes' (Jenkins, 1996, p. 44). Describe the approach which Jenkins used to establish these findings in respect of the UK.[8]

2.3 Inequality of income

The two dimensions of income distribution that spring most readily to the layman's mind are *total* and *spread*. How big is the cake and how is it divided? If we wish to abstract from the issue of population size, then we can ask, what is the mean income, and how unequally are incomes distributed around this average?

The inequality in a typical income distribution is evident from an examination of the measures of central location: the mean, median and mode. These are typically configured as follows:

$$\text{mode} < \text{median} < \text{mean} \tag{2.7}$$

The most common income level is typically less than half-way up the distribution, and the income half-way up the distribution is itself below average. This points to the presence of *positive* (or *right*) *skew* in the distribution: a drawn-out upper tail of high incomes in the frequency density function.[9]

We can gain an impression of the 'degree of inequality' (loosely defined) in an income distribution by examining the shares of total income accruing to various groups of income units. For example, in the summary data presented in *Survey of Personal Incomes* for 1984–5 one can find that there are 2,438,000 incomes of £15,000 and above before tax, contributing £56,090 million to the total pre-tax income, which is £191,000 million. Translated into proportions, *the top 11 per cent of income units receive 29 per cent of all income before tax.* This statement quantifies the unequal command over resources enjoyed by these richest units. In *Economic Trends* for the same year, the pre-tax incomes of £15,000 and above constitute the top $9\frac{1}{2}$ per cent of income recipients, and account for $28\frac{1}{2}$ per cent of allocated income before tax: the populations and income concepts are different in the two data sources, as we have indicated; we may not be talking about the same group of people in both cases; but even if we were, they would account for a reduced fraction of the population in the *Economic Trends* tabulation because of that source's enhanced coverage of low incomes. We may go on to look at the situation after tax of these same income units; we would find reduced shares (27 per cent rather than 29 per cent for *Survey of Personal Incomes*, $25\frac{1}{2}$ per cent rather than $28\frac{1}{2}$ per cent for the *Economic Trends* distribution). The reduced fractions reflect the progressive nature of the income tax: liabilities are proportionately higher for these particular income units than for others lower down the distribution, and their share of the cake is reduced (the cake itself becomes smaller, too).

A standardized approach to measuring income shares is needed if, for example, we wish to see what has happened through time in a given country, or to compare distribution between different countries. If we evaluate the percentage of total income accruing to the top *decile* (10 per cent of income units) in the distribution, rather than working from an income level, like £15,000, the resulting information will be easier to compare between years or countries. For example, Lecaillon *et al.* (1984, pp. 26–27) show top decile shares for 39 countries, all pre-tax, ranging from 56.3 per cent (Kenya, 1969, income unit = economically active person) to 28 per cent (Republic of Korea, 1970, household); in a similar study, Sawyer (1976, p. 14) records a share as low as 23.8 per cent (for Australia, 1966/7, household). Note, of course, that the income share of the top decile must exceed 10 per cent, so long as there is inequality in the distribution! Similarly, the income share of the bottom decile must be less than 10 per cent when there is inequality.

A graph known as the *Lorenz curve* captures all of the quantile share information for a given income distribution. To compute a Lorenz curve, we first order the income units by magnitude of income, starting with the lowest; and

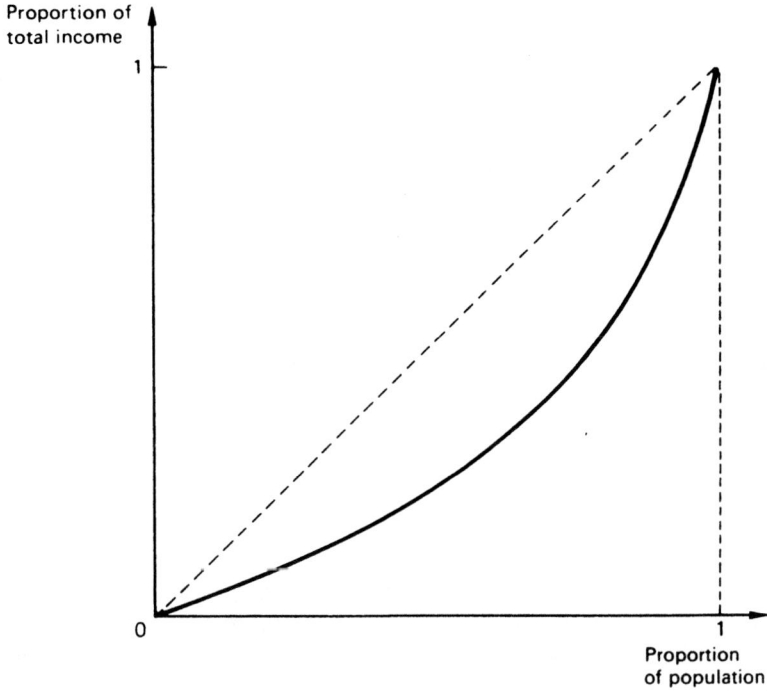

Figure 2.4   Typical Lorenz curve

then plot, against *cumulative proportion of the population* so ordered (running from 0 to 1 along the horizontal axis), the *cumulative proportion of total income* received by these income units. The resultant graph will be a virtually smooth curve for a large microdata set, as shown in figure 2.4. (For grouped data, or just a few incomes, it is conventional to join the smaller number of points determining the Lorenz curve by straight lines.) So long as inequality is present, every 'top quantile' group receives more than its (population) share of total income, and every quantile group that begins with the lowest income receives less than its share. The curve thus lies below the 45° line.

The inequality in two different income distributions can be compared visually by plotting both Lorenz curves on the same graph. The dotted lines in figure 2.5 delimit the boundaries for such curves. If all incomes were equal, the Lorenz curve would run along the 45° line: the bottom quantile would be *any* quantile, and the share in total income equal to the share in the population. We call the 45° line the *line of complete equality* (sometimes the *line of perfect equality*, but this begs the question of what is the ideal distribution, a question to which we shall come). If, at the other extreme, one person held all income, the rest having next-to-nothing, the Lorenz curve would run along the horizontal axis, and then vertically, as also shown.

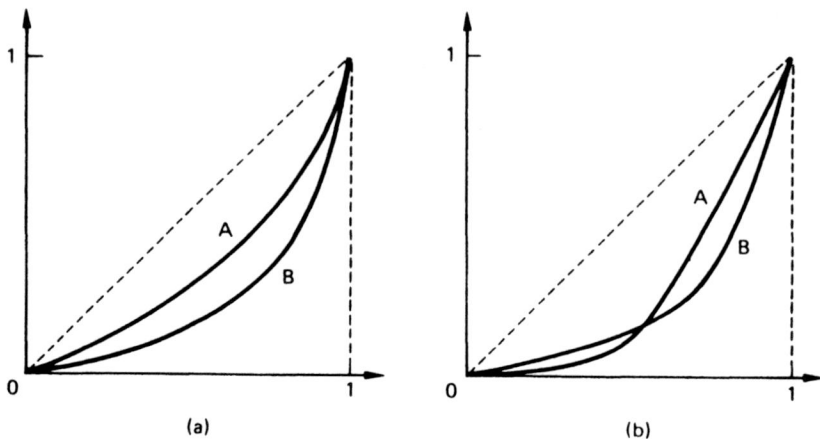

Figure 2.5   Two hypothetical Lorenz curve configurations

Figure 2.5 shows two hypothetical Lorenz curve configurations. The under-lying distributions, A and B, might be for different countries, or for the same country at two different times or, for that matter, for the same country and time period, but for two different populations and/or income concepts. (A could be teachers and B semi-skilled workers; A could be for earned income and B include unearned income; etc.) In case (a) we would describe distribu-tion A as being 'less unequal' than distribution B. In case (b) we would say that A has 'more inequality at the bottom, and less at the top' than B. These are potentially useful insights. However, it is important to add that we are talking about *Lorenz curve inequality*, because there are other facets to inequality too. For example, suppose that two distributions C and D are iden-tical in every respect except that all the incomes in C are double (or ten or fifty times) the corresponding ones in D; then C and D have identical Lorenz curves (can you see why?); but we might not want to judge them as 'equally unequal' if we care about absolute differentials between poor and rich incomes.

It is hard to avoid making (often well-concealed) *value judgements* when assessing inequality – and the Lorenz curve is only suitable if concern is over relative income differentials. We return to this question at several points sub-sequently in the book.

Figure 2.5(a) illustrates a situation of *Lorenz dominance*. We say that A *Lorenz dominates* B. The bottom 100*p* per cent of income units in distribu-tion A have a greater share in total income than do the corresponding group in distribution B, and this is true for every *p* between 0 and 1. Intuitively, one may feel approval for the way the cake is distributed in A relative to the way this is done in B, and hold complete equality in mind as the 'ideal' way to divide a cake – but do not forget that Lorenz curves say nothing about the sizes of the respective cakes, and so cannot tell us which distribution of income is superior in terms of well-being. Non-income characteristics are also suppressed by Lorenz curves. Unless both distributions under consideration are expressed in terms of equivalent income, equal purchasing power of all income units is unlikely to be secured along the 45° line. If populations A and B differ, different unequal distributions may represent the appropriate 'ideals' in the respective cases.

When comparing real-world income distributions, it is often found that Lorenz curves cross. For example, Kakwani (1984b) found Lorenz crossings in more than 30 per cent of 2,556 possible pairwise comparisons between 72 countries. The most prevalent case, that of a single Lorenz crossing, is depicted in figure 2.5(b).

Observers like to encapsulate in a single index number the inequality inherent in an income distribution. This is convenient for comparative purposes, but the question of what is an appropriate index raises many problems. Not least, recalling the earlier reference to absolute and relative income differentials, what is it we want to measure as inequality? Throughout this book, we focus primarily on relative and not absolute income differentials; inequality will be portrayed by the Lorenz curve. Indices of relative inequality will be discussed in some detail in chapter 5, and in chapter 8 the effect of progressive income tax on relative income differentials will be determined analytically.

Two inequality indices which derive from the Lorenz curve are the *Gini coefficient* and *Schutz coefficient*. Each quantifies in a different way how 'far' a given distribution is from the completely equal one whose Lorenz curve lies along the 45° line. We have already discussed the problems which stand in the way of regarding the 45° line as an 'ideal' reference distribution against which to measure inequality. Arguably, these problems of income unit and income concept are a prior concern to that which the Gini and Schutz coefficients address: given an income distribution, how far from equal are the income shares of its income units?

The Gini coefficient G is an *area* measure, and the Schutz coefficient S a *distance* measure, of the extent to which a given Lorenz curve departs from the 45° line (figure 2.6). The Gini coefficient measures the area between the Lorenz curve and the 45° line as a fraction of the total area under the 45° line:

$$G = \frac{A}{A+B} = 2A = 2\left[\frac{1}{2} - B\right] = 1 - 2B \qquad (2.8)$$

while the Schutz coefficient measures the maximum vertical distance between the Lorenz curve and the 45° line:

$$S = \text{distance cd} \qquad (2.9)$$

Clearly each is a number between 0 and 1, taking the value 0 for a completely equal distribution and 1 for a distribution in which inequality is maximal.

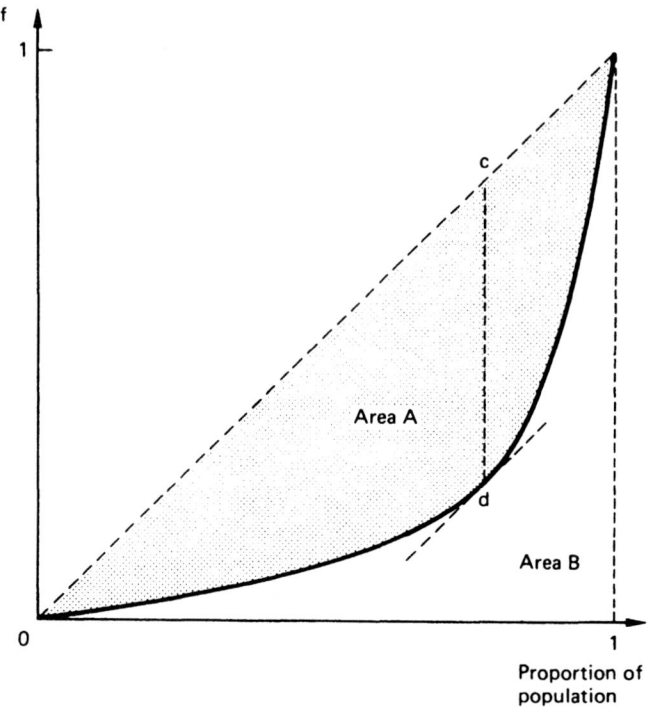

Figure 2.6   The Gini and Schutz coefficients

This property alone is an attractive one for an inequality index, but it is not the only desirable property, and we shall encounter others, some satisfied by these two indices and some not, in chapter 5.

Any device which summarizes inequality by a single number allows a *complete ordering* of income distributions: any pair of income distributions can be unambiguously ranked. By contrast, the Lorenz dominance relationship provides only a *partial ordering:* only some pairs of distributions can be compared. The Gini and Schutz coefficents can thus be used to rank the distributions in figure 2.5(b), whereas Lorenz dominance cannot. In fact, each coefficient ranks distribution B as more unequal than distribution A, as drawn. Can you sketch a pair of Lorenz curves for which the Gini and Schutz coefficient rankings conflict?

Sometimes we may want to know about the income shares of groups of people ordered, not by their income levels, but differently. For example, what is the income share of the 10 per cent of the population whose expenditures on food are the smallest? The graph plotting income shares against position in the distribution of food expenditures would look rather like a Lorenz curve, though it may have a wavy shape (figure 2.7, solid line). This graph is

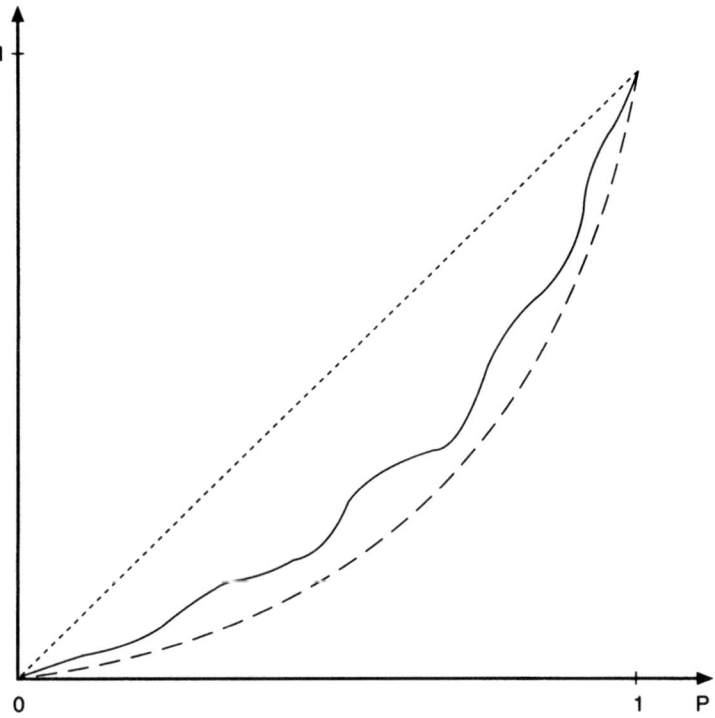

Figure 2.7 Lorenz curve for income (dotted) and concentration curve for income (solid)

called the *concentration curve for income with respect to food expenditure.* Whenever we plot shares of one variate, *x*, against quantiles in the distribution of another, *y* say, the result is called the concentration curve for *x* with respect to *y*.

The concentration curve for any *x* relative to any other *y* must always lie on or above the Lorenz curve for *x*, when both are plotted in the same graph. In figure 2.7, the Lorenz curve for income is shown as a dotted line lying below the concentration curve for income with respect to food expenditure. Values *p* along the horizontal axis stand for positions in the income distribution when drawing the dotted Lorenz curve, and for positions in the food expenditure distribution when drawing the concentration curve. For every *p* between 0 and 1, the income share of the poorest 100*p* per cent of the population is equal to or lower than the income share of any other 100*p* per cent of the population – by definition! – in particular, that of the 100*p* per cent whose expenditures on food are the smallest. Hence, *every concentration curve lies on or above the corresponding Lorenz curve.* The difference between the two curves, if any, is accounted for by differences in the rankings of the distributions in question (of x and y in general; here, of income and food expenditures). Concentration curves can be used, in particular, to analyse the distributive effects of taxes (see section 2.5 and also chapter 10).

Exercises

2.3.1 'Income trends during Mrs Thatcher's reign are usually described as an increase in income levels for most people (the poorest excluded), combined with a substantial growth in inequality. To this should be added a third dimension: income polarisation' (Jenkins, 1995a, p. 412). Describe Jenkins's findings.

2.3.2(a) 'Once we cast aside the socially unrealistic 45° line of equality, we are free to generate new reference lines . . .' (Paglin, 1975, p. 599). Compare Paglin's proposal with Garvy's (1952) suggestion that, in principle at least, Lorenz curve inequality should be measured relative to a reference curve displaying 'the socially desirable minimum of inequality' (p. 30). What are the implications for the Gini coefficient?

2.3.2(b) Discuss Garvy's own reservations on this, and those which followed publication of Paglin's paper (see under Paglin in the bibliography). As Garvy pointed out (p. 38), the Lorenz curve for the income distribution shown below is identical to that generated by a reference distribution allowing $50 per person.

Income unit	No. of persons	Income
A	1	$150
B	2	$100
C	3	$50

How would the use of a concentration curve resolve this difficulty? See Jenkins and O'Higgins (1989).

2.4 Lorenz curves mathematically

A distribution of income in a population of N income units can be represented either in discrete form, as $x_1 \leq x_2 \leq \ldots \leq x_N$, say, or, if N is very large, by a frequency density function $f(x)$. The Lorenz curve and Gini and Schutz coefficients can be defined formally in both cases. For some purposes the continuous formulation is more convenient, yielding insights that are not so readily accessible when incomes are defined discretely; sometimes the reverse is true. We shall adopt whichever convention is the most useful for the context at hand. Generally, this will be the continuous one, because it gives us access to the calculus. Some standard manipulations of integrals and derivatives (notably, the technique of *integration by parts*, see p. 11) are simple counterparts of quite messy combinatorical exercises.

Once we have analytical formulae, we can examine properties of the Lorenz curve and derive interpretations for the Gini and Schutz coefficients which were not apparent from the naive definitions given earlier. Let us call the Lorenz curve $L(p)$, where $0 \leq p \leq 1$. In the discrete case, the data define a sequence of positions $p = 1/N, 2/N, 3/N \ldots$ for adjacent income units (lined up from poorest to richest), whose income shares are

$$L\left(\frac{j}{N}\right) = \sum_{1 \leq i \leq j} \frac{x_i}{X} \qquad 1 \leq j \leq N \tag{2.10}$$

where X is total income. To form a continuous function $L(p)$, $0 \leq p \leq 1$, beginning with $L(0) = 0$ and ending with $L(1) = 1$, we may simply join up the points so generated with straight lines (figure 2.8). However, this makes for a complicated mathematical formula, which is inconvenient for many analytical purposes.

There is more headway to be made using the continuous formulation. Let the frequency density function $f(x)$ be defined over an interval $[0, z]$, with

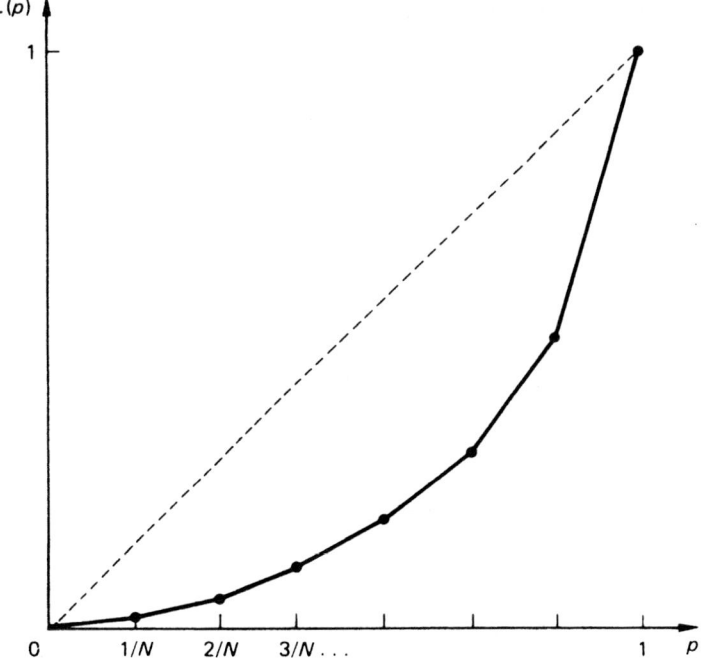

Figure 2.8   A Lorenz curve based on discrete income data

positive density between a lower income $x_1 \geq 0$ and an upper one $x_N \leq z$ (we discussed this modelling convenience on p. 20). For each $p \in (0, 1)$ there is just one income level y with rank p. It lies between x_1 and x_N and is identified by the equation $p = F(y)$. The income of the first $100p$ per cent of income units is $N\int_0^y xf(x)\,dx$, and total income is $N\int_0^z xf(x)\,dx = N\mu$ recall (2.2). Hence we can define the Lorenz curve $L(p)$ at such p-values by

$$p = F(y) \Rightarrow L(p) = \int_0^y \frac{xf(x)\,dx}{\mu} \tag{2.11}$$

A minor complication arises when extending (2.11) to $p = 0$ and $p = 1$. Obviously we want (2.11) to say that $L(0) = 0$ and $L(1) = 1$, but the income level y ranked bottom ($p = 0$) or top ($p = 1$) may not be uniquely identified by the equation $p = F(y)$ if we have extended the domain of the frequency density function. The definition in (2.11) would then appear problematic at $p = 0$ and $p = 1$. However, this is a trivial point: each income outside of the support of $f(x)$ occurs with zero frequency, and contributes nothing to the integral in (2.11).

To distinguish the Lorenz curves associated with two distribution functions $F(x)$ and $G(x)$, we shall denote them $L_F(p)$ and $L_G(p)$, or simply L_F and L_G. We shall say that distribution F *Lorenz dominates* distribution G if

$$L_F(p) \geq L_G(p) \text{ for all } p \in [0, 1], \text{ and } L_F \neq L_G \tag{2.12}$$

Under what circumstances can the Lorenz curves of two distributions F and G be identical? This happens if one distribution is a scaled-up version of the other, but there is no other possibility. In particular, if we know mean income μ and the shape of the Lorenz curve $L(p)$, we can infer the distribution of income. This can be seen from the following, which is our first formal result:

Lemma 2.1

If $p = F(y)$, $0 < p < 1$, then $L'(p) = y/\mu$ and $L''(p) = 1/[\mu f(y)]$

Proof Differentiate (2.11) using the chain rule:

$$\frac{dL}{dp} = \frac{d[L(p)]/dy}{dp/dy} = \frac{yf(y)/\mu}{f(y)} = \frac{y}{\mu}$$

Now differentiate again.   QED

At the two extremities, $p = 0$ and $p = 1$, the proof would fall down. It is nevertheless true that

$$L'(0) = \frac{x_1}{\mu} \quad \text{and} \quad L'(1) = \frac{x_N}{\mu} \tag{2.13}$$

in the case that $f(x)$ has finite support $[x_1, x_N]$. These derivatives must be interpreted as the *right* derivative at $p = 0$, and *left* derivative at $p = 1$; the results are obtained simply by taking limits as $p \downarrow 0$ and $p \uparrow 1$ in the lemma.

Several useful insights flow from the results in lemma 2.1. First, $L(p)$ is upward-sloping and convex, confirming the shape drawn in figure 2.4. Second, as just claimed, the frequency density function can be recovered from a knowledge of mean income and the (curvature of the) Lorenz curve.

A third implication concerns the point on the Lorenz curve where the slope $L'(p)$ is unity. *The Lorenz curve is parallel to, and so farthest from, the line of complete equality at the percentile point corresponding to mean income μ.* Now recall figure 2.6 which shows the Schutz coefficient S as the vertical distance cd between the 45° line and a tangent of slope 1 to the Lorenz curve. It is immediate that

$$S = F(\mu) - L(F(\mu)) \tag{2.14}$$

The Gini coefficient G can also be expressed in terms of the Lorenz curve $L(p)$. Recalling its area definition in equation (2.8), we have

$$G = 1 - 2\int_0^1 L(p)\mathrm{d}p \tag{2.15}$$

Simple transformations of these two expressions bring new insights into the Schutz coefficient S and Gini coefficient G. First, for the Schutz coefficient:

$$S = F(\mu) - L(F(\mu)) = \int_0^\mu f(x)\mathrm{d}x - \int_0^\mu \frac{xf(x)\mathrm{d}x}{\mu} = \int_0^\mu \frac{(\mu - x)f(x)\mathrm{d}x}{\mu} \tag{2.16}$$

This is simply a matter of definition. Second, for the Gini coefficient:

$$G = 1 - 2\int_0^1 L(p)\mathrm{d}p = 2\int_0^1 pL'(p)\mathrm{d}p - 1 = -1 + 2\int_0^\infty \frac{yF(y)f(y)\mathrm{d}y}{\mu} \tag{2.17}$$

For this, we use first integration by parts and then substitution of $p = F(y)$. Interesting interpretations for the Schutz and Gini coefficients are revealed by these new expressions. We state them formally in a theorem:

Theorem 2.1

(a)   The Schutz coefficient measures that proportion of total income which would have to be transferred from incomes above the mean to incomes below it to achieve complete equality.

(b)   The Gini coefficient can be calculated in terms of the covariance between incomes y and their ranks $F(y)$: $G = [2/\mu]\mathrm{cov}\{y, F(y)\}$

Proof (a) Suppose that all of a person's income in excess of the mean level μ could be transferred to others those incomes are below average, and complete equality thereby attained, all income units now having μ. (Such an exercise would raise serious political and practical problems, of course.) Then the amount transferred to an income $x < \mu$ would be $(\mu - x)$; and the total amount transferred to the below average incomes would be $N\int_0^\mu (\mu - x)f(x)\,dx$. As a fraction of total income $X = N\mu$, this is just S.

(b) The covariance between two random variables Y and Z is $E(YZ) - E(Y)E(Z)$, where E is the expectations operator. Taking Y as income, and Z as its rank $F(Y)$, the result follows with a little manipulation from (2.17), because expected rank in any distribution is one half: $E(F(Y)) = \int_0^\infty F(y)f(y)\,dy = \int_0^1 p\,dp = \frac{1}{2}$.   QED

As we originally defined them, the Schutz coefficient was easy to measure (just take a ruler to the Lorenz diagram), and the Gini coefficient was easy to interpret (area measures are like that). The new results show a sort of converse. The Schutz coefficient is, in fact, quite easy to interpret: it measures the 'work to be done' in creating complete equality. The Gini coefficient is easy to compute, at least for a large microdata set (when the continuous formulation for the income distribution is appropriate): any statistical software package which includes sorting and covariance-taking procedures can do it.[10]

It we take the discrete starting-point for income distribution, with the incomes listed as $x_1 \le x_2 \le \ldots \le x_N$ and the Lorenz curve taking the form illustrated in figure 2.8, a formula for the Gini coefficient can be developed by breaking areas up into triangles and rectangles, using some algebra and summing:

$$G = 1 + \frac{1}{N} - \frac{\{x_N + 2x_{N-1} + 3x_{N-2} + \ldots + Nx_1\}}{N^2\mu} \tag{2.18a}$$

A more elegant derivation of this is obtained by considering the discrete analogue of the expression on the right in (2.17). This involves the rank-weighted sum of income levels; the rank of income x_i is $p_i = i/N$; the reader could check that, if N is large, (2.17) and (2.18a) are equivalent. An alternative formula for the Gini coefficient in the discrete case is

$$G = \sum_i \sum_j \frac{|x_i - x_j|}{2N^2\mu} \tag{2.18b}$$

showing that it equals one half of the mean difference between income pairs, divided by mean income (see exercise 2.4.5 below).

The effect on the Lorenz curve and Schutz and Gini coefficients of a small income transfer from a richer to a poorer income unit can be seen most easily using the discrete framework of analysis. Suppose that £1 is transferred from income x_h to income x_k where $h > k$, and that there is no other change in the distribution. What happens to the income shares $L(j/N) = \sum_{1 \le i \le j} x_i/X$, $1 \le j$

$\leq N$? Since total income X is unaffected, we may answer this question by looking at the cumulative sums $\Sigma_{1\leq i\leq j}x_i$, $1\leq j\leq N$. These are obviously unaffected for $j < k$; they increase by £1 for $k\leq j< h$, because the recipient of the transfer is counted in, but not the donor; and they are unaffected for $j\geq h$, because the transfer nets out when the donor is included in the sum as well as the recipient. Hence the Lorenz curve ordinate $L(j/N)$ shifts upwards for $k\leq j< h$ but is otherwise unaffected. The new distribution Lorenz dominates the old one.

It is clear what happens to the Schutz coefficient as a result of this transfer: just consider theorem 2.1(a), alternatively sketch the old and new Lorenz curves and use your ruler. The effect on the Gini coefficient is easily seen by inspecting (2.18a). The long term in parentheses increases by $N + 1 - k$, due to the unit increase in x_k, and falls by $N + 1 - h$, due to the unit decrease in x_h. Thus G falls by $2(h - k)/N^2\mu$. These effects may be summarized as follows:

Theorem 2.2

(a)   The Schutz coefficient is reduced, by the amount $1/X$, by any unit income transfer from an above-average to a below-average income, and is unaffected by transfers *not* across the mean.

(b)   The Gini coefficient is reduced by a small income transfer from a higher to a lower income; it is not sensitive to the levels of the incomes between which the transfer takes place; it *is* sensitive to the difference in rank across which the transfer takes place.

This simple result makes very clear the dangers of using an index of inequality as a criterion for inequality-reducing intervention in the distribution of income: unavoidable, built-in value judgements are involved. If we wish to approve *every* transfer from higher to lower incomes (this is the so-called *Principle of Transfers*), the Schutz coefficient is inappropriate. If we wish to value more a transfer between persons with a given income difference if these incomes are lower than if they are higher (the *Principle of Diminishing Transfers*), the Gini coefficient is also unsuitable. We shall discuss these two principles in some detail in the next chapter.

Exercises

2.4.1(a)   In a population of N persons, suppose that one person has all of the income. Show that the Gini coefficient takes the value $1 - [1/N]$.

2.4.1(b)   Calculate the slope at $p = j/N$, $0\leq j\leq N$, of the Lorenz curve $L(j/N)$ defined in (2.10) by considering figure 2.8. Compare what obtains when N is very large with the values of $L'(p)$ for continuously distributed income given in lemma 2.1 and equations (2.13).

2.4.2   Let $f(y)$ be the frequency density function for income y, with mean μ. What is the frequency density function for $x = y/\mu$? Use lemma 2.1

to conclude that the distribution of y/μ can be deduced from the information contained in the Lorenz curve for y.

2.4.3   In what ways can population growth affect the Lorenz curve and Gini coefficient? Consider Paglin (1975), Petersen (1979) and Lam (1986a).

2.4.4   If one has grouped data, and not microdata, how can the Gini coefficient best be estimated? Refer to Cowell and Mehta (1982). What recommendation do these authors make, to statistical bureaux who may be contemplating the provision of grouped data in greater detail?

2.4.5(a)   Use equation (2.17) and more integration by parts to show that the Gini coefficient can be written $G = \int_0^\infty F(x)[1 - F(x)]\,dx/\mu$. Given that $2F(1 - F)$ is the difference between the distribution functions of the maximum and minimum of two random observations from F (see, for example, Kendall and Stuart (1977, chapter 14)), relate this formula to the discrete one in (2.18b).

2.4.5(b)   Describe Yitzhaki's (1998) 'more than a dozen' alternative ways to express the Gini coefficient.

2.4.6   Let the income distribution $\Omega = \{x_1, x_2, \ldots, x_N\}$ be partitioned into subgroups Ω_k of size N_k and mean μ_k, so that from (2.18b) the Gini coefficient for Ω_k is $G_k = \Sigma_{i \in \Omega_k} \Sigma_{i \in \Omega_k} |x_i - x_j|/2N_k^2 \mu_k$. Write the overall Gini coefficient in the form $G = \Sigma_k[N_k^2 \mu_k/N^2 \mu]G_k + D$ for an appropriate expression D. Now consult Mookherjee and Shorrocks (1982). Show how D can be split into a 'between groups' term and an 'interaction' term. What particular application do Mookherjee and Shorrocks have in mind, and how do they obviate the 'awkward interaction effect' (p. 889)?[11]

2.4.7   '. . . the Gini coefficient . . . can be interpreted in terms of the average expected gain from having the option of receiving the income of someone else selected at random' (Pyatt, 1976, p. 253). Prove this assertion.

2.4.8   Let $\mathbf{x} = (x_1, x_2, \ldots, x_N)$ and $\mathbf{y} = (y_1, y_2, \ldots, y_N)$ be two different ways of distributing the same amount of income $(\Sigma x_i = \Sigma y_i)$ among N people, and suppose that $\mathbf{x}$ Lorenz dominates $\mathbf{y}$: $L_x(j/N) \geq L_y(j/N)$ for all j. Demonstrate that $\mathbf{x}$ can be obtained from $\mathbf{y}$ by a finite sequence of rich-to-poor transfers (adapt Rothschild and Stiglitz, 1973, p. 191).[12]

2.4.9   Show that the variance of an income distribution is raised by every transfer to a better-off income unit; and that only those transfers made to sufficiently less well-off income units cause a reduction in variance.

2.4.10   'It seems then that the Gini coefficient of inequality in lifetime incomes is what economists really need to measure' (Friesen and Miller, 1983, p. 139). Review the arguments in support of this assertion. What are the data requirements for the estimation of a lifetime Gini coefficient? See also Lillard (1977) and Irvine (1981).

2.4.11   '. . . there have been only few attempts to determine the Lorenz ordering within parametric families of income distributions from the values of the respective parameters. For the . . . Pareto, gamma and lognormal families . . . Lorenz curves for different members of the respective families do not intersect . . . for the . . . Sing-Maddala family . . . some curves intersect, and some do not' (Wilfling and Krämer, 1993, pp. 53–54). Summarize Wilfling and Krämer's findings.

2.5   Income tax, the concept of redistribution and reranking

We conclude the chapter with some remarks and preliminary analysis to do with income tax. We shall consider in particular what is meant when it is said that a progressive income tax is *redistributive*. Transferring income from rich to poor is an act of redistribution, in anyone's language – but how can we talk of an income tax, which only takes away from people without necessarily returning the proceeds to others, as 'redistributive'? Since much of the book hangs on the issue of redistribution through progressive income taxation, we had better get this clear.

In the real world, the income tax liability of an individual or household with income x is not determined solely by that income level x. Non-income factors which go towards the determination of taxes typically include marital status, number of children, homeownership (mortgage interest may be allowed against tax for owner-occupiers) and approved items of expenditure such as charitable contributions, life assurance premia, medical and dental expenses. State and local tax payments may also be set against the (federal) income tax in some cases.

These are complicating factors we could well do without from the analytical point of view, and we shall make some simplifying assumptions here for mathematical convenience. Assume (for now) that all population units with the same income x *do* have the same tax liability. Then we may call this liability $t(x)$. We could also assume that the function $t(x)$ is differentiable. The derivative $t'(x)$ would measure the *marginal tax rate*, that rate which applies to a small increase dx in a recipient's income. Typically, an income tax schedule embodies a sequence of fixed, and increasing, marginal tax rates, beginning with zero for the lowest incomes, and with 'steps' at specified threshold values of taxable income. A further assumption we could make is that for taxpayers, both tax and post-tax income increase when pre-tax income increases. Then our function $t(x)$ will satisfy these assumptions:

$$0 \leq t(x) < x \quad \text{and} \quad 0 \leq t'(x) < 1 \tag{2.19}$$

This simplification is not so far removed from what actually pertains, (a) if we confine attention solely to an appropriate sub-population, for example to single or married homeowners; (b) if expenditure-related tax deductions enjoy a systematic relationship with income level; and (c) if we restrict the income measure to that which is taxed on a current 'pay-as-you-earn' basis. At any rate, we shall proceed, noting the problems for realism which are raised by this simplified mathematical structure, and returning to these later.

First, let us aggregate the tax $t(x)$ across the $Nf(x)\,dx$ units with incomes in each infinitesimal range $[x, x + dx]$, to obtain total revenue:

$$T = N\int_0^z t(x)f(x)\,dx \tag{2.20}$$

The overall average tax rate, or fraction of all income taken in tax (this is sometimes called the *total tax ratio*), is

$$g = \frac{T}{X} = \int_0^z \frac{t(x)f(x)\,dx}{\mu} \tag{2.21}$$

Clearly, μg is the average tax liability, and so $\mu(1 - g)$ is mean post-tax income. With a slight change to previous notation, let $L_X(p)$ denote the Lorenz curve for pre-tax income:

$$p = F(y) \Rightarrow L_X(p) = \int_0^y \frac{xf(x)\,dx}{\mu} \tag{2.22}$$

and let L_{X-T} and L_T respectively denote the concentration curves for post-tax income and for tax liabilities with respect to pre-tax income. Each has the same argument p as L_X, since each cumulates the relevant shares (of post-tax income or taxes) by positions in the pre-tax income distribution. Thus

$$p = F(y) \Rightarrow L_{X-T}(p) = \int_0^y \frac{[x - t(x)]f(x)\,dx}{\mu(1-g)} \tag{2.23}$$

and

$$p = F(y) \Rightarrow L_T(p) = \int_0^y \frac{t(x)f(x)\,dx}{\mu g} \tag{2.24}$$

It is straightforward to establish the mathematical relationship between the functions L_X, L_{X-T} and L_T. The numerators of the right-hand sides in (2.23)–(2.24) add up to the one in (2.22). Cross-multiplying in these equations by the respective denominators, and adding, we find

$$L_X \equiv g\,L_T + (1-g)\,L_{X-T} \tag{2.25}$$

The Lorenz curve L_X is a weighted average of tax and post-tax income concentration curves. Therefore

$$L_{X-T} \geq L_X \Leftrightarrow L_T \leq L_X \tag{2.26}$$

Under the assumptions we made in (2.19), there are no differences between the rankings of people by their pre-tax incomes, their post-tax incomes and their taxes. Therefore L_{X-T} and L_T are the Lorenz curves for post-tax income and taxes under these assumptions (recall the discussion about concentration curves and rank differences on p. 29). Hence (2.25) contains a useful insight: *incomes are less unequal after tax than before if and only if taxes are distributed more unequally than the incomes to which they apply.*

You may recognize in this statement a characteristic of progressive income taxation. If the average tax rate $t(x)/x$ is increasing with income, which is what progression entails, then taxes are indeed distributed more unequally than pre-tax incomes (the rich having even more of them than they do of pre-tax income). Hence *a progressive tax exerts an equalizing effect on the distribution of income.* In chapter 7 we shall give formal expression to this line of reasoning.

This equalizing effect is also known as the *redistributive effect* of the tax. Yet redistribution is a term in the English language commonly understood to refer to *the new distribution of a given total.* Why is this terminology used in the case of an income tax, which *reduces* total income, albeit creating more equality in the process? The answer is that we are implicitly making a comparison between what pertains under the existing tax and what would pertain under a proportional tax raising the same revenue (known as an *equal-yield flat tax*). The latter would be have no effect whatever on the Lorenz curve for income (can you see why?), and is a natural benchmark. The upward shift of the Lorenz curve, from L_X to L_{X-T}, which obtains when a progressive tax is applied, is precisely the upward shift which would occur by introducing progression into the equal-yield flat tax. The equalizing effect of a progressive income tax can thus be achieved by first applying the equal-yield flat tax, and then making a sequence of rich-to-poor transfers (exercise 2.4.8); this is why it is called the redistributive effect of the progressive tax.

If the assumptions in (2.19) do *not* hold, then the concentration curve for post-tax income with respect to pre-tax income may not be the same as the post-tax Lorenz curve, and our arguments about equalizing effects must be formulated more carefully. First, an income-determined tax $t(x)$ would fail (2.19) if the marginal tax rate $t'(x)$ exceeded 100 per cent at some income levels; this could happen if benefits are withdrawn against income at the same time as applying taxes, causing the so-called poverty trap (in which one's net income would go down if one's gross income were to increase). Second, as we have noted, there may be no systematic relationship between incomes and taxes at all: for example, in the UK a married couple with both partners working had until recently more than twice the lump-sum tax allowance (tax-free income) of a single person. In this case, a couple can be made better-off by the tax system in money (or even equivalent) income terms than a single with the same or higher pre-tax income.

Whenever non-income characteristics are taken into account in determining tax liabilities, reversals in the ranking of incomes are likely to occur in the transition from pre-tax to post-tax. This is called *reranking*. It means that the concentration curve for post-tax income with respect to pre-tax income, call it $L_{X-T}(p)$ even in the absence of (2.19), will differ from the post-tax Lorenz curve, call this $L^*(p)$.[13] As we know, the concentration curve will dominate:

$$L_{X-T}(p) \geq L^*(p) \text{ for all } p \tag{2.27}$$

and therefore does not measure inequality. The full equalizing effect of the tax is seen in the transformation:

$$\text{pre-tax Lorenz curve } L_X \rightarrow \text{post-tax Lorenz curve } L^* \tag{2.28}$$

and is overstated by the transformation:

$$\text{pre-tax Lorenz curve } L_X \rightarrow \text{post-tax concentration curve } L_{X-T} \tag{2.29}$$

which tracks the incidence of the tax on given groups of income units (quantiles in the pre-tax income distribution). The correction factor is a downward shift:

$$\text{post-tax concentration curve } L_{X-T} \rightarrow \text{post-tax Lorenz curve } L^* \tag{2.30}$$

reflecting the extent of reranking.

Let G_X and G_{X-T} be the Gini coefficients for pre- and post-tax income respectively. Area measures of the extent to which concentration curves depart from the 45° line can be defined in the same way as Gini coefficients, and are known as *concentration coefficients*. The concentration coefficients for post-tax income is

$$C_{X-T} = 1 - 2 \int_0^1 L_{X-T}(p) \mathrm{d}p \tag{2.31}$$

and the one for taxes is

$$C_T = 1 - 2 \int_0^1 L_T(p) \mathrm{d}p \tag{2.32}$$

(compare (2.15)). The various curves and indices which arise for a typical income tax system with reranking are illustrated in figure 2.9. Keeping in mind the warning we sounded after theorem 2.2 about using Gini coefficients to measure inequality reduction, we could quantify the equalizing effect of this tax system in terms of its impact on the Gini coefficient. The reduction brought about by the tax can be decomposed, to correspond to the transformations in (2.28)–(2.30):

$$[G_X - G_{X-T}] = [G_X - C_{X-T}] - [G_{X-T} - C_{X-T}] \tag{2.33}$$

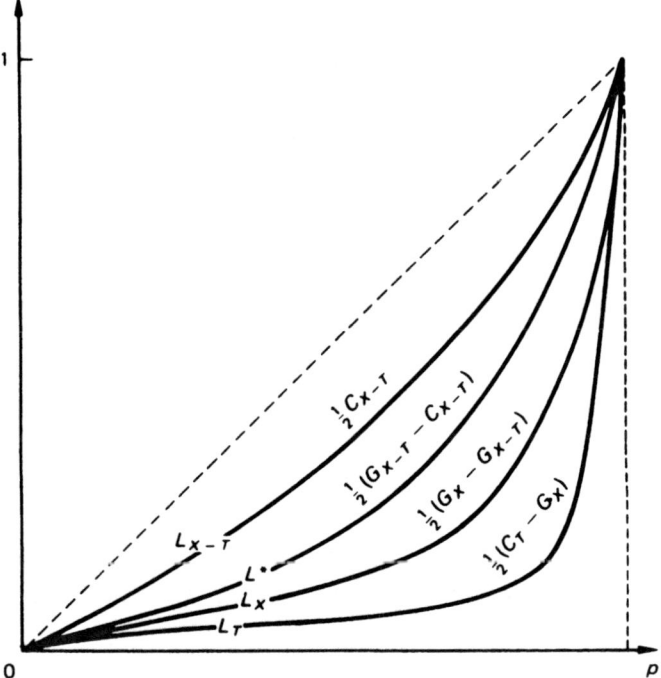

Figure 2.9 Lorenz curves, concentration curves and area measures, in the case of an inequality-reducing income tax

the first term on the right showing how the tax affects the income shares of quantiles of people in the pre-tax distribution, and the latter capturing the negative contribution of reranking. The first term overstates the inequality impact of the tax, by counting in rank reversal effects, in which the tax system merely goes to switch people's positions with no effect on inequality. We shall return to this issue in chapter 10.

Exercises

2.5.1(a) Generalize lemma 2.1 to the concentration curves L_T, L_{X-T}, by showing that if $p = F(y)$ then $L'_T(p) = t(y)/\mu g$ and $L'_{X-T}(p) = [y - t(y)]/\mu(1 - g)$.

2.5.1(b) Can you develop Schutz-type coefficients for the curves L_T and L_{X-T}, with intuitively pleasing properties? See Pfähler (1983).

2.5.1(c) Can you give covariance characterizations of the concentration coefficients C_T and C_{X-T}? See Jenkins (1988a).

2.5.2   Suppose that income x is made up of two components, $x = u + v$ (for example, unearned and earned income). Prove that according to the

Lorenz criterion, inequality in total income is no greater than in the more unequal component. *Hint*: show that the Lorenz curve for x can be written $L_X(p) = \theta L_U(p) + (1 - \theta) L_V(p)$, where L_U and L_V are the concentration curves for u and v with respect to x respectively, and $\theta = \bar{u}/(\bar{u} + \bar{v})$. Now exploit the relationships between these concentration curves and the Lorenz curves L_U^* and L_V^* for u and v, to prove that $L_X(p) \geq \min \{L_U^*(p), L_V^*(p)\}$ for each $p \in [0, 1]$.[14]

Notes

1 For discussion of the problems involved in moving from a distribution of annual income to one of multiyear or even lifetime income, see Benus and Morgan (1975).

2 An additional and quite recent UK microdata source is the *British Household Panel Survey*, published by the Institute of Economic and Social Research at the University of Essex and distributed by their Data Archive in annual 'waves'. These track a fixed group of individuals and related household members over time, and are particularly useful for the analysis of income dynamics.

3 A sizeable sum of income 'unallocated by ranges' is also recorded in ET, whose presence can be inferred only from national accounting procedures (but not tracked down).

4 This is the scale applied to 'income before housing costs'; a slightly different version is applied in case 'income after housing costs' is the chosen measure. The distinction is made, and maintained throughout all of the statistical analysis in HBAI, because of the significant variations in UK housing costs which do not reflect variations in housing quality.

5 The 'income before housing costs' case is the one shown here.

6 A histogram showing amounts rather than numbers is known as an *income density polygon*. One of these (with variable bin widths) is displayed in *Survey of Personal Incomes* for 1984/5.

7 I thank Stephen Jenkins for the provision of both figures. The kernel density estimate was obtained using an adaptive kernel.

8 On this so-called 'vanishing middle' phenomenon, and on other forms of polarization, see also Strobel (1993), Esteban and Ray (1994), Wolfson (1994, 1997), Jenkins (1995a) and Burkhauser *et al.* (1999). Wolfson contains a number of additional references.

9 A measure of skewness that is used for probability distributions is $(\mu - x^*)/\sigma$, where x^* is the median as before. For a typical income distribution, this is positive: hence the terminology *positive skew*.

10 Lerman and Yitzhaki (1984, 1989) derived the result in part (b) of theorem 2.1 and showed how to adapt it for small sample sizes. Jenkins (1988b) pointed out the usefulness of the result for handling microdata.

11 In Lambert and Aronson (1993), graphical analysis is used to reveal interpretations for all three components in the Gini decomposition (the within groups, between groups and interaction effects) in terms of areas on a Lorenz curve and concentration curve diagram. See chapter 5, section 2 for more on this.

12 This result has also been derived using a different (axiomatic) approach by Fields and Fei (1978, theorem 2.1, p. 309). See also Foster (1985).

13 If v is post-tax income and $h(v)$ and $H(v)$ are its frequency density and distribution functions, then $L^*(p)$ is defined as follows: $p = H(u) \Rightarrow L^*(p) = \int_0^u vh(v)\,dv/\mu(1 - g)$. Precisely when v is not an increasing function of x, $h(v)$ and $f(x)$ differ.

14 This result is obtained in Rietveld (1990).

3

Lorenz curves and welfare comparisons

The Lorenz curve shows how the cake is divided, but it does not reveal the size of the cake or the number of mouths. In other words, the mean income and population size cannot be inferred from the information contained in a Lorenz curve. What, then, can be deduced, in terms of well-being, about the dominating distribution when two Lorenz curves do not intersect? What can be said when they cross? Other information is needed, in addition to Lorenz curve configuration, for the relative well-being of two populations of income units to be determined. We shall see that the additional information of mean incomes, and sometimes also variances, can be used to extract considerable normative significance from the information contained in a given pair of Lorenz curves. And we shall go on to consider how non-income information (such as family composition, age, infirmity) can also be brought to bear.

Much of the measurement theory we shall expound was set out by Serge Kolm in 1965 and presented at a Round Table Conference of the International Economic Association at Biarritz in September 1966. An English language exposition surfaced in Kolm (1969), but the terminology used by Kolm in this source is somewhat opaque, and his deductive style, though penetrating and elegant, is condensed and difficult for economists to grasp. Ultimately, it was Tony Atkinson who, in 1970, captured the attention of the profession, with a strikingly clear and illuminating analysis. The paper known as 'Atkinson 1970' has become one of the most widely-cited of all articles written by economists, and is commonly regarded as having laid the foundations for the analysis of welfare and inequality, notwithstanding Kolm's prior contribution, of which there has been at best a patchy recognition.

We begin by describing in section 3.1 of this chapter the so-called Atkinson theorem, according to which one distribution of income is welfare-superior to another with the same mean if and only if it Lorenz dominates. We are then led, in section 3.2, to the theorem of Shorrocks (1983a), according to which dominance of one *generalized Lorenz curve* over another (these being obtained as the products of the respective Lorenz curves and mean incomes) is the appropriate criterion for welfare superiority when mean incomes differ. There are complications when generalized Lorenz curves cross, and these are considered in section 3.3, but information on variances can sometimes be adduced to provide a welfare comparison, as explained in section 3.4.

At this point, we turn to the question of non-income information and its relevance for social welfare. There are two ways to take such information into account. One involves the appropriate use of an equivalence scale and existing dominance methodology. Ebert (1997) has determined what is meant by the word 'appropriate'; we describe what is involved in section 3.5. The other way is to refrain from equivalizing and use a new methodology. Atkinson and Bourguignon (1987) have shown how the generalized Lorenz curve approach can in fact be extended, to allow for systematic differences in the needs of income units, into a sequential dominance criterion. The chapter concludes with a consideration of sequential methods.

3.1   Comparing Lorenz curves

Lorenz curves provide a visual way to assess the inequality in an income distribution and to compare distributions. We might be looking at inequality within a country in two different years, or in two different countries, or before and after an income tax or tax reform. The much-celebrated 'Atkinson theorem', presented in Atkinson (1970) but also formulated earlier by Kolm as we have said, gives the terms under which such a Lorenz curve comparison has normative significance. We state the theorem immediately and discuss its implications. Later, when we have set out some mathematical preliminaries, will we prove it as a special case of a more general result.

Theorem 3.1

Let $F(x)$, $G(x)$ be two income distributions with equal means, $\mu_F = \mu_G$. Then

$$L_F(p) \geq L_G(p) \text{ for all } p \in [0, 1] \Leftrightarrow \int U(x) f(x) \mathrm{d}x \geq \int U(x) g(x) \mathrm{d}x$$

for every strictly increasing and concave function $U(x)$.[1]

In the previous chapter we suggested attributing a level of utility $U(x)$ to each income of x, calling the average utility $\int U(x) f(x) \mathrm{d}x$ across a distribution $F(x)$ *social welfare*, and comparing this between distributions. The Atkinson theorem tells us that, in the case of a strictly increasing and concave utility function $U(x)$, the result of such an exercise will be to prefer the distribution with the dominating Lorenz curve in any equal-mean comparison where the Lorenz curves do not cross. In order to assess the strength of such a recommendation, we had better examine quite closely the assumptions being made.

Non-income factors are entirely neglected by the utility function $U(x)$. This is not surprising: the Lorenz curves $L_F(p)$ and $L_G(p)$ also suppress this aspect of the underlying distributions $F(x)$ and $G(x)$. Population sizes are not relevant for the Atkinson theorem either, since welfares are evaluated as average utility. In the next chapter we shall consider some general issues concerning the formulation of social welfare functions. Taking the average utility-of-income approach as given, the assumption of *concavity* merits attention. The symbol $\Leftrightarrow$ in the theorem shows that welfare superiority according to all increasing and concave utilities is both necessary and sufficient to ensure a more equal division of any cake of a given size. What is it about concavity that guarantees this?

As we shall see in chapter 4, there are a number of quite distinct rationales for evaluating the welfare in an income distribution $F(x)$ as

$$W_F = \int U(x) f(x) \, dx \tag{3.1}$$

and concavity of $U(x)$ has a different interpretation in each case.

One approach to making social judgements, which leads to the form in (3.1), and suggests an appealing interpretation for the concavity of $U(x)$, is through the so-called *ethical observer*. If a socially concerned and personally disinterested individual were to make a choice between income distributions, how would he or she proceed? We may call this person a *social decision-maker*. To rationalize (3.1), let him or her impose on the distribution his or her own (social decision-maker's) utility-of-income function $U(x)$. This will not necessarily be the same function as that of some other social decision-maker. But if each such observer uses a (strictly) concave utility, they will all favour the Lorenz-dominating distribution in any choice where mean incomes are equal and Lorenz curves do not intersect.[2]

What does strict concavity of an imposed decision-maker's utility function mean? It connotes *transfer-approval*. Figure 3.1 shows that if and only if $U(x)$ is everywhere strictly concave, will the deemed loss in utility from taking £1 from any particular income recipient be more-than-compensated by the gain from giving it to somebody else further down the distribution. A social decision-maker for whom $U(x)$ is strictly concave supports the *Principle of Transfers*; later, we shall see how to impose an additional restriction on $U(x)$ so that the social decision-maker favours the more demanding *Principle of Diminishing Transfers*. Both of these principles were mentioned in respect of inequality indices in chapter 2 (p. 35); here, they arise in the context of social choice.

Another rationale for the social evaluation function in (3.1) derives from the veil of ignorance thought-experiment, already described informally on p. 21. Here too, there is a persuasive interpretation for concavity of $U(x)$, to do with the observer's attitude to risk, but we defer its consideration until the next chapter.

Taking as given the average utility approach to measuring social welfare, and concavity of the utility function, what Lorenz configuration guarantees

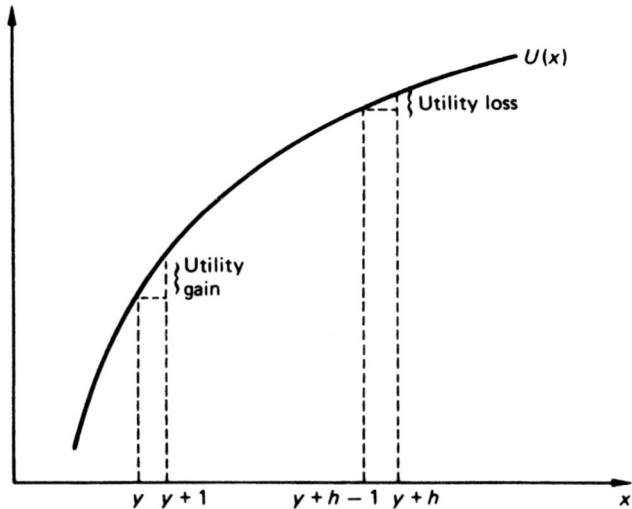

Figure 3.1 Social decision-maker's imposed utility-of-income function

welfare approval when mean incomes are unequal? We shall address this question shortly. It is instructive to ask first: What does the Atkinson theorem *per se* tell us about an unequal-mean comparison where there is Lorenz dominance?

Suppose that distribution 1 Lorenz dominates distribution 2, but mean incomes are not equal. Specifically, suppose $\mu_1 = k\mu_2$ for some $k \neq 1$. Now form a new income distribution 3 from distribution 2 by multiplying all the incomes in it by k. Then 3 has the same mean as 1 and the same Lorenz curve as 2. Now we can apply the Atkinson theorem to 1 and 3. Hence distribution 1, with the inner Lorenz curve, is preferred to 3, the mean-adjusted version of 2, according to all social welfare functions based on strictly increasing and concave utility of income functions $U(x)$. We have found a formal way to say that, making allowance for sizes, the way cake 1 is divided up is preferred to the way cake 2 is divided up.

What we have done is to scale the incomes in 2, without affecting the Lorenz curve, to create an equal-mean Lorenz comparison. We argued in exactly this way in section 5 of the previous chapter, when discussing redistribution. Instead of comparing the Lorenz curve for pre-tax income (call it 2) with the dominating Lorenz curve for income after application of a progressive income tax (call this 1), we scaled down pre-tax incomes by means of an equal-yield flat tax (this gives 3). By the Atkinson theorem, welfare approval is thus secured for progressive *vis-à-vis* equal-yield flat tax. This argument is taken up again in chapter 8.

Returning to comparison of income distributions 1 and 2 which do not have the same mean incomes but which do have non-intersecting Lorenz curves, what insight does the conclusion just reached in respect of the mean-adjustment procedure bring? To take a real-world example: in 1970, national income (GDP) per capita in the Philippines was about twice that in India (both expressed in US dollar terms), but India had a higher Lorenz curve (Kakwani, 1980a, p. 204). We can say from this, using the Atkinson theorem, that the distribution of Indian incomes is unambiguously welfare superior to the distribution of {one half of Philippine incomes}. This does *not* amount to a recommendation for the Indian over the Philippine distribution; but it does bring some normative insight to statistical fact.

In this example, the size of the cake and the way it is divided are in conflict. The Philippine cake is larger – twice as large – but the Indian cake is more equally divided. Can we say which cake is preferable? Later, it will emerge that we can, in this particular case though not generally when the larger cake is more unequal. In cases where the larger cake also has the more equal slices, there is a definitive answer, provided in Atkinson (1970):

Corollary 3.1

Let $F(x)$, $G(x)$ be two income distributions. Then

$$\mu_F > \mu_G \text{ and } L_F(p) \geq L_G(p)$$
$$\text{for all } p \in [0,1] \Rightarrow \int U(x)f(x)\mathrm{d}x \geq \int U(x)g(x)\mathrm{d}x$$

for every strictly increasing and concave function $U(x)$.

This result is obvious in terms of the mean-adjustment procedure we have been using. The distribution of {incomes in F} is preferred to the distribution of {μ_F/μ_G times the incomes in G} and (in fact, for any strictly increasing utility, not just concave ones), the distribution of {μ_F/μ_G times the incomes in G} is preferred to the distribution of {incomes in G}. The recommendation follows.

Lorenz curves may cross one or more times (see figure 2.5(b) on p. 26). Shorrocks and Foster (1987) have derived a result rather like the one in the Atkinson theorem, if the means of two distributions are equal and their Lorenz curves cross once. The distribution whose Lorenz curve crosses the other *from above* is welfare-superior for all utility functions $U(x)$ respecting the Principle of Diminishing Transfers if and only if this distribution has a lower coefficient of variation than the other.[3] When the Lorenz curves for two unequal mean distributions 1 and 2 cross once, and the curve crossing from above has a lower coefficient of variation, the welfare comparison holds between distributions 1 and 3 (3 being the scaled version of 2), just as in the case of the Atkinson theorem. Davies and Hoy (1995) have generalized Shorrocks and Foster's result to the case of multiple Lorenz curve crossings.

We shall return to these results in section 4, once we have defined the Principle of Diminishing Transfers explicitly and cast it in the form of a restriction on the utility function.

Exercise

3.1.1 The UK's Lorenz curve for 1967 lies inside the Tunisian one for 1970. In 1970 terms, UK real GDP per capita in 1967 was $4\frac{1}{2}$ times Tunisian real GDP per capita in 1970. What normative significance do theorem 3.1 and corollary 3.1 respectively lend to these bare statistical facts? Which result provides the stronger recommendation for the UK 1967 distribution? What other factors do you think ought to be relevant to the judgement of comparative well-being in this case?

3.2   Generalized Lorenz dominance and social welfare

The Atkinson theorem says that, for equal mean comparisons, Lorenz dominance carries with it welfare approval according to every strictly increasing and concave utility-of-income function $U(x)$ – though, remember, we have not yet proved this theorem. The same welfare result obtains if the Lorenz-dominating distribution has higher mean income than the dominated one: this was corollary 3.1. What can be said more generally? What if Lorenz curves cross, or if the dominating one has the lower mean income? Can we find a simple criterion in terms of mean incomes and Lorenz configuration which is necessary and sufficient for unanimous welfare approval?

The answer is 'yes', and the criterion has become known as that of Shorrocks (1983a). Shorrocks defines the *generalized Lorenz curve* for a distribution $F(x)$ as follows:

$$p = F(y) \Rightarrow GL_F(p) = \int_0^y x f(x) \, dx = \mu_F L_F(p) \tag{3.2}$$

(recall the definition of the Lorenz curve $L_F(p)$ in (2.11) on p. 32). Generalized Lorenz dominance is precisely the criterion that is necessary and sufficient for the robust welfare approval we seek.

Theorem 3.2

Let $F(x)$, $G(x)$ be two income distributions. Then $\int U(x) f(x) \, dx \geq \int U(x) g(x) \, dx$ for every increasing and strictly concave $U(x) \Leftrightarrow GL_F(p) \geq GL_G(p)$ for all $p \in [0, 1]$.

This theorem was obtained earlier by Kolm: its statement can be found in Kolm (1969, p. 193), where generalized Lorenz dominance is termed *isophily*.[4]

A different and independent proof is also given in Kakwani (1984b). Hence the ownership of the result is at least threefold. Following established convention, we shall call it 'the Shorrocks theorem'. The theorem tells us how to proceed: given two income distributions, we simply compute (mean income) × (ordinary Lorenz curve values) and plot new curves to see whether we have a configuration for which a robust welfare distinction is available (figure 3.2). The generalized Lorenz curve cumulates income (per capita of the whole population) upwards from $p = 0$ to $p = 1$ (see exercise 3.2.1). Plotted against p, $GL_F(p)$ is convex; the slope $GL_F'(p)$ at any point $p = F(y)$ is just y (recall lemma 2.1, p. 32).

Shortly we shall prove the Shorrocks theorem in a sequence of easy steps. The proof of the Atkinson theorem will follow, because Lorenz dominance and generalized Lorenz dominance are identical requirements for distributions with the same mean. For unequal mean comparisons in which the distribution with the higher mean also has a dominating Lorenz curve, the

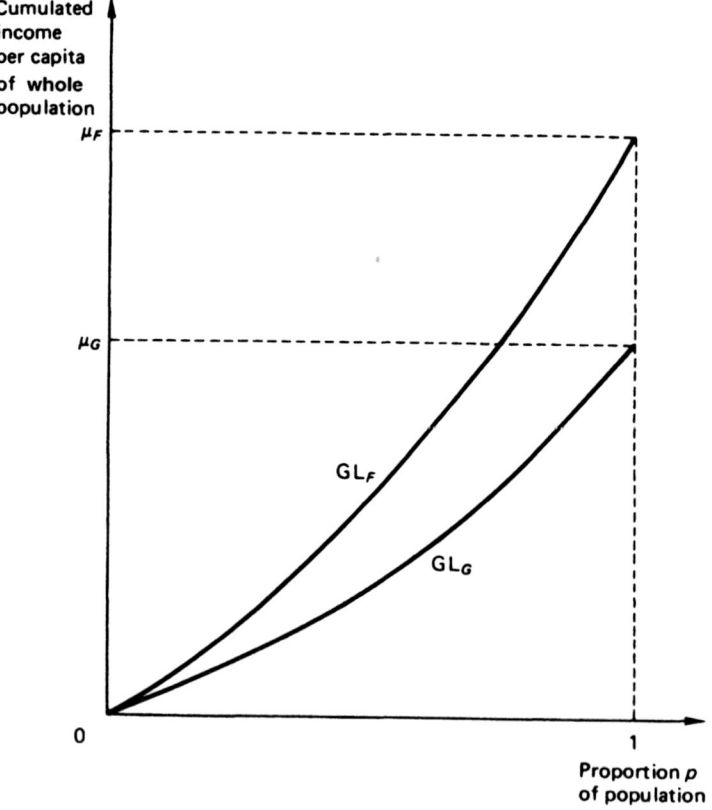

Figure 3.2   Generalized Lorenz curves (showing dominance)

Shorrocks theorem tells us the same as corollary 3.1, because the conditions $\mu_F > \mu_G$ and $L_F(p) \geq L_G(p)$ in corollary 3.1 imply generalized Lorenz dominance, $GL_F(p) \geq GL_G(p)$; welfare superiority of F follows from either result. But we can say more in such a case. For example, refer back to exercise 3.1.1, in which we said that

$$\mu_{\text{UK}} \simeq 4\frac{1}{2}\mu_{\text{Tunisia}} \text{ and } L_{\text{UK}}(p) > L_{\text{Tunisia}}(p) \text{ for all } p \in (0,1) \tag{3.3}$$

The inference from corollary 3.1 is that the distribution of income in the UK is welfare superior to that in Tunisia; but scaling the incomes as we did before (p. 47), we can conclude from the Atkinson theorem that the distribution of UK income is in fact welfare superior to the distribution of *four-and-a-half times* Tunisian income – a much stronger statement.

The contribution of the Shorrocks theorem is to resolve *some* income distribution comparisons for which Lorenz curves cross, and *some* comparisons where there is Lorenz dominance but it is the smaller cake which is more equally divided. Kakwani (1984b) has studied the success rate of generalized Lorenz dominance, demonstrating its capacity to resolve cases where the Atkinson theorem and corollary 3.1 fail. For example, for the India-Philippines example we cited earlier, in which

$$\mu_{\text{Philippines}} \simeq 2\mu_{\text{India}} \text{ but } L_{\text{Philippines}}(p) < L_{\text{India}}(p) \text{ for all } p \in (0,1) \tag{3.4a}$$

Kakwani found that

$$GL_{\text{Philippines}}(p) > GL_{\text{India}}(p) \text{ for all } p \in (0,1) \tag{3.4b}$$

so that the Philipppine distribution, with the higher mean, can be recommended despite having more inequality. Below we summarize Kakwani's findings for 248 pairwise comparisons between the 1970 distributions of real GDP in US dollar terms of 23 countries. Comparisons are between F and G and show the number of cases in the various circumstances.[5]

1	$\mu_F > \mu_G$ and $L_F \geq L_G$	116
2	$\mu_F > \mu_G$, $L_F \leq L_G$ but $GL_F \geq GL_G$	46
3	L_F and L_G cross but GL_F and GL_G do not	46
4	GL_F and GL_G cross	40

The Shorrocks theorem resolves all cases of types 2 and 3, and the Atkinson theorem and corollary deal with cases of type 1; as yet we have no results which deal with cases of type 4. As an example of the sort of international comparison which can now be established, consider the following chain, derived from Kakwani's classification, where the numbered arrow connotes in each case a welfare improvement of the indicated type:

Malawi 3→ India 1→ Pakistan 2→ Korea 2→ Costa Rica 2→
Chile 3→ Canada 1→ USA

It is clear from the number of 2s and 3s in this chain that generalized Lorenz dominance has delivered a significant increase in power. There nevertheless remain many interesting pairwise comparisons in Kakwani's sample for which generalized Lorenz curves cross. For example, no pair of countries among the following:

{Australia, Canada, West Germany, New Zealand, USA}

except for Canada $1 \rightarrow$ USA can be unambiguously ranked in welfare terms according to every strictly increasing and concave utility of income function $U(x)$. Before we turn to the problem of extracting normative conclusions in such cases as these, we address ourselves to the proof of the Atkinson and Shorrocks theorems.

A simple mathematical condition on the income distribution pair {$F(x)$, $G(x)$} is necessary and sufficient to ensure that social welfare is higher under F than under G according to every strictly increasing and concave utility function. Our approach will be to isolate this condition, and then identify it with generalized Lorenz dominance.

The initial step is to evaluate the difference in social welfare using integration by parts. For this, we need to assume that $U(x)$ is differentiable, an assumption we shall maintain throughout.

$$W_F - W_G = \int U(x)f(x)\mathrm{d}x - \int U(x)g(x)\mathrm{d}x = \int_0^z U'(x)[G(x) - F(x)]\mathrm{d}x \quad (3.5)$$

where, as previously, z is any income level in excess of the highest one occurring in either distribution. We need to specify z here, because integration by parts involves evaluating terms at the upper limit of integration. Now integrate by parts again:

$$W_F - W_G = -\int_0^z U''(x)S(x)\mathrm{d}x + U'(z)S(z) \quad (3.6)$$

where $S(x)$ is the function defined by

$$S(x) = \int_0^x [G(y) - F(y)]\mathrm{d}y \quad (3.7)$$

which evaluates cumulatively the area between the two distribution functions (figure 3.3).

The function $S(x)$ has some very useful properties. First:

$$S(0) = 0 \text{ and } S(z) = \mu_F - \mu_G \quad (3.8)$$

(recall exercise 2.2.1). Second, $S(x)$ is differentiable on the interval $[0, z]$ and has the derivative

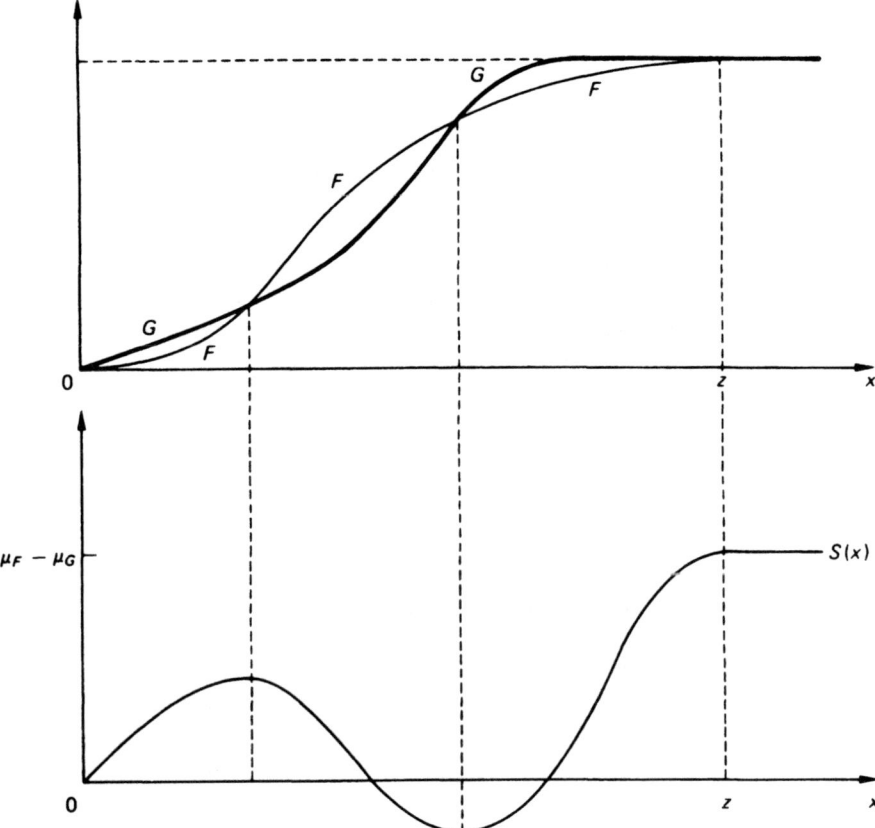

Figure 3.3 $S(x)$ and the crossings of $F(x)$ and $G(x)$

$$S'(x) = G(x) - F(x) \tag{3.9}$$

so that its stationary values correspond with the crossing points of $F(x)$ and $G(x)$ (see figure 3.3). Third, we obtain a result whose usefulness will become apparent later on:

$$\int_0^{\bar{z}} S(x)\,dx = \frac{1}{2}[(\sigma_G^2 - \sigma_F^2) + (\mu_F - \mu_G)(2z - \mu_F - \mu_G)] \tag{3.10}$$

This can be shown by making repeated applications of integration by parts (try it: go from $\int S(x)\,dx$ via $-\int x S'(x)\,dx$ to $\int x^2 S''(x)\,dx$).

To return to our pursuit of the welfare superiority criterion, it is almost immediate from (3.6) that nonnegativity of $S(x)$ is both necessary and sufficient for F to be welfare superior to G.

Lemma 3.1

$\int U(x)f(x)\,\mathrm{d}x \geq \int U(x)g(x)\,\mathrm{d}x$ for all strictly increasing and concave $U(x)$ $\Leftrightarrow$ $S(x) \geq 0$ for all $x \in [0, z]$.[6]

Proof $\Leftarrow$ By assumption, both terms on the right in (3.6) are non-negative for every strictly increasing and concave utility function. The result follows. To prove the $\Rightarrow$ assertion, first note that welfare superiority implies $\mu_F \geq \mu_G$. This is because the linear utility function $U(x) = x$ is among those which do not favour G. Now suppose for a contradiction that $S(x)$ becomes negative somewhere. Then there exists a number $k > 0$ and an interval (v, w) on which $S(x) < -k$. By choosing a utility function $U(x)$ which is linear for $x < v$, and also for $x > w$, and is concave and differentiable everywhere (figure 3.4), we have, from (3.6) and using (3.8),

$$W_F - W_G < k\int_v^w U''(x)\,\mathrm{d}x + U'(z)(\mu_F - \mu_G) = (k + \mu_F - \mu_G)U'(w) - kU'(v)$$

(3.11)

We could obviously make the right-hand side of this negative (for example, by choosing $U'(w) = 1$ and $U'(v) = 2 + (\mu_F - \mu_G)/k$). But $U(x)$ is increasing and concave, so (3.11) must be positive. This is the required contradiction.

QED

The vital link between generalized Lorenz curves and the function $S(x)$ that we need for our proof of the Shorrocks theorem can now be given. It shows that the signing of $S(x)$ is closely related to the crossing or non-crossing of the generalized Lorenz curves $GL_F(p)$ and $GL_G(p)$.[7]

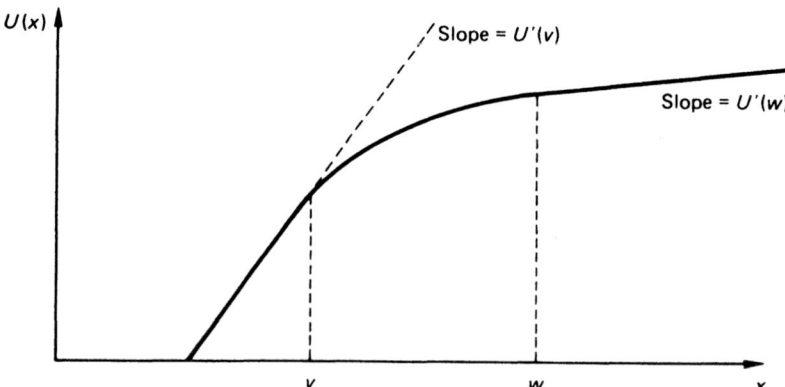

Figure 3.4   The utility function $U(x)$ used in the proof of lemma 3.1

Lemma 3.2

If $p = F(y) = G(w) \in [0, 1]$, then

$$S(w) \leq GL_F(p) - GL_G(p) \leq S(y)$$

Proof If $p = F(y) = G(w)$, then from (3.2) we have

$$GL_F(p) - GL_G(p) = \int\limits_0^y x f(x) dx - \int\limits_0^w x g(x) dx \qquad (3.12)$$

which we can write as

$$GL_F(p) - GL_G(p) = \int\limits_0^w G(x) dx - \int\limits_0^y F(x) dx - wG(w) + yF(y) \qquad (3.13)$$

using integration by parts. Now re-express this in two different ways, and apply the intermediate value theorem for integration (p. ••) to each. We have

$$GL_F(p) - GL_G(p) = S(y) - \left[\int\limits_w^y G(x) dx - (y - w)G(w) \right] \leq S(y) \qquad (3.14a)$$

and

$$GL_F(p) - GL_G(p) = S(w) + \left[(y - w)F(y) - \int\limits_w^y F(x) dx \right] \geq S(w) \qquad (3.14b)$$

QED

Now we are ready to prove the Shorrocks theorem.

Theorem 3.2

Let $F(x)$, $G(x)$ be two income distributions. Then $\int U(x)f(x) dx \geq \int U(x)g(x) dx$ for every increasing and strictly concave $U(x) \Leftrightarrow GL_F(p) \geq GL_G(p)$ for all $p \in [0, 1]$.

Proof $\Rightarrow$ From lemma 3.2, generalized Lorenz curves cannot cross if the function S does not change sign. Thus, by lemma 3.1, welfare superiority of F implies generalized Lorenz dominance. For $\Leftarrow$, since $[GL_F(p) - GL_G(p)] \geq 0$ for all p there can be no income level y for which $S(y) < 0$: otherwise, set $p = F(y)$ and apply lemma 3.2. Thus $S(x) \geq 0$ for all x. Now apply lemma 3.1.

QED

Thus we prove, at a stroke, not only the Shorrocks theorem but also the Atkinson theorem. This is simply the $\mu_F = \mu_G$ case of the Shorrocks theorem.

Exercises

3.2.1   Prove that for each $p \in [0, 1]$, $GL_F(p)/p$ is income per capita among the $100p\%$ poorest in the distribution F (whilst $GL_F(p)$ is the cumulated income of this group per capita of the overall population).

3.2.2(a) Use (3.5), (3.9) and an argument like that in lemma 3.1 to show that $\int U(x)f(x)\,dx \geq \int U(x)g(x)\,dx$ for all strictly increasing $U(x) \Leftrightarrow S'(x) \geq 0$ for all $x \in [0, z]$.[8]

3.2.2(b) *Rank dominance* of distribution F over distribution G obtains when the income at each position p in F is higher than the corresponding income in G: $p = F(y) = G(w) \Rightarrow y > w$. See Saposnik (1981). Prove that rank dominance obtains if and only if $S'(x) \geq 0$ for all x, and that rank dominance implies generalized Lorenz dominance. Now explain Bishop *et al.*'s (1991, p. 1399) finding that '. . . much of the power of generalized Lorenz dominance [in international comparisons] is due to efficiency preference . . . equity preference adds only marginally to the ability to order income distributions'.

3.2.2(c) Explain Saposnik's (1993) finding that '. . . the generalized Lorenz criterion can be 'factored' into an efficiency component – in the form of the rank criterion – and an equity component – in the form of the Lorenz criterion'.

3.2.3   For what class of income distributions does Levy (1991) prove that mean-variance analysis *alone* is decisive for welfare comparisons in terms of concave utility functions (i.e. without taking generalized Lorenz configuration into account)?

3.2.4(a) If $F(x)$ is the distribution function for x, let $A_F(p)$ be the generalized Lorenz curve for $x - \mu_F$. Moyes (1987) calls $A_F(p)$ the 'absolute Lorenz curve' for F. Show that $A_F(p)$ is invariant to equal additions to all incomes. Prove that $A_F(p) = \mu_F[L_F(p) - p]$. What is the welfare result which can be deduced from Shorrocks (1983a) when absolute Lorenz curves do not intersect?

3.2.4(b) Let B_F be the 'absolute Gini coefficient', given as twice the area between the absolute Lorenz curve $A_F(p)$ and the p-axis. Prove that $B_F = \mu_F G_F$ where G_F is the regular Gini coefficient.

3.2.5(a) Let $H(x)$ be the distribution function for income when two populations, with distribution functions $F(x)$ and $G(x)$, are combined. Asssume that $f(x)$ has support $[a_f, b_f]$ where $a_f > 0$, $f(a_f) \neq 0 \neq f(b_f)$, and $g(x)$ has support $[a_g, b_g]$ where $a_g > 0$, $g(a_g) \neq 0 \neq g(b_g)$. Prove that if $L_H(p) \geq L_G(p)$ for all $p \in [0, 1]$ then $\mu_F = \mu_G$, $b_f \leq b_g$ and $a_f \geq a_g$. *Hint*: sign $L_H'(p) - L_G'(p)$ at $p = 0, 1$ referring back to exercise 2.2.2 on p. 23 and using equation (2.13) on p. 33.

3.2.5(b) Now use the Shorrocks theorem to prove that $GL_H(p) \geq GL_G(p)$ for all $p \in [0, 1] \Leftrightarrow GL_F(p) \geq GL_G(p)$ for all $p \in [0, 1]$.

3.2.5(c) Finally, use parts (a) and (b) above to prove that $L_H(p) \geq L_G(p)$ for all $p \in [0, 1] \Leftrightarrow \mu_F = \mu_G$ and $L_F(p) \geq L_G(p)$ for all $p \in [0, 1]$. Explain why this result constitutes '. . . a powerful statement of an inherent tendency for changes in population composition to produce ambiguous inequality comparisons' (Lam, 1986a, p. 1107).[9]

3.2.6(a) Let $F_u(x)$ and $F_r(x)$ be the distribution functions and $GL_u(p)$ and $GL_r(p)$ the generalized Lorenz curves in the urban and rural sectors of a developing country. Suppose that a fraction α of the population lives in the urban sector, so that the overall distribution function is $F(x, \alpha) = \alpha F_u(x) + (1 - \alpha)F_r(x)$ (exercise 2.2.2, p. 23). Show that the overall generalized Lorenz curve $GL(p, \alpha)$ is defined as follows: $p = F(x, \alpha) \Rightarrow GL(p, \alpha) = \alpha GL_u(F_u(x)) + (1 - \alpha)GL_r(F_r(x))$.

3.2.6(b) By reproducing Kakwani's (1988) proof that $GL_u(p) \geq GL_r(p)$ for all $p \Rightarrow \partial GL(p, \alpha)/\partial \alpha \geq 0$ for all p, and interpreting appropriately, conclude that if welfare is unambiguously higher in the urban sector than the rural one then further urbanization is welfare-enhancing.

3.2.7 Explain Howes' (1996) remark, in respect of generalized Lorenz dominance, that '. . . aggregation increases the probability of attaining a ranking'.

3.2.8(a) A *Yaari social welfare function* (YSWF) is additive and linear in peoples' income levels x, with weights determined by a function $w(p) \geq 0$ of their positions $p = F(x)$: $W_F = \int x w(F(x))f(x)\,dx$ (see Yaari, 1987). Explain why rich-to-poor transfers which do not affect peoples' positions are welfare-improving if and only if $w(p)$ is decreasing in p.

3.2.8(b) Use integration by parts and substitution to show that an alternative expression for Yaari social welfare is $W_F = w(1)\mu_F - \int_0^1 GL_F(p)w'(p)\,dp$

3.2.8(c) Prove that $W_F \geq W_G$ for all YSWFs having the transfer property in (a) $\Leftrightarrow$ F generalized Lorenz dominates G. *Hint*: obtain an expression for $W_F - W_G$ using (b), and adapt the method used to prove lemma 3.1.

3.3 Generalized Lorenz curve configuration and attitude to inequality

If the generalized Lorenz curves GL_F and GL_G intersect, neither distribution can be ranked as welfare-superior to the other according to *every* strictly increasing and concave (transfer-approving) utility function $U(x)$. Of course, we could specify a particular utility function $U(x)$, and check which of F and G is preferred. However, the strength of the Shorrocks theorem lies in the unanimity of prescription which generalized Lorenz dominance brings. By restricting the class of utility functions, can we derive meaningful unanimous preference results for scenarios where generalized Lorenz curves intersect?

The answer is 'yes, in some cases'. The principal restriction is to narrow the class of transfer-approving utilities to those favouring the Principle of Diminishing Transfers. We shall discuss this in the next section. However, an additional, and more severe, restriction is necessary whenever generalized Lorenz curves cross an odd number of times and mean incomes are unequal: it is to this that we turn now.

The unanimity of preference in the Atkinson and Shorrocks theorems covers the whole spectrum of aversion to inequality. Strict concavity of $U(x)$ means that every rich-to-poor income transfer provides a net utility gain. Look again at figure 3.1 on p. 47. Can you see that the more concave, or arched, is $U(x)$ (in a sense not yet defined mathematically), the greater will be the net gain from each such transfer? Also, the 'flatter' is $U(x)$, the less will be this gain. Depending on 'how concave' $U(x)$ is, transfers are valued, or equivalently the presence of inequality is abhorred, to a different degree. We shall formalize this argument in chapter 4, and develop an appropriate measure of the degree of concavity, which we shall call *inequality aversion*.

However there are two extremes of attitude to inequality we can discuss relatively informally. Moreover, for these two, the generalized Lorenz curve configuration alone determines preference between income distributions. We cannot expect unanimity of preference across the whole spectrum of utilities if these two disagree; and they do disagree whenever generalized Lorenz curves cross an odd number of times and mean incomes are unequal. Therefore, in such cases, we have to limit significantly the spectrum of inequality attitudes if we want to secure a robust welfare prescription for one or other income distribution.

One extreme attitude to inequality is indifference. This is where the utility function loses all concavity, becoming linear in income. Then rich-to-poor income transfers involve zero gain in utility. Social welfare is evaluated simply in terms of total income, or rather income per capita:

$$U(x) = a + bx \Rightarrow W_\Gamma = a + b\mu_\Gamma \tag{3.15}$$

This attitude is called *inequality neutrality* (and sometimes also 'efficiency preference'). For this utility function, a larger cake is always preferred, regardless of how it is sliced (i.e. regardless of equity considerations).

If $\int U(x)f(x)\,dx \geq \int U(x)g(x)\,dx$ for all inequality-averse utilities, then $\mu_F \geq \mu_G$ must hold. This derives from the limiting case as $U(x)$ approaches linearity, but we can also see it from the generalized Lorenz curve relationship. By the Shorrocks theorem, $GL_F(p) \geq GL_G(p)$ must hold for all $p \in [0, 1]$, and so

$$GL_F(1) = \mu_F \geq \mu_G = GL_G(1) \tag{3.16}$$

must also hold.

Quite generally, from (3.16), the preference of the inequality-neutral utility function is determined by the generalized Lorenz curve configuration at the 'top end' of the scale, namely at $p = 1$.

At the other extreme of inequality aversion, imagine that the utility function in figure 3.1 becomes more and more arched, until it forms virtually a right angle (see figure 3.5). Then the only income transfer which is valued is a transfer to the poorest income unit (no matter from whom). Such an attitude to inequality is not representable by an increasing and differentiable utility function, as the mathematics of this chapter demands, but it does allow us to introduce a *non-utilitarian* approach to social choice at this point, known as *Rawlsian leximin*.

Rawls (1971) has argued that an ethically justifiable approach to social choice of income distribution is to seek to improve the position of the least well-off income unit regardless of all else. In formal terms, the criterion is as follows.

Definition 3.1

Rawlsian leximin ranks distribution F higher than distribution G if under F the poorest income is greater than under G, or if under F it is the same but occurs with a lower frequency:

$$F >_R G \Leftrightarrow \exists\,(0, y] \text{ on which } F \neq G \text{ and } F(x) \leq G(x)$$

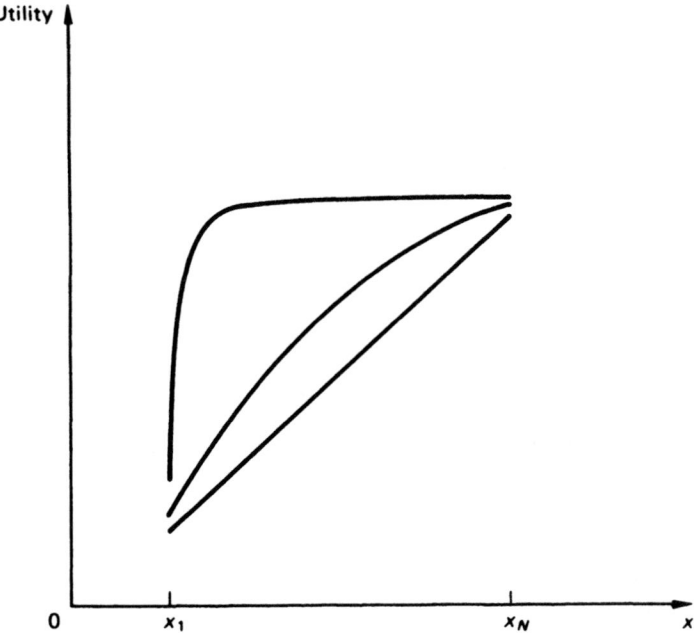

Figure 3.5   Degrees of concavity

Under the Rawlsian criterion, that cake whose smallest slice is larger is preferred, regardless of all other considerations. We shall characterize this criterion as equivalent to *infinite inequality aversion* in a precise sense in the next chapter: to anticipate, if $F >_R G$ then for a range of the most inequality averse utility functions $U(x)$, $\int U(x)f(x)\,dx \geq \int U(x)g(x)\,dx$. Hence Rawlsian leximin commands the support of the most inequality averse utility functions.

The mathematical reader will recognize that the weaker version of this relationship between income distributions:

$$F \geq_R G \Leftrightarrow F \equiv G \text{ or } F >_R G \tag{3.17}$$

is reflexive, anti-symmetric and transitive, and fails only to rank pairs of distribution functions $\{F(x), G(x)\}$ for which it would be impossible to compare smallest incomes or their frequencies. An example of this strange mathematical pathology has been exhibited by Meyer (1975, p. 128, footnote 9), but the possibility need not concern us here. We can eliminate it entirely by imposing a minor technical restriction on pairs of distributions to be considered, namely that each such pair $\{F(x), G(x)\}$ cross at most a finite number of times. In terms of real-world applicability, this restriction does not involve a significant sacrifice.[10]

What is the link between Rawlsian leximin and generalized Lorenz curve configuration? It is almost obvious. Generalized Lorenz curves cumulate incomes from the smallest upwards; whichever of GL_F and GL_G is dominant in the neigbourhood of $p = 0$ has more income among the poorest; this is the one which is ranked higher by Rawlsian leximin:

Theorem 3.3

$F >_R G \Leftrightarrow \exists (0, q]$ on which $GL_F \neq GL_G$ and $GL_F(p) \geq GL_G(p)$.

Proof   In view of (3.9), we can transcribe definition 3.1 as

$$F >_R G \Leftrightarrow \exists (0, y] \text{ on which } S \neq 0 \text{ and } S'(x) \geq 0 \tag{3.18}$$

which is evidently equivalent to

$$F >_R G \Leftrightarrow \exists (0, y_1] \text{ on which } S \neq 0 \text{ and } S(x) \geq 0 \tag{3.19}$$

Now use lemma 3.2 (p. 55): the details are left to the reader.   QED

The inequality-neutral ranking criterion is efficiency-preferring, regardless of equity considerations, and Rawlsian leximin has a reverse property. As we have seen, the preferences between income distributions F and G of both of these extreme attitudes are determined by the configuration of the generalized Lorenz curves GL_F and GL_G. Inequality neutrality focuses on the $p = 1$ end of the scale and Rawlsian leximin on the $p = 0$ end of the scale. Figure

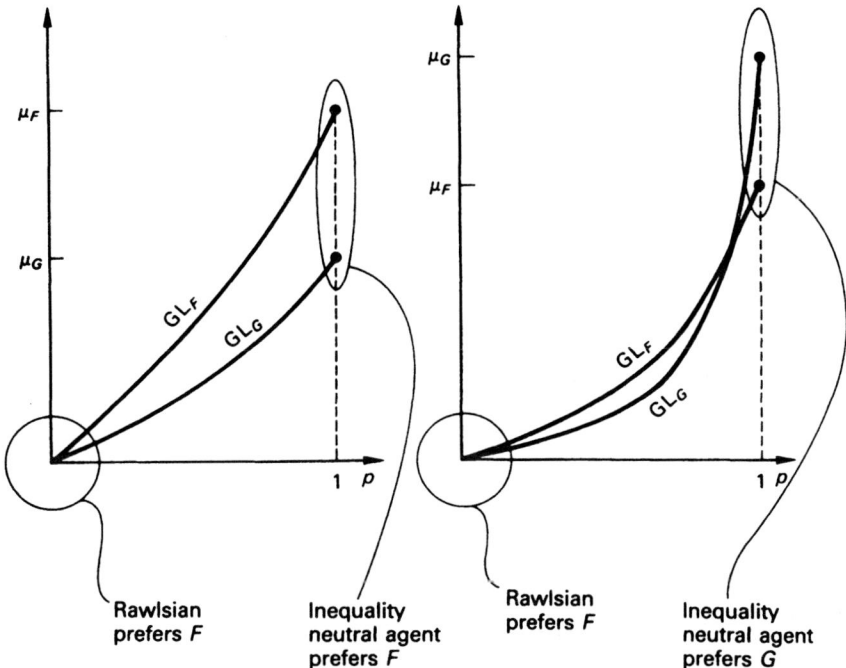

Figure 3.6   Generalized Lorenz configuration, Rawlsian leximin and inequality neutrality

3.6 illustrates this situation in the cases of generalized Lorenz dominance and of unequal-mean single generalized Lorenz curve crossing.

It is precisely when generalized Lorenz curves cross an *odd* number of times, and mean incomes are unequal, that these two criteria are in conflict. For then and only then does the distribution whose generalized Lorenz curve first intersects the other from above terminate, at $p = 1$, below the other. Therefore, precisely in such cases, we know in advance of all other considerations that we will have to restrict the spectrum of attitudes to inequality, excluding either the least inequality-averse or the most inequality-averse utilities, if we wish to secure a unanimous preference recommendation for one or other income distribution.

Exercises

3.3.1 What is Rawls's difference principle? See Rawls (1971, pp. 76–78, 302–303). Is it the same thing as Rawlsian leximin? See also Lambert and Weale (1981, p. 111).

3.3.2 'Gandhian social welfare function is very near to Rawlsian one . . . Sarvodaya conveys that the good of all is served by promoting the good of the poorest – the lowliest and lost' (Chaubey, 1993, p. 70). Explain.

3.4   Social welfare when generalized Lorenz curves cross

Any further restriction we might place on the class of utility functions, beyond the requirement that they be strictly increasing and concave (transfer-approving), will of course reduce the strength of the resulting welfare recommendations, but by the same token it will also permit more comparisons to be successfully made. When generalized Lorenz curves cross, welfare comparisons can sometimes be made by restricting attention to those utilities favouring the Principle of Diminishing Transfers. We consider first the case of a single generalized Lorenz curve crossing. To make headway mathematically, we need to restrict attention to the sub-class of utility functions for which the third derivative is positive.

Definition 3.2

Denote by U the following class of utility functions:

$$U = \{U : U'(x) > 0, U''(x) < 0 \text{ and } U'''(x) > 0 \text{ for all } x > 0\}$$

How may we interpret this sign restriction on the third derivative? Does it convey something intuitively understandable and acceptable about attitude to inequality? Why should we be interested in the approval of this class of utilities? One interpretation, and justification for finding unanimous preference according to U a worthwhile pursuit, arises when we consider the effect of income transfers from rich to poor. Recall that strict concavity of $U(x)$ is necessary and sufficient to ensure that every transfer from richer to poorer increases welfare, i.e. to make the resulting welfare function obey the Principle of Transfers. The class U contains precisely those strictly concave utilities which also obey the more demanding Principle of Diminishing Transfers.

'Whereas a mild egalitarian will certainly appreciate a small transfer from a rich person to a poorer one' says Kolm (1976, p. 87) of the Principle of Transfers, '. . . he may go one step further and value more such a transfer between persons with a given income difference if these incomes are lower than if they are higher. Thus, he would prefer to transfer £1 from a person who earns £500 a month to one who earns only £100, than to transfer £1 from a £900 earner to a person who already earns £500'. Thus Kolm sets out his Principle of Diminishing Transfers. The appeal is clear if we are contrasting transfers from super-rich to rich with transfers from middle-incomes to poor; but an inescapable conclusion is that the most effective small transfer across a small income gap is one from poor to very poor. Do you go along with this idea?

The equivalence of the Principle of Diminishing Transfers to a positive third derivative of the utility function $U(x)$ is easy to see. Suppose an amount Δy is transferred from an income of $y + h$ to an income of y. The net increase in utility is

$$\Delta U = [U(y + \Delta y) - U(y)] - [U(y + h) - U(y + h + \Delta y)] \qquad (3.20)$$

The first square-bracketed term is the recipient of the transfer's utility gain, and the second the donor's utility loss. If Δy is very small relative to y, then

$$\Delta U \simeq [U'(y) - U'(y + h)]\Delta y \qquad (3.21)$$

To satisfy the Principle of Transfers, this has to be positive for all y and all $h > 0$; this is true if and only if U' is strictly decreasing, i.e. $U'' < 0$ (strict concavity). The more demanding Principle of Diminishing Transfers requires ΔU also to be decreasing in y. Differentiating (3.21), this requires

$$U''(y) < U''(y + h) \qquad (3.22)$$

which is so for all y and all $h > 0$ if and only if U'' is strictly increasing; in other words, if and only if $U \in U$. In chapter 4, we will examine further the restriction on inequality aversion which is implied by $U''' > 0$.

Given two income distributions F and G, the criterion for unanimous preference for F over G by all utilities $U \in U$ can be expressed in terms of the familiar function $S(x)$.

Lemma 3.3

$\int_0^z U(x) f(x) \, dx \geq \int_0^z U(x) g(x) \, dx$ for all $U \in U \Leftrightarrow S(z) \geq 0$ and $\int_0^y S(x) \, dx \geq 0$ for all $y \in [0, z]$.

Here, as before, z is some income level exceeding the highest one that occurs with non-zero frequency in either distribution. A proof of this lemma could be devised along the same lines as that given for the analogous lemma 3.1.[11] This time, integrate by parts *three* times in (3.5):

$$W_F - W_G = S(z)U'(z) - \left[\int_0^z S(x) \, dx \right] U''(z) + \int_0^z U'''(y) \left[\int_0^y S(x) \, dx \right] dy \qquad (3.23)$$

and use this instead of (3.6) in constructing the proof.

Lemma 3.3 specifies a much weaker requirement of F and G than non-intersection of generalized Lorenz curves. By lemma 3.1, non-intersection happens if and only if $S(x) \geq 0$ for all $x \in [0, z]$. We shall be able to use this weaker condition to maximum benefit when generalized Lorenz curves cross *once*. Notice, though, that the new condition on $S(x)$ still requires mean income to be no lower in the preferred distribution, since $S(z) = \mu_F - \mu_G$ (see

(3.8)); and it still involves the approval of Rawlsian leximin, since $S(x)$ could not be negative on any $[0, y)$ (see (3.19)). Unanimous approval by U also places a restriction on the *variances* of the income distributions:

$$W_F - W_G \text{ for all } U \in U \Rightarrow \sigma_F^2 \leq \sigma_G^2 + (\mu_F - \mu_G)(2z - \mu_F - \mu_G) \qquad (3.24)$$

This derives from equation (3.10).

When generalized Lorenz curves cross once, the criterion for unanimous preference by all utilities $U \in U$ is expressed very simply in terms of means and variances.

Theorem 3.4

If the generalized Lorenz curves for F and G cross once, then

$$\int U(x)f(x)\,dx \geq \int U(x)g(x)\,dx$$

for all $U \in U \Leftrightarrow \mu_F = \mu_G$, $F >_R G$ and $\sigma_F^2 \leq \sigma_G^2$.

Proof ⇒ The necessary conditions $F >_R G$ and $\mu_F \geq \mu_G$ together imply $\mu_F = \mu_G$ in the case that GL_F and GL_G cross once (see figure 3.6). The result follows in view of (3.24). For the ⇐ proof, note that under the given conditions, $S(z) = 0$ and $\int_0^z S(x)\,dx \geq 0$. Thus, it is enough to show that $\int_0^y S(x)\,dx \geq 0$ for all $y < z$. By theorem 3.3, $\exists p_0$: $GL_F(p) \gtrless GL_G(p)$ for $p \lessgtr p_0$. Now let $p_0 = F(x_F) = G(x_G)$. From lemma 3.2, we have

$$x \leq x_F \Rightarrow S(x) \geq 0 \text{ and } x \geq x_G \Rightarrow S(x) \leq 0 \qquad (3.25)$$

If $x_F < x_G$ then for $x \in (x_F, x_G)$ we have $G(x) \leq G(x_G) = p_0 = F(x_F) \leq F(x)$, so that $S'(x) \leq 0$. If $x_F > x_G$, $S \equiv 0$ on (x_G, x_F). In any case, $\exists w$: $S(x) \gtrless 0$ for $x \lessgtr w$. Since $\int_0^z S(x)\,dx \geq 0$, it follows readily that $\int_0^y S(x)\,dx \geq 0$ for all $y < z$.

QED

When generalized Lorenz curves cross once and mean incomes differ, unanimous preference by all $U \in U$ cannot possibly obtain. As the discussion in section 3.3 demonstrated, another restriction on the class of utility functions must also be made in this case.

Suppose, then, that GL_F and GL_G cross once, that $F >_R G$ and $\mu_F < \mu_G$ (just as in figure 3.6). F is equity superior to G and G is efficiency superior to F. It turns out that means and variances are also decisive for welfare results in this case. Provided that the variance in F is *sufficiently* less than that in G, we find that when the least inequality-averse utility functions are excluded from U, the remainder favour F unanimously; and, furthermore, that the more the variance of F falls below that of G, the smaller the set of utilities that need to be excluded – i.e. the stronger the welfare recommendation for F.[12] The formal result is given in theorem 3.5. In this theorem, we denote by $q_U(x)$ the negative of the elasticity of marginal utility:

$$q_U(x) = -e^{U'(x), x} = -\frac{xU''(x)}{U'(x)} \qquad (3.26)$$

This is positive because when utility is strictly concave, marginal utility is decreasing in income, The function $q_U(x)$ will be shown to be a measure of inequality aversion in chapter 4.

Theorem 3.5

Suppose that $\mu_F < \mu_G$, $F >_R G$ and GL_F, GL_G cross once. If $\sigma_F^2 < \sigma_G^2 - (\mu_G - \mu_F)(2z - \mu_F - \mu_G)$, then $\int_0^z U(x)f(x)\,dx \ge \int_0^z U(x)g(x)\,dx$ for all $U \in U$ such that $q_U(z) \ge 2z(\mu_G - \mu_F)/[(\sigma_G^2 - \sigma_F^2) - (\mu_G - \mu_F)(2z - \mu_F - \mu_G)]$

Proof Because of (3.10), the relationship supposed between means and variances is equivalent to $S(z) < 0$ and $\int_0^z S(x)\,dx > 0$. We can infer, following exactly the line of reasoning used in the proof of the $\Leftarrow$ part of theorem 3.4, that $\int_0^y S(x)\,dx > 0$ for all $y < z$. From (3.23), it is therefore sufficient for $W_F \ge W_G$ for all $U \in U$ that

$$[-S(z)]U'(z) \le \left[\int_0^z S(x)\,dx\right][-U''(z)] \qquad (3.27)$$

(which is written so that the terms in square brackets are all positive); the result is immediate from (3.8) and (3.10). QED

The criterion is expressed in terms of inequality aversion at the highest income level z. We will return to this result in chapter 4. It is enough for now to note that, in a sense which will become more meaningful, the mean-variance expression is the lower bound on inequality aversion which permits unanimous preference for F over G by utilities belonging to U. The larger is the gap

$$[\sigma_G^2 - (\mu_G - \mu_F)(2z - \mu_G - \mu_F)] - \sigma_F^2 \qquad (3.28)$$

i.e. the more the variance of F falls below that of G, the nearer to zero is this lower bound, and (since zero connotes inequality neutrality) the larger the sub-class of U which favours F over G.

In chapter 9 we shall re-examine these results in the context of income taxation, and discover the significance of variance reduction as a criterion in tax reform. Some tax reforms which raise more revenue for the government can be recommended on social welfare grounds – the more strongly, the larger the reduction in the variance of post-tax income which is secured by the reform.

Finally, we turn our attention to cases where generalized Lorenz curves cross more than once. Such configurations are empirically quite uncommon. Although multiple crossings of *ordinary* Lorenz curves are sometimes found, they are, according to Shorrocks and Foster (1987, p. 491) 'in practice . . . less common than single intersections', and Kakwani (1984b, p. 205) finds that generalized Lorenz curves '. . . are likely to cross less often than . . . [ordinary] Lorenz curves'. Nevertheless, we can deal with these configurations. There are two distinct cases to consider.

First, if the generalized Lorenz curves GL_F and GL_G cross an *even* number of times, then by appropriate labelling, we may take it that both $F >_R G$ and $\mu_F \geq \mu_G$. In these circumstances, unanimous approval by the utilities in U for F is possible. One could compute the function $S(x)$ and check whether the condition in lemma 3.3 holds to find out whether this is so. However, is there an operationally less demanding condition in terms of generalized Lorenz curves?

Second, the generalized Lorenz curves may cross an *odd* number of times. In this case, we know that if mean incomes are unequal, then unanimous approval by U for either distribution is impossible. What support from U can we give to the Rawlsian leximin criterion?

Answers to both questions are available if we follow an interesting construction which has been enunciated by Davies and Hoy (1995). This amounts to comparing variances for appropriate sub-populations, defined by the points of intersection of the generalized Lorenz curves, and piecing together the normative implications rather like the parts of a jigsaw puzzle.

For the technically bold, here is a sketch of the bare details. Suppose that GL_F and GL_G cross $n > 1$ times and that $F >_R G$, so that GL_F crosses GL_G first from above. Define $p_0 = 0$ and p_i as the point at which the $2i$th intersection of GL_F and GL_G takes place, where i runs from 1 to $n/2$ if n is even and $(n-1)/2$ if n is odd. Finally, let $p_{(n+1)/2} = 1$ if n is odd (already $p_{n/2} = 1$ if n is even). Now define the ith *sub-population* to consist of those income units belonging to the poorest $100p_i\%$ but not the poorest $100p_{i-1}\%$ of the population, for each $i > 0$. Figure 3.7 illustrates the cases $n = 2$ and $n = 3$. Finally, let F_i and G_i be the distribution functions for sub-population i income which are induced by F and G respectively.

The nature of this construction ensures several things: (a) if $p_i < 1$, then $\mu_{Fi} = \mu_{Gi}$; (b) if $p_i = 1$, $\mu_{Fi} \gtrless \mu_{Gi}$ according to $\mu_F \gtrless \mu_G$, i.e. according to n even (>) or odd (<), and $\mu_{Fi} - \mu_{Gi}$ if $\mu_F - \mu_G$; (c) for all i, $F_i >_R G_i$; (d) if $p_i < 1$, GL_{Fi} and GL_{Gi} cross once; and (e) if $p_i = 1$, either GL_{Fi} dominates GL_{Gi} (n even) or GL_{Fi} and GL_{Gi} cross once (n odd).

The first two of these observations follow because of the generalized Lorenz intersections which take place at $p = p_{i-1}$ and $p = p_i$. Cumulated income per capita is the same under F as under G for both the poorest $100p_{i-1}\%$ and the poorest $100p_i\%$ of income units: it is therefore the same for the sub-population we have defined. The other observations follow essentially because the generalized Lorenz curves GL_{Fi} and GL_{Gi} are just the relevant portions of GL_F and GL_G 'writ large' (see exercise 3.4.2).

In the light of (a)–(e), we can apply theorem 3.4 to every sub-population except possibly the last; and we can apply either theorem 3.2 or theorem 3.5 to the last. Then we know how utilities in U rank the restricted distributions F_i and G_i. Putting together the pieces of this jigsaw, we obtain the following result.

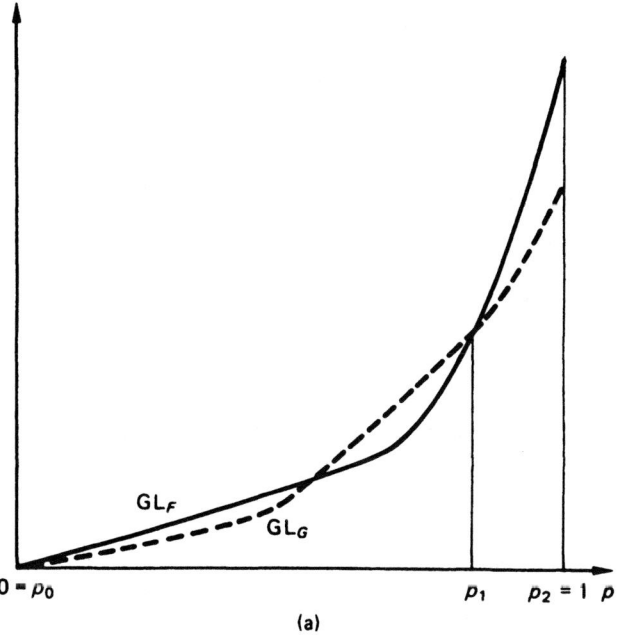

(a)

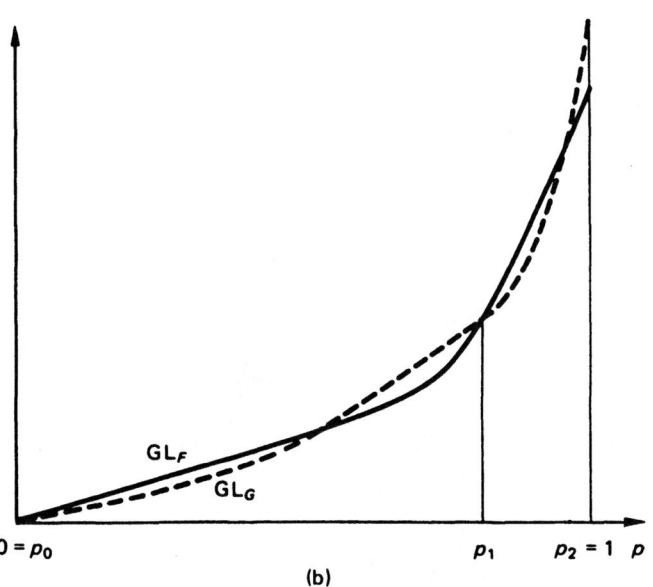

(b)

Figure 3.7   Multiple generalized Lorenz curve crossings (*n* crossings; unequal means illustrated): (a) *n* = 2; (b) *n* = 3

Theorem 3.6

(a) If $F >_R G$ and GL_F, GL_G cross an even number of times, and if under F variance is less for each sub-population but the last than it is under G, then F is preferred to G by all utilities in U.

(b) If $F >_R G$ and GL_F, GL_G cross an odd number of times, and if under F variance is less for each sub-population but the last, the strength of the recommendation for F, by all but the least inequality-averse utilities in U, depends on the mean-variance relationship in the last sub-population.

Exercises

3.4.1   Show that the condition on $S(x)$ in lemma 3.3 is equivalent to $\int_0^y S(x)\,dx \geq 0$ for all $y \in [0, \infty)$ (the graph of $S(x)$ in figure 3.3 may help).

3.4.2   Suppose that $F(y_i) = G(w_i) = p_i$, where p_i, $1 \leq i \leq n$, are the intersection points of GL_F and GL_G as in theorem 3.6. Show that

$$F_i(x) = \frac{F(x) - p_{i-1}}{p_i - p_{i-1}} \qquad \text{for } x \in (y_{i-1}, y_i)$$

$$G_i(x) = \frac{G(x) - p_{i-1}}{p_i - p_{i-1}} \qquad \text{for } x \in (w_{i-1}, w_i)$$

What is the relation between GL_{Fi} and GL_F, and similarly, between GL_{Gi} and GL_G?

3.4.3   Suppose that $L_F(p)$ crosses $L_G(p)$ once from above. Let G^* be the distribution of $\{\mu_F/\mu_G\}$ times the incomes in G. Use theorem 3.4 to show that $W_F \geq W_{G^*}$ for all $U \in U \Leftrightarrow \sigma_F/\mu_F \leq \sigma_G/\mu_G$. State a corresponding result for the case in which Lorenz curves cross more than once, drawing on theorem 3.6.

3.4.4   How do the sub-populations used for theorem 3.6 differ from those used by Davies and Hoy (1995)? For equal-mean comparisons, which variance criterion is less demanding?

3.4.5(a) Compare Shorrocks and Foster's (1987) *favourable composite transfers* with Davies and Hoy's (1994) *Rawlsian composite transfers* and their (1995) *mean-variance preserving transformations*.

3.4.5(b) In exercise 2.4.8(a), p. 36, you demonstrated that a Lorenz-dominating income distribution can be obtained from a Lorenz-dominated one with the same mean by a finite sequence of rich-to-poor transfers. What corresponding results do Shorrocks and Foster (1987) and Davies and Hoy (1995) draw out, in the cases of equal-mean single and multiple Lorenz curve intersections respectively?

3.4.6   'During the Thatcher years in Britain, the poorest have lost out and inequality has increased, but the cake has become larger and as a result overall well-being has risen'. How did Jenkins (1991c) structure the investigation which leads to this conclusion?

3.4.7(a) Explain the *Positional Principle of Transfers* as enunciated by Zoli (1999a). Reproduce Zoli's proof that a Yaari social welfare function (YSWF) $W_F = \int xw(F(x))f(x)\,dx$ satisfies the Positional Principle of Transfers if and only if $w'' \geq 0$. Compare with the result in exercise 3.2.8(a), p. 57.

3.4.7(b) What dominance condition does Zoli show ensures $W_F \geq W_G$ for all YSWFs which satisfy both the Principle of Transfers and Positional Principle of Transfers?

3.4.7(c) 'When generalized Lorenz curves cross once, the Gini coefficient is decisive in determining welfare rankings if we strengthen the Principle of Transfers applying a Positional version . . .' (Zoli, 1999a, p. 183). Compare and contrast the conditions in Zoli's propositions 3 and 4, for YSWF dominance when generalized Lorenz curves cross once, with those in our theorems 3.4 and 3.5. What is the main difference? Compare also the corresponding results for multiple generalized Lorenz curve crossings.

3.5   Using equivalence scales

In the dominance theorems of this chapter so far, we have been rather vague about the income concept and the income unit. Simply, x has been income and $U(x)$ the utility attributed to an income unit having that income. This is well and good if the population is *socially homogeneous*. If money income x is held to be the only socially relevant source of difference between income units, then indeed we can compare well-being in different populations or time periods by applying the same utility function $U(x)$ to all of the incomes in the alternative distributions of x, and aggregating. Our dominance theorems delineate the distributional conditions under which unambiguous comparisons obtain for wide classes of such utility functions.

But what if the populations being compared are *socially heterogeneous* – comprising, for example, a mix of households of differing sizes and compositions? No account is taken of non-income factors in our dominance theorems; distributions of *money* income cannot be the basis for welfare comparisons in these circumstances; complete equality in household *money* income is unlikely to be the ideal among families of differing sizes and composition; yet the class of social welfare functions we have been working with is equality-seeking, as the Atkinson theorem shows.

In order to make welfare comparisons in the presence of social heterogeneity, additional value judgements are needed to take into account non-income factors such as family size and composition, age, handicap, urban/rural location. A popular approach among practitioners has been to use an equivalence scale to deflate money incomes, and simply apply the dominance methodology to the resulting distributions of household equivalized income. Some analysts go further, and change the income unit from the household to the individual, having equivalized, attributing to each individual in each household the living standard achieved by that household, before applying the dominance methodology (recall exercise 2.1.1, p. 19).

This is a deceptively simple procedure, intended to salvage applicability of the Atkinson–Shorrocks methodology, but it actually raises many questions. It amounts to making several value judgements: (i) that equivalizing can take full account of non-income factors to determine living standards; (ii) that the equivalence scale to hand is the right one for the job; and (iii) that well-being in alternative scenarios can be compared by applying a strictly increasing and concave function to distributions of household or individual living standards and aggregating. Each of these judgements can be contested. As exercises 3.5.1–3.5.3 below show, there have been a medley of objections to equivalizing and the use of particular scales, but at least the normative assumptions implicit in any particular scale can now be drawn out and exposed to scrutiny (exercise 3.5.4). We concentrate here on the last assumption, focusing in particular on concavity of the assumed utility-of-equivalent-income function.

One cannot swallow the Atkinson–Shorrocks methodology whole, for equivalized income distributions, without accepting the transfer principle, which is at the heart of it. Concavity of the utility function amounts in this context to approving small transfers *of living standard* from the better-off to the worse-off. We have already noted in the case of households that this kind of transfer cannot always be implemented (p. 17); still less can it be implemented at the individual level, for one cannot take a unit of living standard from *one* member of a household without also taking from the others, nor give a unit of living standard to one member of another worse-off household, and not the others! Yet all such transfers are 'a good thing'; the methodology is purpose-designed to embody this value judgement.

What can be done to rectify matters? Ebert (1997) has addressed this issue, and found the solution. The answer is that, when equivalizing, one must also create a population of artificial income units, known variously as standard adults, equivalent adults and even fictional adults. Having done that, application of the Atkinson–Shorrocks methodology reflects a sensible transfer principle: *money income transfers from households with high living standards to households with low living standards are 'a good thing'.*

To clarify and explain matters, suppose for simplicity that the population comprises single person households (S), married couples without children (M), and couples with one child (C), and that the equivalence scale deflators are z_S, z_M and z_C where $z_C > z_M > z_S = 1$. This tells us that couples with a child need a higher money income than childless couples to achieve a given living standard, and childless couples need more than singles; and that all living standards are measured by reference to single persons' actual purchasing power. In order to apply the Atkinson-Shorrocks methodology to distributions of equivalent income across *households*, the welfare function must take the form

$$W = \frac{\sum_S U(x) + \sum_M U\left(\frac{x}{z_M}\right) + \sum_C U\left(\frac{x}{z_C}\right)}{N_S + N_M + N_C}$$

to use an obvious notation, whilst for the distribution over *individuals* it has to be

$$W = \frac{\sum_S U(x) + 2\sum_M U\left(\frac{x}{z_M}\right) + 3\sum_C U\left(\frac{x}{z_C}\right)}{N_S + 2N_M + 3N_C}$$

Can you see why? Ebert's proposal is to create an artificial population, in which *a houseold of type i (i = S, M, C) gets replaced by a set of z_i equivalent adults*. These 'adults' have been called 'fictional' because, of course, z_i is in general non-integer. For the practitioner, it is simply a matter of re-weighting the sample observations by the equivalence scale factors. The welfare function becomes

$$W = \frac{\sum_S U(x) + z_M\sum_M U\left(\frac{x}{z_M}\right) + z_C\sum_C U\left(\frac{x}{z_C}\right)}{N_S + z_M N_M + z_C N_C}$$

Of these three possible forms for the welfare function, *only the last satisfies the modified transfer principle*, according to which money transfers from those with high living standards to those with lower living standards are 'a good thing' (see exercise 3.5.5). If this is what the practitioner believes in, or is the value judgement he or she wishes to represent, then Ebert's fictional adults must be created; it is the only correct way to conduct distributional analysis using an equivalence scale.[13]

Exercises

3.5.1 Explain Blackorby and Donaldson's (1993, p. 143) finding that: 'scaled income . . . is an ordinal index of household well-being if and only if preferences are homothetic'

3.5.2 How does Conniffe (1992, p. 442) make his case that: 'scales change with income . . . constant scales are not plausible and their use needs reconsidering'?

3.5.3 On what basis did Banks and Johnson (1994a, p. 22) assert that: 'while the construction of an ideal equivalence scale is likely to defeat even the ingenuity of economists, the [McClements] scale used in official statistics appears to be as good as any, despite its dubious theoretical underpinnings'?

3.5.4 'This paper deals with the comparison of living standards and investigates two normative methods of deriving equalizing transformations ... the methods can determine the implicit normative assumptions involved in conducting distributional analysis using any equalizing transformation' (Ebert, 2000a, p. 619). Summarize Ebert's two methods. Can income-dependent equivalence scales be founded in Ebert's normative framework?

3.5.5 Let $v(x, y)$ be the contribution to total utility of a single person having x and a married couple having y in a socially heterogeneous population. Explain why $v(x, y)$ takes the value $U(x) + U(y/z_M)$ if the income unit is the household, $U(x) + 2U(y/z_M)$ if the income unit is the individual, and $U(x) + z_M U(y/z_M)$ if the income unit is the equivalent adult. Use the calculus to demonstrate that the effect on social welfare of taking a small amount of money income from the single and giving it to the couple is proportional to $[\partial v/\partial y - \partial v/\partial x]$, and conclude that if U is strictly concave, then only in the case of the equivalent adult is such a transfer unambiguously a good thing if $x > y/z_M$ and a bad thing if $x < y/z_M$.

3.5.6 Let F and G be two alternative distributions across households of the same total amount of money income. Let F^* and G^* be the associated distributions of equivalent income in the artificial populations of equivalent adults. Show that F^* and G^* have equal means. Will the associated distributions of household and individual equivalized income have equal means, in general?

3.5.7 'If the social welfare of households of different demographic type has to be evaluated, we observe considerable disagreement about the way the composition of households is to be taken into account' (Ebert, 1997, p. 233). Describe the four methods Ebert considers. Which do you find the most appealing?

3.5.8 Reproduce Glewwe's (1991) example showing that rich-to-poor money income transfers can be disequalizing in their effect on the distribution of equivalent income. Can you 'cure' the problem by redefining the income unit to be the equivalent adult?

3.6   Sequential dominance criteria

There is an alternative to using equivalence scales for making welfare comparisons in the presence of social heterogeneity. Analysis can be carried out in money income terms; the essential elements of the average utility approach to measuring welfare can be retained; and the analysis can be conducted using generalized Lorenz curves. This alternative methodology is due to Atkinson and Bourguignon (1987), and gained popularity throughout the 1990s. It involves *sequential methods*.

The basic idea is to attribute different utility-of-money-income functions to households of different types, endowing these utility functions with systematic differences to reflect the differing needs (or 'social merits') of the relevant households, and then to average the resulting utility levels across the entire population to form a social welfare function. Figure 3.8 illustrates some possible utility functions for the case discussed in the preceding section of the chapter, where the population comprised three homogeneous subgroups: single person households (S), married couples without children (M), and couples with one child (C).

The utility functions suggested in figure 3.8 are all concave. This means that rich-to-poor transfers would be approved *within groups*: according to these utility functions, it is a good thing to redistribute from rich singles to poor singles, from rich couples to poor couples and so on. Some value judgements about relative social merit *as between the groups* can also be seen in figure 3.8. Specifically, as between households all having a given money income of x: (a) single person households are judged best-off, then couples then families; (b) the utility gain that would derive from an additional unit of income is judged highest among families, then couples, then singles; let us call the extra utility gain experienced by a needier household relative to a less needy one at the same income level the 'social premium' that comes from directing resources toward the needier; and (c), these social premia decline with increases in the income level x at which they are manifested: it matters

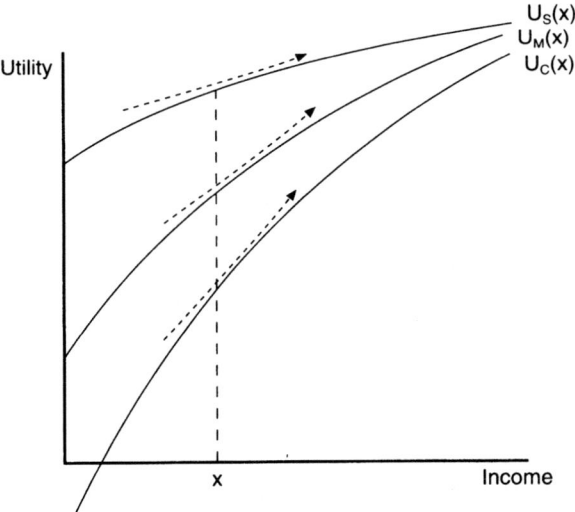

Figure 3.8   Utility functions for Atkinson–Bourguignon theorem

less among rich people, and hardly at all among millionaires, whether an extra unit of resource would be directed to a single person, a childless couple or a family. Do you concur with all these value judgements?

Formally, the restrictions we have suggested on the bundle of utility functions $\langle U_S(x),\ U_M(x),\ U_C(x)\rangle$ can be expressed like this: (a) $U_S(x) > U_M(x) > U_C(x)$ for all x; (b) $U'_S(x) < U'_M(x) < U'_C(x)$ for all x; and (c) $0 > U''_S(x) > U''_M(x) > U''_C(x)$ for all x, the latter because the social premia $[U'_M(x) - U'_S(x)]$ and $[U'_C(x) - U'_M(x)]$ are decreasing in x; condition (c) also takes care of concavity. In a moment, we will see that for many purposes (a) can be dropped. To compute social welfare, we aggregate utility levels and average across the whole population:

$$W = \frac{\sum_S U_S(x) + \sum_M U_M(x) + \sum_C U_C(x)}{N_S + N_M + N_C}$$

(Compare this with the three forms given on p. 71 using equivalence scale deflators z_S, z_M and z_C, and a common utility-of-equivalent-income function U; can you see a connection? (See exercise 3.6.7.) Writing W_S, W_M and W_C for average utility within the relevant groups, an alternative expression for overall welfare is

$$W = p_S W_S + p_M W_M + p_C W_C$$

where p_S, p_M and p_C are the proportions in the overall population of households of each type.

Economists hesitate to make interpersonal comparisons of utility levels (though they are less worried by marginal utility comparisons). Our condition (a) above could be taken as implying that singles are judged happier than couples at each income level, and couples happier than families. Of course we do not claim this. In fact, we could replace the three utility functions by upward shifts of themselves, and also incorporate a scale change, without affecting any welfare comparison between income distributions F and G across a fixed population. Can you see that, if $U_S(x)$, $U_M(x)$ and $U_C(x)$ were to be replaced by $a_S + bU_S(x)$, $a_M + bU_M(x)$ and $a_C + bU_C(x)$, where $b > 0$, then overall welfares for F and G would change from W_F and W_G to $p_S a_S + p_M a_M + p_C a_C + bW_F$ and $p_S a_S + p_M a_M + p_C a_C + bW_G$, i.e. the comparison would not be affected? We shall drop (a), at least until we consider the issue of demographic change.

Atkinson and Bourguignon's (1987) sequential procedure rests upon identifying a set of homogeneous subgroups of the population whose different degrees of need or social merit can be ranked, just as we have been doing with the groups S, M and C above. Having identified the groups and the needs ranking, alternative distributions of income F and G across the overall population can be compared by making *sequential generalized Lorenz curve comparisons*. For this, we start with the neediest group, and look for dominance – of F over G, say. Then we go to the two neediest groups taken together, and again check for dominance of F over G; and so on until all groups are included. If dominance of F over G occurs at all stages in the sequence, then $W_F > W_G$ for all welfare functions in the Atkinson-Bourguignon class. In the remainder of the chapter, we formalize this strikingly simple procedure, prove the theorem and mention some extensions which have followed upon publication of the original article in 1987.

Let us be slightly more general than before, and index the subgroups by $i = 1, 2, \ldots, n$, in *descending order of need*. Atkinson and Bourguignon cite as an example, with $n = 5$, the following classification of household types which, we might readily agree, is ranked from the neediest ($i = 1$) downwards:

> $i = 1$: families with three or more children
> $i = 2$: families with two children
> $i = 3$: families with one child
> $i = 4$: couples
> $i = 5$: single persons

This needs structure is modelled by restrictions on utility functions. Let $U_i(x)$ be the utility-of-income function for households of type i, $1 \le i \le n$. The bundle of utility functions $\langle U_1, U_2, \ldots, U_n \rangle$, which specify the welfare function, will be called a *utility profile*.

Definition 3.3

Let U_{AB} be the class of utility profiles $\langle U_1, U_2, \ldots, U_n \rangle$ satisfying the following two properties:

(i)   each U_i is strictly increasing and concave; and
(ii)   for each $i = 1, 2, \ldots, n - 1$, $U_i' - U_{i+1}'$ is positive and decreasing.

The value judgement in (i) is that more income is a good thing and so are transfers from rich to poor within groups; (ii) says that at each given income level, members of group i are judged more deserving of additional resources than those of group $i + 1$, and the marginal utility differential reflecting this difference in social desert decreases with income. A consequence is that welfare functions based on utility profiles in U_{AB} approve not only of transfers of income from rich to poor within type, but also of certain forms of transfer between types. For example, transfers from single people at any given income level to families at the same income level are approved, as are transfers from smaller to larger families at the same income level. Of course, transfers from single millionaires to married ones with families, etc., hardly matter.

Consider two alternative distributions of money income across households, with overall distribution functions $F(x)$ and $G(x)$. Let $F_i(x)$ and $G_i(x)$ be the type-specific distribution functions associated with F and G, and let

$f_i(x)$ and $g_i(x)$ be the corresponding density functions, $1 \leq i \leq n$. The proportion of households belonging to each type i will be assumed the same in F and G for the time being, and written p_i. In extending the results to allow for demographic differences later, we will rewrite these proportions p_{iF} and p_{iG}. The social welfare function is additive, with utility functions $U_i(x)$ from profiles in U_{AB} being applied to the different types:

$$W_F = \sum_{1 \leq i \leq n} p_i \int_0^z U_i(x) f_i(x) \mathrm{d}x, \qquad W_G = \sum_{1 \leq i \leq n} p_i \int_0^z U_i(x) g_i(x) \mathrm{d}x \qquad (3.29)$$

Here, as elsewhere previously, z can represent any income level equal to or exceeding the maximum one present in either distribution with non-zero density.

It is a lot less demanding for the analyst to determine a ranking of household types by need, than to draw up an equivalence scale in order to apply the Atkinson–Shorrocks methodology to distributions of equivalized income. Corresponding to the luxury of this lesser input, the criterion to ensure welfare superiority in the Atkinson–Bourguignon framework is more involved. It is known as *sequential generalized Lorenz dominance*.

Theorem 3.7

$W_F \geq W_G$ for all utility profiles $\langle U_1, U_2, \ldots, U_n \rangle \in U_{AB}$ if and only if there is generalized Lorenz dominance of F over G in each of the sub-populations comprising the j most needy groups, $j = 1, 2, \ldots, n$.

The procedure to follow is, take first the most deserving group, then add the next most deserving group, and so on, until all groups are included, checking at each stage for generalized Lorenz dominance. If this always obtains, one distribution can be recommended over the other. The sequential generalized Lorenz dominance criterion demands conventional generalized Lorenz dominance, $GL_F \geq GL_G$, at the final stage – but it demands a lot more as well. Nevertheless, it has been found to work well in practice in studies which examine, for example, alternative systems of child support (see exercise 3.6.4). When it fails, the cause of failure can be revealing too. If the failure (first instance of a generalized Lorenz curve intersection) is far along the sequence of tests, one can say that F is 'better than G among the neediest groups but not overall', and pinpoint where the problem arises.

Atkinson (1990) contains a very readable account of the sequential generalized Lorenz dominance criterion. In Jenkins and Lambert (1993) and Chambaz and Maurin (1998) this criterion is extended to allow different proportions of households of each type in the distributions F and G being compared, and we shall come to this. Without such an extension, the technique hardly applies to intertemporal and international comparisons, where needs structures (partitions into types i) can differ considerably between regimes.

We turn to the proof of the Atkinson–Bourguignon theorem. To demonstrate that sequential dominance implies welfare superiority, we use combinatorics and the ubiquitous S-function, our intermediary between unanimous preference and generalized Lorenz curves in all previous results. Remember that generalized Lorenz dominance holds in a population if and only if the relevant S-function is everywhere non-negative (pp. 54–55). Let $S_i(x)$ be the S-function for households of type i:

$$S_i(x) = \int_0^x [G_i(y) - F_i(y)]\,dy \tag{3.30}$$

Generalized Lorenz dominance of F over G in the sub-population comprising the j most needy groups corresponds to $\Sigma_{1\leq i\leq j} p_i S_i(x) \geq 0$ for all x (see exercise 3.6.1(b)). It will be enough to show that when this holds for each j, the welfare difference $W_F - W_G$, which can be written as

$$W_F - W_G = \sum_{1 \leq i \leq n} p_i \int_0^{\bar{z}} U_i(x)[f_i(x) - g_i(x)]\,dx$$

$$= -\sum_{1 \leq i \leq n} \int_0^{\bar{z}} U_i(x) p_i S_i''(x)\,dx \tag{3.31}$$

is unambiguously positive for all utility profiles $\langle U_1, U_2, \ldots, U_n \rangle \in U_{AB}$. To show this, we first integrate by parts twice in (3.31), to yield

$$W_F - W_G = \sum_{1 \leq i \leq n} U_i'(z) p_i S_i(z) + \sum_{1 \leq i \leq n} \int_0^{\bar{z}} [-U_i''(x)] p_i S_i(x)\,dx \tag{3.32}$$

and then change the order of summation and integration:

$$W_F - W_G = \sum_{1 \leq i \leq n} U_i'(z) p_i S_i(z) + \int_0^{\bar{z}} \left\{ \sum_{1 \leq i \leq n} [-U_i''(x)] p_i S_i(x) \right\} dx \tag{3.33}$$

The right-hand side of this expression involves two sums, each in the general form $\Sigma_{1 \leq i \leq n} u_i s_i$ for appropriate values u_i and s_i. A simple combinatorial result makes the next step straightforward.

Lemma 3.4

Given real numbers u_i and s_i, $1 \leq i \leq n$, set $d_j = u_j - u_{j+1}$ for $1 \leq j \leq n-1$, $d_n = u_n$, and $t_j = \Sigma_{1 \leq i \leq j} s_i$ for $1 \leq j \leq n$. Then $\Sigma_{1 \leq i \leq n} u_i s_i = \Sigma_{1 \leq j \leq n} d_j t_j$.

Proof   This is just a matter of rearrangement: $\Sigma_{1 \leq i \leq n} u_i s_i = u_n \Sigma_{1 \leq i \leq n} s_i + (u_{n-1} - u_n)\Sigma_{1 \leq i \leq n-1} s_i + (u_{n-2} - u_{n-1})\Sigma_{1 \leq i \leq n-2} s_i + \ldots + (u_1 - u_2)s_1 = d_n t_n + d_{n-1} t_{n-1} + d_{n-2} t_{n-2} + \ldots + d_1 t_1 = \Sigma_{1 \leq j \leq n} d_j t_j$.   QED

When we apply lemma 3.4 to each summation in (3.33), with the us and ss defined appropriately, we obtain the alternative decomposition:

$$W_F - W_G = \sum_{1 \leq j \leq n} D_j(z)T_j(z) + \int_0^{\bar{z}} \left\{ \sum_{1 \leq j \leq n} [-D_j'(x)]T_j(x) \right\} dx \qquad (3.34)$$

in which, corresponding to the definitions of the ds and ts in the lemma, we have set

$$D_j(x) = U_j'(x) - U_{j+1}'(x) \text{ for } 1 \leq j \leq n-1, D_n(x) = U_n'(x) \qquad (3.35)$$

and

$$T_j(x) = \sum_{1 \leq i \leq j} p_i S_i(x) \text{ for } 1 \leq j \leq n \qquad (3.36)$$

Now consider the terms in the right-hand side of (3.34). For utility profiles in U_{AB}, for each j we have $D_j(z) > 0$ and $[-D_j'(x)] \geq 0$ for all x (see definition 3.3). Also, each $T_j(x)$ is non-negative for all x by our earlier assumption. Hence all terms are non-negative: $W_F \geq W_G$ for all utility profiles belonging to U_{AB}, as required.

The converse result, that welfare superiority demands sequential generalized Lorenz dominance, can be proved by contradiction. An intuitive argument is this. Supposing that some $T_k(x)$ in (3.34) is negative for some x, 'fix' the utility profile to be such that the corresponding $[-D_k'(x)]$ is large and all other marginal utility differentials are vanishingly small, forcing $W_F - W_G < 0$ for this particular utility profile, a contradiction. Brief details of a more formal approach can be found in Atkinson and Bourguignon (1987, pp. 369–370).

We turn finally to the issue of demographic change. The needs structure will vary between income distributions in both intertemporal and international comparisons, and so far we have ruled this possibility out of court. To adapt Atkinson and Bourguignon's sequential generalized Lorenz dominance criterion for situations in which there are demographic differences in the distributions being compared, we must go back to the drawing board. Not least, this is because, in the manipulations that led us from (3.29) on p. 76 to the crucial (3.34) above, from which we identified sequential generalized Lorenz dominance as sufficient for welfare dominance, the proportions of income units of each type i were written simply p_i, and must now become p_{iF} and p_{iG}. The starting-point for these manipulations is therefore now

$$W_F = \sum_{1 \leq i \leq n} p_{iF} \int_0^{\bar{z}} U_i(x)f_i(x)dx \qquad W_G = \sum_{1 \leq i \leq n} p_{iG} \int_0^{\bar{z}} U_i(x)g_i(x)dx \qquad (3.29a)$$

We can get a long way just replacing $p_i S_i(x)$, wherever it occurs in the manipulations, by $\int_0^x [p_{iG}G_i(y) - p_{iF}F_i(y)]dy$, which is closely related (see (3.30)). Try it: starting from the modified version of (3.31), you will reach a version of (3.34) in which $T_j(x)$ must be replaced by

$$T_j^*(x) = \sum_{1 \leq i \leq j} \int_0^{\bar{z}} [p_{iG}G_i(y) - p_{iF}F_i(y)]\mathrm{d}y \qquad (3.36a)$$

but you will have gained an extra term, $\Sigma_{1 \leq i \leq j}U_i(z)[p_{iG} - p_{iF}]$, arising from the integration by parts.

With an additional normative assumption, already anticipated to some extent, a sequential criterion which is appropriate for welfare dominance can be identified – though it is not sequential generalized Lorenz dominance. It is enough to eliminate the extra (unwanted) term that, for each admissible utility profile $\langle U_1, U_2, \ldots, U_n \rangle$, $U_1(z) = U_2(z) = \ldots = U_n(z)$. Taken along with the other properties assumed of utility profiles, in definition 3.3, this implies $U_1(x) \leq U_2(x) \leq \ldots \leq U_n(x)$ for all $x \leq z$, an assumption we avoided up to now. Remember that z can be any very high income level, so long as it is higher than any occurring in either F or G with non-zero density; actually, it would be enough that the $U_i(z)$ all converge to the same value as $z \to \infty$. In figure 3.8 one can imagine convergence to such an income level; it means that the social decision-maker does not care about the family types of the super-rich. Let us define as U_{AB}^* the subclass of U_{AB} in which the utility profiles satisfy this restriction. For such utility profiles, the modified version of (3.34) which we reach from (3.29a) is

$$W_F - W_G = \sum_{1 \leq j \leq n} D_j(z)T_j^*(z) + \int_0^{\bar{z}} \left\{ \sum_{1 \leq j \leq n} [-D_j'(x)]T_j^*(x) \right\} \mathrm{d}x \qquad (3.34a)$$

The sequential criterion for welfare dominance can be identified from this.

Theorem 3.8

In the presence of demographic differences, $W_F \geq W_G$ for all utility profiles $\langle U_1, U_2, \ldots, U_n \rangle \in U_{AB}^*$ if and only if $T_j^*(x) \geq 0$ for each j and for all x.

Sufficiency is clear, and is demonstrated in Jenkins and Lambert (1993). A proof of necessity can be found in Chambaz and Maurin (1998, appendix C). These tests are not expressible in terms of generalized Lorenz curves. They require the analyst to use numerical integration techniques to compute areas under distribution functions.

Exercises

3.6.1(a) In the sub-population comprising the j most needy subgroups, $1 \leq j \leq n$, let the distribution functions for income be $^jF(x)$ and $^jG(x)$. Show that $[\Sigma_{1\leq i\leq j}p_i]$ $^jF(x) = \Sigma_{1\leq i\leq j}p_iF_i(x)$ and $[\Sigma_{1\leq i\leq j}p_i]$ $^jG(x) = \Sigma_{1\leq i\leq j}p_iG_i(x)$. *Hint*: Recall exercise 2.2.2, p. 23.

3.6.1(b) Deduce that the *S*-function $^jS(x) = \int_0^x[^jG(y) - ^jF(y)]\,dy$ for this sub-population satisfies $[\Sigma_{1\leq i\leq j}p_i]$ $^jS(x) = \Sigma_{1\leq i\leq j}p_iS_i(x)$.

3.6.2(a) Explain why the condition $T_j'(x) \geq 0$ for all x corresponds to rank dominance of *F* over *G* in the sub-population comprising the *j* most needy groups. *Hint*: Refer back to exercise 3.2.2(b), and make use of the results in exercise 3.6.1 above.

3.6.2(b) Integrate by parts in (3.34) to show that

$$W_F - W_G = \sum_{1 \leq j \leq n}\left\{\int_0^{\bar{z}}D_j(x)T_j'(x)\,dx\right\}$$

Conclude that $W_F \geq W_G$ for all utility profiles $\langle U_1, U_2, \ldots, U_n\rangle$ for which (i) each U_i is strictly increasing, and (ii) each $U_i' - U_{i+1}'$ is positive, if and only if *F* sequentially rank dominates *G* (i.e. there is rank dominance of *F* over *G* in each of the sub-populations comprising the *j* most needy groups, $j = 1, 2, \ldots, n$).[14]

3.6.3   Show that if no restriction is placed on the class of utility profiles $\langle U_1, U_2, \ldots, U_n\rangle$ save that each $U_i(x)$ be strictly increasing and concave, then the necessary and sufficient condition for *F* to be unambiguously welfare superior to *G* is that *F* generalized Lorenz dominates *G* in each needs group. *Hint*: Sufficiency is easy using (3.32) and non-negativity of each $S_i(x)$. For necessity, argue by contradiction. Suppose that generalized Lorenz dominance fails in the *k*th needs group, so that there is a strictly increasing and concave $u(x)$ such that $\int u(x)f_k(x)\,dx < \int u(x)g_k(x)\,dx$. Now choose a utility profile in which each $U_i(x)$ is a multiple of $u(x)$, in such a way as to make $W_F - W_G$ go negative.[15]

3.6.4   Describe Atkinson and Bourguignon's (1987, p. 360) simple example, showing how the sequential generalized Lorenz dominance criterion can be used to recommend an improved child benefit financed by changes in the income tax.

3.6.5   Joe has an annual income of $50,000, all for himself, whilst Jon and Julie get $60,000 between them. Sketch utility-of-income functions $U_S(x)$ and $U_M(x)$ (like those in figure 3.8) according to which an annual transfer of $5 from Joe to Jon and Julie would be socially approved. Show too, however, that the sequential generalized Lorenz criterion would fail to endorse this transfer. Why?

3.6.6   'The present paper ... provides a characterization of the sequential generalized Lorenz ordering by transfer principles ... and demonstrates that the underlying value judgements about transfers are rather weak' (Ebert, 2000b, p. 114). Discuss, paying particular attention to Ebert's principles of progressive and diminishing transfers between groups.

3.6.7   Consider a population whose household types are ranked by need from $i = 1$ to $i = n$ in the Atkinson–Bourguignon sense. Let Z be the set of equivalence scales $\{z_1, z_2, \ldots, z_n\}$ which respect this needs ranking, i.e. for which $z_1 > z_2 > \ldots > z_n$. Let E be a social evaluation function defined as the average of a strictly increasing and concave utility-of-equivalent-income function $U(\alpha)$ over the fictitious population of equivalent adults, there being z_i such beings occupying each household of type i: $E_F = \Sigma p_i z_i \int_0^z U(x/z_i) f_i(x) \, dx$, etc. Show that the utility profile $\langle U_1, U_2, \ldots, U_n \rangle$ formed by setting $U_i(x) = z_i U(x/z_i)$ will belong to U_{AB} for all equivalence scales in Z if and only if $U''(\alpha) + \alpha U'''(\alpha) > 0$ for all α. *Hint*: Show that $D_j(x) = U'(x/z_j) - U'(x/z_{j+1})$ for this profile, and deduce that $D_j'(x) < 0 \; \forall x$ for all equivalence scales if and only if $U''(x/z)/z$ decreases with z given x.

3.6.8   Bourguignon (1989) identifies a dominance criterion for the class of utility profiles satisfying two out of three of the requirements for U_{AB}: each U_i is strictly increasing and concave, and for $i = 1, 2, \ldots, n-1$, $U_i' - U_{i+1}'$ is positive (though not necessarily decreasing). Explain why Bourguignon's criterion will succeed in some cases in which sequential rank dominance fails, but never when sequential generalized Lorenz dominance fails. Use your findings from the previous exercise to account for Bourguignon's remark that his criterion is 'quite close to what would result from the direct application of the equivalence scale approach to one-dimensional dominance . . . using not a precise set of equivalence scales but a range of them under the restriction that [the] equivalence scale must increase . . . with family size' (p. 76).

3.6.9   'Between the generalized Lorenz criterion applied to equivalent incomes proposed by Ebert, and the sequential generalized Lorenz criterion of Atkinson and Bourguignon, there is room for a middle-way criterion' (Fleurbaey *et al.*, 2000). Evaluate Fleurbaey *et al.*'s criterion with particular reference to that of Bourguignon (1989) cited in the previous exercise.

3.6.10   'The impact on social welfare of income distribution changes . . . may be reinforced – or offset – by population composition changes' (Jenkins and Lambert, 1993, p. 340). Rewrite the dominance conditions $T_j^*(x) \geq 0$ of theorem 3.8 in such a way as to demonstrate this claim, using the same technique as Jenkins and Lambert.

Notes

1 The expressions $\int U(x) f(x) \, dx$ and $\int U(x) g(x) \, dx$ are shorthand for the less convenient ones, $\int_0^z U(x) f(x) \, dx$ and $\int_0^z U(x) g(x) \, dx$ where z is an income level equal to or exceeding the maximum present with non-zero density in either distribution. We shall use shorthand versions in presenting results, but not, of course, in

proving them. For the proofs, we shall assume differentiability of $U(x)$. Under the restrictions $U'(x) > 0$ and $U''(x) < 0$ for all $x > 0$, the inequalities on the right-hand side in theorem 3.1 can be made strict provided the two Lorenz curves are not identical.

2 If the utility of income function $U(x)$ has a linear segment, say of the form $U(x) = a + bx$ for $x \in [c, d]$, then for all distributions of income $F(x)$ whose support lies in the interval $[c, d]$, average utility is the same, $W_F = a + b\mu_F$, regardless of inequality. Hence our use of the word 'strictly' in this statement.

3 The coefficient of variation is defined as the standard deviation σ divided by the mean μ. If two distributions have the same mean, the one with the lower coefficient of variation is the one with the lower variance. The coefficient of variation is invariant to scaling all the incomes in a distribution.

4 The Atkinson theorem and corollary 3.1 can be found on the same page. Kolm called the dominance conditions in these two results *constant-sum isophily* and *super-isophily* respectively.

5 Kakwani's categorization of $_{23}C_2 = 253$ pairwise generalized Lorenz curve comparisons between 23 countries contains errors. At most 248 comparisons are reliable because: (i) he cites 255 comparisons, not 253; (ii) Philippines/Brazil and Korea/UK each appear twice in mutually contradictory categories; (iii) Philippines/Honduras, Philippines/Hong Kong and Sri Lanka/Brazil are missing; (iv) there are three apparently spurious comparisons involving Uruguay.

6 The function $S(x)$ is well known in the risk literature, and the criterion of lemma 3.1 is known in this context as *second degree stochastic dominance*; see Hanoch and Levy (1969). Some wordings of this result include *strict* concavity of $U(x)$. Every non-strictly concave utility function $U(x)$ can be expressed as the limit as $n \to \infty$ of a sequence of strictly concave utilities $U_n(x)$ (just try sketching in such a sequence on figure 3.4). If none of these utilities $U_n(x)$ favours G then nor, in the limit, can $U(x)$. Thus welfare superiority in the strictly concave setting amounts to the same thing as in ours.

7 An improved version of this result is to be found in proposition 2.2 in Spencer and Fisher (1992).

8 This criterion, equivalent to $G(x) \geq F(x)$ for all x, is known as *first degree stochastic dominance* in the risk context.

9 The sequence of exercises 3.2.5(a)–(c) derive from the results of Lam (1986b). Some of Lam's results are also obtained in Stark and Yitzhaki (1988).

10 The finite crossing restriction does not rule out of consideration any distribution function $F(x)$ *per se*. Note that if $\{F(x), G(x)\}$ satisfy the finite crossing restriction and $\{G(x), H(x)\}$ do, it cannot be guaranteed that $\{F(x), H(x)\}$ will.

11 For a version of this lemma in the risk context, see Whitmore (1970).

12 This material, and much of that preceding it in this section, is drawn from Dardanoni and Lambert (1988).

13 Pyatt (1990, p. 251) has also pointed this out: 'households must be weighted in proportion to their needs . . . a failure to weight households correctly will result in a social evaluation function which violates the principle of transfers'. Ebert (1999a) gives examples to show how redistribution between household types works, and how Lorenz curves must be constructed, using these weights.

14 Sequential rank dominance was considered in Atkinson and Bourguignon (1987) along with sequential generalized Lorenz dominance and the test which is

expounded in exercise 3.6.3 to follow. Jenkins and Lambert (1993) and Chambaz and Maurin (1998) extend sequential rank dominance to situations of demographic change.

15 An explicit proof is given on p. 84 in the second (1993) edition of this book.

4

Social welfare and inequality aversion

The social welfare function

$$W_F = \int U(x)f(x)\mathrm{d}x \tag{3.1}$$

is central to the Atkinson (1970) and Shorrocks (1983a) theorems, as well as to the results addressing situations in which Lorenz or generalized Lorenz curves intersect. The analogous form for the case of differences in need,

$$W_F = \sum_{1 \le i \le n} p_{iF} \int_0^{\bar{z}} U_i(x)f_i(x)\mathrm{d}x \tag{3.29}$$

is central to the Atkinson and Bourguignon (1987) theorem. (Not least, these forms are central because all of our proofs rested upon them, through the use of S-functions. As we will see, though, each can be relaxed somewhat.) So far, the $U(x)$ figuring in (3.1) and the utility profile $\langle U_1, U_2 \dots, U_N \rangle$ underpinning (3.29) have been described as imposed by a social decision-maker. In this chapter we shall examine some different rationales that can give rise to these forms.

We shall go on to develop a measure of inequality aversion for the utility function $U(x)$, and to explore its properties and relationship with Rawlsian leximin. This will enable us to return to a result in section 3.4 of the previous chapter, and reconsider the nature of the restriction in terms of inequality aversion that is needed for unanimous preference results when unequal-mean income distributions have generalized Lorenz curves which cross an odd number of times.

4.1 The veil of ignorance

One interpretation for the welfare function in (3.1), which we alluded to in chapter 2 (p. 21), involves individuals judging between income distributions *for themselves*, rather than employing a social decision-maker. The resulting evaluations are rendered free from the effects of self-interest by engaging the individuals in the so-called *veil of ignorance thought-experiment*. The idea is, to appeal to actual or potential participants in the income distributions concerned, to make a choice as if from a hypothetical 'original state' in which they would be ignorant of their own (future) positions. Which of two alternative distributions of income $F(x)$ and $G(x)$ would you prefer, if you were going to be parachuted from a very great height into the relevant society, to assume the rôle of the first person you came across? As Harsanyi (1953, p. 434) has argued, such a value judgement on income distributions 'would show ... impersonality to the highest degree'.

According to this thought-experiment, one has an equal chance of occupying any rôle in society. Hence the relative frequency with which any given income level occurs is the probability of assuming an income of that magnitude. Inequality is represented as *risk*: one may find oneself occupying either extreme of the distribution, or a central position, and must weigh up this risky prospect for each distribution under consideration. Von Neumann and Morgenstern, in 1944, proposed a set of 'preference axioms', according to which individual choice under uncertainty amounts to maximizing the expected value of a utility function $U(x)$ defined over possible outcomes x. Vickrey (1945, p. 329) was quick to see the the the scope for application to matters of income distribution:

> If utility is defined as that quantity the mathematical expectation of which is maximized by an individual making choices involving risk, then to maximize the aggregate of such a utility function over the population is equivalent to choosing that distribution of income which the individual would select were he asked which of various variants of the economy he would like to become a member of, assuming that once he selects an economy with a given distribution of income he has an equal chance of landing in the shoes of each member of it.

If $U(x)$ is a von Neumann–Morgenstern utility function defined over the incomes x from a distribution F, which provide the risky outcomes for the parachutist, the frequency density function $f(x)$ for incomes becomes the probability density function for the prospect. From all available alternative prospects, the F will be chosen for which expected utility,

$$E_F[U(X)] = \int U(x)f(x)\mathrm{d}x \tag{4.1}$$

is the greatest. This is precisely the form our social welfare function takes in (3.1).

What does concavity mean in this context? To answer this, consider figure 4.1. Suppose that the individual is contemplating a gamble which yields x_1 with probability p, and x_2 with probability $1 - p$. The expected return is $px_1 + (1 - p)x_2$, and the individual's expected utility if he gambles is $pU(x_1) +$

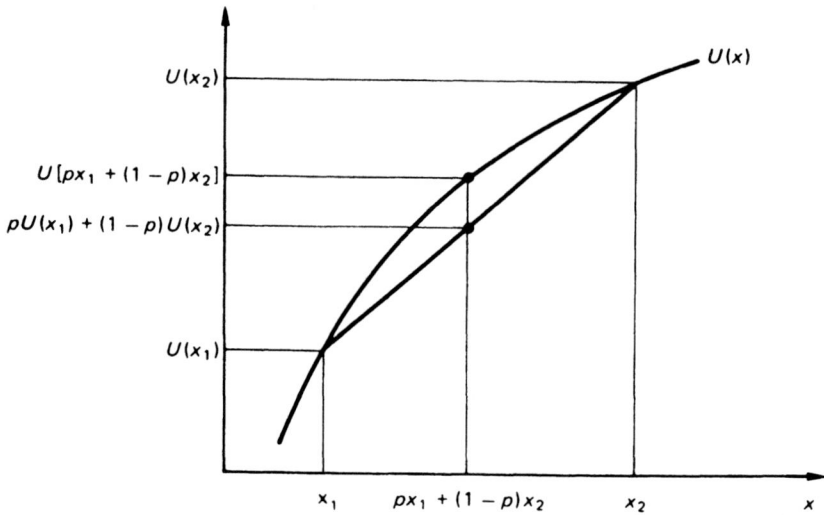

Figure 4.1   von Neumann–Morgenstern utility function

$(1-p)U(x_2)$. If and only if $U(x)$ is strictly concave, will the individual prefer to receive with certainty the expected return from any such gamble, than to take that gamble. We can extend this to arbitrary non-degenerate random prospects X, using Jensen's inequality:

$$E(U(X)) < U(E(X)) \text{ for all } X \Leftrightarrow U \text{ strictly concave} \qquad (4.2)$$

Concavity is known as *risk aversion* in the context of individual choice under uncertainty. The Atkinson and Shorrocks theorems show that *generalized Lorenz dominance is the criterion to ensure the unanimous preference of all risk-averse individuals from behind the veil of ignorance.*

Rawlsian leximin can also be seen as a veil of ignorance approach to social choice. As we shall see later, it corresponds to the choice that would be made by an extreme risk-averter – somebody whose only concern is to do as well as possible in the worst situation that could befall him.

Exercises

4.1.1   Describe the von Neumann–Morgenstern axioms for expected utility theory, as reviewed in Hey (1984, pp. 436–441). What do they say in the specific context of income distributions and the veil of ignorance thought experiment? Do you find them acceptable in this case?

4.1.2   'It has often been suggested that vNM [= von Neumann–Morgenstern] utility functions have no place in *welfare economics* and in *ethics* because they merely indicate people's attitudes towards gambling, and these have no moral significance ... I will argue that this suggestion would be valid only if these vNM utility functions indicated people's *intrinsic* attitudes toward gambling, which is, however, not the case. In fact, people's vNM utility functions are an important piece of information for welfare economics and ethics because they are natural measures for the *intensity* of people's desires, preferences and wants' (Harsanyi, 1987, pp. 546–7). Describe Harsanyi's view of the economic meaning of vNM utility functions.

4.1.3 Describe Buchanan and Faith's (1980) concept of 'veil of ignorance bargaining'. Explain how the Rawlsian outcome can emerge even when individuals behind the veil are risk-neutral. Can you change the numbers slightly in their numerical example (figure 1, p. 27) to refute their claim on p. 30 that '... there is a distinct bias in favor of such an outcome due to the structure of the [bargaining] process itself'?

4.1.4(a) 'Risky prospects are evaluated in this theory by a cardinal numerical scale which resembles an expected utility, except that the roles of payments and probabilities are reversed' (Yaari, 1987, p. 95). Outline Yaari's dual theory of choice under risk as it applies to income distributions and the veil of ignorance thought experiment.

4.1.4(b) Explain Yaari's (1988, p. 385) 'measure for measure theorem' establishing the YSWF of exercises 3.2.8 and 3.4.7, pp. 57 and 69, as the utility representation of a preference ordering over income distributions satisfying six axioms. Why does he call his theorem 'measure for measure'?

4.2 Some general considerations

The social decision-maker is not personally involved in the income distributions under consideration; the risk-averter, if involved, is parachuted in from behind a veil of ignorance. Can we give legitimacy to participants' assessments of their own well-being in making social evaluations?

Social choice theory, which has developed to quite a sophisticated degree, is concerned with the business of aggregating individual preferences into a social preference ordering. We consider here what is involved in representing the Atkinson form (3.1) as an individualistic social welfare function.

Take a fixed population of N persons, and let S be the set of all conceivable income distributions over this population. Suppose that each person i, $1 \leq i \leq N$, has a preference relation P_i defined over S. Specifically, let P_i be weak preference, and denote by I_i indifference:

$$\mathbf{x} I_i \mathbf{y} \Leftrightarrow \text{both } \mathbf{x} \, P_i \mathbf{y} \text{ and } \mathbf{y} P_i \mathbf{x} \tag{4.3}$$

This formulation allows that people might care about entire income distributions – about their fellows' fortunes as well as their own – but we shall focus on *self-interested preferences*, according to which,

$$\mathbf{x} P_i \mathbf{y} \Leftrightarrow x_i \geq y_i \qquad (4.4)$$

Each individual judges distributions solely in terms of 'what is in it for him', and more is preferred to less. A more saintly quality would be *disinterest*:

$$\mathbf{x} I_i \mathbf{x}_\sigma \text{ for all permutations } \sigma \qquad (4.5)$$

An individual holding such preferences would care nothing for his own position in the distributions before him. The social decision-maker is such a person. We aim here to arrive at a disinterested *social* preference relation P, starting with self-interested private ones P_i. Such a social ordering is also called *impersonal*.

How should we go about combining the profile of private preferences $\langle P_1, P_2, \ldots, P_N \rangle$ into a social preference ordering P? Arrow's famous impossibility theorem warns that there are severe problems: four separately innocuous properties one might want the aggregation procedure to satisfy are jointly contradictory.[1] Approaching the problem from a different angle, we could represent the preference relations P_i by utility functions $U_i(\mathbf{x})$:

$$\mathbf{x} P_i \mathbf{y} \Leftrightarrow U_i(\mathbf{x}) \geq U_i(\mathbf{y}) \qquad (4.6)$$

and seek to identify, not a social ordering P on the basis of $\langle P_1, P_2, \ldots, P_N \rangle$, but a representation of such an ordering, $v: S \rightarrow R$ based on the profile $\langle U_1, U_2, \ldots, U_N \rangle$ of private utility realizations. Such a representation,

$$v(\mathbf{x}) = W(U_1(\mathbf{x}), U_2(\mathbf{x}), \ldots, U_N(\mathbf{x})) \qquad (4.7)$$

in which $W: R^N \rightarrow R$ aggregates the individual information, is called a social welfare functional or SWFL.

Another problem raises its head at this point. Any increasing transformation $\emptyset_i(U_i(\mathbf{x}))$ would serve just as well as U_i to identify how P_i ranks income distributions, $1 \leq i \leq N$, and yet substitutions of such transformations in (4.7) would evidently affect v and change the implied social ordering.[2] Therefore we must pin the U_is down, ruling out transformations. This admits a degree of interpersonal comparability, something economists have been reluctant about, as we noted in the previous chapter. But if we are intent on using the form (4.7), then there is no getting away from it: trading utility units among the arguments of W is anyhow going to be mathematically valid.

What properties would we want to endow $W: R^N \rightarrow R$ with? Certainly, it should be a strictly increasing function, so that if $\mathbf{x}$ is preferred to $\mathbf{y}$ by all individuals then $v(\mathbf{x}) > v(\mathbf{y})$, i.e. $\mathbf{x}$ is ranked socially superior to $\mathbf{y}$. Before going further, let us assume self-interest again. Then each U_i defines an increasing $u_i: R \rightarrow R$ such that

$U_i(\mathbf{x}) = u_i(x_i)$ for all $\mathbf{x}$ \hfill (4.8)

Now our focus is upon SWFLs satisfying

$$v(\mathbf{x}) = W(u_1(x_1), u_2(x_2), \ldots, u_N(x_N)) \tag{4.9}$$

We shall want v to be *symmetric*:

$$v(\mathbf{x}) = v(\mathbf{x}_\sigma) \tag{4.10}$$

for all $\mathbf{x} \in S$ and for all permutations σ. This is because socially we should not care which income attaches to which individual: social preferences should be disinterested or impersonal. This is guaranteed in (4.9) only if identical utility representations $u_1(x) = u_2(x) = \ldots = u_N(x)$ $(= u(x)$, say) are chosen for all individuals, and if also W is symmetric over utilities,

$$v(\mathbf{x}) = W(u(x_1), u(x_2), \ldots, u(x_N)) \quad \text{and} \quad W \text{ symmetric} \tag{4.11}$$

Notice that although we needed to pick out identical utility representations here, to make the mathematics yield an ethical social ordering, this is not quite the same thing as positing identical tastes over consumption goods for all individuals. The only taste that is assumed identical for all individuals here is a taste for more rather than less income.

We are getting close to where we want to be. The final step is to make W *additively separable*. This is a very strong restriction. Forgetting the symmetry just imposed, it means

$$W(\mathbf{w}) = \emptyset\left(\sum W_i(w_i)\right) \tag{4.12}$$

for all $\mathbf{w}$, where $\emptyset$ and the W_i, $1 \le i \le N$, are monotonic functions. Taking symmetry of W into account, we need $W_1(\ ) = W_2(\ ) = \ldots = W_N(\ )$ in (4.12), and could then substitute from (4.12) into (4.11). Defining $V = \emptyset^{-1} \circ v/N$, a monotonic transformation of v which does not change the social ordering of income distributions, and setting $U = W_i \circ u$ for all i, we arrive at the form

$$V(\mathbf{x}) = \frac{1}{N}\sum U(x_i) \tag{4.13}$$

which corresponds exactly to the social welfare function in (3.1).

It will not have escaped the discerning reader that, starting with merely ordinal utility representations $U_i: S \to R$ for individual preference relations P_i, we have ended up with cardinality – full comparability in level terms between persons of a common utility-of-own-income function $U(x)$. What has emerged, from a carefully reasoned argument, is an end-product known as *classical utilitarianism*: simply, the overall good is identified with the total (actually, the average) of people's own good. How has this transition come about? First, we insisted that a social evaluation function $v(\mathbf{x})$ be defined over utility values $U_i(\mathbf{x})$; second, we demanded symmetry; given self-interested preferences, this compelled us to select a common utility-of-own-income function $u(x)$ representing each individuals preference for more rather than less own-income x; finally we imposed additive separability and made certain monotonic transformations.

To this brew we only need to add concavity of the function $U(x)$, to accord with the Principle of Transfers, to end up exactly where we wanted to be. Giving it its full title, we have rationalized the form $W_F = \int U(x)f(x)\mathrm{d}x$ in (3.1), where U is strictly increasing and concave, as an *individualistic, additively separable, symmetric and inequality-averse social welfare function*.

Additive separability can be relaxed while retaining the property of inequality aversion, and the Atkinson and Shorrocks theorems actually hold good for a wider class of social welfare functions than the additively separable one (see exercise 4.2.3). One final ingredient is still lacking. So far, we have assumed a fixed population. An extension to variable population size is needed to support most uses of the Atkinson and Shorrocks theorems (see exercise 4.2.4).

Exercises

4.2.1   'For classical utilitarians, then, the individual utilities $u_1, u_2, \ldots, u_n$ may be taken, at the outset, as measured in terms of a common unit. End of story? Not quite' (Yaari, 1981, p. 15). How does Yaari complete the story? Explain his interpretation of classical utilitarianism.

4.2.2   What criticism has 'the naive concept of social welfare as a sum of intuitively measurable and comparable individual cardinal utilities ... been found unable to withstand' (Harsanyi, 1955, p. 309)? What are Harsanyi's and Pattanaik's (1968) contributions? How does Sen (1970b) deal with the comparability issue?

4.2.3(a) Suppose that $u(x)$ is concave and $v(\mathbf{x}) = W(u(x_1), u(x_2), \ldots, u(x_N))$ as in (4.11). Does W have to be additively separable for v to be equality-preferring? Explain the significance in this context of *quasi-concavity*. See Rothschild and Stiglitz (1973), also Dasgupta *et al.* (1973).

4.2.3(b) How do these authors extend the Atkinson theorem? What similar extensions to the Shorrocks theorem are possible? See Shorrocks (1983a) and Saposnik (1993).

4.2.4   'We have laid out the ethical and informational postulates for a social welfare function that is additively separable, quasi-concave, welfaristic and respects the Pareto principle. Furthermore, postulates can be invoked to make the social welfare function symmetric and homothetic. In this case it can be represented by

$$W = \sum_{1 \le h \le H} \frac{(u^h)^{1-\rho}}{1-\rho}$$

where u^h is a utility indicator of household h and ρ is an equity parameter' (Boadway and Bruce, 1984 p. 191). Review the steps by which Boadway and Bruce lead the reader of their book to this particular form for the social welfare function. Explain carefully the distinction they make between *measurability* and *comparability* of utility functions.

4.2.5(a) An individual has preferences over two goods Y and Z represented by the utility function $v(y, z) = y^\alpha z^\beta$. Let $V(x, pq)$ be the indirect utility function, where p and q are the prices of Y and Z and x is income. Show that V is strictly concave in x if and only if $\alpha + \beta < 1$.

4.2.5(b) Could this indirect utility function be substituted for $U(x)$ in the welfare function (3.1) for the Atkinson and Shorrocks theorems? To what extent would this offend against Hume's Law, according to which one cannot draw normative conclusions from positive premises? Review the so-called 'is/ought controversy'. Start with Hume's own writings (in section I of book III: *Moral Distinctions not deriv'd from Reason*, especially pp. 468–470, see Hume, 1990), and then browse in Hudson (1969).

4.2.6 Describe Blackorby and Donaldson's (1984b) axiomatic discussion of the problems involved in choosing a social evaluation function when the population size can vary. See also Dasgupta *et al.* (1973, pp. 184–185).

4.3 Lerner's probabilistic social welfare function

An interesting way to avoid assuming that the utility-of-own-income functions $u_1(x)$, $u_2(x)$, ..., $u_2(x)$ of (4.8) are identical, and nevertheless arrive at the additively separable symmetric form for the welfare function, is through the concept of *probable social welfare* proposed by Lerner (1944, p. 29): 'If it is impossible, on any division of income, to discover which of any two individuals has a higher marginal utility of income, the probable value of total satisfactions is maximized by dividing income evenly'.

Suppose that the utility functions $u_1(x)$, $u_2(x)$, ..., $u_2(x)$ are known to the planner, and that each possibility as to which income recipient i has which utility function $u_j(\ )$ is held to be equally likely. Each possible pairing $i \leftrightarrow u_j(\ )$ of individuals i with utility functions $u_j(\ )$ is, in fact, defined by a permutation σ of $\{1, 2, \ldots, N\}$:

$$i \leftrightarrow u_{\sigma(i)}(\ ) \qquad 1 \le i \le N \tag{4.14}$$

Given an income distribution $\mathbf{x} \in S$, this pairing by σ yields average utility:

$$v^\sigma(\mathbf{x}) = \frac{1}{N} \sum u_{\sigma(i)}(x_i) \tag{4.15}$$

Each of the N! permutations σ is equally likely, so probable (expected) social welfare is

$$V(\mathbf{x}) = \frac{1}{N!} \sum_\sigma v^\sigma(\mathbf{x}) \qquad (4.16)$$

In this summation, each term $u_i(x_i)$ occurs precisely $(N-1)$! times; whence $V(\mathbf{x})$ can be written as

$$V(\mathbf{x}) = \frac{1}{N} \sum U(x_i) \qquad (4.17)$$

where $U(x) = \Sigma u_i(x)/N$. The function $U(x)$ is, given the state of ignorance that prevails, the expected utility of any person who has income x. The form in (4.17) is identical to that in (4.13). Concavity of each $u_i(x)$ is sufficient, but not necessary, to ensure concavity of $U(x)$ and thence inequality-aversion of $V(\mathbf{x})$; and just as before additivity (in this case, of the social evaluation function v^σ) can be relaxed.

Exercises

4.3.1 '. . . the maximizing property of the equal distribution holds for probable social welfare even if it is not of the additive form' (Sen, 1973b, p. 223). Reproduce the very simple argument used by Sen in proving his theorem 1.

4.3.2 'Lerner and most subsequent analysts have studied the "equal numbers" case, where the number of possible utility functions equals the number of individuals in the population . . . It seems plausible that the number of possible utility functions may be (much) larger than the population size . . . [and] that the planner may have some information regarding the possible assignment of utility functions to individuals' (Thistle, 1997, pp. 2–3). Evaluate Thistle's extension to Lerner's probabilistic approach.

4.4 Differences in need

In the preceding three sections we explained some alternative rationales for the additively separable, symmetric and inequality-averse social welfare function of the Atkinson (1970) and Shorrocks (1983a) theorems. These did not rely on asserting $U(x)$ to be a social decision-maker's imposed utility-of-income, as we had it in chapter 3. Here we sketch the corresponding rationales for the differences-in-need social evaluation function of the Atkinson and Bourguignon (1987) theorem.

First of all, the veil of ignorance thought-experiment can be carried through if we admit *state-dependent utility functions*. These figure, for example, in life insurance models, when it is reasonably assumed that an individual would have a different utility-of-wealth function conditional on surviving, than he would conditional on having died (and leaving his wealth as a bequest). In our context, the parachutist could be assumed to have a different utility function contingent on different 'states of the world' being revealed – a state of the world being the event that he will transform into a household of particular composition upon coming to earth. Once the state of the world is revealed, the parachutist then faces the risky prospect of receiving the income of one or another houshold of that type. Jumping from the aeroplane is a now a *compound lottery*. With appropriate assumptions about preferences over compound lotteries, expected utility theory extends (see Mas-Collel *et al.*, 1995, chapter 6, section E), accounting for the Atkinson–Bourguignon form. Risk aversion at the second stage accounts for concavity of the state-dependent utility functions $U_i(x)$, $1 \le i \le n$. The other properties of the utility profile $\langle U_1, U_2, \ldots, U_n \rangle$ enumerated in definition 3.3, p. 75, relate to the parachutist's attitude to risk were the two stages of the lottery reversed. If you were to come to earth *with an income of x guaranteed*, which state of the world would you most like to be revealed? In which state would you be most pleased to receive a given increment to that income x?

The development of the additively separable, symmetric and inequality averse social welfare function $W_F = \int U(x)f(x)\,dx$ from social choice considerations in section 4.2 falls down in the presence of differences in need. However, two modifications do the trick. First, we replace symmetry by *partial symmetry* (Cowell, 1980), according to which there should be social indifference to permutations of incomes *among households of each given type*, but not necessarily between the types. This is achieved by restricting the permutations σ for which (4.10) is valid, and fairly clearly leads to the form $W_F = \Sigma_{1 \le i \le n} p_{iF} \int U_i(x)f_i(x)\,dx$, though not to the particular assumptions about utility profiles spelt out in definition 3.3. These come about when we specify transfer principles. These include the standard one about rich-to-poor transfers within each type (implying concavity of $U_i(x)$, $1 \le i \le n$), and certain others about transfers between the types (see exercise 4.4.1).

Lerner's (1944) probabilistic approach can be moulded to yield the form of the Atkinson–Bourguignon social welfare function, if not the full content. Friedman (1947) commented, in his review of the book in which Lerner set out his approach, that 'the amount of income an individual receives is statistically independent of his capacity for enjoying it . . . any actual unequal division of income must therefore involve a random association of income with innate efficiency as a pleasure machine'. This is what accounts for the equiprobable pairings of all possible individuals with all possible utility functions in (4.16) on p. 92. Friedman went on to remark, critically, that things would change dramatically if 'a feasible technique is devised to determine each individual's capacity to enjoy satisfaction' (p. 310). A weaker supposition would be that income units could be classified *into types* by their capacities for satisfaction, but that ignorance would still prevail as to which particular pairing of income unit and utility function was appropriate within a type. Can you see how the form $W_F = \Sigma_{1 \leq i \leq n} p_{iF} \int U_i(x) f_i(x) \, dx$ would emerge?

Exercises

4.4.1 'The present paper ... provides a characterization of the sequential generalized Lorenz ordering by transfer principles. This axiomatization ... demonstrates that the underlying value judgements are rather weak.' (Ebert, 2000b, p. 114). Explain Ebert's principles of progressive and diminishing transfers between groups.

4.4.2 'A heterogeneous income distribution seqentially generalized Lorenz dominates another if and only if the former yields higher social welfare than the latter in terms of all (and only) increasing and needs-based SWFs for any given admissible utility profile' (Ok and Lambert, 1999, p. 46). What is a *needs-based SWF*? In what sense is this a non-utilitarian extension of Atkinson and Bourguignon's result? How does it compare with the extensions of the Atkinson and Shorrocks theorems indicated in exercise 4.2.3(b)?

4.4.3 Review Bourguignon's (1989) model of income allocation within the household in which families behave as 'utilitarian micro-societies'. Under what assumptions about household types, family formation and the relative values of members' private marginal utilities of consumption does Bourguignon show that family-level indirect utility functions $U_i(x)$ emerge which satisfy the properties in definition 3.3?

4.5   Measuring inequality aversion

Now, taking as given the welfare form

$$W_F = \int U(x) f(x) \, dx \tag{3.1}$$

where $U(x)$ is strictly increasing and concave, we address the question of how to measure the degree of inequality aversion represented by W. What change in the utility function $U(x)$ would make W more inequality-averse – and in what sense, and with what consequences?

Given the several diverse rationales we have acquired for (3.1), we can look at this question from more than one angle.

First, and fundamental to all approaches, it is declining marginal utility of income which causes W to favour less unequal distributions. We might therefore capture the degree of inequality aversion in some measure of the way marginal utility declines with income. The elasticity of marginal utility:

$$q_U(x) = -\frac{xU''(x)}{U'(x)} \tag{4.18}$$

is a candidate. Intuitively, this records, at income x, the percentage reduction in marginal utility that occurs when that income is increased by 1 per cent. It is invariant to linear transformations of the utility function:

$$q_{a+bU}(x) \equiv q_U(x) \text{ for all } a \text{ and all } b > 0 \tag{4.19}$$

Linear transformations $U \rightarrow a + bU$ are the only monotonic transformations of U which affect welfare without changing at all the ranking of income distributions: $W_F \rightarrow a + bW_F$. We might say that the form $\hat{W}_F = \int \hat{U}(x) f(x) \, dx$ is more inequality averse than $W_F = \int U(x) f(x) \, dx$ if

$$q_{\hat{U}}(x) > q_U(x) \text{ for all } x > 0 \tag{4.20}$$

Second, observe from figure 3.1, p. 47, that, loosely, the more concave or arched a social decision-maker's imposed utility function $U(x)$ is, the greater the net utility gain from any given rich-to-poor income transfer. We might reasonably say that a social decision-maker with utility $\hat{U}$ is more egalitarian than one with U if $\hat{U}$ is a concave transformation of U:

$$\exists \, \varphi \text{ such that } \varphi' > 0, \varphi'' < 0 \text{ and } U(x) = \varphi[U(x)] \text{ for all } x \tag{4.21}$$

Third we have the veil of ignorance rationale for the welfare function, in which $U(x)$ is the von Neumann-Morgenstern utility function of a risk-averse individual. There is a well-developed literature on the measurement of attitude to risk which we can draw upon. From Jensen's inequality, for any non-degenerate prospect X, there is a realization $\xi < E(X)$ such that

$$E[U(X)] = U(\xi) \tag{4.22}$$

(Refer back to figure 4.1, p. 86; for the prospect illustrated there, ξ lies vertically below the intersection of the horizontal line at $pU(x_1) + (1 - p)U(x_2)$ and the curve; can you see why?) The value ξ is known as the 'certainty equivalent' of the prospect X; it is the smallest cash amount for which the individual would exchange the risk. If $\hat{U}$ would always exchange risks for less than U, $\hat{U}$ could be said to be more risk-averse than U:

$$\hat{\xi} < \xi \text{ for all prospects } X \tag{4.23}$$

In our context, (4.22) says that, for each income distribution F, there is an income level ξ_F such that

$$W_F = \int U(x) f(x) \, dx = U(\xi_F), \text{ where } 0 < \xi_F < \mu_F \tag{4.24}$$

This identifies ξ_F as the level of income which, if distributed equally to all individuals, would generate the same welfare (average utility) as the existing distribution F. We call ξ_F the *equally distributed equivalent income* for F.[3] Now let

$$C_F = \mu_F - \xi_F > 0 \tag{4.25}$$

C_F is the income per head, equivalently (if N is the population size) NC_F is the total income, which could be sacrificed with no loss of social welfare if the rest were to be distributed equally. Kay and King (1984, p. 221) call NC_F the *cost of inequality* in F, and give a clear and intuitive link with attitude to inequality:

> How much commission would we pay Robin Hood to transfer £1 from the rich to the poor? The answer will depend on our view of inequality . . . We can imagine a continuing series of such transfers which eventually bring us to a wholly egalitarian outcome, and measure the amount of income which we would be willing to give up in order to bring about this result. This total amount is the 'cost of inequality': the reduction in aggregate income which we would accept in order to achieve complete equality in its distribution . . . The size of these costs depends on how much we are offended by inequality.

Thus we have another possible criterion for increased inequality aversion. We might say that $\hat{U}$ is more inequality averse than U if

$$\hat{\xi}_F < \xi_F, \text{ equivalently } \hat{C}_F > C_F, \text{ for all distributions } F \tag{4.26}$$

Because of an important theorem of Pratt (1964) in the risk literature, we are in the happy position of being able to confirm that all three of our possible criteria (4.20), (4.21) and (4.26), are equivalent.

Theorem 4.1

Given two strictly increasing and concave utility functions $U(x)$ and $\hat{U}(x)$, the following statements are equivalent:

(a) $q_{\hat{U}}(x) > q_U(x)$ for all $x > 0$.
(b) $\exists \, ø$ such that $ø' > 0$, $ø'' < 0$ and $\hat{U}(x) = ø[U(x)]$ for all x.
(c) $\hat{\xi}_F < \xi_F$, equivalently $\hat{C}_F > C_F$, for all distributions F.

Proof (a) $\Leftrightarrow$ (b). For any $U(x)$ and $\hat{U}(x)$ we can always find a strictly increasing function $ø$ such that $\hat{U}(x) = ø[U(x)]$ (set $ø(t) = \hat{U}[U^{-1}(t)]$ and differentiate $\hat{U}(x) = ø[U(x)]$ to obtain $ø'[U(x)] = \hat{U}'(x)/U'(x) > 0$). Since

$$q_{ø(U)}(x) = q_U(x) - x \frac{ø''[U(x)]U'(x)}{ø'[U(x)]}$$

the equivalence of (a) and (b) is clear.
    (b) $\Rightarrow$ (c). For random variables,

$$\hat{U}(\hat{\xi}) = E[\hat{U}(X)] = E\{ø[U(x)]\} < ø\{E[U(X)]\} = ø[U(\xi)] = \hat{U}(\xi)$$

by Jensen's inequality (applied to $ø$). The result follows.

(c) $\Rightarrow$ (a). Given (c), suppose that (a) is false. Then either (i) $q_{\hat{U}}(x) \equiv q_U(x)$, or (ii) $q_{\hat{U}}(x) < q_U(x)$ on some interval $x \in [z_1, z_2]$. If (i), integrate to obtain $\hat{U} \equiv a + bU$ for some a and some $b > 0$; however, then $\hat{\xi}_F \equiv \xi_F$ for all F, which is a contradiction. If (ii), then $\varnothing$ as defined above is convex on $[U(z_1), U(z_2)]$. Reversing Jensen's inequality as used above, $\hat{\xi}_F > \xi_F$ for those F whose support is $[z_1, z_2]$, also a contradiction.   QED

This important theorem validates our choice of the function $q_U(x)$ as a measure of inequality aversion. The property of being 'more inequality averse' according to $q_U(x)$ has the intuitively attractive cost-of-inequality consequence. The interpretation in terms of concavity also brings useful insights: see exercise 4.5.2(b) for an application.

Of course, two utility of income functions $U(x)$ and $\hat{U}(x)$ need not be ordered by inequality aversion; $\hat{U}(x)$ might be more inequality averse in one range of incomes and $U(x)$ more so in another range of incomes. In that case, we know how to compare the respective costs they place upon inequality *for distributions centred in these different ranges* (just consider what we did in the (c) $\Rightarrow$ (a) part of the proof above).

Exercises

4.5.1   What two separate interpretations of inequality aversion does Cowell (1985b, p. 569), say are conflated by adopting the utilitarian framework for social choice? What remedy does he propose?

4.5.2(a) 'In social choices we are interested not only in the mathematical expectation of welfare with impersonality, but also with the exact distribution of that welfare over individuals' (Sen, 1970a, p. 143). Review Sen's argument.

4.5.2(b) Suppose that a social decision-maker with utility function $U(x)$ is indifferent between two income distributions F and G: $\int U(x)f(x)\,dx = \int U(x)g(x)\,dx$. Suppose further that under F, utility $u = U(x)$ is *itself* distributed more equally than under G according to the Lorenz criterion; and that the social decision-maker decides to recommend F on this basis to break the tie. By applying the Atkinson theorem to the distribution of u, prove that his choice is in accord with the preferences of all social decision-makers more egalitarian than himself.

4.6   Constant inequality aversion and Rawlsian leximin

There is a class of utility functions $U(x)$ which are deserving of our particular attention. These are the utility functions whose inequality aversion $q_U(x)$ is constant for all $x > 0$. In order to make the case which commends these utilities, we take a short diversion.

In his 1970 paper, as well as presenting theorem 3.1, p. 45, which imparts normative significance to Lorenz dominance, Atkinson also suggested the following as an index of the inequality in an income distribution F:

$$I_F = 1 - \frac{\xi_F}{\mu_F} \qquad (4.27)$$

From (4.25), $I_F = C_F/\mu_F = [N.C_F]/[N.\mu_F]$, i.e. I_F measures the fraction of total income which could be sacrificed with no loss of social welfare if the rest were to be distributed equally. In fact, the equally distributed equivalent income and cost of inequality concepts, along with this index I_F, were all proposed first in Kolm (1969, pp. 186–7), where I is termed *relative injustice per dollar of social income*. However, I_F has become widely known as 'the Atkinson index' and that is what we shall call it in this book. Like the Gini coefficient and Schutz coefficient we have already encountered, the Atkinson index takes a value between 0 and 1 (so long as $U(x)$ is concave, i.e. inequality averse), and is zero if income is distributed equally. It is not so clear that I_F would take the value of unity if inequality were maximal: we shall come to this. Where the Atkinson index differs from our presentation thus far of the Gini and Schutz coefficients is in its explicitly ethical foundation: it is based upon a social welfare function, rather than having a statistical origin. In the next chapter we shall explore further this issue of the link between social welfare functions and indices of inequality.

The case for constant inequality aversion,

$$q_U(x) = -\frac{xU''(x)}{U'(x)} = e > 0 \text{ for all } x > 0 \qquad (4.28)$$

is made by requiring of the Atkinson index a property we have already noted in respect of Lorenz curve inequality. As we said on p. 26, the Lorenz curve is invariant to equal proportionate changes in all incomes. It detects only changes in relative income differentials. The restriction we must place on the utility function $U(x)$ in order that the Atkinson index also responds only to changes in relative inequality is precisely that inequality aversion $q_U(x)$ must be the same at all positive income levels. This result follows readily from the work of Pratt (1964), and is also stated on pp. 194–5 in Kolm (1969).

Theorem 4.2

ξ_F/μ_F is invariant to equal proportionate changes in all incomes, for every distribution F, if and only if there exists an $e > 0$ such that $q_U(x) = e$ for all $x > 0$; namely, if and only if $U(x) \equiv U_e(x)$ where

$$U_e(x) = a + b\frac{x^{1-e}}{1-e} \qquad \text{if } e \neq 1 \qquad (4.29a)$$

and

$$U_1(x) = a + b \ln x \qquad (4.29b)$$

and a and $b > 0$ are constants.

Proof Suppose ξ_F/μ_F is invariant to a change in incomes of the form $x \to kx$, where $0 < k \neq 1$. Then because $\mu_F \to k\mu_F$, we must have $\xi_F \to k\xi_F$, i.e.

$$U(k\xi) = \int U(kx) f(x) dx \qquad (4.30)$$

(since the right-hand side expresses welfare after this change). Now let $\hat{U}(x) = U(kx)$. It is immediate from (4.30) that $\hat{U}(\xi_F) = \hat{U}(\hat{\xi}_F)$, i.e $\hat{\xi}_F = \xi_F$ for all distributions F. We can conclude that $q_{\hat{U}}(x) \equiv q_U(x)$, following the line taken in the (c) $\Rightarrow$ (a) proof of theorem 4.1. But $q_{\hat{U}}(x) \equiv q_U(kx)$ (the reader should check this). So for all x, and for all $0 < k \neq 1$, $q_U(x) = q_U(kx)$. This forces $q_U(x)$ to be constant. If $q_U(x) \equiv e$, integration shows that $U(x)$ takes the form stated. Conversely, given this form, when each $x \to kx$, $\xi_F \to k\xi_F$ also: just consider (4.30) above.   QED

It is important to stress that this result does not invalidate non-constant inequality aversion $q_U(x)$. Utilities $U(x)$ for which $q_U(x)$ varies with x represent entirely feasible attitudes towards inequality. As a result of theorem 4.2, however, we know that such utilities do not view equiproportionate income growth neutrally in cost-of-inequality terms.

The two limiting cases of constant inequality aversion, $e \to 0$ and $e \to \infty$, are of considerable interest.

The first of these, $e \to 0$, is the polar case of inequality neutrality. The utility function becomes

$$U_0(x) = a + bx, b > 0 \qquad (4.29c)$$

for which $q_U \equiv 0$. Linearity, i.e. constant marginal utility b, means that this utility cares nothing for inequality, preferring one distribution F over another G if and only if under F there is more income per capita than under G:

$$\int U_0(x) f(x) dx > \int U_0(x) g(x) dx \Leftrightarrow \mu_F > \mu_G \qquad (4.31)$$

No loss of total income would be accepted in exchange for complete equality:

$$\xi_F = \mu_F, C_F = 0 \text{ and } I_F = 0 \text{ for all } F \qquad (4.32)$$

(this follows from (4.24), (4.25) and (4.27)).

At the other end of the spectrum of inequality aversion, we can consider what happens as $e \to \infty$. It is not very helpful to consider the limit at $e = \infty$ of the utility function $U_e(x)$ (what is this?). However, it can be shown that decision-making behaviour as $e \to \infty$ approaches Rawlsian leximin.

Recall first the definition of the Rawlsian leximin ranking criterion $>_R$, given in chapter 3.

Definition 4.1

Rawlsian leximin ranks distribution F higher than distribution G if under F the poorest income is greater than under G, or if under F it is the same but occurs with a lower frequency:

$$F >_R G \Leftrightarrow \exists (0, y] \text{ on which } F \neq G \text{ and } F(x) \leq G(x)$$

The formal result connecting preferences as $e \to \infty$ with Rawlsian leximin is this. If and only if Rawlsian leximin ranks F higher than G do the most inequality-averse of the constant-inequality-aversion utility functions also favour F over G.

Theorem 4.3

Let F and G be any two income distributions:

$$F >_R G \Leftrightarrow \exists e_0 > 1 : e > e_0 \Rightarrow \int U_e(x) f(x) \mathrm{d}x > \int U_e(x) g(x) \mathrm{d}x$$

Proof $\Rightarrow$ With $y > 0$ as the income level given by definition 3.1, we have

$$\int_0^y [G(x) - F(x)] \mathrm{d}x = K \tag{4.33}$$

for some $K > 0$. Now let z be any income level in excess of the highest one occurring in either distribution. If $e > 1$ then, integrating by parts:

$$\int U_e(x) f(x) \mathrm{d}x - \int U_e(x) g(x) \mathrm{d}x = \int U_e(x) [f(x) - g(x)] \mathrm{d}x$$

$$= \int_0^z U_e'(x) [G(x) - F(x)] \mathrm{d}x = b \int_0^z x^{-e} [G(x) - F(x)] \mathrm{d}x$$

$$= b \left\{ \int_0^y x^{-e} [G(x) - F(x)] \mathrm{d}x + \int_y^z x^{-e} [G(x) - F(x)] \mathrm{d}x \right\}$$

$$> b \left\{ K y^{-e} - \int_y^z x^{-e} \mathrm{d}x \right\} > b y^{-e} \left\{ K - \frac{y}{e-1} \right\} \tag{4.34}$$

since for $x \in (0, y)$, $x^{-e} > y^{-e}$ and for $x \in (y, z)$, indeed anywhere, $G(x) - F(x) \geq -1$. It is clear that this last expression is positive if e is large enough. For the $\Leftarrow$ proof, note that if not $F >_R G$ then either (i) $F \equiv G$ or (ii) $G >_R F$; and then either (i) every U is indifferent between F and G, a contradiction, or (ii), using the $\Rightarrow$ proof, G is preferred to F by the most inequality-averse utilities, another contradiction.   QED

Hammond (1975) states and proves this theorem in the $\Rightarrow$ direction. The proof given above is modelled on one given by Meyer (1975) for a stronger result in the risk literature, linking Rawlsian leximin with what pertains when inequality aversion is high. Specifically, Meyer proved the following theorem.

Theorem 4.4

Let F and G be any two income distributions. Then

$$F >_R G \Leftrightarrow \exists U: \text{ for all } V \text{ for which } q_V \geq q_U, \int V(x)f(x)\mathrm{d}x \geq \int V(x)g(x)\mathrm{d}x$$

Thus the ranking of income distributions by Rawlsian leximin carries with it the unanimous approval of the most egalitarian of social decision-makers and the most risk-averse of individuals behind the veil of ignorance. Nevertheless, the case for this criterion was not made on utilitarian grounds by Rawls (see exercise 4.6.2).

We have established that the criterion $>_R$ determines the social welfare ranking of income distributions by constant-inequality-aversion utilities $U_e(x)$ as $e \to \infty$. What, then, happens to the equally distributed equivalent income ξ_F, the cost-of-inequality measure C_F and the Atkinson index I_F as $e \to \infty$?

To see this, note first that, for $e > 1$, the discrete version of equation (4.24) implies the definition

$$\xi = \left[\sum N^{-1} x_i^{1-e} \right]^{1/(1-e)} \tag{4.35}$$

for the equally distributed equivalent income level. Second, within the summation, each term $x_i^{1-e} \leq x_1^{1-e}$ (assuming the smallest income x_1 to be positive), whilst the sum exceeds $N^{-1}x_1^{1-e}$. Hence

$$N^{1/(e-1)}x_1 \geq \xi \geq x_1 \tag{4.36}$$

Now let $e \to \infty$, and use (4.24), (4.25) and (4.27). For any income distribution F, with smallest income $x_{1F} > 0$,

$$\xi_F \to x_{1F}, C_F \to \mu_F - x_{1F} \text{ and } I_F \to 1 - \frac{x_{1F}}{\mu_F} \text{ as } e \to \infty \tag{4.37}$$

If income is modelled as continuously distributed, we must interpret x_{1F} as $\sup_x\{x: F(x) = 0\}$, which could be zero. The message is plain: as inequality aversion approaches the extreme, almost all income would be sacrificed in order to equalize the distribution at the income level of the worst-off income recipient.

In the next chapter, we shall examine in detail the properties of the Atkinson index corresponding to the constant-inequality-aversion utility function $U_e(x)$. Denoting this index $I_F(e)$, note that in the discrete case we have

$$I_F(e) = 1 - \left[N^{-1} \sum \left(\frac{x_i}{\mu_F} \right)^{1-e} \right]^{1/(1-e)}$$

(4.38a)

for $0 < e \neq 1$ (from (4.35) above), whilst for $e = 1$ we have

$$I_F(1) = 1 - \frac{x_F}{\mu_F}$$

(4.38b)

where x_F is geometric mean income. Can you see why?

Exercises

4.6.1 What is Sen's (1973b) 'probable leximin' result?

4.6.2 What does Alexander (1974, p. 609) describe as 'the conflation problem'? Explain his use of 'The Parable of the Two Sons' to show that the Rawlsian rule is but a form of utilitarianism. What is Rawls's response (see under Alexander (1974) in the bibliography)?

4.6.3 '. . . what attitude to distributive justice must be assumed for these changes (in UK income distribution, 1961 to 1973) to be welfare improving?' (Harrison and Papageorgiou, 1987, p. 23). How do the authors formulate their question analytically, and what significance can be attached to their answers?

4.6.4 Consider a socially heterogeneous population comprising n household types indexed by i, $1 \leq i \leq n$. Let the welfare function for type i be additively separable and symmetric with constant inequality aversion e_i. Let ξ_{Fi} denote the equally distributed equivalent income for type i when the income distribution is F. Define

$$\xi_F = \left[\sum_{1 \leq i \leq n} \alpha_i \xi_{Fi}^{1-e} \right]^{1/(1-e)}$$

where each $\alpha_i > 0$ and $\Sigma \alpha_i = 1$. Now define

$$F >_W G \Leftrightarrow \xi_F > \xi_G$$

Show that $>_W$ satisfies partial symmetry. Describe the transfer principle and aggregation property according to which, Ebert (1995) shows, $e_1 = e_2 = \ldots = e_n = e$ and ξ_F is the equally distributed equivalent income for the additively separable and [fully] symmetric social welfare function, with constant inequality aversion e, defined over the artificial population of equivalent adults according to an equivalence scale defined by the α_i.

4.7   Generalized Lorenz curve configurations again

We return to the question of generalized Lorenz curve configuration, and to social welfare recommendations taking the form of unanimous preference. When generalized Lorenz curves do not intersect, we know that all individualistic, additively separable, symmetric and inequality-averse social welfare functions favour the dominating distribution. When they do intersect, the mean-variance relationship between the distributions is crucial, and we have to restrict attention to certain utilities in the class U, whose members satisfy the Principle of Diminishing Transfers, in order to derive a unanimous preference result. Here we comment briefly on the restriction this represents in terms of the inequality aversion measure $q_U(x)$.

The utility functions in U are the ones with a positive third derivative. This includes the utility functions $U_e(x)$ which have constant inequality aversion:

$$e > 0 \Rightarrow U_e \in U \tag{4.39}$$

You can verify this by differentiating the formula for $U_e(x)$ in (4.29), to show that $U_e'''(x) = e(e + 1) b x^{-e-2} > 0$. In fact, all utility functions exhibiting non-increasing inequality aversion belong to U:

$$\frac{d[q_U(x)]}{dx} \leq 0 \text{ for all } x \Rightarrow U \in U \tag{4.40}$$

To see this, note that

$$\frac{d[q_U(x)]}{dx} = \frac{x U''(x)^2 - U'(x) U''(x) - x U'(x) U'''(x)}{U'(x)^2} \tag{4.41}$$

Since the first two terms in the numerator on the right are positive, $U'''(x)$ must be positive if the whole is to be non-positive. One property of such utility functions, following from Pratt's (1964) analysis, is that equiproportionate income growth reduces the perceived cost of inequality relative to the mean. Do you find it appealing that, if all incomes were doubled, we should be prepared to pay *less than* twice as much to eliminate inequality? Atkinson (1970, p. 251) suggests that, to the contrary, increasing inequality aversion would be a reasonable assumption if 'as the general level of incomes rises we are more concerned about inequality'. The class U is wide enough to accommodate some, but not all, of the utility functions exhibiting increasing inequality aversion.

We discussed informally in chapter 3 the further restriction on utility functions $U \in U$ which is necessary for unanimous preference results in unequal-mean comparisons where generalized Lorenz curves cross an odd number of times. As we said, precisely in such unequal-mean odd-crossing cases, Rawlsian leximin and inequality neutrality conflict in their prescriptions:

$$F >_R G \text{ and } \mu_F < \mu_G \tag{4.42}$$

Unanimous preference by all $U \in U$ cannot possibly obtain for either F or G if the utility functions $U_e(x)$, $0 < e \neq 1$, do not all agree about which is the preferred distribution; and they do not; for the welfare differential

$$\Delta W = \left[\int U_e(x) f(x) dx - \int U_e(x) g(x) dx \right] \tag{4.43}$$

goes negative as $e \to 0$ (see (4.31)) and positive as $e \to \infty$ (theorem 4.3).

Hence a further restriction on utility functions is indeed in order. We showed in theorem 3.5, p. 65, that in case (4.42) holds and generalized Lorenz curves cross once, if a mean-variance criterion is satisfied:

$$\sigma_F^2 < \sigma_G^2 - (\mu_G - \mu_F)(2z - \mu_F - \mu_G) \tag{4.44}$$

then, setting

$$e_0 = \frac{2z(\mu_G - \mu_F)}{(\sigma_G^2 - \sigma_F^2) - (\mu_G - \mu_F)(2z - \mu_F - \mu_G)} \tag{4.45}$$

which is positive, F is preferred to G by all utilities $U \in U$ for which $q_U(z) \geq e_0$.

In particular, e_0 is a lower bound on inequality aversion permitting unanimous preference for F over G by utilities with constant inequality aversion:

$$q_U(x) \equiv e \in [e_0, \infty) \Rightarrow W_F > W_G \tag{4.46}$$

In fact, e_0 is also a lower bound on inequality aversion for utilities with decreasing inequality aversion, because the criterion $q_U(z) \geq e_0$ is expressed at the highest income level:

$$\frac{d[q_U(x)]}{dx} \leq 0 \text{ for all } x \text{ and } q_U(x) \in [e_0, \infty) \text{ for all } x \Rightarrow W_F > W_G \tag{4.47}$$

The more the variance of F falls below that of G, the bigger the denominator in the expression defining e_0 in (4.45) above, and so the nearer to zero is e_0 and therefore the larger the sub-class of U which favours F over G.

Exercises

4.7.1 '. . . the set of downside risk averters can be characterized as all individuals whose von Neumann–Morgenstern utility functions have a positive third derivative' (Menezes *et al.*, 1980, p. 926). Describe the *downside risk* and *downside risk aversion* concepts of Menezes *et al.*, with particular reference to income distributions and social choice from behind the veil of ignorance.

4.7.2 Define $W_F(e) = \int U_e(x)f(x)dx$. Howes (1996) defines *e-dominance* of F over G as occurring when $W_F(e) > W_G(e)$ for all e between two limits, suggesting illustratively $e_{min} = 0$ and $e_{max} = 5$. What welfare ranking of income distributions does Thistle (1994) equate with unrestricted *e*-dominance? By examining Moore's (1996) findings in the case of Denmark and the UK, or otherwise, show that *e*-dominance is a less restrictive requirement of two income distributions than generalized Lorenz dominance.

Notes

1 The technically adventurous reader could consult Arrow (1963, pp. 96–97) on this.

2 In fact, the Arrow impossibility conditions can be transcribed to this scenario: the reader who has followed up the Arrow reference could also benefit from reading Sen's (1977) interesting essay.

3 The construction of the equally distributed equivalent income level ξ does not depend crucially on the utilitarian framework. As Sen (1973a, p. 42) notes, we can define an equally distributed income ξ in respect of any symmetric social evaluation function $v(\mathbf{x})$, by $v(x_1, x_2, \ldots, x_N) = v(\xi, \xi, \ldots, \xi)$. The essence of equation (4.24), namely $\xi < \mu$, follows if quasi-concavity of $v(\mathbf{x})$ is assumed.

5

Abbreviated social welfare functions and inequality indices

What are the things that matter about a cake? Its size and the way it is sliced. In this chapter we examine rationales for making per capita income and some index of the inequality in an income distribution the twin objects of social concern. The end-product we seek is a social evaluation function of the form

$$v(\mathbf{x}) \equiv V(\mu, I) \tag{5.1a}$$

where $\mu = \mu(\mathbf{x}) = \Sigma x_i/N$ and $I = I(\mathbf{x})$ is the inequality index in question. Given such a function, we can use it to rank any pair of income distributions, F and G. Either $V(\mu_F, I_F) > V(\mu_G, I_G)$ or $V(\mu_F, I_F) < V(\mu_G, I_G)$ (or there could be a tie, $V(\mu_F, I_F) = V(\mu_G, I_G)$). In other words, V provides a *complete ordering* of income distributions, as distinct from the *partial orderings* by unanimous preference which we saw in chapter 3. Of course, we lose the strength of the unanimity by this abbreviation but, provided $V(\mu, I)$ has a convincing rationale, we gain the ability to make meaningful welfare comparisons in situations where unanimous preference is not attainable.

To be convincing, V should at the very least be increasing in its first argument and decreasing in its second:

$$\frac{\partial V}{\partial \mu} > 0, \qquad \frac{\partial V}{\partial I} < 0 \tag{5.1b}$$

That is to say, given the way the cake is to be sliced, a bigger cake should be better than a smaller one; and, given the size of the cake, a more equal slicing should be preferred. But we shall want a lot more of the function V than merely these two properties. Can we develop *intuitively agreeable and convincing* ways to rank one sliced cake above another in welfare terms, which confine attention to the size of the cake and an index of the way it is divided?

Such an evaluation function would have many uses. Not least, it would allow the economist to address the so-called 'big trade-off' (see Okun, 1975, 1979). We cannot use generalized Lorenz dominance to recommend a reduction in the size of a cake, no matter what gains might follow (see p. 61). But a function V, as in (5.1), can be used to recommend a reduction in the size of the cake for the sake of more equality. Namely, this scenario can occur:

$$\Delta\mu < 0, \Delta I < 0 \text{ and } \Delta V = \frac{\partial V}{\partial \mu}\Delta\mu + \frac{\partial V}{\partial I}\Delta I > 0 \qquad (5.2)$$

Efficiency can be traded for equity; the disincentive effects of redistributive taxation can be more than offset by the gains to the poor, for example.

There are implications for the design of an inequality index posed by the requirement that it figure in a social evaluation function of the form (5.1). How can we appropriately encapsulate the detailed picture of inequality, as portrayed by the Lorenz curve, into a single index number I? Can the Gini coefficient and Atkinson index, already described, be used along with mean income to summarize social welfare? If so, how? That is, what functional form should V take?

Many statistical indices of spread in a distribution have no proven place in a convincing social evaluation function, and their use in policy analysis is therefore questionable. Some inequality indices have been identified as the result of enumerating sets of axioms (see Cowell, 2000, and references cited therein). The axiomatic approach ensures that value judgements and other requirements get 'built in', but typically does not tell us how the resulting indices should be used along with mean income in making social welfare judgements. Here we take the view that an index of inequality is given normative content by establishing a conforming, and ethically founded social evaluation function V as in (5.1). Ideally, we would like to find such functions V for *all* inequality indices which are in popular use, and/or have been designed to meet the needs of application. But we are in difficulty on this point, as we shall see.

To be defensible, the social evaluation function $V(\mu, I)$ should be constructed to conform with principles of social choice. In the following section, we consider what is involved in abbreviating a full-blown social welfare function $v(\mathbf{x})$ into the form $V(\mu, I)$. This will reveal some limitations upon the sort of inequality index I one can hope to use in conjunction with mean income to make social welfare recommendations, and also upon the evaluation function V. In section 5.2, we discuss issues concerning the design and construction of inequality indices, and identify the main families of indices that are in common use. In section 5.3 we show how the familiar Gini coefficient, and an extension of it, can be used in social evaluations, and in section 5.4 we consider the suitability of the Atkinson index, which, as we have seen, was constructed from a social welfare function in the first place. Many of the indices we will consider in this chapter crop up again in later chapters, when we seek to measure the impact of the tax system on income distribution.

5.1 Abbreviating the social welfare function

Let us begin with the general form of social welfare function,

$$v(\mathbf{x}) = W(U_1(\mathbf{x}), U_2(\mathbf{x}), \dots, U_N(\mathbf{x}))$$

considered in chapter 4 (p. 88), where $U_i(\ )$ is a utility representation of individual i's preference relation P_i over income distributions $\mathbf{x}$. The question we ask is this: in what circumstances can social welfare $v(\mathbf{x})$ be summarized by mean income μ and a scalar index I of inequality? We could also put it another way: if we take a given inequality index $I: R^N \to R$, and make it and mean income μ the twin concerns of a social evaluator, with what social welfare function or functions $v(\mathbf{x})$ does this conform?

In (4.7) we supposed that W was increasing and v symmetric (see p. 89). We then considered what was implied by assuming each $U_i(\mathbf{x})$ to be individualistic, in which case $v(\mathbf{x})$ is also an increasing function. What emerged was the additively separable form. With the additional assumption of concavity of the common utility-of-own-income function, inequality aversion was secured. What limits do these suppositions place on the type of inequality index I which could, with mean income, summarize social welfare?

Two very reasonable and natural requirements for I arise straightaway. Suppose that $v(\mathbf{x})$ is symmetric, increasing and transfer-approving, and that the abbreviating function $V(\mu, I)$ of (5.1a) is increasing in its first argument and decreasing in its second, as in (5.1b). Since the mean $\mu = \mu(\mathbf{x}) = \Sigma x_i/N$ is symmetric, for symmetry of v, $I = I(\mathbf{x})$ must also be symmetric, otherwise $v(\mathbf{x}) \equiv V(\mu, I)$ cannot possibly hold. Also, since rich-to-poor transfers raise social welfare $v(\mathbf{x})$, and do not affect mean income, they must reduce $I = I(\mathbf{x})$ in order that the identity continue to hold. That is, *I inherits impersonality (symmetry) from the full social welfare function, and must obey the Principle of Transfers.* These requirements are forced by the abbreviating requirement. They stem directly from the specification of what is good and what is bad, through the welfare function $v(\mathbf{x})$, rather than being imposed directly on I as a matter of description or belief (e.g. through statements such as: 'it should not matter for inequality what order the incomes are listed in' and 'inequality ought to fall if a rich-to-poor transfer is made').

In an interesting paper, Kondor (1975) addresses the question of restrictions implied by abbreviating social welfare according to (5.1). His penetrating analysis focuses on the structural implications of the identity $v(\mathbf{x}) \equiv V(\mu, I)$, and in particular upon the requirement that $v(\mathbf{x})$ be increasing in each x_k. We reproduce some of Kondor's arguments here. He assumes that the functions v, V and I in (5.1) are all differentiable. The trade-off between equity I and efficiency μ in V may be expressed by the *marginal rate of substitution M* between them when $V(\mu, I)$ is held constant. Differentiating totally

$$0 = \mathrm{d}V \frac{\partial V}{\partial \mu} \mathrm{d}\mu + \frac{\partial V}{\partial I} \mathrm{d}I \tag{5.3}$$

and rearranging, we obtain

$$M = \frac{\mathrm{d}I}{\mathrm{d}\mu}\bigg|_V = -\frac{\partial V/\partial \mu}{\partial V/\partial I} > 0 \tag{5.4}$$

Similarly, the marginal rate of substitution m_{ij} between two incomes x_i and x_j in the full social welfare function $v(\mathbf{x})$ is

$$m_{ij} = \frac{\mathrm{d}x_i}{\mathrm{d}x_j}\bigg|_v = -\frac{\partial v/\partial x_j}{\partial v/\partial x_i} < 0 \tag{5.5}$$

Now differentiate throughout the identity $v(\mathbf{x}) \equiv V(\mu, I)$ with respect to an income x_k:

$$\frac{\partial v}{\partial x_k} = \frac{\partial V}{\partial \mu}\frac{\partial \mu}{\partial x_k} + \frac{\partial V}{\partial I}\frac{\partial I}{\partial x_k} > 0 \tag{5.6}$$

(for this we need I to be differentiable, an assumption to which we shall return). In some intricate analysis, which the reader may reproduce by following the steps outlined in exercise 5.1.1, Kondor shows that (5.3)–(5.6) imply

$$M > N\frac{\partial I}{\partial x_k} \qquad \forall k \tag{5.7}$$

$$M = \frac{N[\partial I/\partial x_j + m_{ij}(\partial I/\partial x_i)]}{1 + m_{ij}} \qquad \forall i \neq j \tag{5.8}$$

and

$$x_i > x_j \Rightarrow 1 < |m_{ij}| < \frac{\partial I/\partial x_k - \partial I/\partial x_j}{\partial I/\partial x_k - \partial I/\partial x_i} \qquad \forall k \neq i, j \tag{5.9}$$

These are significant joint restrictions on the form of the abbreviating function V and the inequality index I. In particular, in (5.8) the right-hand side must be independent of i and j since the left-hand side is; and in (5.9), to maintain the strict inequality, $\partial I/\partial x_k$ is forced to be bounded as $x_k \to \infty$ for each k. The variance σ^2 obviously fails this test. All in all, Kondor's investigations led him to conclude gloomily that, although for any specific $v(\mathbf{x})$, an inequality index I can indeed be constructed permitting $v(\mathbf{x})$ to be abbreviated, 'this possibility is . . . not enough to make our abbreviated welfare functions usable in social discussion and planning of the income distribution'.

Exercises

5.1.1(a) Use (5.3) and (5.5) to show that (5.7) is equivalent to $\partial v/\partial x_k > 0$.

5.1.1(b) Set $\partial \mu/\partial x_k = 1/N$ in (5.6) and substitute from (5.6) into (5.5), first with $k = i$ and then with $k = j$. Now use (5.4) and rearrange to obtain (5.8).

5.1.1(c) Show that if I satisfies the Principle of Transfers then $x_i > x_j \Rightarrow \partial I/\partial x_i > \partial I/\partial x_j$. Use this along with (5.8) to establish (5.9).

5.1.2   What were Kondor's (1975) conclusions in respect of the four 'conventional inequality measures' he investigated (the variance of income, the variance of the logarithm of income, the Gini coefficient and the Schutz coefficient)? Outline the case which emerges for the Gini coefficient.

5.1.3   Suppose that a social evaluator, with preferences over income distributions x which are unknown to you, the welfare economist, wishes for ease of policy analysis to summarize alternative distributions by mean income and a certain inequality index I. By what sort of questioning could you determine from him whether or not the inequality index I fits his underlying social welfare function $v(x)$? See Kondor (1975, p. 312).

5.1.4   What concerns, in addition to mean income and inequality, does Kondor (1975, p. 320) suggest as candidates for a 'less severe abbreviation' of the social welfare function?

5.1.5   Discuss the relationship that exists between social welfare functions and measures of inequality. In particular, explain and contrast the approaches of Blackorby and Donaldson (1978), Ebert (1987) and Dutta and Esteban (1992).

5.2   Indices of relative inequality

Our purpose here is to describe some of the indices most commonly used to measure income inequality, and in doing so to highlight their particular features and deficiencies. We do this with an eye to their possible rôle in an abbreviated social welfare function, but the measurement of inequality *per se* forms a considerable area of recent and ongoing research endeavour. There are treatments at many levels to which the reader could refer, from the readable short text of Cowell (1995) to the weighty monograph of Nygård and Sandström (1981). Informative surveys can be found in Foster (1985), Jenkins (1991a) and Cowell (2000).

We have already seen that an index of income inequality should both be symmetric and satisfy the Principle of Transfers, if it is to appear in an abbreviated social welfare function. These two requirements are appealing *per se*, though Cowell (1980) has sensibly suggested substituting partial symmetry for the former in case the population is socially heterogeneous (recall the discussion on p. 93 in respect of partially symmetric social welfare functions). Here, we will assume homogeneity and full symmetry (but see exercise 5.2.12: the indices we shall describe can perfectly well be applied to distributions of equivalent income). The responsiveness to transfers is, as Shorrocks (1988, p. 432) says, 'the most fundamental defining characteristic of an inequality index'. If we add scale invariance, which says that the inequality index should not be affected by equiproportionate (scale) changes in all incomes, then (with some other technical requirements, see Shorrocks 1988 for details) we arrive at the class of indices of relative inequality.

Indices of relative inequality reflect what, in chapter 2, we called 'Lorenz curve inequality' – in the sense that they are reduced if the Lorenz curve shifts inwards, and unaffected when the Lorenz curve is unaffected. We can see this as follows. Suppose that income distribution **y** Lorenz dominates income distribution **x**. Now consider the transition from **x** to **y** in two stages:

$$x_i \to z_i = \frac{\mu_y}{\mu_x} x_i \to y_i \tag{5.10}$$

If I is an index of relative inequality then $I(\mathbf{z}) = I(\mathbf{x})$ because of scale invariance. The move from **z** to **y** involves an inward shift of Lorenz curve and no change in mean income: can you see why? Now such a change can always be replicated by performing a sequence of income transfers from higher to lower incomes: recall exercise 2.4.8 on p. 36. Therefore by the transfers property, $I(\mathbf{y}) < I(\mathbf{z})$. Combining, we have $I(\mathbf{y}) < I(\mathbf{x})$: the Lorenz dominant distribution displays reduced inequality according to any index I of relative inequality.

An index of absolute inequality would demand invariance to equal additions to all incomes rather than scale invariance. Although we shall concentrate in this book on indices of relative inequality, it is by no means clear that the relative inequality concept perfectly captures what is commonly perceived as inequality. A literature has grown up around alternative inequality concepts, and is referred to in exercise 5.2.17.

A compelling property for an inequality measure as a descriptive tool is one known as subgroup decomposability. We may wish to account for overall inequality – or trends in inequality through time, for example – in terms of the inequality (or trends) prevailing within and between specified population subgroups, for example occupations, social groupings, age groups, sexes or geographical regions. One way to conduct such an accounting is to use an 'additively decomposable' inequality index I. Such an index has the property that, for any population and any partition into subgroups (indexed by $k = 1$, $2, \ldots , K$, say), overall inequality can be expressed as a weighted sum of the inequality values calculated for the subgroups, call these I_k, plus a term I_B capturing 'between-group inequality':

$$I = \sum_k \alpha_k I_k + I_B \tag{5.11a}$$

In this, the weights α_k depend on the proportion of the population in group k, call this p_k, and their share in total income, call this q_k:

$$\alpha_k = \alpha(p_k, q_k) \tag{5.11b}$$

for some function $\alpha\colon [0, 1] \times [0, 1] \to \mathbf{R}_+$. The index I_B measures inequality in the hypothetical distribution in which each income in each group k, $1 \le k \le K$, is replaced by the mean for that group, call it μ_k. I_B thus captures that part of overall inequality which is accounted for by differences in the general levels of income in the different groups, all within-group inequalities having been 'smoothed out'.

The choice of index is severely limited if one requires additive decomposability. We saw in exercise 2.4.6 that the Gini coefficient is not additively decomposable; we shall return to this shortly. In fact, the only indices of relative inequality which satisfy (5.11a–b) are the members of the so-called *generalized entropy family* (and scalar multiples of these). This is a parametric family of inequality indices, $E(c)$, $c \in \mathbf{R}$, defined when $c \neq 0, 1$ by

$$E(c) = \left\{ \frac{1}{Nc(c-1)} \right\} \sum_i \left[\left(\frac{x_i}{\mu} \right)^c - 1 \right] \tag{5.12a}$$

In the excluded cases $c = 0, 1$ special expressions obtain. These are

$$E(0) = \frac{1}{N} \sum_i \ln \frac{\mu}{x_i} \tag{5.12b}$$

which is known as the *mean logarithmic deviation*, and

$$E(1) = \frac{1}{N} \sum_i \frac{x_i}{\mu} \ln \frac{x_i}{\mu} \tag{5.12c}$$

which is known as *Theil's entropy index* (Theil, 1967). In all cases, the weights α_k for the decomposition in (5.11a) are given as

$$\alpha_k = \alpha(p_k, q_k) = p_k^{1-c} q_k^c \tag{5.12d}$$

Thus only for the two special cases $c = 0, 1$ do the weights for the subgroup inequality contributions sum to unity, a desirable property from an accounting point of view. Only in the case of the mean logarithmic deviation ($c = 0$) are these weights independent of income shares. In this case, and this case only, within-groups inequality is simply the population shares-weighted sum of subgroup contributions.

Interestingly, there is a strong connection between the generalized entropy indices $E(c)$ and the Atkinson indices $I(e)$:

$$0 < e \neq 1 \Rightarrow I(e) = 1 - [e(e-1)E(1-e) + 1]^{1/1-e} \tag{5.13}$$

(to see this, go back to equation (4.38a) on p. 102). An equivalence also holds between $E(0)$ and $I(1)$: can you express it formally? Thus the inequality rankings of income distributions by the Atkinson and corresponding generalized entropy measures are the same, even though the former are not additively decomposable.

There are a number of other ways in which subgroup decomposability could be formulated. One could ask merely that overall inequality be *some function of* subgroup inequalities I_k, population shares p_k and income shares q_k (Shorrocks, 1984). Or, one could demand the additive form but seek to measure between-group inequality I_B by smoothing out within-group inequalities *in some other way* than replacing incomes by subgroup means (see on, also see Ebert, 1999b, and Foster and Shneyerov, 1999). One could even seek to measure within-group inequality differently – in the same spirit as for the between-groups component of inequality – by *first* eliminating between-groups inequality and *then* measuring within-groups inequality as the residual (this involves re-scaling subgroup incomes so that all the means become the same, see Foster and Shneyerov, 2000). We note all of these variants in passing, and turn now to a more careful consideration of the Atkinson index.

As Blackorby *et al.* (1981) have shown, the Atkinson index $I(e)$ enjoys a decomposability property of its own across subgroups. For this, one has to measure between-groups inequality differently – not by averaging out within-group inequalities, as for additive decomposability, but instead by eliminating within-group inequalities *with social indifference*. This involves passing to an artificial income distribution in which everybody in subgroup $k = 1, 2, \ldots, K$ gets the equally distributed equivalent income for that group rather than the mean, in order to measure the component $I_B(e)$. When this is done, a multiplicative decomposition emerges, in which the weights on the within-group inequalities are income shares:

$$[1 - I(e)] = [1 - I_B(e)]\left[1 - \sum_k q_k I_k(e)\right] \tag{5.14}$$

To see this, let ξ be equally distributed equivalent income in the population as a whole, and let ξ_k be equally distributed equivalent income in subgroup k. That is, $U_e(\xi)$ is average utility overall and $U_e(\xi_k)$ is average utility in subgroup k, where $U_e(x)$ is the constant-inequality-aversion utility function defined in theorem 4.2 on p. 98. When within-group inequalities are eliminated by passing to the artificial income distribution in which everybody in subgroup k gets ξ_k, $1 \leq k \leq K$, the income wasted, or cost of inequality per capita, in subgroup k is $C_k = \mu_k - \xi_k$. If *all* inequality were to be eliminated with social indifference, by moving from the original position to the perfectly equal distribution in which everybody got ξ, the income wasted, or cost of inequality per capita, would be $C = \mu - \xi$. If we passed to perfect equality from the artificial distribution, the income wasted, or cost of inequality per capita, would be $C_B = \Sigma p_k \xi_k - \xi$. It follows simply that

$$C = C_B + \sum_k p_k C_k \tag{5.15}$$

This decomposition of the per capita cost of inequality is additive. Recall that for the relevant Atkinson indices:

$$I(e) = \frac{C}{\mu} = 1 - \frac{\xi}{\mu}, \ I_k(e) = \frac{C_k}{\mu_k} = 1 - \frac{\xi_k}{\mu_k}, \ I_B(e) = \frac{C_B}{\sum_k p_k \xi_k} \tag{5.16}$$

we have the multiplicative decomposition in (5.14). Can you see the relationship between these two decompositions?

The Gini coefficient fails to decompose additively into between and within-group components in general. In case the subgroup income ranges overlap, one has to add an extra term to make the decomposition work:

$$G = \sum_k p_k q_k G_k + G_B + R \tag{5.17}$$

In Bhattacharya and Mahalanobis (1967) an interpretation for the extra term is given in terms of concentration areas (p. 150). Mehran (1975, p. 148) explained R in terms of 'income domination of one group over the other', Pyatt (1976) in terms of the expected value of a game, and Silber (1989) in terms of rank changes using a matrix-theoretic approach. There have been very many papers written over the years on this and other possible subgroup decompositions of the Gini index (see exercise 5.2.8, for example, and also Dagum, 1997). Graphical analysis provides the key to understanding the residual term R as a measure of overlap.

Starting from complete equality, where everybody gets μ, imagine a three-step conceptual procedure by means of which the actual inequality in incomes is introduced. *First, introduce between-group inequality.* This means passing to the smoothed distribution in which each person in subgroup k gets μ_k, $1 \leq k \leq K$. Let the Lorenz curve for this smoothed distribution be $L_B(p)$. This curve is shown in figure 5.1 for the case $K = 3$. The ranking of income units assumed for $L_B(p)$ begins with all members of the poorest subgroup, then all members of the second-poorest group, etc. *Second, introduce inequality within groups,* by moving to people's actual incomes, keeping them lined up by subgroups as before, and within subgroups from poorest to richest. Let $C(p)$ be the concentration curve measuring the proportion of total income received by the first $100p$ per cent of people in this 'lexicographic income parade'. *Finally, take account of the overlapping which occurs between subgroup income distributions,* by reranking people as necessary to form the true income parade, from the overall poorest person to the overall richest. Thus we arrive at the true Lorenz curve $L(p)$, measuring the income share of the $100p$ per cent poorest overall. The transformation

$$p \to L_B(p) \to C(p) \to L(p) \tag{5.18}$$

records first the introduction of between group inequality, then within-group inequalities neglecting overlappings, and finally overlappings, and at each stage the shift is a downwards one (see p. 29). As demonstrated by Lambert and Aronson (1993), the areas enclosed in the Lorenz diagram by these shifts are equal to one half of G_B, $\Sigma_k p_k q_k G_k$ and R respectively (and of course they sum to one half of G, the overall Gini coefficient). We shall return to the Gini decomposition in chapter 10, when, for a particular partition of the population, the contributions G_B, $\Sigma_k p_k q_k G_k$ and R to the post-tax Gini coefficient

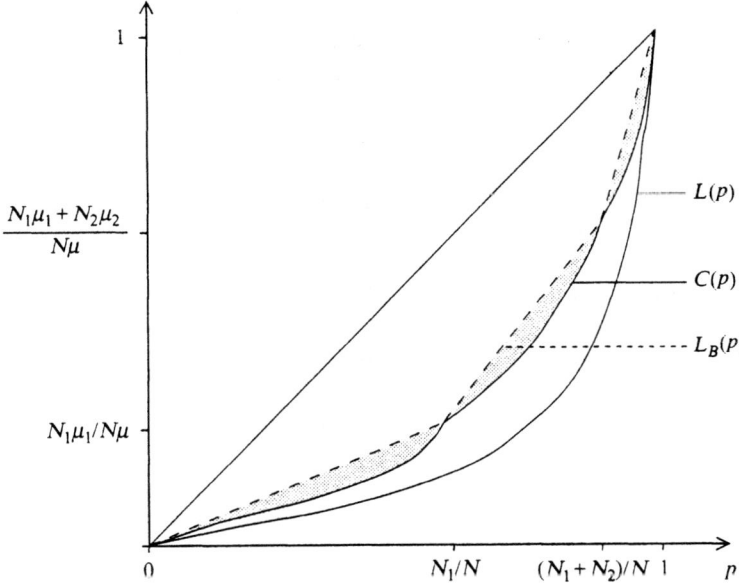

Figure 5.1 Introducing inequality in stages
Source: Lambert and Aronson (1993) with permission

will be shown to convey vital information about the equity characteristics of the income tax system.

An interesting extension of the Gini coefficient has been proposed by Yitzhaki (1983). Recall that the Gini coefficient for F is defined as $G_F = 1 - 2\int_0^1 L_F(p)\,dp$, where $L_F(p)$ is the Lorenz curve. Yitzhaki has suggested the extended version:

$$G_F(v) = 1 - v(v-1)\int_0^1 (1-p)^{v-2} L_F(p)\,dp \tag{5.19}$$

in which $v > 1$ is a 'distributional judgement parameter' to be selected by the analyst. Plainly $G(2)$ is the ordinary Gini coefficient. For $v \neq 2$, Lorenz ordinates $L_F(p)$ are weighted in the computation of $G(v)$.[1] Yitzhaki's (1983, p. 617) claim is that '... this extension has most of the properties of Atkinson's index'. Certainly the behaviour of $G_F(v)$ in the extremes, $v \to 1$ and $v \to \infty$, resembles uncannily that of the Atkinson index $I_F(e)$ at the extremes $e \to 0$ and $e \to \infty$ of inequality aversion. Integrate by parts twice in (5.19):

$$G_F(v) = 1 - v\int_0^1 (1-p)^{v-1} L_F'(p)\,dp = 1 - L'(0) - \int_0^1 (1-p)^v L_F''(p)\,dp \tag{5.20}$$

From the middle expression, as $v \to 1$ the index $G_F(v)$ approaches zero – just as the Atkinson index $I_F(e)$ does when $e \to 0$. As $v \to \infty$, $G_F(v) \to 1 - L'(0)$ from the final expression (the integral vanishes because $|1 - p| < 1$ within the range of integration). Recalling (2.13) on p. 33, we see that $G_F(v) \to 1 - x_{1F}/\mu_F$ as $v \to \infty$, where x_{1F} is the lowest income in F – again, just like the Atkinson index $I_F(e)$ as $e \to \infty$ (see p. 101).

The rôle of v in determining a complete ordering by $G_F(v)$ of the set of income distributions is similar in some other significant respects, too, to the rôle of the inequality aversion parameter e defining the Atkinson index. An obvious attraction over the ordinary Gini coefficient, for applied work, is that the analyst may select the value of v, or a range of values for v to check the robustness of the implied inequality ranking to different distributional judgements. We discuss criteria which might guide the choice of e or v in section 5.4 ahead.

In this fairly compressed treatment of inequality indices, the generalized entropy measures, Atkinson indices and (extended) Gini coefficient have been most prominent. Each family of indices has its particular recommendations and uses. In the latter part of the book we shall want to measure the redistributive impact of taxes and benefits using inequality indices. How should we choose in any particular context between the indices which present themselves? We have to balance statistical attractiveness against ease of interpretation and normative content.

We must add some qualifications to what we have done in this section of the chapter, lest it be thought that we have covered, even sketchily, all of the significant issues in the measurement of inequality. First, we have rather taken it for granted that economic inequality is a unidimensional phenomenon; clearly it is not; for treatments of inequality as a multidimensional phenomenon, see especially Kolm (1977), Atkinson and Bourguignon (1982), Dardanoni (1995) and Tsui (1995, 1998), in the latter of which many other relevant papers are also cited. Second, we have similarly taken it for granted that incquality is *relative* – about people's *shares* in the cake – but there are other equally important and valid inequality concepts: see exercise 5.2.17 on this. Finally, we have used a static framework; our indices are snapshot measures of inequality at a moment in time, in terms of income accruing to recipients over a fixed but unspecified accounting period; this is at best a very partial view; see exercise 5.2.18.

Exercises

5.2.1(a) 'Students' views on the meaning of inequality comparisons were elicited by means of a questionnaire ... The responses suggest that two important axioms ... are not universally accepted' (Amiel and Cowell, 1992, p. 3). Which axioms are these?

5.2.1(b) Which other axiom suffers a similar fate in Harrison and Seidl's (1994) study using 1773 German university students: 'the rejection

... has far-reaching consequences: all measures of ... [relative] inequality ... are paralyzed' (*ibid.*, p. 78)?

5.2.1(c)   What do you consider to be the implications of these findings for the measurement theorists?

5.2.2   Explain the thinking behind Kolm's (1996) comment: 'The goodness of a progressive transfer is a banal view ... but the proposition that a progressive transfer diminishes inequality is a bold, audacious and original one indeed'. See also Kolm (1999).

5.2.3   Describe Mosler and Muliere's (1996) *principle of transfers about θ* and *starshaped principle of transfers at θ*, where θ may be a given constant, a function of mean income or a quantile of the income distribution, and describe the classes of inequality indices which are consistent with these principles.

5.2.4   If the Lorenz curves for distributions **x** and **y** cross, indices of relative inequality can be found which rank **x** and **y** differently. If attention is restricted to the subset of indices which obey the Principle of Diminishing Transfers, in what circumstances is a unanimous ranking attainable? Evaluate the contributions of Shorrocks and Foster (1987) and Davies and Hoy (1995) in this respect.

5.2.5(a)   Show that the effect on the variance of logarithms J of a small transfer of dy from an income y to an income $y - h$ is proportional to $V'(y) - V'(y - h)$ where $V(x) = [\ln\{x/x_m\}]^2$ and x_m is geometric mean income. Now show that $V'(x)$ has a unique local maximum at $x = \exp(1) x_m \simeq 2.718 x_m$. What do you conclude?

5.2.5(b)   '... It is therefore suggested that the fact that the variance of logarithms *can* violate the principle of transfers need be regarded as no more than a *curiosum*' (Creedy, 1977, p. 157). Explain Creedy's defence of the variance of logarithms as a convenient inequality measure.

5.2.5(c)   'In this note we offer a strikingly different picture of the potential conflict between the variance of logarithms and the Lorenz criterion ... the following "worst-case scenario" can occur: One distribution, whose Lorenz curve approximates the 45° line of equality, Lorenz dominates a second distribution, whose Lorenz curve approximates the L-shaped curve of complete inequality, and yet V_L [the variance of logarithms] concludes that the second is more equal than the first' (Foster and Ok, 1999, p. 901). Describe the 10-person numerical example of Foster and Ok which demonstrates the bizzarre behaviour of the variance of logarithms, whose logic they extend to provide the 'worst-case scenario'.

5.2.6   Trace the path of development of the generalized entropy family of inequality measures, by describing briefly the contributions of Bourguignon (1979), Cowell (1980), Shorrocks (1980), Toyoda (1980), Cowell and Kuga (1981), Zagier (1983, pp. 104–105) and Shorrocks (1984).

5.2.7   Adapt the theorem of Chakravarty and Eichhorn (1994) to show that overall inequality I exceeds between-group inequality I_B for all non-decomposable as well as decomposable indices of relative inequality.

5.2.8   Explain how Yitzhaki (1988, 1994a) and Yitzhaki and Lerman (1991) have used a covariance version of the Gini decomposition to measure stratification and segmentation.

5.2.9   'Choosing "decomposable" measures . . . over "non-decomposable" ones . . . on grounds of the merits of general decomposability is not as sound a reasoning as is frequently claimed' (Sen, 1999, p. xxv). Explain Sen's reservation about the GE family, which led him to declare that 'in the demanding universal form . . . decomposability is surely an over-kill'.

5.2.10   'A set of acceptable axioms convinces us of the use of the GE class; so our basic policy is that we use the GE class; but the simple clarity of the Gini coefficient is enchanting as well. How, then, can we reconcile these circumstances?' (Kuga, 1980, p. 217). Describe Kuga's definition of 'alikeness' between inequality measures, his Monte Carlo study showing that among the GE class the Theil measure gives the highest alikeness value with the Gini coefficient, and his theory explaining why among the GE class the Theil measure is most close to the Gini coefficient.

5.2.11(a) Explain what Cowell and Jenkins (1995, pp. 427–428) mean when, in their search for explanations of US income inequality trends, they say 'we used both forms of the between-groups inequality definition in order to check the sensitivity of our results to the specification of the aggregation procedure'.

5.2.11(b) 'If the focus is on income (describing opportunities) μ-decomposable generalized entropy measures seem to be more suitable; if the distribution of living standards is relevant, dual ξ-decomposable indices should be preferred . . . two examples are presented demonstrating that the choice between additive μ-decomposability and ξ-decomposability is of decisive importance' (Ebert, 1999b, pp. 237, 243). Explain the relationship between Ebert's dual decomposable inequality indices and the Atkinson and generalized entropy indices, and show that his decomposition procedure can be derived from the one given in equation (5.15) for the cost of inequality. Reconstruct Ebert's two examples. What exactly do they show?

5.2.12(a) A population comprises households of types $i = 1, 2, \ldots, n$. Let $I = I_B + \Sigma \alpha_i I_i$ be the decomposition of overall inequality of household equivalent income across types, where I is a member of the GE family. Discuss whether the within-groups term $\Sigma \alpha_i I_i$ is invariant to changes in equivalence scale relativities (see Coulter et al., 1992a). Would a similar invariance property hold for the artificial population of equivalent adults?

5.2.12(b) Describe the exchange between Banks and Johnson (1994b) and Cowell and Jenkins (1994) exploring the sensitivity of UK income inequality findings to changes in the choice of equivalence scale.

5.2.13   Compare Shorrocks's (1982) view of the usefulness of the Gini coefficient for decomposing inequality across income sources with that of Lerman and Yitzhaki (1985). See also Shorrocks (1983b).

5.2.14   'I have examined the veracity of eight explanations for the change in UK income inequality between 1971 and 1986 by pooling the results of a large number of inequality index decompositions by population subgroup and income source' (Jenkins, 1995b, p. 55). Describe Jenkins's methodology and findings.

5.2.15   How does Cowell (1985a) distinguish inequality measurement from the 'analysis of distributional change'? What are the 'features one would like to see respected by an index of the distributional change involved in going "from" a distribution x "to" a distribution y' (*ibid.*, p. 136)?

5.2.16(a) Let $k(p)$ be a function such that $\int_0^1 pk(p)\,dp = 1$, and define

$$M_F = \int\limits_0^1 [p - L_F(p)]k(p)\,dp$$

as the weighted area between the Lorenz curve for distribution F and the line of equality. Use integration by parts to demonstrate that M_F can also be expressed as a normalized average deviation of incomes from the population mean:

$$M_F = \frac{1}{\mu_F} \int (x - \mu_F)W(F(x))f(x)\,dx$$

using a weighting function $W(\ )$ such that $W(1) = 1$ and $\int_0^1 W(p)\,dp = 0$.

5.2.16(b) Demonstrate that $W(p)$ is strictly increasing if and only if $k(p)$ is positive for all p.

5.2.16(c) Prove that M_F is an index of relative inequality in this and only this case. *Hint*: examine the effect on M_F of a small transfer dy from an income y to an income $y - h$.

5.2.16(d) The measures M_F as above form Mehran's (1976) 'general class of linear measures of income inequality'. Show that the Gini coefficient and extended Gini coefficient can both be regarded as members of this class, by appropriate choice of weighting functions $k(p)$.

5.2.16(e) Prove that if M_F belongs to Mehran's class, then $\mu_F[1 - M_F]$ is a Yaari social welfare function (YSWF) as defined in exercise 3.2.8 with weighting function $w(p) = 1 - W(p)$.

5.2.17(a) Explain the *intermediate* and *absolute inequality* concepts with the help of the simple graphical illustration used by Pfingsten (1986b) for a two-person income distribution. Describe the indices of intermediate inequality which have been proposed in Eichhorn (1988), Bossert and Pfingsten (1990) and Seidl and Pfingsten (1997). In what sense do these indices make a compromise between relative and absolute inequality judgements? See also Kolm (1976, 1996).[2]

5.2.17(b) An *inequality equivalence criterion* (IEC) specifies how, given an income distribution **x**, an additional amount of income should be distributed in order to leave inequality unchanged. Trace the development of the absolute IEC and intermediate IEC from Kolm (1976) to Besley and Preston (1988), Bossert and Pfingsten (1990), Zoli (1999b) and Del Rio and Ruiz-Castillo (2000). Explain in particular Zoli's *flexible IEC*, according to which 'the inequality perception could move from positions close to the relative and approach the absolute equivalence as the average income in society increases' (*ibid.*, p. 429).

5.2.17(c) How have transformations of Lorenz curves been used to provide dominance criteria for intermediate inequality comparisons? See Besley and Preston (1988), Chakravarty (1988) and Zoli (1999b).

5.2.18(a) 'Some of the *dynamic* changes are therefore incorporated in the *static* inequality value, and the distinction between the static and dynamic aspects becomes very blurred' (Shorrocks, 1978, p. 377). Describe the problems that arise and, with particular reference to the Atkinson index $I(e)$, sketch Shorrocks's clarification of the situation.

5.2.18(b) 'Intuitively one would expect . . . that a ranking between two distributions in one snapshot would give little information on the rankings in the next snapshot. But can this intuition be made precise?' (Kanbur and Stromberg, 1988, pp. 408–409). Describe the approach and conclusions of Kanbur and Stromberg.

5.2.18(c) '. . . we will derive a partial order of social mobility matrices which can be considered as the natural extension of the Lorenz order [from static inequality measurement] to mobility measurement' (Dardanoni, 1993b). Describe Dardanoni's contribution, paying particular attention to the parallels which he obtains with results in Atkinson (1970).

5.3 Social welfare and the (extended) Gini coefficient

The Gini coefficient G is a popular index of inequality and much attention has been focused on its normative properties. The question we address here is whether a convincing story can be told which allows a social welfare function of the form considered earlier:

$$v(\mathbf{x}) = W(U_1(\mathbf{x}), U_2(\mathbf{x}), \ldots, U_N(\mathbf{x})) \tag{4.7}$$

where W is strictly increasing and v symmetric, to be summarized as

$$v(\mathbf{x}) \equiv V(\mu, G) \tag{5.1a}$$

where V is increasing in μ and decreasing in G. Recall that the utility function $U_i(\mathbf{x})$ represents individual i's preferences over income distributions $\mathbf{x}$, and may or may not be individualistic.

We look in the first place at what pertains for individualistic preferences. In this case, symmetry of v demands that a commmon utility of income function $u(x)$ be employed for each i:

$$v(\mathbf{x}) = W(u(x_1), u(x_2), \ldots, u(x_N)) \tag{4.11}$$

and that W be symmetric and strictly increasing. As matter of notational convenience, we shall write $v = W \circ u$, or

$$v(\mathbf{x}) = W \circ u(\mathbf{x}) \tag{5.21}$$

for (4.11).

On p. 89 we showed that any additively separable and inequality-averse social welfare function can be written as $v = W_A \circ U$, where $U(x)$ is strictly concave and

$$W_A(u_1, u_2, \ldots, u_N) = \sum_i \frac{u_i}{N} \tag{5.22}$$

We know from the Atkinson theorem that each such $W_A \circ U$ ranks equal-mean distributions with non-intersecting Lorenz curves as does (the negative of) the Gini coefficient; could one or more of these social welfare functions be summarized by mean income and the Gini coefficient? If so, then *a fortiori* the welfare and inequality rankings of alternative distributions with a fixed mean, say μ_0, will be the same. Let $S = \{\mathbf{x}: \Sigma x_i = N\mu_0\}$. We could ask more generally: Do there exist a symmetric and increasing W and an increasing u such that the rankings induced on S by $W \circ u$ and by $-G$ are the same? Newbery (1970) was the first to address this question. His conclusion was negative in the additively separable case.

Theorem 5.1

There is no differentiable strictly concave $U(x)$ such that for $\mathbf{x}, \mathbf{y} \in S$, $W_A \circ U(\mathbf{x}) > W_A \circ U(\mathbf{y}) \Leftrightarrow G_x < G_y$.

Newbery's proof is very simple. Given any $a \in (0, 1)$ and $x \in (a, 1)$, for a population of which a proportion x of income recipients each have incomes of $1 - a/x$ and the remainder $1 + a/(1 - x)$, the mean income is $\mu_0 = 1$ and the Gini coefficient is $G = a$. Assuming that the theorem is false, there must exist a differentiable function of a and x of the form $xU(1 - a/x) +$

$(1 - x)U[1 + a/(1 - x)]$ which is decreasing in a and constant with respect to x. Newbery contradicts this. Can you?

In fact, W_A can be replaced by any differentiable W and concavity of $U(x)$ dropped in the statement of Newbery's theorem.

Theorem 5.2

There do not exist differentiable functions W and U such that for $\mathbf{x}, \mathbf{y} \in S$, $W \circ U(\mathbf{x}) > W \circ U(\mathbf{y}) \Leftrightarrow G_x < G_y$.

The proof goes a little beyond the level of presentation in this book, but can be found in Lambert (1985b). Note that the Gini coefficient is not differentiable as a function of $\mathbf{x}$, because it involves terms $|x_i - x_j|$ (see equation (2.18b), p. 34) which are not differentiable at $x_i = x_j$. It is this which causes ordinal equivalence to a differentiable $v = W \circ U$ to break down.

These results are not very encouraging to the individualistic case. Differentiability is a familiar economists' assumption (just recall the mathematics of Kondor (1975) presented in section 2), but it is ruled out of court if we want to use the Gini coefficient in a utilitarian evaluation function.

A potentially interesting social evaluation function involving the Gini coefficient arises by considering the area beneath the generalized Lorenz curve. From (2.15), p. 33, this area, call it A, is given by

$$A = \int GL_F(p)\mathrm{d}p = \mu_F \int L_F(p)\mathrm{d}p = \frac{1}{2}\mu_F(1 - G_F) \qquad (5.23)$$

Hence we might consider the form $A(\mu, G) = \mu(1 - G)$ as a social evaluation function. If *every* egalitarian social decision-maker prefers F to G then for sure $A_F > A_G$ (because $GL_F(p) \geq GL_G(p)$ for all p, theorem 3.2, p. 49). However the evaluation function $A(\mu, G)$ does not rank income distributions in the same way as *any particular* social decision-maker, egalitarian or not; this is implied by theorem 5.2. Can we defend the form $A(\mu, G) = \mu(1 - G)$ as a social evaluation function on non-individualistic welfare grounds?

A neat rationale for this particular form stems from a welfare criterion called *pairwise maximin* suggested by Sen (1973a, p. 33): 'Suppose the welfare level of any pair of individuals is equated to the welfare level of the worst-off person of the two. Then if the total welfare of the group is identified with the sum of the welfare levels of all pairs, we get the welfare function underlying the Gini coefficient'. We can see this as follows. First, recall an earlier definition of the Gini coefficient in the discrete case (p. 34):

$$G = \sum_i \sum_j \frac{|x_i - x_j|}{2N^2\mu} \qquad (2.18b)$$

Now set $|x_i - x_j| = x_i + x_j - 2\min\{x_i, x_j\}$ and manipulate this expression:

$$\mu(1-G) = \mu - \sum_i \sum_j \frac{|x_i - x_j|}{2N^2} = \sum_i \sum_j \frac{\min\{x_i, x_j\}}{N^2} \tag{5.24}$$

The welfare-generating unit is a pair of individuals, $\{i, j\}$, of which there are N^2 in all; the contribution to welfare of each such pair $\{i, j\}$ is the lesser income of the two, $\min\{x_i, x_j\}$; overall welfare is the averaged value across all pairs $\{i, j\}$ of these contributions, and is equal to $\mu(1 - G)$.

We can pursue other non-individualistic possibilities using the continuously-distributed framework. Suppose that an individual with income x has utility functional $U(x, F)$ when $F(x)$ is the income distribution. That is, he cares not only about his own income but also about the distribution he inhabits. Keeping to the additively separable form, for what $U(x, F)$ is welfare $W_F = \int U(x, F)f(x)\mathrm{d}x$ summarized by mean income μ_F and the Gini coefficient G_F? There are at least two different stories to tell, both of which lead to a generalized version of the Sen evaluation function of the form

$$V(\mu, G) = \mu(1 - kG) \tag{5.25}$$

where $0 < k \le 1$. One story tells of the individual's feeling of deprivation relative to the incomes of others better off, and the other of his altruistic concern for the positions of those worse off than himself. We examine each in turn.

Let the *deprivation* felt by an individual with income x in respect of an individual with income y be $D(x; y)$ where

$$D(x; y) = y - x \qquad \text{if } x \le y \tag{5.26}$$

and $D(x; y) = 0$ if $x \ge y$. This follows the thinking of Runciman (1966, p. 10) in his well-known book *Relative Deprivation and Social Justice*: 'The magnitude of a relative deprivation is the extent of the difference between the desired situation and that of the person desiring it'. The overall deprivation felt by an individual with income x, when F is the income distribution, is

$$D_F(x) = \int D(x; y)f(y)\mathrm{d}y \tag{5.27}$$

Now let the utility of an individual with income x in distribution $F(x)$ be

$$U(x, F) = ax - bD_F(x) \qquad a, b > 0 \tag{5.28}$$

i.e. linear in own income, less the disutility conferred by the feeling of deprivation. The following result confirms that mean income and the Gini coefficient summarize aggregate social welfare in this case.

Theorem 5.3

When $U(x, F) = ax - bD_F(x)$, $W_F = \int U(x, F)f(x)\mathrm{d}x = \mu_F(a - bG_F)$ for every income distribution F.

Proof We have $W_F = a\mu_F - b\int_0^z [\int_x^z (y-x)f(y)\,dy]f(x)\,dx$ for any finite z equal to or exceeding the highest income. Now let $p = F(x)$, so that $\mu_F[1 - L_F(p)] = \int_x^z yf(y)\,dy$ and $x = \mu_F L_F'(p)$ (recall lemma 2.1, p. 32). Substituting, we find

$$W_F = \mu_F\left\{a - b\int_0^1 [1 - L_F(p) - (1-p)L_F'(p)\,dp]\right\}$$

$$= \mu_F\left\{a - b\int_0^1 [pL_F'(p) - L_F(p)\,dp]\right\}$$

from which the result follows using integration by parts (see (2.17), p. 33).

QED

Dividing W_F by a and setting $k = b/a$, theorem 5.3 rationalizes a family of social evaluation functions of the type $V(\mu, G) = \mu(1 - kG)$, $k > 0$. In order that $\partial V/\partial\mu > 0$, k must be less than $1/G$. If the deprivation effect is strong, in that $k > 1$ (i.e. $b > a$ in (5.28)), then perversely, for income distributions which are very unequal ($G > 1/k$ being the criterion, certainly satisfied in the extreme as $G \to 1$), a reduction in mean income would be judged a good thing; a scaling down of all incomes would raise welfare by reducing the deprivation effect more than the own-income effect. By restricting k to the interval $(0, 1]$, we avoid this possibility, and arrive at the form $V(\mu, G) = \mu(1 - kG)$ where $0 < k \leq 1$. The rationale for this does not depend on empirical validity of the deprivation effect at the individual level; $U(x, F)$ could be a social decision-maker's imposed utility functional, in which case the value judgement is that society should be organized so people are not put in the position where they could suffer such deprivation effects.

A different story yielding this same family of social evaluation functions depends not on deprivation effects, but rather on altruism. If we accept the argument of Layard (1980, p. 740), that '. . . what matters is a person's percentile rank-order in the earnings distribution', we are led to a utility functional of the form $U(x, F)$ whose arguments are own income x and rank $F(x)$. Suppose that this is multiplicative:

$$U(x, F) = x[a - bF(x)] \qquad a > 0, b > 0 \tag{5.29}$$

so that, given a person's own income level, he prefers to be in a distribution with a smaller proportion of people less well-off than himself. This is clearly a form of altruism, albeit temepered by concern for self.[3] Then we have

$$W_F = \int U(x, F)f(x)\,dx = \mu_F\left[a - \frac{1}{2}b(1 + G_F)\right] \tag{5.30}$$

for every income distribution F. (This is immediate from (2.17), p. 33, where it is shown that $\mu_F(1 + G_F) = 2\int_0^z xF(x)f(x)\,dx$. In order that W_F be increasing in μ_F, we need $a \geq b$. This is reasonable, because for utility to be increasing in own income, the derivative

$$\frac{dU}{dx} = a - b\,F(x) - bx\,f(x) \tag{5.31}$$

must be positive, and this will not be so unless a is big enough relative to b. Then $W_F/(a - \frac{1}{2}b) = \mu_F(1 - kG_F)$ with $0 < k = b/(2a - b) \leq 1$, in the same form as before. See exercise 5.3.3 for another specification of $U(x, F)$ incorporating an altruism effect which also leads to this form.

We now have several rationales for the family

$$V(\mu, G) = \mu(1 - kG) \qquad 0 < k \leq 1 \tag{5.25}$$

of abbreviated social welfare functions containing the Gini coefficient. Can we find a place for the extended Gini coefficient $G(v)$ in an abbreviated social welfare function? Re-expressing equation (5.20), p. 115, using lemma 2.1, we have

$$G_F(v) = 1 - v \int_0^1 (1 - p)^{v-1} L_F'(p)\,dp = 1 - v \int \frac{x[1 - F(x)]^{v-1} f(x)\,dx}{\mu_F} \tag{5.32}$$

from which it follows that

$$\mu_F[1 - G_F(v)] = v \int x[1 - F(x)]^{v-1} f(x)\,dx \tag{5.33}$$

If v is an integer there is a very attractive welfare rationale for this expression. Just note that the distribution function, call it $F(x\,|\,v)$, for the minimum income in a random sample of v incomes drawn from F satisfies

$$1 - F(x|v) = [1 - F(x)]^v \tag{5.34}$$

(on the left is the probability that this minimum exceeds x; on the right is the probability that each of the v incomes exceeds x; these probabilities are the same). Differentiating (5.34) and substituting into (5.33), we find

$$\mu_F[1 - G_F(v)] = \int xf(x|v)\,dx \tag{5.35}$$

so that $\mu_F[1 - G_F(v)]$ measures the expected value of the minimum income in a random sample of v incomes drawn from F. This result extends Sen's pairwise maximin rationale for the form $\mu_F(1 - G_F)$ (which is just the $v = 2$ version: see p. 123). The new criterion, which is due to Muliere and Scarsini (1989), could be called *v-wise maximin*. Mimicking Sen (1973a, p. 33) we may describe it thus: 'Suppose the welfare level of any v-tuple of individuals is equated to the income level of the worst-off member. If the welfare of the group is identified with the average of the welfare levels of all v-tuples, we get the welfare function underlying the extended Gini coefficient'.

The role played by v as distributional judgement parameter is rendered particularly clear by this criterion. As v is increased (through integer values), the 'net is cast wider' in forming the basic welfare-generating unit, a v-tuple, within which concern is for the poorest-off member. As $v \to \infty$ welfare becomes, simply, the poorest income of all: $\mu_F[1 - G_F(v)] \to x_{1F}$. This fact has already been established, albeit in a slightly different form, on p. 116.[4]

Exercises

5.3.1 Recall from exercise 4.2.3 that we may replace W_A by any quasi-concave W and still uphold the Atkinson theorem. Can W_A be replaced by any quasi-concave W in Newbery's theorem? Consult Dasgupta *et al.* (1973, p. 186) and/or Blackorby and Donaldson (1978, p. 69).

5.3.2 Following Sheshinski (1972), show that for each strictly increasing function $u(x)$, not necessarily concave, a symmetric W can be found, call it W_u, such that for all **x** and **y**, $W_u \circ u(\mathbf{x}) > W_u \circ u(\mathbf{y}) \Leftrightarrow \mu_x(1 - G_x) < \mu_y(1 - G_y)$. Explain why this does not gainsay theorem 5.2.

5.3.3 Suppose that an individual's utility functional takes the form $U(x, F) = ax + b\int_0^x yf(y)\,dy$, $a > 0$, $b > 0$, so that the individual cares about those less fortunate than himself and includes in his utility function the incomes of such individuals. Prove that this form of altruism leads to a social evaluation function of the form $\mu(1 - kG)$, $0 < k \le 1$. *Hint*: Use (3.2), p. 49 and (5.23), p. 122 to prove that $W_F = \int U(x, F)f(x)\,dx = b\mu_F(1 - kG_F)/k$ for an appropriate value of k.[5]

5.3.4 Describe Kakwani's (1986, p. 200) alternative derivation of the social evaluation functions $V(\mu, G) = \mu(1 - kG)$, and his (1980a, pp. 75–79) axiom set leading to the social evaluation function $V(\mu, G) = \mu/(1 + G)$.

5.3.5 Describe Bishop *et al.*'s (1991) study of international welfare and deprivation using the index $V(\mu, G) = \mu(1 - kG)$. How sensitive is their ranking to changes in the parameter k?

5.3.6 Berrebi and Silber (1985) say that many inequality indices can be interpreted as relative deprivation aggregates. Evaluate their argument, taking into account also Paul (1991), Chakravarty and Mukherjee (1999) and the result in proposition 1 of Duclos (2000).

5.3.7 'To capture the role of exclusion and isolation in the measurement of social welfare, we use the expected resources (or income) of economically isolated individuals as our social evaluation function' (Duclos, 1998, p. 105). Describe the thought-experiment underlying Duclos' social evaluation function, which takes the form $\mu[1 - J(v)]$ where $J(v)$ is an inequality index and $v > 1$ is a parameter, and explain the relationship with the form $\mu[1 - G(v)]$ where $G(v)$ is the extended Gini coefficient.

5.3.8 Explain how $\mu(1 - G)$ can be interpreted as the equally distributed equivalent income measure for the Gini coefficient when the method of deriving SWFs from inequality indices suggested in Blackorby and Donaldson (1978) is applied.

5.3.9 Replicate Zoli's (1999a, p. 186) proof that 'the welfare function $\mu(1 - kG)$, where $0 \le k \le 1$, can be considered as a linear transformation of a ... Yaari SWF where the weights $v(p)$ are linear and non-increasing in p' (refer back to exercises 3.2.8, p. 57, and 5.2.16, p. 119).

5.4 Social welfare and the Atkinson index

To give the Gini coefficient normative content, we had to make very special assumptions, and could then rescue the additively separable social welfare formulation from Newbery's impossibility theorem. No such problem presents itself in respect of the normatively-founded Atkinson index, however: an abbreviated SWF is immediately available, as we will see in a moment. Nevertheless, some economists have strong reservations about the capacity of the Atkinson index to describe inequality. We address this matter after deriving the abbreviated social welfare function associated with the index and then considering the influence of inequality aversion e on inequality and welfare.

The Atkinson index $I(e)$ obtains from the utility function $U_e(x)$ defined in theorem 4.2 on p. 98, where e is inequality aversion. Specifically, for a distribution F we have

$$I_F(e) = 1 - \frac{\xi_F}{\mu_F} \tag{5.36}$$

where μ_F is mean and ξ_F is the equally distributed equivalent income. The latter is defined by

$$U_e(\xi_F) = W_F(e) = \int U_e(x)f(x)\,\mathrm{d}x \tag{5.37}$$

It is immediate that welfare can be abbreviated in terms of μ_F and $I_F(e)$. Just substitute for ξ_F from (5.36) into (5.37):

$$W_F(e) = U_e(\mu_F[1 - I_F(e)]) \tag{5.38}$$

The simplest thing is to use

$$V(\mu_F, I_F(e)) = \mu_F[1 - I_F(e)] \tag{5.39}$$

as a social evaluation function, since (5.38) shows that $W_F(e)$ is a monotonic function of this indicator. This has exactly the same form as the v-wise maxmin welfare indicator $\mu_F[1 - G_F(v)]$ for the extended Gini coefficient!

Changes in the inequality aversion parameter e have a pronounced effect on measured inequality $I(e)$. We saw in chapter 4 that for any fixed distribution F, with smallest non-zero income x_{1F}, $I_F(e) \to 0$ as $e \to 0$ and $I_F(e) \to 1 - x_{1F}/\mu_F$ as $e \to \infty$: recall (4.32) and (4.37), pp. 99 and 101 respectively. In fact, $I_F(e)$ increases monotonically with e: this is shown in figure 5.2. The effect of changes in e upon the welfare in a given income distribution is more complicated, however. As e increases, $\mu_F[1 - I_F(e)]$ falls, and as $e \to \infty$, $\mu_F[1 - I_F(e)] \to x_{1F}$, i.e. this indicator approaches the Rawlsian one. However, welfare

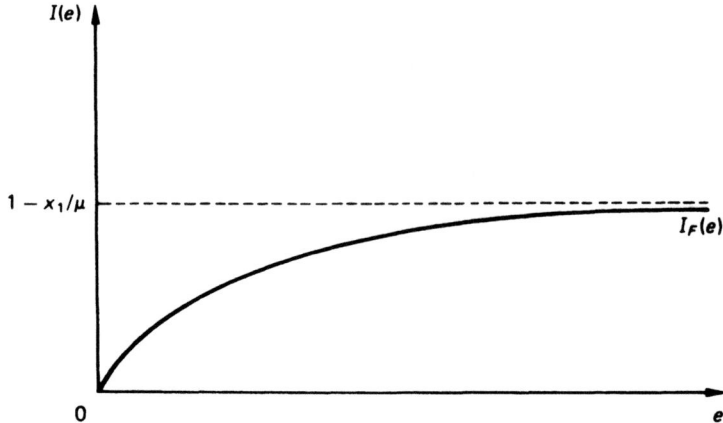

Figure 5.2 The Atkinson index $I_F(e)$ for a fixed income distribution $F(x)$

$W_F(e)$ depends on e as well as on $\mu_F[1 - I_F(e)]$. In making ordinal welfare comparisons between distributions, this is not a problem: for each e, $W_F(e)$ $> W_G(e)$ if and only if $\mu_F[1 - I_F(e)] > \mu_G[1 - I_G(e)]$, as (5.38) shows.

Atkinson (1970, p. 261) shows how the inequality ranking by $I(e)$ of 12 countries changes as e is increased. We give below the rankings which obtain for a subset of eight of these countries, for four different values of e (though Atkinson displays an ingenious graph with e varying continuously):

$e = 1$ Mexico → Ceylon → Sweden → India → Denmark → USA
            → Italy → UK

$e = 1\frac{1}{2}$ Mexico → Sweden → Denmark → Ceylon → India → USA
            → Italy → UK

$e = 2$ Mexico → Sweden → Denmark → Ceylon → USA → India
            → UK → Italy

$e = 2\frac{1}{2}$ Sweden → Denmark → Mexico → Ceylon → USA → UK
            → Italy → India

The arrow → indicates a decrease in inequality as measured by $I(e)$. Atkinson attributes some of the rank reversals which occur as e increases to the increasing tendency of $I(e)$ to focus on the relative incomes x/μ at the bottom of the distributions in question: see exercise 5.4.1. The ranking of these countries by welfare according to (5.39) also depends on inequality aversion, and has been studied by Mondragon-Barreto (2000):

$e = 1$ Ceylon → India → Mexico → Italy → UK → Denmark
            → Sweden → USA

$e = 1\frac{1}{2}$ Ceylon → India → Mexico → Italy → Denmark → UK
       → Sweden → USA

$e = 2$ Ceylon → India → Mexico → Italy → Denmark → UK
       → Sweden → USA

$e = 2\frac{1}{2}$ Ceylon → India → Mexico → Italy → Denmark → Sweden
       → UK → USA

We can see clearly here the overriding effect of mean income differences between the countries for low values of inequality aversion. As inequality aversion rises, the increase in inequality in some better-off countries relative to others less well-off is big enough to cause a rank reversal in the welfare indicator $\mu[1 - I(e)]$. Denmark and the UK change places at around $e = 1.4$. Extending the range for e beyond that shown here, Mondragon-Barreto shows that Denmark and Italy change places around $e = 3$, and Sweden and Italy around $e = 4\frac{1}{2}$. The final ranking that emerges as $e \to \infty$ is the one in place just after $e = 4\frac{1}{2}$: Ceylon → India → Mexico → Denmark → Sweden → Italy → UK → USA. This shows the order in which the lowest incomes from the respective countries line up.[6]

What range of values of e should the analyst select for empirical work? There is no authoritative answer to this question. Moore (1996) gives welfare rankings for a range of countries for $e = \frac{1}{2}$, 1 and 2. Amiel *et al.* (1999) inferred $e \approx \frac{1}{4}$ from a questionnaire addressed to students. Jenkins (1997) found that, for Britain between 1979 and 1990/91, the welfare indicator in (5.39) rose by 35 per cent for $e = 0$ (i.e. mean income rose by 35 per cent, since inequality counts for nothing when $e = 0$), by 14 per cent for $e = \frac{1}{2}$, by 4 per cent for $e = 1$ and actually fell, by 46 per cent, if $e = 2$ is assumed.[7] There is a literature in which the social decision-maker's value of e is inferred from government policies. Gouveia and Strauss (1994) infer e-values for the US between 1979 and 1989 in the range $1.72 \le e \le 1.94$ by assuming that effective federal income taxes were designed to cause each income unit an equal loss of utility (we explain equal sacrifice theory in chapter 7). Young (1990) finds US values $e = 1.61$ for 1957, $e = 1.52$ for 1967 and $e = 1.72$ for 1977 using a similar methodology. For West German nominal income taxes in 1984, Young finds $e = 1.63$; for Italy in 1987, $e = 1.40$; and for Japan in 1987, $e = 1.59$. Stern (1977) finds $e = 1.97$ for the UK in 1973/4. Stern's paper also contains a comprehensive survey of many different approaches to evaluating e, reporting values found by a range of authors for different countries using various methodologies as high as $e = 10$ and as low as $e = 0.4$. See also Lambert *et al.* (2001).

Within the Atkinson utilitarian framework, inequality gets manifested as a social welfare loss. Because of concavity, average utility $\int U_e(x) f(x)\,\mathrm{d}x$ falls short of what would pertain if the distribution were equal (i.e. $\int U_e(x) f(x)\,\mathrm{d}x < U_e(\mu)$; recall (4.24) on p. 95). The more it falls short, the more unequal the distribution is judged; this is the basis of the Atkinson index. Sen (1978,

pp. 421–422) sees this entire approach as problematic: 'The attempt to identify 'greater inequality' with 'lower social welfare' leads to contradictions
arising from the fact that both inequality and social welfare are 'primitive'
notions, and they cannot be arbitrarily declared to be identical without some
genuine loss of meaning'. He says that concern for inequality should focus
not on *inequality in incomes* but on *inequality in utility levels*, complaining
that because utility levels are merely averaged, '. . . the social welfare ranking
couldn't care less about distribution as such'. He is especially concerned
about the influence of the parameter e on measured inequality, producing an
example in which '. . . the ethical measure of inequality seems to head in
the opposite direction to the description of inequality' as e is varied. See
exercises 5.4.4(a) and 5.4.6(b) below.

What is it that we are trying to describe when we measure inequality? If
we assign utility $U_e(x)$ to income x, is it the level of x or the level of $U_e(x)$
that should count – or neither? In a thought-provoking essay, Broome (1989)
explores this question further: 'Utilitarianism identifies the overall goodness
of a distribution with the total of people's good . . . What a modified utilitarianism needs to do is to produce a way of giving the quantity of a person's
good a meaning independently of how much it counts in aggregation across
people'.

Exercises

5.4.1   '. . . the conclusions reached about the relative degree of inequality
in advanced and developing countries depend on the degree of
inequality aversion . . . none of the reversals of ranking as e increases
involve a developing country falling relative to an advanced country'
(Atkinson, 1970, p. 261). Explain how Atkinson accounts for this
observation. Could we expect a similar property to be true in respect
of welfare reversals?

5.4.2(a) Show that the marginal rate of substitution m_{ij} between two incomes
x_i and x_j in the Atkinson SWF $W_A \circ U(\mathbf{x}) = \Sigma_i U_e(x_i)/N$ is $m_{ij} = (x_i/x_j)^e$
(recall equation (5.5), p. 109). Now explain Jenkins's (1991a, p. 28)
statement: 'A tax-transfer policy that paid \$1 to some poor person
P via a tax of \$1 on a richer person R would certainly be approved
by all inequality-averse people (those with $e > 0$). But many would
endorse giving \$1 to P even if it meant that R was taxed by more
than this and the extra was "lost" (for example in administrative
costs)'.

5.4.2(b) Describe Jenkins's illustrations of the socially tolerable amounts
lost, when \$1 is transferred to a poor person from someone four
times richer, implied by various choices of inequality aversion e.
See also Atkinson (1980a, p. 42). Compare with Duclos' (2000,
pp. 149–150) discussion, in the context of the extended Gini coeffi-

cient $G(v)$, of how the parameter v determines the 'size of the bucket leak' which is socially tolerable. What are the considerations which led Duclos to suggest using values of v ranging from 1 to 4 in empirical work?

5.4.3   How does Stern (1977, pp. 236–237) answer his own question, 'What is the use of deriving values [of inequality aversion e] from policies if the only point of having explicit values is to derive policies?'

5.4.4(a) Consider two incomes x_P and $x_R > x_P$. Choose utility functions $U_e(x)$ $= a(e) + bx^{1-e}/(1 - e)$, $e < 1$, for which the constant $a = a(e)$ is selected to make $U_e(x_P)$ the same for every e. Using Sen's (1978) diagrammatic approach, confirm that as $e \to 0$ the divergence $U_e(x_R) - U_e(x_P)$ between utilities increases, whereas the inequality between x_P and x_R, as measured by the Atkinson index, goes to zero.

5.4.4(b) Now suppose that x_P and x_R are not the smallest and biggest incomes in the distribution respectively. Show that after a small income transfer from x_R to x_P, the new Lorenz curve for utility values intersects the old one once from below. *Hint*: what happens to the shares in total utility of the poorest ($x < x_P$) and the richest ($x > x_R$)?[8]

5.4.5   What are Broome's (1989) reservations about utilitarianism? Explain what he means by the *inefficiency* and the *unfairness* of inequality. How, re-framing the utilitarian social welfare function in the form $W = \Sigma_i[U_i(x_i) - c_i(\mathbf{x})]$ where $c(\ )$ is a *complaint function* specifying 'the amount of unfairness suffered', does Broome show that 'Atkinson's measure . . . is evidently aimed at inefficiency. The Gini coefficient is aimed at unfairness'.

5.4.6(a) Suppose that welfare is measured by a Yaari social welfare function (YSWF) which is additive and linear in peoples' *utilities* $U_e(x)$ where x is income and e is inequality aversion, with weights determined by a function $w(p) \geq 0$ of their positions $p = F(x)$ in the income parade: $W_F = \int U_e(F^{-1}(p))w(p)\,dp$ (recall the definition and properties of a YSWF as delineated in exercise 3.2.8, p. 57). Show that when the weighting function is $w(p) = v(1 - p)^{v-1}$, welfare can equivalently be written $W_F = \bar{u}_F[1 - \gamma_F(v)]$ where $\bar{u}_F = \int U_e(x)f(x)\,dx$ and $\gamma_F(v)$ is the extended Gini coefficient for utility levels. *Hint*: Refer back to exercise 5.2.16, p. 119, and note that the Mehran index of inequality corresponding to this weighting function is the extended Gini coefficient.

5.4.6(b) Deduce that this welfare function embodies concern not only with average utility but also with the spread of utility values. Does it thereby meet the concerns of Sen (1978) (see p. 130)?

5.4.6(c) Show that if $v = 2$ and $e = 0$, $W_F = \mu_F[1 - G_F(v)]$ where μ_F is the mean income and $G_F(v)$ is the extended Gini coefficient for income, and that if $v = 1$, W_F is a monotonic transformation of $\mu_F[1 - I_F(e)]$ where $I_F(e)$ is the Atkinson index of income inequality.[9]

Notes

1 The weighting scheme at different percentiles $p = F(y)$ which is implicit in the definition of $G_F(v)$ is illustrated for $v = 1.1$ to $v = 6$ in an Appendix in Yitzhaki (1994b, pp. 464–5).

2 For indices of absolute inequality, see Kolm (1976) and Blackorby and Donaldson (1980a). The subgroup decomposable indices of absolute and intermediate inequality have been characterized by Chakravarty and Tyagarupananda (1998, 1999).

3 If $b < 0$ in (5.29) then the individual prefers to be high up in the distribution, given his income level, reflecting care for status perhaps. In this case, the weight attaching to position rises as we go up the income scale. In consequence, if income is redistributed from poor to rich, increasing the Gini coefficient, welfare will rise.

4 Much of the unascribed material on the Gini coefficient in this section of the chapter stems from Hey and Lambert (1980) and Lambert (1985b). For additional material on extended Gini coefficients, see Donaldson and Weymark (1980, 1983), Weymark (1981) and Chakravarty (1988).

5 I thank Yves Duclos for pointing out this interesting result.

6 Mondragon-Barreto also studied the rankings of these same countries by the extended Gini coefficient $G(v)$ and associated welfare indicator $\mu_F[1 - G_F(v)]$ for $1 \le v \le 20$.

7 The Gini-based indicator $\mu(1 - G)$ rose by 20 per cent.

8 The results in exercises 5.4.5(a)–(b) are demonstrated on pp. 134–135 in the second (1993) edition of this book.

9 A discrete version of the welfare function of this exercise can be found in Berrebi and Silber (1981). Some of its properties are explored in Araar and Duclos (1998).

6
Poverty

In this chapter we discuss how to measure poverty and make poverty comparisons – just as we did for inequality and welfare in the preceding chapters. In his 1976 paper 'Poverty: an ordinal approach to measurement', Amartya Sen pioneered an axiomatic approach to the construction of poverty measures. Just as the Atkinson (1970) paper 'On the measurement of inequality' became the cornerstone for an entire literature on inequality and welfare, Sen's article on poverty led to an industry of subsequent research, and has been cited by almost all subsequent writers as the cornerstone for measurement theory in this area. Sen framed a set of axioms that led to a unique poverty measure, but in doing so he opened up a Pandora's box. By now, more than 20 different axioms have been proposed, many of which are not compatible with each other, and subsets of these are satisfied by the various poverty measures since proposed or identified. Recently the emphasis of theoretical poverty research has changed, and now concerns the devising of dominance conditions for telling when one distribution has less poverty than another according to all indices adhering to 'core axioms' (those felt to be incontrovertible).

In section 6.1 of this chapter we briefly consider some of the conceptual and methodological preliminaries underpinning the measurement of poverty, and give the flavour of Sen's founding contribution. In section 6.2 we consider the connections which exist between inequality, welfare and poverty. In section 6.3 we describe some of the most widely-used families of poverty indices, and in sections 6.4 and 6.5 we turn to dominance conditions.

6.1 Who is poor and what is poverty?

There is much debate about the essential preliminaries for the conduct of poverty analysis. The most fundamental question concerns the identification of the poor. We need to know who is poor! Second to that, if we want to make poverty comparisons or formulate an anti-poverty policy, we need to ask, how poor are the poor? This second question is about the intensity of poverty. These two questions require choices to be made about the definition of living standards, the appropriate cut-off or 'poverty line' in the distribution of living standards for identifying who is poor, and the depth of poverty a person or household below the poverty line experiences (and whether this matters). The third question to arise is, how should we aggregate poverty across a distribution? An answer to this question is needed in order to arrive at a statistic or other procedure in terms of which to make poverty comparisons, and also to formulate an objective or criterion function for the design of poverty alleviation policies.

There are many sources in which you could read about these conceptual and methodological issues. Atkinson (1989, chapter 1) is a good starting point: 'one of the main points of the chapter is to bring out the different enterprises on which people may be embarked when they set out to "measure poverty"' (p. 9). Ravallion (1994a) is another: 'Poverty comparisons . . . are typically clouded in conceptual and methodological uncertainties . . . This monograph surveys the issues that need to be considered . . . The exposition is oriented toward the needs of an economist or student new to this field'. The first two chapters in Johnson (1996) can also be recommended. In Lipton and Ravallion (1995) you will find a historical perspective on poverty, and an emphasis on underdeveloped countries: 'we provide a "snapshot" of poverty in the developing world today, looking first at the global picture, and then turning to the village and household levels'. We will not go deeply into all of the issues surrounding the measurement of poverty here, but we will address some of the most germane very shortly.

To cut to the chase, take a socially homogeneous population, say that comprising all single persons or all married childless couples. Their money incomes may be continuously distributed, with distribution function $F(x)$ and density function $f(x)$, or discrete and listed in ascending order, $x_1 \le x_2 \le \ldots \le x_N$ say. An income level Z will specify the poverty line, and everything will depend on this choice. A function $\theta(x|Z)$ will measure the poverty of an income unit having income x, conditional on the chosen poverty line Z. This function will satisfy $\theta(x|Z) = 0$ if $x \ge Z$: it is only people *below* the poverty line who are poor. For such people, $\theta(x|Z)$ could be a function of the income shortfall or *poverty gap* $Z - x$, interpretable as the deprivation felt by someone with x in respect of another with a just sufficient standard of living, Z (recall equation (5.27), p. 123). Although it is widely held that poverty is about lack of access to the good life, or deprivation, we shall not presuppose that $\theta(x|Z)$ is necessarily a function of the poverty gap at this early stage. Aggregate poverty, conditional on the selected poverty line, is

$$P(F|Z) = \int_0^Z \theta(x|Z) f(x) \, dx \qquad (6.1a)$$

if incomes are continuously distributed, and

$$P(\mathbf{x}|Z) = \sum_j \frac{\theta(x_j|Z)}{N} \tag{6.1b}$$

in the discrete case. This bare mathematical outline anticipates some of the steps which are to come, but also invites a number of questions. We shall turn to these shortly.

The extension to a socially heterogeneous population, e.g. one comprising families of various sizes, can take one of two forms. We might choose to equivalize (x now being equivalent income) and set the poverty line as a minimum standard of living below which people will be judged poor (this being Z); then the same analytics can be adopted (with some care when we come to discuss the transfer principle). Alternatively, we might choose to refrain from equivalizing, working with money income distributions and household types $i = 1, 2, \ldots, n$ having distinct needs. Then we must specify money income poverty lines, Z_i for households of type i, which are related in some way with each other: $Z_i > Z_{i+1}$ would be natural if type i is needier than type $i + 1$. We might want to vary the Z_is, one relative to another, to see how poverty is affected under different assumptions about relative needs. Aggregate poverty takes the form

$$P(F|\mathbf{Z}) = \sum_{1 \le i \le n} p_{iF} P_i(F_i|Z_i) \tag{6.2a}$$

in this scenario, where $\mathbf{Z}$ is the vector of poverty lines, F_i is the component distribution function for the money income of type i households when the overall distribution is F, and p_{iF} is the proportion of the overall population belonging to group i in this case. Finally, just as before, individual deprivation functions $\theta_i(x|Z)$ can be used to measure contributions to poverty in the subgroups:

$$P_i(F_i|Z_i) = \int_0^{Z_i} \theta_i(x|Z_i) f_i(x) \mathrm{d}x \tag{6.2b}$$

The functional forms in (6.1)–(6.2) show how *some* of the mathematics will look, later in the chapter (but not all, as we shall very soon see). First, let us take a step back, to consider some of the assumptions which are inherent in the structures we have just mapped out.

Idenitifying the poor by means of a poverty line, or minimum living standard, is itself a significant step. Can a single number Z possibly serve to determine who is poor and who is not – who *feels* poor and who does not – in a society? Is Z intended to describe in this way, or is it to be taken prescriptively, as specifying a living standard below which people *ought not* to fall? To escape poverty, is it enough to be able to buy food, clothing and shelter? Or should poverty be defined relative to contemporary living standards? Those who believe the latter would say that there should be a higher poverty threshold in a developed and generally affluent society than in a lesser-developed and poor country, and that the poverty line should be updated as an economy grows. Such observers see poverty as a *relative* concept. Those who would set Z in stone, as the minimum needed for physical subsistence, and hold it fixed (in real terms), possibly over a long time period and no matter where poverty would be measured, see poverty as strictly an *absolute*.

There are elements of the relative *and* the absolute in most people's perceptions of poverty. Sen (1983, p. 159) puts his finger on it: 'There is, I would argue, an irreducible absolutist core in the idea of poverty'. Sen acutely observes that '*absolute* deprivation in terms of a person's *capabilities* relates to *relative* deprivation in terms of commodities, incomes and resources', and he cites Adam Smith in 1776 in support of the mixed bag: 'By necessaries I understand not only the commodities which are indispensably necessary, for the support of life, but what ever the custom of the country renders it indecent for creditable people, even the lowest order, to be without'. Sen believes that the capabilities to live without shame, to participate in the activities of the community and to have self-respect are absolutes which have 'extremely variable resource requirements' (p. 163), militating towards a relativist perception of poverty in terms of incomes – it being more costly to buy one's way out of poverty and thereby enjoy participation in an affluent society than in a poor one.

Thus poverty is about deprivation and lack of access to the good life. Townsend (1985, p. 662) also puts his finger on this: 'There seems to be not just a *continuum* of deprivation in accordance with ranked income (or total resources). Below an approximate threshold of income, deprivation seems to intensify, accelerate or multiply disproportionately. It is as if people strive to conform with what is expected of them when income shrinks (they economise in what they do but still undertake the same activities) but once it shrinks below a particular level they withdraw (or withdraw their children) from fulfilling certain social obligations or well-established customs or activities'.

Having agreed that there should be a poverty line, expressed as a minimum acceptable living standard Z (or set of threshold income values Z_i for different household types i), next comes the question, how poor is a poor person or household – and does this matter? Let Z be the poverty line for a given population and let $F(x)$ be the distribution of income in that population. (We could be talking about money income or equivalent income here, depending on the scenario.) The *headcount ratio*

$$H(F|Z) = F(Z) \qquad (6.3a)$$

tells us the proportion of the population who are poor in F. For a discrete population comprising the N incomes $x_1 \leq x_2 \leq \ldots \leq x_N$, suppose that x_Q is the largest poor income: $x_1 \leq x_2 \leq \ldots \leq x_Q < Z \leq x_{Q+1} \leq \ldots \leq x_N$. Then the headcount ratio is[1]

$$H(\mathbf{x}|Z) = \frac{Q}{N} \tag{6.3b}$$

If we do not care *how poor* these people are, this is a sufficient statistic for aggregate poverty. But the headcount ratio tells us nothing about the extent of deprivation the poor people experience. If used as a target for poverty reduction, the headcount would sanction a redistributive policy that helped the least poor people first – even at the expense of the most poor. Despite this obvious drawback, it is the most widely quoted poverty statistic in applied work.

We already mentioned the income shortfall or poverty gap $Z - x$ of a poor person or household (having $x < Z$), and said that this bore the interpretation of deprivation. Aggregated across the population, we have the *poverty deficit*

$$D(F|Z) = \int_0^Z (Z - x) f(x) \mathrm{d}x = H(F|Z)[Z - \mu_F^p] \tag{6.4a}$$

where μ_F^p is the mean income of the poor in F. In discrete terms, the formula for the poverty deficit is

$$D(\mathbf{x}|Z) = \sum_{1 \leq i \leq Q} \frac{Z - x_i}{N} = H(\mathbf{x}|Z) \left[Z - \sum_{1 \leq i \leq Q} \frac{x_i}{Q} \right] \tag{6.4b}$$

which corresponds. The average income shortfall among the poor is the square-bracketed term in (6.4). Expressed as a fraction of the poverty threshold Z, this term is known as the *income gap ratio*:

$$I(F|Z) = 1 - \frac{\mu_F^p}{Z} \tag{6.5}$$

and is another widely quoted poverty statistic.[2] The normalized poverty deficit can be written as the product of the headcount ratio and income gap ratio:

$$\frac{D(F|Z)}{Z} = H(F|Z) I(F|Z) \tag{6.6}$$

As Foster and Sen (1997, p. 169) say, 'gap measures add a second dimension to the picture of poverty . . . However, like the headcount measure, the gap measures too are best seen as partial indicators'. The problem lies in what these indices capture and what they fail to capture. The headcount ratio $H(F|Z)$ is insensitive to the extent of shortfall of incomes from the poverty line, which is plainly unsatisfactory if the intensity of poverty matters as well as the incidence of it. The income gap ratio $I(F|Z)$ is silent about the proportion of the population who may share a given average income below the poverty line, which is not satisfactory either. The product of these two measures, the normalized poverty deficit $D(F|Z)/Z$, has neither of these problems but still this measure is completely insensitive to the distribution of income among the poor. Income could be taken from the poorest of the poor, and given to anybody less poor, and provided the transfer did not lift the recipient out of poverty then $D(F|Z)/Z$ would stay exactly the same. Sen (1976) argued that the *incidence, intensity* and *inequality* of poverty should all matter. These three concerns have subsequently become known as *the three I's of poverty*.

Sen outlined some axioms under which the appropriate measure of poverty could be identified as a mix of the headcount ratio, the income gap ratio and the Gini coefficient of income among the poor, call this G_F^p:

$$P^{SEN}(F|Z) = H(F|Z)\{I(F|Z) + [1 - I(F|Z)]G_F^p\} \tag{6.7}$$

We will not dwell on the axioms themselves, which Sen himself admitted were to some extent arbitrary (for example, placing a weight $Q - i + 1$ on the income shortfall $Z - x_i$, $1 \le i \le Q$, and demanding also that the index take the value $H(F|Z)I(F|Z)$ if all poor incomes are the same); it is the very fact that Sen took an axiomatic stance which has so profoundly influenced subsequent work.

The three most widely accepted poverty axioms, those of *focus, monotonicity* and *transfers*, are all satisfied by Sen's measure $P^{SEN}(F|Z)$, though none were explicitly invoked by him to obtain $P^{SEN}(F|Z)$. The focus axiom says that the incomes of the non-poor are irrelevant for the calculation of poverty.[3] There are, by now, several variants of the monotonicity and transfer axioms[4] – Zheng (1997) is an excellent source for all of these, and for very many other poverty axioms (he lists 22 in total). The simplest version of the monotonicity axiom says that if a poor person or household's income is reduced, then poverty should increase; the simplest transfer axiom, that if an income transfer is made from a poor to an even poorer income unit, then poverty should fall.[5]

Transfers and income changes which take people across the poverty threshold need very careful consideration. These have a non-obvious effect on overall poverty. If the absoluteness of poverty in capabilities space is accepted, then something highly significant happens when an income unit crosses the poverty line. Sen (1982, p. 33) suggested that 'a reduction of the number of the poor might under certain circumstances compensate a rise in the extent of penury of those who remain below the poverty line'. His index $P^{SEN}(F|Z)$ has this property, because it gives what Foster and Sen (1997, p. 174) call 'a constitutive rôle' to the headcount ratio. Look again at its definition in (6.7) above. However, many of the poverty indices subsequently developed do not share this 'constitutive rôle' feature, as we shall see in section 6.3.

Exercises

6.1.1   'If all commodities were perfectly divisible, and yielded direct consumption benefits captured by a utility function that was differentiable, strictly increasing, strictly concave and identical for all consumers, then as we compared the expenditure patterns of consumers on different incomes, we would see these varying in a continuous fashion . . . Within such a framework there is nothing in the consumption behaviour of consumers nor in the construction of the individual or social welfare functions that gives one particular level of income the characteristics and significance that the poverty line has in the poverty literature' (Lewis and Ulph, 1988, p. 119). How do Lewis and Ulph modify this framework, and what do they achieve?[6]

6.1.2(a) Distinguish between Sen's (1983) *nutritional* and *cultural* poverty lines.

6.1.2(b) 'It seems useful to define a single poverty line that takes into account both these aspects of poverty. One such poverty line is $Z(\beta) = Z_0 + \beta(m - Z_0)$ where Z_0 is the nutritional poverty line income and m denotes either the median or mean income of the society . . . The value of β depends on the society's judgement about the minimum standard of living that all its members must enjoy. The problem is that of obtaining social preferences about the alternative values of β from the individual preferences' (Kakwani, 1986, p. 240). How does Kakwani propose to derive an overall poverty index from the poverty indices $P(\mathbf{x}|Z(\beta_j))$ of different individuals j?

6.1.3 'There are several ways in which relative and absolute considerations enter into poverty measurement. We offer a simple taxonomy including the *threshold* and *equivalence scale* choices in the identification step, and the treatment of *population*, *scale* and *individual deprivation* in the aggregation step' (Foster, 1998, p. 336). Explain each of these 'several avenues for relative and absolute concepts to enter into poverty evaluations' as enumerated by Foster.

6.1.4 '. . . there can be no distribution-sensitive poverty index that is relative and absolute' (Zheng, 1994, p. 1453). Explain Zheng's characterization of relative and absolute poverty in terms of scale and translation invariance. What index does Zheng identify as essentially the only poverty index which is both relative and absolute?

6.1.5 Continuity is an axiom which says that gradual income changes, including those that would have people slip across the poverty threshold, should have only gradual effects on measured poverty. Define $\mathbf{x}^*(u)$ as the vector $\mathbf{x}$ censored at the income level u – i.e. the vector obtained from $\mathbf{x}$ by replacing each income in excess of u by u itself. Let $P(\mathbf{x}|Z)$ be a focused poverty measure. If $P(\mathbf{x}|Z)$ differs from $P(\mathbf{x}^*(Z)|Z)$, deduce that (a) people at the poverty line count as poor and contribute to overall poverty, (b) $P(\mathbf{x}|Z)$ cannot be continuous in all incomes, and (c) the measure $P^*(\mathbf{x}|Z) = P(\mathbf{x}^*(Z)|Z)$ *is* continuous. *Hint:* The focus axiom tells you that

$P(x|Z) = P(x^*(Z + \varepsilon)|Z)$ for all $\varepsilon > 0$. If P were continuous, you could take the limit as $\varepsilon \to 0$.[7]

6.1.6   Show that $GL_F(p) \geq GL_G(p)$ for all $p \Leftrightarrow D(F|Z) \leq D(G|Z)$ for all Z. *Hint:* integrate $D(G|Z) - D(F|Z)$ by parts and use results in section 3.2 of chapter 3.

6.1.7(a) 'People – not households or families – experience poverty yet it is standard practice to measure poverty at the level of the household or family. Household members are assumed to receive equal shares of their household's income . . . The alternative measurement strategy, often recommended but rarely implemented systematically, is to open up the "black box" that is the household' (Jenkins, 1991b, p. 457). Describe Jenkins's arguments and his 'agenda for action'.

6.1.7(b) How do Borooah and McKee (1994) relax the equal sharing assumption?

6.1.8   Describe the findings of Coulter *et al.* (1992a,b) and Duclos and Mercader-Prats (1999) on the influence of the choice of equivalence scale on measured poverty in the UK and Spain.

6.2   Poverty, inequality and welfare

What are the connections between the measurement procedures for welfare, inequality and poverty, and are these three phenomena conceptually distinct or closely related? Ravallion (1994b) characterizes social welfare functions as *inclusive* measures of well-being (i.e. including the whole population) and poverty indices as *exclusive* measures (setting zero weight on the incomes of the non-poor). There is nothing in an inclusive measure that explains where the poverty line comes from; this has to be set exogenously – and then, for sure, an inclusive measure can be applied to the distribution of incomes among the poor, or to incomes which have been truncated at the poverty line, to provide an exclusive measure. Watts (1968), Vaughan (1987) and Pyatt (1987) have all taken this sort of approach, and found links between poverty and welfare, the latter two using the equally distributed equivalent income concept. Lewis and Ulph (1988) sought to explain the poverty line using microeconomic theory, and came up with a social welfare function in which inequality and poverty provide distinct subtractions from a well-being measure based only on the size of the cake.

We shall briefly describe the analyses of these authors here. The work of other writers who have considered the links that can be drawn between welfare, inequality and poverty will be referred to in exercises. Thus, Atkinson (1987) discusses the relationship between the size of the cake, the cost of inequality and the 'cost of poverty', considering in particular a Rawlsian theory of poverty (exercise 6.2.1); Yitzhaki (2001) argues that an inequality index can do anything a poverty index can do, and more (see exercise 6.2.4); Ravallion

(1994b) investigates empirically the correlations between measures of poverty we have not yet introduced and social welfare in developing countries, finding these to be very high and giving reasons (see exercise 6.3.14, p. 152); and Kakwani (1999) shows how to derive inequality and poverty indices from common underpinnings in terms of deprivation (exercise 6.2.5).

In a far-sighted contribution, Watts (1968) proposed to use the social welfare function subsequently popularized by Atkinson (1970) to measure welfare:

$$W_F = \int_0^\infty U(x) f(x) \, dx \tag{6.8}$$

in which $U(x)$ is concave. Watts decomposed overall welfare into contributions from the non-poor ($x \geq Z$) and the poor ($x < Z$):

$$W_F = W_F^a + W_F^p \tag{6.9}$$

where the first summand,

$$W_F^a = \int_Z^\infty U(x) f(x) \, dx \tag{6.10}$$

is unambiguously positive and the balance, $W_F^p = \int_0^Z U(x) f(x) \, dx$, is unambiguously negative. This sign property follows from Watts's particular choice of utility function:

$$U(x) = \ln \frac{x}{Z} \tag{6.11}$$

The absolute value of W_F^p is the poverty index, call it $P^{\text{WATTS}}(F|Z)$, proposed by Watts:

$$P^{\text{WATTS}}(F|Z) = -\int_0^Z \ln \frac{x}{Z} f(x) \, dx > 0 \tag{6.12}$$

whence

$$W_F = W_F^a - P^{\text{WATTS}}(F|Z) \tag{6.13}$$

Watts calls W_F^a 'the affluence level of society, part of which is "wasted" as an offset to . . . [poverty] in the calculation of total utility' (p. 328).

Vaughan (1987) also uses this poverty–affluence dichotomy, arguing that 'without an adequate contrast between poverty and riches within a society, it may be argued, an important dimension of deprivation is open to neglect'. He uses the constant inequality aversion utility function $U_e(x)$ of theorem 4.2 (p. 98) for the measurement of welfare as average utility, as in (6.8). Letting ξ, ξ^p and ξ^a be the equally distributed equivalent (EDE) income values for the whole population, the poor and the non-poor (affluent) respectively, (6.9) translates into

$$\xi^{1-e} = H(F|Z)[\xi^{\mathrm{p}}]^{1-e} + (1 - H(F|Z))[\xi^{\mathrm{a}}]^{1-e} \tag{6.14}$$

in Vaughan's case, where $H(F|Z)$ is the headcount ratio. Can you see why? Vaughan obtains corresponding expressions for the overall EDE after two hypothetical exercises to remove poverty, one in which all poor incomes are topped up to Z by means of new resources from outside (call this ξ_g, g for 'gross') and the other after the topping-up is done with the proceeds of a proportional tax levied on the affluent (ξ_n, n for 'net'). He proposes to measure poverty gross by the difference between ξ_g and ξ, and net by the difference between ξ_n and ξ, claiming that the latter approach has 'a clear advantage . . . in ensuring that welfare gains arise solely from the elimination of poverty within a society of fixed initial resources' (Vaughan 1987, p. 164). Vaughan conducts various comparative static exercises to determine the effects of inequality, and mean income change among the poor and the affluent, on overall poverty; see exercise 6.2.2.

Pyatt (1987) also concerns himself with a poverty–affluence distinction, but he takes a very different line: 'it is income, not the population, which is dichotomised' (p. 459). Thus Pyatt breaks an income x_i into two components, one part being person or household i's *basic income*:

$$b_i = \min\{x_i, Z\} \tag{6.15}$$

and the balance, if any, namely income over and above the poverty line, being characterized as i's *affluence*:

$$a_i = x_i - b_i = \max\{0, x_i - Z\} \tag{6.16}$$

He argues that poverty should be represented by a well-being measure defined over the vector of basic incomes – that is, over incomes truncated at the poverty line. Assuming a general form of social evaluation function, Pyatt resorts to EDE incomes (see note 3 in chapter 4, p. 105 on this). Letting ξ, ξ_b and ξ_a be the EDE incomes for **x**, **b** and **a**, Pyatt makes a critical assumption of additivity in these:

$$\xi = \xi_b + \xi_a \tag{6.17}$$

and this severely restricts the welfare function which can be adopted (see exercise 6.2.3(a)). Defining poverty as

$$P^{\mathrm{PYATT}}(\mathbf{x}|Z) = 1 - \frac{\xi_b}{Z} \tag{6.18}$$

simple manipulation gives

$$\xi = Z + \xi_a - Z\, P^{\mathrm{PYATT}}(\mathbf{x}|Z) \tag{6.19}$$

whence Pyatt's (1987, p. 464) remark: 'the mean equivalent income measure of social welfare can be decomposed into the poverty level Z, *plus* the gain in social welfare due to affluence and *minus* the loss in social welfare due to poverty'. Pyatt also connects inequality with poverty and affluence: 'if the poverty line is set equal to the average level of income, then the inequality measure is simply the net difference between the index of poverty and a normalized measure of affluence'; see exercise 6.2.3(b).

In Lewis and Ulph (1988), the utility-of-income function derives from a model of consumer choice in which an absolute utility loss, g, is predicted by the microeconomics to come from being poor. Utility is thus $U(x)$ if $x \geq Z$ and $U(x) - g$ if $x < Z$,[8] and overall welfare can accordingly be written as

$$W_F = U(\mu_F) - \left[U(\mu_F) - \int_0^\infty U(x) f(x) \, dx \right] - g H(F|Z) \qquad (6.20)$$

where μ_F is mean income (size of the cake). The bracketed term, which is positive because $U(x)$ is concave, is a subtraction representing the cost of inequality and the final term, involving the headcount ratio, is a subtraction for the cost of poverty. Lewis and Ulph are unrepentant about coming up with a distribution-insensitive poverty measure in (6.20): 'none of the writers who have tried to incorporate the distribution of income amongst the poor into their measure of poverty have adequately explained why this feature of income distribution should matter when measuring poverty (as distinct from inequality)' (p. 129).

We shall consider a number of additional families of poverty indices in the next section of this chapter. In the main, these have been set up by their designers to share common underpinnings with social welfare functions and inequality indices, but they have not been introduced as welfare components.

Exercises

6.2.1 '... sceptics have been heard to complain that those concerned about poverty are really confusing poverty and inequality ... the sceptics are touching on a raw nerve, since in my view the literature on the measurement of poverty has done little to illuminate the relationship between these two concepts' (Atkinson, 1987, p. 26). Describe Atkinson's discussion of four separate schools of thought about the relation between poverty and inequality.

6.2.2 Write each EDE income ξ_* in (6.14) in the form $\mu_*[1 - I_*(e)]$ where μ_* and $I_*(e)$ are the relevant mean and Atkinson index. Do the same for ξ_g and ξ_n. Now investigate the effects on Vaughan's measures of making small changes in inequality and mean income among the rich. Vaughan found that an equal proportionate increase in the incomes of the rich leads to a reduction in his gross poverty index. How does he explain this?

6.2.3(a) What is the special form of welfare function required to validate Pyatt's (1987, p. 463) assumption of additivity of EDE income components, as in (6.17)?

6.2.3(b) Let inequality be defined as $I = 1 - \xi/\mu$ and write the EDE basic income and affluence levels as $\xi_b(Z)$ and $\xi_a(Z)$ to show their dependence on the choice of poverty line Z. Confirm that $I = P^{PYATT}(x|\mu) - \xi_a(\mu)/Z$, thereby proving Pyatt's assertion about the link between poverty, inequality and affluence quoted in the text.

6.2.4   '. . . all the informational content of a poverty index can be derived from a decomposition of an appropriate inequality index. Moreoever, the decomposed inequality index supplies additional information that is useful in poverty measurement' (Yitzhaki, 2001). Evaluate Yitzhaki's claim, and reproduce his figure 1 which decomposes the Lorenz area into components of Sen's poverty index, similar components of an analogous affluence index and a measure of inequality between the poor and the affluent.

6.2.5(a) Let $d(x, y)$ be the deprivation a person with income x feels relative to one with y, assumed positive for $x < y$, zero for $x = y$ and negative for $x > y$. Assume that $d(x, y) = d(\lambda x, \lambda y)$ for all $\lambda > 0$. Kakwani (1999, p. 621) defines an index of relative inequality as $J_F = \int_0^\infty d(x, \mu_F) f(x)\, dx$: 'in the measurement of inequality, we may assume that individuals compare their incomes with the average income of the society'. Now let Z be the poverty line and let $\theta(x|Z) = \max\{0, d(x, Z)\}$ be the poverty contribution of a person with x. Define overall poverty as $P(F|Z) = \int_0^Z \theta(x|Z) f(x)\, dx$. Show that inequality among the poor, J_F^p, can be written as $\int_0^Z d(x, Z[1 - I(F|Z)]) f(x)\, dx / H(F|Z)$ where $I(F|Z)$ and $H(F|Z)$ are the income gap and headcount ratios.

6.2.5(b) Show that if $d(x, y) = \ln(y/x)$ then J_F is the mean logarithmic deviation (see p. 112) and $P(F|Z) = P^{WATTS}(F|Z) = H(F|Z)[J_F^p - \ln(1 - I(F|Z))]$.

6.2.5(c) Can you write Kakwani's poverty measure $P(F|Z)$ for the inequality measure J_F *in general* as a function of the headcount ratio, income gap ratio and inequality among the poor? See Kakwani (1999, p. 622). What axioms does Kakwani propose that such a function should obey, and what leads him to say that the failure of two of these axioms for all known poverty measures 'is a serious drawback of the entire poverty literature' (p. 626)? Sketch Ravallion's (1999) objection to Kakwani's line of argument.

6.3   Indices of poverty

There are a number of survey articles describing the families of poverty indices which have appeared in the literature since the publication of Sen's (1976) article. Zheng (1997) is the most up-to-date and comprehensive. There are also valuable insights in Foster and Sen (1997), Seidl (1988), Hagenaars (1987) and Foster (1984).

We already said poverty was about deprivation and that the poverty gap

$$g_i = \max\{Z - x_i, 0\} \tag{6.21}$$

could measure this. Many poverty indices are in fact expressed in terms of *normalized* poverty gaps, call these Γ_i:

$$\Gamma_i = \frac{g_i}{Z} = \max\left\{1 - \frac{x_i}{Z}, 0\right\} \tag{6.22}$$

The normalized gaps tell, on a scale from 0 to 1, the fractional shortfall of a poor person's or household's income from the poverty line. A particular attraction of using normalized poverty gaps to make poverty comparisons between countries, regions or time periods is that the analyst need not worry about the appropriate exchange rate or price index for rendering the incomes in one regime (country, region or year) commensurate with those in the other: scalar conversion factors do not affect normalized gaps.

Let **g** be the vector of poverty gaps and let Γ be the vector of normalized poverty gaps. In the case that incomes are continuously distributed, let $\Gamma(x)$ be the function which evaluates peoples' normalized poverty gaps:

$$\Gamma(x) = \max\left\{\frac{1-x}{Z}, 0\right\} \tag{6.23a}$$

To be more general we could indicate by a subscript 'F' the distribution $F(x)$ in which the gaps are evaluated, and write

$$\Gamma_F(x) = \max\left\{\frac{1-x}{Z_F}, 0\right\} \tag{6.23b}$$

to allow for a distribution-specific poverty line Z_F. This will not become important until section 6.4, and we shall avoid it in the meantime. From now on though, we shall paint everything in terms of normalized poverty gaps, where possible, even when the original indices may have been cast in terms of un-normalized gaps.

The general form Sen (1976) began with was in terms of un-normalized gaps g_i:

$$P^{SEN}(\mathbf{x}|Z) = A(N, Q, Z) \sum_{1 \leq i \leq Q} v_i(x_i, Z) g_i \tag{6.24}$$

but Sen reduced this, using carefully tailored axioms, to

$$P^{SEN}(\mathbf{x}|Z) = \frac{2}{\{(Q+1)N\}} \sum_{1 \leq i \leq Q} (Q + 1 - i)\Gamma_i \tag{6.25a}$$

which, as you can see, is indeed defined over normalized poverty gaps Γ_i, being linear in these with weights that depend on peoples' positions. In a continuous formulation, taking N as very large, this index has been written, e.g. by Kakwani (1999, p. 610), as

$$P^{SEN}(F|Z) = 2\int_0^Z \Gamma(x)\frac{[F(Z)-F(x)]f(x)\mathrm{d}x}{F(Z)} \qquad (6.25b)$$

in which $F(Z)$ is of course the headcount ratio $H(F|Z)$. Can you see how the formula for $P^{SEN}(F|Z)$ given in (6.7), involving the Gini coefficient G_F^p among the poor, emerges from (6.25b)? Try to, using the formula in (2.17), p. 33, for the Gini coefficient and noting that the distribution function for poor incomes is $F(x)/F(Z)$.[9]

Kakwani (1980b) generalizes Sen's index, introducing a 'sensitivity parameter' κ, essentially by raising Sen's weight $v_i(x_i, Z)$ in (6.24) to the power κ, $\kappa \geq 1$, to make the index more sensitive to transfers among those with large poverty gaps and also more sensitive to small income changes at the bottom end of the distribution (see exercise 6.3.1). Kakwani's index is

$$P^{KAK}(x|Z, \kappa) = \frac{Q}{\{Ni_{Q,\kappa}\}}\sum_{1\leq i\leq Q}(Q+1-i)^{\kappa}\Gamma_i \qquad (6.26a)$$

in discrete form, where $i_{Q,\kappa} = \Sigma_{1\leq i\leq Q}i^{\kappa}$. It takes the form

$$P^{KAK}(F|Z, \kappa) = (\kappa+1)\int_0^Z \Gamma(x)\frac{[F(Z)-F(x)]^{\kappa}f(x)\mathrm{d}x}{F(Z)^{\kappa}}, \qquad \kappa \geq 1 \qquad (6.26b)$$

when income is continuously distributed. As you can see, this index reduces to Sen's when $\kappa = 1$. Like Sen's, it takes peoples' positions (or ranks) into account and gives a 'constitutive rôle' to the headcount ratio.

Clark, Hemming and Ulph (1981) also propose a parametric family of poverty indices in which the headcount ratio has a 'constitutive rôle', but for them the ranks of the poor do not matter. They base their poverty measure on a *loss function*, defined over the poor sub-population, which is averse to inequality in poverty gaps with inequality-aversion parameter α. Normalizing, we may write Clark *et al.*'s loss function as

$$L(x|Z, \alpha) = \frac{1}{\alpha}\sum_{1\leq i\leq Q}\frac{\Gamma_i^{\alpha}}{Q} \qquad \alpha \geq 1 \qquad (6.27)$$

$L(x|Z, 1)$ is the income gap ratio of equation (6.5), which is not sensitive to the distribution of poor incomes, but for $\alpha > 1$ more weight is placed on bigger poverty gaps, i.e. smaller incomes, by $L(x|Z, \alpha)$, and as $\alpha \to \infty$ only the biggest gap of all (smallest income) matters. Clark *et al.* use an analogue of the EDE income level to measure poverty. Thus, let $\Gamma^* = g^*/Z$ be the *equally distributed equivalent normalized poverty gap*:

$$[\Gamma^*]^{\alpha} = \sum_{1\leq i\leq Q}\frac{\Gamma_i^{\alpha}}{Q} \qquad (6.28)$$

Clark *et al.* define their poverty index as 'the aggregate gap of the poor which, if equally shared, would yield the same level of welfare of the poor as the actual aggregate gap distributed as it is, expressed as a proportion of the aggregate gap when each member of the population has a zero income' (p. 520). In other words, they propose to measure poverty as[10]

$$P^{CHU}(x|Z, \alpha) = \frac{Qg^*}{NZ} = H(x|Z)\Gamma^* = \frac{Q^{1-1/\alpha}}{N}\left[\sum_{1 \le i \le Q} \Gamma_i^\alpha\right]^{1/\alpha} \tag{6.29}$$

Notice that the headcount ratio figures in P^{CHU} in addition to, and separately from, the distribution of normalized poverty gaps Γ.

The 'constitutive rôle' given to the headcount ratio by the indices $P^{SEN}(x|Z)$, $P^{KAK}(x|Z, \kappa)$ and $P^{CHU}(x|Z, \alpha)$ has been seen as a difficulty by some authors. The problem stems from the transfer axiom. Many observers would say that if an income transfer is made from any poor person to somebody richer, overall poverty should rise. However, if a transfer of income from a very poor to a less poor (but still poor) person causes the latter to cross the poverty line, thereby reducing the number of poor, poverty indices having the 'constitutive rôle' feature may record a reduction in poverty – notwithstanding their distributional sensitivity to income changes among the poor. A simple numerical example illustrates the point. Suppose the economy has six persons, with incomes $x = (\$7, \$8, \$9, \$10, \$20, \$30)$ and that the poverty line is $Z = \$10$. Then three persons are poor. Now suppose that the poorest person gives $1 to the one with $9. The incomes become $y = (\$6, \$8, \$10, \$10, \$20, \$30)$. If you calculate values, you will find that P^{SEN}, P^{KAK} and P^{CHU} all fall, for all parameter values;[11] this is entirely due to the reduction in the headcount ratio (from $\frac{1}{2}$ to $\frac{1}{3}$).

Clark, Hemming and Ulph in fact proposed two parametric families of poverty measures in their 1981 paper. Their 'type I' family is the one developed above, based on the EDE poverty gap. They also suggested a second form of index, also based on an EDE concept, which denies any role to the headcount ratio *per se*. This index, known subsequently as their 'type II' index, takes as its starting point a social evaluation function defined over the *whole* population (rather than the subpopulation of the poor as before), but caps individual incomes at the poverty threshold – i.e. it sets aside all affluence, being defined over the censored income distribution **b** comprising basic incomes $b_i = \min\{x_i, Z\}$. When normalized by the poverty threshold Z, basic incomes can be expressed in terms of normalized poverty gaps:

$$\frac{b_i}{Z} = 1 - \Gamma_i \qquad \text{for all } i \tag{6.30}$$

Let us then define

$$W(x|Z, \beta) = \frac{1}{\beta} \sum_{1 \le i \le N} \frac{\{1 - \Gamma_i\}^\beta}{N} \qquad 0 \ne \beta \le 1 \tag{6.31}$$

as the corresponding type II evaluation function, and extend this to include the case $\beta = 0$ by specifying

$$W(\mathbf{x}|Z,0) = \sum_{1 \le i \le N} \frac{\ln\{1-\Gamma_i\}}{N} \tag{6.32}$$

The coefficient β, which may be negative, measures inequality aversion over basic incomes and has been called 'aversion to inequality in poverty' by Foster and Sen (1997, p. 178). The same steps as before lead us to an EDE income level ξ^* such that $W(\mathbf{x}|Z, \beta) = W(\xi^*\mathbf{1}|Z, \beta)$ where $\mathbf{1}$ is a vector of ones, and to Clark et al.'s type II poverty index:

$$P^{\mathrm{CHU2}}(\mathbf{x}|Z, \beta) = 1 - \frac{\xi^*}{Z} \tag{6.33}$$

This comes down to

$$P^{\mathrm{CHU2}}(\mathbf{x}|Z, \beta) = 1 - \left\{ \frac{1}{N} \sum_{1 \le i \le N} (1-\Gamma_i)^\beta \right\}^{1/\beta} \tag{6.34a}$$

for $0 \ne \beta \le 1$ and to

$$P^{\mathrm{CHU2}}(\mathbf{x}|Z, 0) = 1 - \left\{ \prod_{1 \le i \le N} (1-\Gamma_i) \right\}^{1/N} \tag{6.34b}$$

when $\beta = 0$. This latter is an increasing transformation of the Watts index: can you see why? Consult exercise 6.3.3. As is evident, nowhere does the head-count ratio appear as an argument in $P^{\mathrm{CHU2}}(\mathbf{x}|Z, \beta)$.

Chakravarty (1983a) defines a wide class of poverty indices in the same form as Clark et al.'s type II family, beginning with a general evaluation function $W(\mathbf{b})$ defined over basic incomes and an EDE income level ξ_b satisfying $W(\mathbf{b}) = W(\xi_b\mathbf{1})$. His class of poverty indices take the form

$$P^{\mathrm{CHAK}}(\mathbf{x}|Z) = 1 - \frac{\xi_b}{Z} \tag{6.35}$$

there being one index for each W that is feasible. Chakravarty observes that 'these indices will differ only in the manner in which the amount of relative inequality in the censored income distribution is taken into account' and that they are 'a fairly natural translation of a relative inequality index of a censored income distribution into a relative poverty index' (p. 81). Under Chakravarty's assumptions about W, his indices are in fact inequality-averse functions of normalized poverty gaps Γ_i (see his equation (17), p. 79). He cites $P^{\mathrm{CHU2}}(\mathbf{x}|Z, \beta)$ as one example. For another, see exercise 6.3.4.

It is easy to see that each of the indices P^{CHU2} and P^{CHAK} records an unambiguous *increase* in poverty for the numerical example sketched earlier. This is because the vector of basic incomes becomes unambiguously more unequal as a result of the transfer, going from $\mathbf{b}_x = (7, 8, 9, 10, 10, 10)$ to $\mathbf{b}_y = (6, 8,$

10, 10, 10, 10), and both families of indices are inequality-averse over the set of basic incomes and pay no attention to changes in the headcount ratio.

The family of poverty indices introduced by Foster, Greer and Thorbecke (1984) takes the form

$$P^{\text{FGT}}(\mathbf{x}|Z, \alpha) = \frac{1}{N} \sum_{1 \le i \le N} \Gamma_i^{\alpha} \qquad (6.36\text{a})$$

and

$$P^{\text{FGT}}(F|Z, \alpha) = \int_0^Z \Gamma(X)^{\alpha} f(x) \mathrm{d}x \qquad (6.36\text{b})$$

in the case of discrete and continuous income distributions respectively, where $\alpha \ge 0$. For $\alpha = 0$, this index is simply the headcount ratio and for $\alpha = 1$ it is the normalized poverty deficit, or product of the headcount and income gap ratios (see equation (6.6), p. 137). Its value for $\alpha = 2$ involves the headcount ratio, income gap ratio and coefficient of variation of income among the poor (see exercise 6.3.5 ahead). For $\alpha > 1$, $P^{\text{FGT}}(\mathbf{x}|Z, \alpha)$ is averse to transfers of income from a poor person to a less poor one whether or not the latter crosses the poverty threshold; it does not give a 'constitutive rôle' to the headcount ratio. As $\alpha \rightarrow \infty$, $P^{\text{FGT}}(\mathbf{x}|Z, \alpha)$ approaches a Rawlsian measure: only the normalized poverty gap of the poorest person matters in poverty comparisons. Foster *et al.* describe the parameter α as an indicator of 'aversion to poverty' (*ibid.*, p. 761).

The Foster-Greer-Thorbecke family (henceforth FGT family) has gained wide popularity. A particular attraction is that the indices of this family are *subgroup decomposable*. If the population is partitioned into demographic groups, indexed by $k = 1, 2, \ldots, K$ say, then overall poverty can be expressed as a sum of contributions from these groups:

$$P^{\text{FGT}}(F|Z, \alpha) = \sum_{1 \le k \le K} p_k P^{\text{FGT}}(F_k|Z, \alpha) \qquad (6.37)$$

where p_k is the fraction of the overall population belonging to group k and F_k is the distribution of income in that group. This feature, which is very useful for tracking the sources of poverty and poverty change, distinguishes the FGT family from almost all other poverty indices previously described in this chapter. Another attraction of the FGT family is that it comes equipped with a poverty dominance test; a simple distributional criterion can be used to verify reduced poverty according to *all* indices in the family. We shall come to this in section 6.4 ahead.

The poverty indices in the FGT family are all in the form

$$P(F|Z) = \int_0^Z \theta(x|Z) f(x) \mathrm{d}x \qquad (6.1\text{a})$$

if incomes are continuously distributed, and

$$P(\mathbf{x}|Z) = \sum_j \frac{\theta(x_j|Z)}{N} \tag{6.1b}$$

in the discrete case, where $\theta(x|Z) = \Gamma(x)^\alpha$ for $x < Z$. We anticipated this general form, which has been called 'canonical' by Foster and Shorrocks (1991), at the start of the chapter! In fact the headcount ratio is in this form too (trivially; just take $\theta(x|Z)$ equal to 1 if $x < Z$), and so is the index $P^{\text{WATTS}}(F|Z)$, for which $\theta(x|Z) = \ln(Z/x)$ (see (6.12) on p. 141). Another index in this form, due to Chakravarty (1983b), is given in exercise 6.3.4 ahead, and an increasing transformation of $P^{\text{CHU2}}(F|Z, \beta)$ is also in this form (exercise 6.3.7). As Foster and Shorrocks (1991, p. 696) say, there is a 'vast array of possible functional forms' for the function $\theta(x|Z)$ defining a canonical poverty index; so what is special about such indices?

Foster and Shorrocks (1991) have shown that all canonical poverty indices, *and only such indices*, are additively decomposable in the FGT sense (i.e. into a weighted average of subgroup poverty measures, the weights being population shares).[12] They go much further than this in fact, proposing a weaker requirement of a poverty index, *subgroup consistency*, according to which overall poverty should fall if one subgroup's poverty level falls *ceteris paribus*, and showing that essentially the only poverty indices satisfying subgroup consistency are the increasing transformations of canonical indices.[13] For example, $P^{\text{WATTS}}(F|Z)$ is decomposable because it is canonical, whilst its increasing transformation $P^{\text{CHU2}}(F|Z, 0)$ is merely subgroup consistent (see exercise 6.3.3).

Exercises

6.3.1   Describe Kakwani's (1980b) three 'sensitivity axioms'. For what ranges of values of the parameter κ does his index satisfy these axioms? What are Clark *et al.*'s (1981, pp. 517–518) reservations about Kakwani's poverty index?

6.3.2   How do Blackorby and Donaldson (1980b) portray Sen's index as based on an equally distributed equivalent income concept, and then generalize it? What is Chakravarty's (1983a, p. 79) criticism of Blackorby and Donaldson (1980b)?

6.3.3   Verify that when incomes are continuously distributed, $P^{\text{CHU2}}(F|Z, \beta) = 1 - [\int_0^\infty (1 - \Gamma(x))^\beta f(x) \, dx]^{1/\beta}$ for $0 \neq \beta \leq 1$ and $P^{\text{CHU2}}(F|Z, 0) = 1 - \exp\{\int_0^Z \ln(1 - \Gamma(x)) f(x) \, dx\} = 1 - \exp\{-P^{\text{WATTS}}(F|Z)\}$.

6.3.4   Chakravarty (1983b) proposes the poverty index $P^{\text{CHAK2}}(F|Z, e) = \int_0^Z [1 - (x/Z)^e] f(x) \, dx$ for $0 < e < 1$. Write $P^{\text{CHAK2}}(F|Z, e)$ in terms of the normalized poverty gap function $\Gamma(x)$. Show that it is an increasing transformation of $P^{\text{CHU2}}(F|Z, \beta)$ for an appropriate value of β.

What are the merits claimed by Chakravarty for his index? See also Chakravarty (1990, p. 191).

6.3.5   Show that $P^{\mathrm{FGT}}(F|Z, 2) = H[I^2 + (1 - I)^2(C^{\mathrm{p}})^2]$ where H is the headcount ratio, I is the income gap ratio and C^{p} is the coefficient of variation of income among the poor. Conclude that when $\alpha = 2$, 'the effect of a given-sized regressive transfer between two poor persons who are a given 'income distance' apart is the same regardless of the absolute levels of income' (Foster and Sen, 1997, p. 179). What transfer sensitivity property does $P^{\mathrm{FGT}}(F|Z, \alpha)$ satisfy for $\alpha > 2$, and how does it relate to those of Kakwani (1980b) (exercise 6.3.1 above)? See Foster *et al.* (1984, p. 763).

6.3.6   Prove that $P^{\mathrm{CHU}}(F|Z, \alpha)$ and $P^{\mathrm{FGT}}(F|Z, \alpha)$ are linked by the relationship $P^{\mathrm{CHU}}(F|Z, \alpha) = H(F|Z)^{(\alpha-1)/\alpha} P^{\mathrm{FGT}}(F|Z, \alpha)^{1/\alpha}$.

6.3.7   Let $\mathbf{P}_{\mathrm{NG}}$ be the class of poverty indices of the form $P(F|Z) = \int_0^Z \theta(x|Z) f(x) \mathrm{d}x$ as in (6.1a), where $\theta(x|Z)$ is an increasing and convex function of the normalized poverty gap $\Gamma(x)$: $\theta(x|Z) = \Phi(\Gamma(x))$ where $\Phi(0) = 0$ and $\Phi'(\Gamma) > 0$ and $\Phi''(\Gamma) > 0$ for all $\Gamma > 0$. Let $\mathbf{P}_{\mathrm{NG}}^*$ be the sub-class for which also $\Phi'''(\Gamma) > 0$ for all $\Gamma > 0$, and let $\mathbf{Q}_{\mathrm{NG}}^*$ be the subset of $\mathbf{P}_{\mathrm{NG}}^*$ in which $\Phi'(0) > 0$. By considering the function $\Phi(\Gamma) = 1 - (1 - \Gamma)^\beta$ show that the index $[1 - \{1 - P^{\mathrm{CHU2}}(F|Z)\}^\beta]$ belongs to $\mathbf{Q}_{\mathrm{NG}}^*$ for $0 \neq \beta \leq 1$. Show that $P^{\mathrm{WATTS}}(F|Z)$ belongs to $\mathbf{Q}_{\mathrm{NG}}^*$. Show that $P^{\mathrm{FGT}}(F|Z, \alpha)$ belongs to $\mathbf{P}_{\mathrm{NG}}$ for all $\alpha \geq 1$ and to $\mathbf{P}_{\mathrm{NG}}^* \backslash \mathbf{Q}_{\mathrm{NG}}^*$ for $\alpha > 2$. Under what condition does $P^{\mathrm{PYATT}}(F|Z)$ belong to $\mathbf{P}_{\mathrm{NG}}$?

6.3.8   Bourguignon and Fields (1997) introduce the class of 'poverty line discontinuous' poverty measures, which are in canonical form with $\theta(x|Z)$ positive, decreasing and convex for $x < Z$, zero for $x > Z$ and discontinuous at $x = Z$. Explain the rationale for this specification. The specific form $\theta(x|Z) = \Gamma(x)^\alpha + \delta$ for $x < Z$ and $\theta(x|Z) = 0$ for $x > Z$ is suggested, where $\alpha > 1$ and $\delta > 0$. Show that the resultant poverty index is $P^{\mathrm{BF}}(F|Z, \alpha, \delta) = P^{\mathrm{FGT}}(F|Z, \alpha) + \delta H(F|Z)$. Describe the properties of this index and some of the reasons why Bourguignon and Fields recommend it.

6.3.9(a)   'This modified version of the Sen index is still not subgroup consistent. But it is an ideal measure of poverty in all other respects' (Shorrocks, 1995). Relate Shorrocks's modified Sen index to those of Thon (1979) and Takayama (1979).

6.3.9(b)   What is the link between Shorrocks's modified Sen index and $P^{\mathrm{CHAK}}(x|Z)$? Consult Chakravarty (1997).

6.3.10   'We say that a relative index and an absolute index are "compatible" if, at any fixed poverty line, they give the same ranking of distributions, although not necessarily the same values . . . if a pair of continuous subgroup consistent indices is compatible, then the relative index must be an increasing transformation of a member of the Foster *et al.* class' (Foster and Shorrocks, 1991, p. 689). What form does the compatible absolute index take? Explain the nature of the axiomatic characterization of the FGT family which this result represents, and compare it with that of Zheng (1994) given in exercise 6.1.4, p. 139.[14]

6.3.11 '... whilst all axioms are arbitrary and the intellectual prejudices of authors apparent within them, it turns out that rather weak and appealing requirements do impose an interesting and readily interpretable structure on the general mathematical representation of a poverty measure' (Cowell, 1988, p. 149). Account for the various families of poverty indices described in this chapter within Cowell's axiomatic framework (see *ibid.*, pp. 162–163). How does Cowell treat decomposability?

6.3.12 'If we would know what the individual welfare function looks like, the general Dalton and Atkinson indices for poverty measurement may be even further argued to be the proper indices to use: they simply aggregate individual welfare of the poor, and compare it to the welfare threshold at which the poverty line is set' (Hagenaars, 1987, p. 599). Describe the two classes of poverty indices which Hagenaars defines over censored income distributions. Which classes of indices defined in this chapter can be represented as members of one or other of Hagenaars' two classes?

6.3.13 'In the simple case where only one poverty line is defined for all income units and where individual income units have the same implicit weighting, the new poverty index is a member of the Dalton class of indexes described by Hagenaars ... The index is ... very similar to another member of the Dalton class, the FGT index ... but has two main differences ... each unit is allowed to have its own poverty line and a weighting parameter h is included ... these differences necessitate a more general version of the transfer axiom which is called the distribution axiom' (Johnson, 1996, p. 46). Describe Johnson's proposed index and the axioms it satisfies. On what grounds do Johnson and Dixon (1999) claim that Johnson's index is preferable to $P^{\text{FGT}}(F|Z, \alpha)$?

6.3.14 '... inclusive [social welfare] measures with only quite modest inequality aversion yield very similar rankings to poverty measures, even though on average two-thirds of the population is given zero weight by the latter' (Ravallion, 1994b, p. 363). Describe Ravallion's investigation into the links between measures of poverty and social welfare in developing countries, using the constant inequality aversion SWF of Atkinson (1970) and the FGT family of poverty indices. What does he identify as the factors which in practice tend to blur the theoretical differences between exclusive (poverty) and inclusive (social welfare) measures?

6.3.15 'Unlike the income approach, human deprivation is visualized *not* through income as an intermediary of basic needs but in terms of shortfalls from minimum levels of basic needs themselves' (Tsui,

2001). Describe Tsui's axiom system and extension of the class of subgroup consistent poverty indices to the multidimensional context. See also Chakravarty *et al.* (1998).

6.4   Poverty dominance criteria

A number of dominance criteria appeared in the literature of the 1990s which enable robust poverty comparisons to be made whilst allowing for a diversity of judgements about the identification of the poor and the aggregation of their poverty. This literature is well described in Zheng's (2000a) panoramic survey. There are two different cases to consider, depending on how social heterogeneity is to be dealt with.

In the first case, which we address in this section of the chapter, we assume that social heterogeneity in the population (if present) can be satisfactorily taken account of by equivalizing, using an agreed equivalence scale. In this context (and also in the context of a socially homogeneous population), a fixed poverty line Z (denominated in units of equivalent income when there is heterogeneity) must be specified to determine which income units in a given distribution are poor, whatever their household type. There may be disagreement about the appropriate value for Z; the dominance criteria we describe allow room for such disagreement.

A second strand of analysis, deferred until section 6.5 ahead, addresses the case in which, although the population is socially heterogeneous, the analyst wishes to refrain from equivalizing, perhaps because of doubt about the appropriate equivalence scale relativities. This is a very different scenario; now money income distributions must be retained, and the poverty line specified differently for income units of different types. We indicated such a line of analysis in equations (6.2a,b) on p. 135, using a vector of poverty lines, $Z = (Z_1, Z_2, \ldots, Z_n)$, which varied with household composition. An appropriate dominance criterion for this scenario would allow for a range of possible configurations of the type-specific poverty lines Z_i, $1 \le i \le n$.

Suppose, then, that the income distributions to be compared are F and G, each denominated in units of equivalent income using an appropriate equivalence scale. We compared the welfare in two such distributions in chapter 3. The first issue to confront here is whether the *same* poverty line, Z, should be set in F and G – or whether *different* poverty lines, Z_F and Z_G, would be appropriate. Different poverty lines may be appropriate when comparing poverty in different countries or regions, and at different points in time,[15] but if these different lines correctly reflect differences in costs of living between the sectors or dates being compared, one may of course normalise the income distributions by them and then apply a common poverty line: it would take the value $Z = 1$. For the present, we shall assume agreement that a common poverty line Z should be applied to both F and G, but not necessarily agreement about its magnitude.

Later, we will extend the analysis to allow for different poverty lines, Z_F and Z_G. This will be important empirically so long as there is scope for disagreement about the appropriate normalization, e.g. about the appropriate exchange rate, purchasing-power-parity index or inflation rate in international and intertemporal comparisons. The advantages of extending the methodology to permit the setting of different fixed poverty lines, and also to permit flexibility in the relativity between these, will then become apparent.

To fix ideas and illustrate what is at stake, let us look at how F and G are ranked by a few of the most familiar poverty measures when the poverty lines are both set at Z. From the definitions of the headcount ratio and poverty deficit in (6.3a) and (6.4a), pp. 136–137, we have

$$H(G|Z) - H(F|Z) = G(Z) - F(Z) = S'(Z) \tag{6.38}$$

and

$$D(G|Z) - D(F|Z) = \int_0^Z (Z - x)[g(x) - f(x)]\mathrm{d}x = S(Z) \tag{6.39}$$

respectively, where $S(x) = \int_0^x [G(y) - F(y)]\mathrm{d}y$ is the ubiquitous S-function of chapter 3 (to obtain (6.39), use integration by parts). For the case $\alpha = 2$ of the FGT family (see (6.36b), p. 149), we have

$$P^{\mathrm{PGT}}(G|Z, 2) - P^{\mathrm{PGT}}(F|Z, 2) = \int_0^Z (Z - x)^2 [g(x) - f(x)]\mathrm{d}x = 2\int_0^Z \frac{S(x)\mathrm{d}x}{Z^2} \tag{6.40}$$

(using integration by parts twice). Applying results from chapter 3, we obtain immediately the following poverty dominance criteria.

Theorem 6.1

(i) $H(F|Z) \leq H(G|Z)$ for all common poverty lines Z if and only if F rank dominates G;

(ii) $D(F|Z) \leq D(G|Z)$ for all common poverty lines Z and if and only if F generalized Lorenz dominates G;

(iii) $P^{\mathrm{FGT}}(F|Z, 2) \leq P^{\mathrm{FGT}}(G|Z, 2)$ for all common poverty lines Z if F generalized Lorenz dominates G, and also in equal-mean comparisons in which GL_F and GL_G cross once if $F >_R G$ and $\sigma_F^2 \leq \sigma_G^2$.

To prove these results, refer for (i) to exercise 3.2.2(b), p. 56, for (ii) to lemma 3.1 and theorem 3.2, pp. 54–55, and for (iii) to lemma 3.3. and theorem 3.4, pp. 63–64.

These dominance tests for less poverty according to the headcount ratio, poverty deficit and $\alpha = 2$ version of the FGT index give the flavour of the sort of poverty ordering results available. Each is for a single index and a range of common poverty lines, and each in fact makes a link between poverty and welfare.[16] Recall Ravallion's (1994b) characterization of social welfare functions as *inclusive* measures of well-being and poverty indices as *exclusive* measures. Allowing the poverty line to take all possible values effectively equates the two. Zheng (1999, 2000a) distinguishes poverty orderings *for a fixed poverty measure and range of poverty lines* from those *for a fixed poverty line and range of poverty measures*, and we shall come to the latter shortly. In fact, the distinction is hazy in the literature, some orderings holding both for a class of poverty measures *and* for a range of poverty lines.

Atkinson (1987) focuses on poverty orderings which should hold for all poverty lines Z in a restricted range, say $Z \in [Z^-, Z^+]$. It is immediate from (6.38) that $H(F|Z) \le H(G|Z)$ for all common poverty lines $Z \in [Z^-, Z^+]$ if and only if

$$S'(Z) \ge 0 \quad \text{for all } Z \in [Z^-, Z^+] \tag{6.41}$$

and from (6.39) that $D(F|Z) \le D(G|Z)$ for all common poverty lines $Z \in [Z^-, Z^+]$ if and only if

$$S(Z) \ge 0 \quad \text{for all } Z \in [Z^-, Z^+] \tag{6.42}$$

Atkinson also examines what is required in order that F have less poverty than G for poverty lines in this restricted range for the class of poverty indices which are in canonical form,

$$P(F|Z) = \int_0^z \theta(x|Z) f(x) \mathrm{d}x \tag{6.1a}$$

As we have already noted, the Watts index and FGT family are in this form, with $\theta(x|Z) = \ln(Z/x)$ and $\theta(x|Z) = (1 - x/Z)^\alpha$ respectively. Assuming only that the poverty contribution function $\theta(x|Z)$ is continuous and decreasing in x, integration by parts once in

$$P(G|Z) - P(F|Z) = \int_0^z \theta(x|Z)[g(x) - f(x)] \mathrm{d}x \tag{6.43}$$

yields the appropriate distributional condition to make $P(G|Z) - P(F|Z)$ positive. Under the additional assumption that $\theta(x|Z)$ is convex in x (as is the case for the Watts index and for the FGT family for $\alpha > 1$), integation by parts twice can be used, to obtain a second distributional condition which is, naturally, weaker. The conditions which emerge as necessary and sufficient are, in the first case

$$S'(Z) \ge 0 \quad \text{for all } Z \in [0, Z^+] \tag{6.44}$$

and in the second case

$$S(Z) \ge 0 \quad \text{for all } Z \in [0, Z^+] \tag{6.45}$$

Can you verify these conditions, which correspond to those in (6.41)–(6.42) for the headcount and poverty deficit but are a little stronger?[17]

By letting $Z^- \to 0$ and $Z^+ \to z$ in Atkinson's results, where z is the highest income present in either distribution with non-zero frequency density, we see that rank dominance and generalized Lorenz dominance respectively are, in fact, necessary and sufficient to ensure reduced poverty for all common poverty lines Z *for all indices in two wide classes* – not just for the headcount ratio and poverty deficit as in Theorem 6.1.

Theorem 6.2

Let $\mathbf{P_A}$ be the class of poverty indices of the form $P(F|Z) = \int_0^Z \theta(x|Z) f(x)\,dx$ where $\theta(x|Z)$ is continuous and decreasing in x, and let $\mathbf{P_A^*}$ be the sub-class of $\mathbf{P_A}$ in which $\theta(x|Z)$ is also convex in x. Then:

(i) $P(F|Z) \leq P(G|Z)$ for all common poverty lines Z and for all $P \in \mathbf{P_A}$ if and only if F rank dominates G; and

(ii) $P(F|Z) \leq P(G|Z)$ for all common poverty lines Z and for all $P \in \mathbf{P_A^*}$ if and only if F generalized Lorenz dominates G.

These results show that rank and generalized Lorenz dominance guarantee much more than simply a reduced headcount ratio and reduced poverty deficit. The headcount ratio and poverty deficit have already been noted to be entirely insensitive to the distribution of income among the poor. The classes $\mathbf{P_A}$ and $\mathbf{P_A^*}$ contain many distribution-sensitive poverty indices, including the Watts index and members of the FGT family.[18]

In respect of the FGT family, the sufficiency of generalized Lorenz dominance to ensure reduced poverty is almost transparent. Just note that

$$P^{\mathrm{PGT}}(G|Z, \alpha) - P^{\mathrm{PGT}}(F|Z, \alpha) = \alpha \int_0^Z \frac{(Z - x)^{\alpha-1} S(x)\,dx}{Z^\alpha} \tag{6.46}$$

Foster and Shorrocks (1988a,b) advocate a procedure to test for reduced poverty according to all members of the FGT class which can be seen as a weakening of the generalized Lorenz dominance test. To implement their test, a computational algorithm is required, to search for the least integer ρ for which 'ρ^{th} degree stochastic dominance' of F over G holds.[19] Having found this least value of ρ, call it ρ_0, the conclusion is that $P^{\mathrm{FGT}}(F|Z, \alpha) \leq P^{\mathrm{FGT}}(G|Z, \alpha)$ for all common poverty lines Z and all $\alpha \geq \rho_0 - 1$. Moreover, when some finite upper bound is placed on the choice of poverty line (as in Atkinson's paper), these results 'remain substantially intact, except that comparisons are now made in terms of a censored distribution in which all incomes above Z^* [the upper bound] are replaced by Z^* itself' (Foster and Shorrocks, 1988b, p. 181).[20]

The dominance results we have described thus far deal with situations where there is a common poverty line Z in the distributions F and G being compared, whose value may vary freely or in an interval. We turn now to some weaker dominance conditions that can be applied when the common poverty line takes on a *known* value Z. As we shall see, this methodology will also cater for cases in which the analyst wishes to specify *different and known* poverty lines Z_F and Z_G. It can even be adapted for cases in which the poverty lines Z_F and Z_G are *different and can vary*, freely or in an interval.

Generalized Lorenz dominance of one income distribution, F, over the other, G, is a strong requirement, guaranteeing less poverty in F than in G whatever the common poverty line Z (for the class $\mathbf{P}^*_\Lambda$: recall theorem 6.2). Suppose now that Z is common *and fixed* – known to the analyst and, for the moment, beyond dispute. For a special class of poverty indices, we can invoke a variant of the generalized Lorenz dominance methodology, to produce a much weaker test for reduced poverty. This class comprises poverty indices $P(F|Z)$ that are, at one and the same time, in canonical form, so that $P(F|Z) = \int_0^Z \theta(x|Z) f(x)\, dx$ for some $\theta(x|Z)$, *and* expressed in terms of the normalized poverty gap function $\Gamma(x) = \max\{1 - x/Z, 0\}$. Specifically, let $\mathbf{P}_{NG}$ be the class of poverty indices in the form

$$P(F|Z) = \int_0^Z \Phi(\Gamma(x)) f(x)\, dx \qquad (6.47)$$

where $\Phi(0) = 0$ and $\Phi'(\Gamma) > 0$ and $\Phi''(\Gamma) > 0$ for all $\Gamma > 0$. Notice that $\mathbf{P}_{NG} \subset \mathbf{P}^*_\Lambda$.

$\mathbf{P}_{NG}$ contains a number of the poverty indices we have already encountered, and yet others are monotonic functions of indices in $\mathbf{P}_{NG}$ (see exercise 6.3.7, p. 151, on this). What is special about the structure of such indices, that can lead us to a new dominance test for reduced poverty? Notice that the poverty contribution function $\theta(x|Z)$ is an increasing and convex function of the normalized poverty gap $\Gamma(x)$ for indices in $\mathbf{P}_{NG}$. Convexity of Φ means that 'transfers of poverty gap' from someone with a big gap to someone with a smaller gap, i.e. transfers of income from a poor person to someone less poor or even non-poor, raise measured poverty. You can think of $\mathbf{P}_{NG}$ as the class of additively separable, symmetric and *inequality-preferring* social evaluation functions defined over the entire distribution of normalized poverty gaps (the upper limit of integration in (6.47) could perfectly well have been infinite since $\Phi(\Gamma(x)) = 0$ for $x > Z$). This means that a turned-on-its-head version of the Shorrocks theorem, tailored to the case of inequality-preferring social evaluation functions, can be invoked, to tell precisely under what conditions one distribution of poverty gaps is 'preferred to' (i.e. judged to have more poverty than) another.

Generalized Lorenz curves cumulates peoples' incomes from the lowest upwards, and dominance of one curve over another yields higher social welfare for the class of additively separable, symmetric and inequality-averse SWFs. To cater for inequality-*preferring* social evaluation functions, defined over the distribution not of incomes but of normalized poverty gaps, we need to cumulate normalized poverty gaps *from the biggest one downwards* and then test for dominance. Spencer and Fisher (1992) were the first to have this insight, and it has been developed further by Jenkins and Lambert (1997) and Shorrocks (1998).

Let us be slightly more general than we need at the moment, and extend the notation to allow the setting of different poverty lines, Z_F and Z_G, in the two distributions. The normalized poverty gap functions become

$$\Gamma_F(x) = \max\left\{1 - \frac{x}{Z_F}, 0\right\}, \qquad \Gamma_G(x) = \max\left\{1 - \frac{x}{Z_G}, 0\right\} \tag{6.48}$$

Let the induced distributions of normalized poverty gaps in F and G have density functions denoted by $f^*(\Gamma)$ and $g^*(\Gamma)$ and distribution functions denoted by $F^*(\Gamma)$ and $G^*(\Gamma)$ respectively in all that follows.

Jenkins and Lambert (1997) define the *three I's of poverty* (or *TIP*) *curve* for F, $TIP_F(p)$ for $0 \leq p \leq 1$, as the cumulated value, per head of the population, of the first $100p$ per cent of normalized poverty gaps Γ starting with the biggest. In formal terms, we have

$$F^*(\Gamma_0) = 1 - p \Rightarrow TIP_F(p) = \int_{\Gamma_0}^{1} \Gamma f^*(\Gamma) d\Gamma \tag{6.49}$$

and similarly for G.

Why do we call this function the 'three I's of poverty' curve? Recall our discussion on p. 138 of Sen's three I's of poverty: these were the incidence, intensity and inequality of poverty. The TIP curve is typically as shown in Figure 6.1. The length of the non-horizontal portion of the TIP curve reveals the *incidence* of poverty; it is simply the headcount ratio $H(F|Z_F)$. The *intensity* dimension of poverty is summarized by the height of the TIP curve: the value at which $TIP_F(p)$ terminates, which occurs at $p = H(F|Z_F)$ and beyond, is just the normalized poverty deficit, $D(F|Z)/Z = P^{FGT}(F|Z_F, 1)$. The degree of concavity of the curved section, or rate at which the gaps decrease as income rises, summarizes the *inequality* dimension of poverty.

By analogy with inequality measurement for which the cases of maximum and minimum inequality yield bounding Lorenz curves, there are also maximum and minimum poverty reference situations and bounding TIP curves. Define maximum poverty as being when each person or household has an income of zero and hence a poverty gap of Z. In this case the TIP curve follows the 45° line. At the other extreme, when no-one is poor, the TIP curve coincides with the horizontal axis.

Spencer and Fisher (1992, p. 120) call the TIP curve the 'absolute rotated Lorenz curve for poverty gaps' and Shorrocks (1995, 1998) calls it the

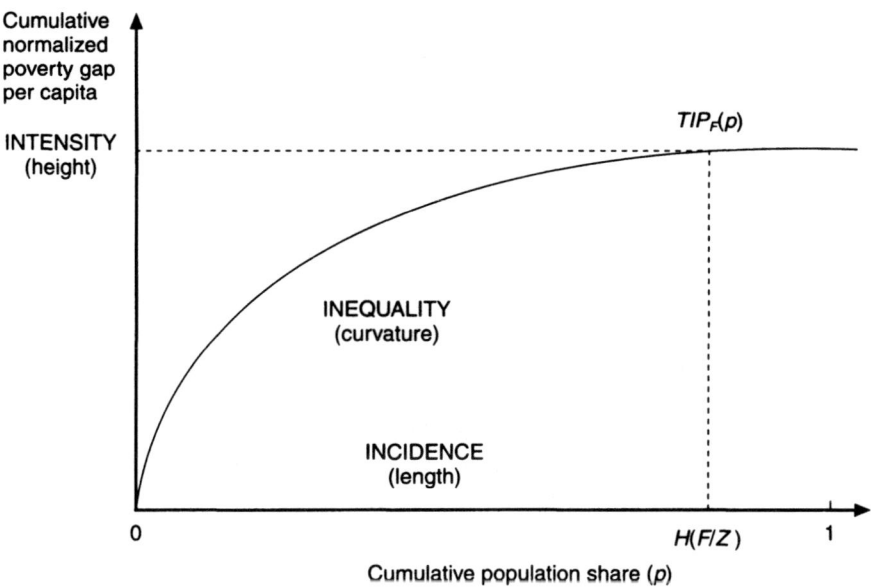

Figure 6.1   The TIP curve and the three 'I's of poverty

'poverty gap profile'. Reverting to the case of a common and known poverty line Z in the distributions being compared, the main property is that dominance of one TIP curve over another, which we shall henceforth refer to as *TIP dominance*, is the criterion which reveals an unambiguous poverty comparison for the class $\mathbf{P_{NG}}$. Remarkably, TIP dominance for the poverty line Z also guarantees that the poverty comparison remains valid at all lower common poverty lines Z'; observers wishing to set a more stringent poverty line than Z are catered for by TIP dominance at Z.

Theorem 6.3

Given income distributions F and G and a common poverty line Z, TIP dominance of G over F, $TIP_G(p) \geq TIP_F(p)$ for all $p \in [0, 1]$, is necessary and sufficient to ensure $P(F|Z') \leq P(G|Z')$ for all common poverty lines $Z' \in (0, Z]$ and for all poverty measures $P \in \mathbf{P_{NG}}$.

Proof   It will be enough to prove that TIP dominance of G over F is *equivalent to* less poverty in F for the poverty line Z, and that it *implies* less poverty in F for a lower poverty line Z'. Can you see why? For the equivalence, just follow the steps that led to the proof of theorem 3.2 in chapter 3 (showing the equivalence of generalized Lorenz dominance and welfare superiority). Namely, using (6.47) and integration by parts twice, write

$$P(G|Z) - P(F|Z) = \int_0^1 \Phi(\Gamma)[g^*(\Gamma) - f^*(\Gamma)]d\Gamma$$

$$= T(0)\Phi'(0) + \int_0^1 \Phi''(\Gamma)T(\Gamma)d\Gamma \qquad (6.50)$$

where

$$T(\Gamma) = \int_\Gamma^1 [F^*(\Gamma_0) - G^*(\Gamma_0)]d\Gamma_0 \qquad (6.51)$$

so that the poverty ranking between G and F depends on the sign property of the function $T(\Gamma)$. Following very similar steps to those in lemma 3.1, p. 54, you will find that $P(F|Z) \leq P(G|Z)$ for all $P \in \mathbf{P_{NG}}$ if and only if $T(\Gamma) \geq 0$ for all Γ. The final step makes use of an analogue of lemma 3.2, p. 55: if $1 - p = F(\Gamma_F) = G(\Gamma_G)$, then $T(\Gamma_F) \geq TIP_G(p) - TIP_F(p) \geq T(\Gamma_G)$ (compare lemma 3.2). The equivalence of the condition $T(\Gamma) \geq 0$ for all Γ with TIP dominance of G over F follows in the same way that theorem 3.2 followed from lemma 3.2. When the poverty line is reset at $Z' = Z(1 - u)$, $u \in (0, 1)$, the poverty gap for an income of x changes from $\Gamma = \Gamma(x) = \max\{1 - x/Z, 0\}$ to $\delta_u(\Gamma)$ where $\delta_u: \mathbf{R} \to \mathbf{R}$ is defined by $\delta_u(\gamma) = 0$ for $\gamma \leq u$ and $\delta_u(\gamma) = (\gamma - u)/(1 - u)$ for $\gamma \geq u$, which is a convex and increasing function of γ. Thus $P(G|Z') - P(F|Z')$ $= \int_0^1 \Phi \circ \delta_u(\Gamma)[g^*(\Gamma) - f^*(\Gamma)]d\Gamma$ in which $\Phi \circ \delta_u$ is convex and increasing. TIP dominance of G over F implies that this expression is positive.   QED

TIP dominance for a fixed common poverty line Z is a much weaker requirement of two income distributions than generalized Lorenz dominance. Hence the TIP dominance criterion is extremely useful for empirical poverty analysis. We can see exactly how strong the generalized Lorenz dominance criterion is, compared to TIP dominance, from the following result:

Lemma 6.1

$GL_F(p) \geq GL_G(p)$ for all $p \in [0, 1] \Leftrightarrow TIP_G(p) \geq TIP_F(p)$ for all $p \in [0, 1]$ and all common poverty lines Z.

Proof For the $\Rightarrow$ direction, note that by theorem 6.2(ii) generalized Lorenz dominance of F over G implies $P(F|Z) \leq P(G|Z)$ for all common poverty lines Z and for all $P \in \mathbf{P_A^*}$. Since $\mathbf{P_{NG}} \subset \mathbf{P_A^*}$, it then follows from theorem 6.3 that G must TIP dominate F for all common poverty lines Z. For the proof in the $\Leftarrow$ direction, note that TIP dominance of G over F for all common poverty lines Z implies in particular that the terminal TIP curve value is no less in G than in F, or that $D(F|Z) \leq D(G|Z)$, for all common poverty lines Z. Theorem 6.1(ii) then implies generalized Lorenz dominance of F over G.   QED

This result shows generalized Lorenz dominance to be equivalent to *the conjunction of* the TIP dominance conditions for all possible poverty lines.[21]

We turn now to situations in which different but known poverty lines, Z_F and Z_G, are specified. As we said earlier, different poverty lines may be appropriate when comparing poverty in different countries or regions, and at different points in time, but if these different lines correctly reflect differences in costs of living between the sectors or dates being compared, one may normalize the income distributions by them and apply a common poverty line, whose value would be $Z = 1$. Look again at the definitions of normalized poverty gaps when poverty lines differ:

$$\Gamma_F(x) = \max\left\{1 - \frac{x}{Z_F}, 0\right\}, \quad \Gamma_G(x) = \max\left\{1 - \frac{x}{Z_G}, 0\right\} \tag{6.48}$$

It is just as if we had normalized the incomes x in F and G, by Z_F and Z_G respectively, and then applied a poverty line of $Z = 1$! So we are in luck. Because the normalized poverty gaps are unit-free, and the poverty lines used to compute them are internal to the construction of the relevant TIP curves, nothing within the proof of theorem 6.3 needs to be changed to cater for this new scenario! Only a slight modification in the statement of the result is needed, and, within the proof, replacement of $P(F|Z)$ and $P(G|Z)$, wherever they occur, by $P(F|Z_F)$ and $P(G|Z_G)$ respectively.

Theorem 6.4

Given income distributions F and G and poverty lines Z_F and Z_G, TIP dominance of G over F is necessary and sufficient to ensure $P(F|kZ_F) \leq P(G|kZ_G)$ for all $k \in (0, 1)$ and for all poverty measures $P \in \mathbf{P}_{\mathbf{NG}}$.

The poverty conclusion thus holds also for poverty lines lower than Z_F and Z_G but held in the same relativity. Another result covers cases where this relativity itself might be open to dispute. If the separation between the TIP curves is big, so that intuitively poverty is *much* higher in the TIP-dominating distribution, then the poverty comparison can be upheld even when the poverty line in this much poorer distribution is reduced somewhat.

Theorem 6.5

Suppose that, with the poverty lines set at Z_F and Z_G, not only is $TIP_G(p) \geq TIP_F(p)$ for all $p \in [0, 1]$ but also $\inf_{p \in (0,1)}\{[TIP_G(p) - TIP_F(p)]/[p - TIP_G(p)]\} = \tau > 0$.

(a)   If $H(G|Z_G) > H(F|Z_F)$, and $Z_0 < Z_G$ is such that $H(G|Z_0) = H(F|Z_F)$, then $P(F|Z_F) \leq P(G|Z')$ for all poverty lines $Z' \in [\max\{Z_0, Z_G/(1 + \tau)\}, Z_G]$ and for all $P \in \mathbf{P}_{\mathbf{NG}}$.

(b)   Let $Z_1 < Z_G$ be such that $P^{FGT}(G|Z_1, 1) = P^{FGT}(F|Z_F, 1)$. Then $P(F|Z_F)$ $\leq P(G|Z')$ for all poverty lines $Z' \in [\max\{Z_1, Z_G/(1 + \tau)\}, Z_G]$ and for all $P \in \mathbf{P}_{NG}$.

The proof of this theorem is omitted but can be found in Jenkins and Lambert (1998a, pp. 53–54). The result can, of course, also be applied in cases in which a common poverty line Z is (initially) chosen for both distributions; just set $Z_F = Z_G = Z$ in the statement of the theorem; a reduction in the poverty line for G is then sanctioned, with that in F held at Z. The potential for lowering Z_G while maintaining the poverty comparison is greater the bigger is τ, i.e. the larger the vertical distance between $TIP_G(p)$ and $TIP_F(p)$ at each p, and also the closer $TIP_G(p)$ is to the 45° line of maximum poverty.

A good example of the applicability of this theorem is afforded by Gustafsson and Shi's (1998) study of poverty in rural and urban China. See figure 6.2, which shows the initial portions of the relevant TIP curves in 1988. Poverty in rural China is so much higher (Gustafsson and Shi report a head-count ratio some fifty times higher in the rural areas than the urban areas),

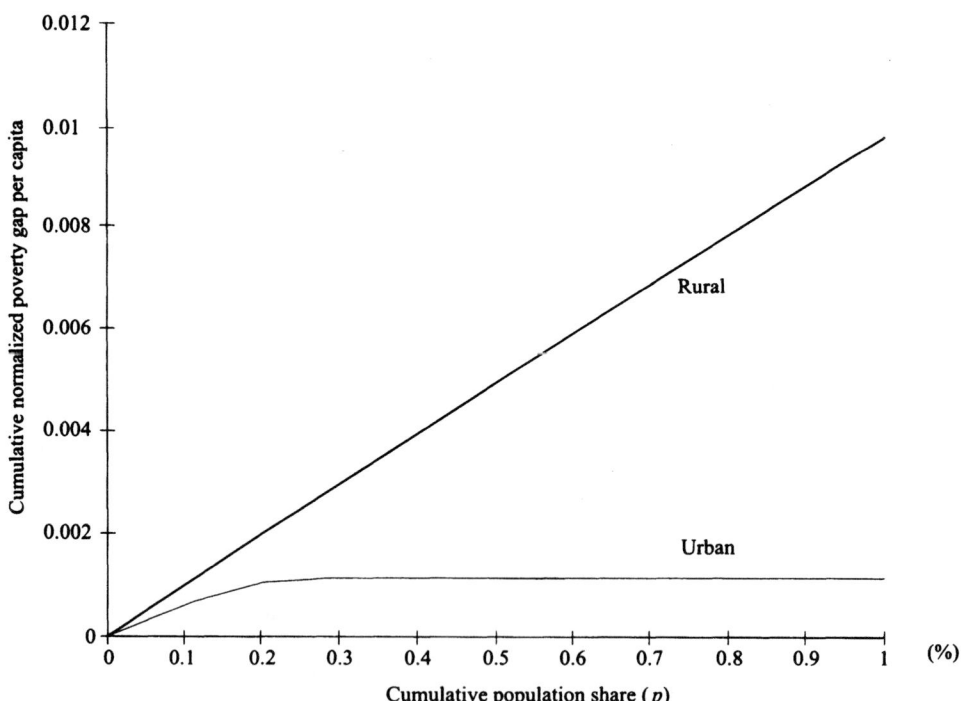

Figure 6.2   TIP curves for rural and urban China, 1988
Source: Gustafsson and Shi (1998) with permission

and the rural TIP curve so close to the line of maximum poverty, that, clearly, their conclusion that 'poverty in China is almost entirely a rural phenomenon' (p. 397) would be robust even to a substantial downrating of the rural poverty line. For other applications of theorem 6.5, see exercises 6.4.8 and 6.4.9 ahead.

What can be said if two TIP curves cross? This question is examined in Jenkins and Lambert (1998b). In the case of a single crossing, an unambiguous poverty ranking may still obtain, just as it did in section 3.4 of chapter 3 when generalized Lorenz curves crossed, by restricting attention to evaluation functions with a positive third derivative and verifying appropriate mean-variance conditions on the distributions of normalized poverty gaps. Let $\mathbf{P}^*_{\mathrm{NG}}$ be the sub-class of $\mathbf{P}_{\mathrm{NG}}$ for which $\Phi'''(\Gamma) > 0$ for all $\Gamma > 0$, and let $\mathbf{Q}^*_{\mathrm{NG}}$ be the subset of $\mathbf{P}^*_{\mathrm{NG}}$ for which also $\Phi'(0) > 0$. As shown in exercise 6.3.7, p. 151, an increasing transformation of P^{CHU2} belongs to $\mathbf{Q}^*_{\mathrm{NG}}$, as does P^{WATTS}, whilst $P^{\mathrm{FGT}} \in \mathbf{P}^*_{\mathrm{NG}} \backslash \mathbf{Q}^*_{\mathrm{NG}}$ for $\alpha > 2$.

Theorem 6.6

Suppose that, with the poverty lines set at Z_F and Z_G, TIP_G crosses TIP_F once from above and also $P^{\mathrm{FGT}}(G|Z_G, 2) \geq P^{\mathrm{FGT}}(F|Z_F, 2)$.

(i) If $P^{\mathrm{FGT}}(F|Z_G, 1) = P^{\mathrm{FGT}}(G|Z_F, 1)$ then $P(F|Z_F) \leq P(G|Z_G)$ for all $P \in \mathbf{P}^*_{\mathrm{NG}}$.

(ii) If $P^{\mathrm{FGT}}(F|Z_G, 1) > P^{\mathrm{FGT}}(G|Z_F, 1)$ then (a) $P(F|Z_F) \leq P(G|Z_G)$ for all $P \in \mathbf{P}^*_{\mathrm{NG}} \backslash \mathbf{Q}^*_{\mathrm{NG}}$ and (b) if also $P^{\mathrm{FGT}}(G|Z_G, 2) > P^{\mathrm{FGT}}(F|Z_F, 2)$ then $P(F|Z_F) \leq P(G|Z_G)$ for all $P \in \mathbf{Q}^*_{\mathrm{NG}}$ for which $\Phi''(0)/\Phi'(0) \geq 2[P^{\mathrm{FGT}}(F|Z_F, 1) - P^{\mathrm{FGT}}(G|Z_G, 1)]/[P^{\mathrm{FGT}}(G|Z_G, 2) - P^{\mathrm{FGT}}(F|Z_F, 2)]$.

These results may be understood as follows (the proof will come in a moment). If $TIP_F(p)$ and $TIP_G(p)$ cross once with TIP_G initially dominant, then clearly $P^{\mathrm{FGT}}(G|Z_G, 1) \leq P^{\mathrm{FGT}}(F|Z_F, 1)$ (these being the terminal TIP values for F and G, i.e. the respective normalized poverty deficits). Unless the two normalized poverty deficits are the same, the initial and terminal comparisons reveal conflict between the equity and efficiency aspects of poverty – who has it worst (judged by the largest percentage income shortfall from the poverty line) and how much of it there is in total. The poverty ranking, in favour of the initially dominant distribution G, will hold for all measures in $\mathbf{P}^*_{\mathrm{NG}}$ if the normalized poverty deficits are the same, subject to an appropriate variance condition, and for a restricted class of measures if the normalized poverty deficits differ. The variance criterion over distributions of normalized poverty gaps involves the comparison of FGT indices for $\alpha = 2$, and the restriction that is needed when normalized poverty deficits differ takes the form of a lower bound on poverty aversion, which is always satisfied by the FGT indices for $\alpha > 2$ (and by the other indices in the class

$P^*_{NG}\backslash Q^*_{NG}$) but more generally must be checked at the poverty threshold, i.e. at $\Gamma = 0$ (see exercise 6.4.10(b) on this).

Proof of theorem 6.6   Integrate by parts in (6.50), allowing now for different poverty lines, and set $V(\Gamma) = \int_\Gamma^1 T(\Gamma_0)\,d\Gamma_0$:

$$P(G|Z_G) - P(F|Z_F) = T(0)\Phi'(0) + V(0)\Phi''(0) + \int_0^1 V(\Gamma)\Phi'''(\Gamma)\,d\Gamma \qquad (6.52)$$

It is thus sufficient for $P(F|Z_F) \le P(G|Z_G)$ for all $P \in P^*_{NG}$ that $T(0) \ge 0$ and $V(\Gamma) \ge 0$ for all Γ. Now verify that $T(0) = P^{FGT}(G|Z_G, 1) - P^{FGT}(F|Z_F, 1)$ and $V(0) = \frac{1}{2}[P^{FGT}(G|Z_G, 2) - P^{FGT}(F|Z_F, 2)]$. Under the assumptions in the theorem, therefore, $T(0) \le 0$ and $V(0) \ge 0$. Moreover $V'(\Gamma) = -T(\Gamma)$ changes sign once, being first positive,[22] and $V(1) = 0$. Hence $V(\Gamma) \ge 0$ for all Γ and the result in (i) follows. For the results in (ii), note that when $T(0) < 0$ the condition $T(0)\Phi'(0) + V(0)\Phi''(0) \ge 0$, along with $V(\Gamma) \ge 0$ for all Γ, ensures $P(F|Z_F) \le P(G|Z_G)$. For $P \in P^*_{NG}\backslash Q^*_{NG}$ this condition is satisfied (because $\Phi'(0) = 0$) and for $P \in Q^*_{NG}$ it reduces to the one stated in (b).   QED

Exercises

6.4.1   Suppose that $\mu_F < \mu_G$, $F > G_R$ and GL_F, GL_G cross once. By examining the proof of theorem 3.5, p. 65, prove that if $\sigma_F^2 < \sigma_G^2 - (\mu_G - \mu_F)(2z - \mu_F - \mu_G)$, then $P^{FGT}(F|Z, 2) \le P^{FGT}(G|Z, 2)$ for all possible poverty lines Z.

6.4.2   'Our main result characterizes the variable-line poverty orderings for the Dalton utility-gap measures. It is shown that distribution **x** has more poverty than distribution **y** at some poverty line, and no less at all poverty lines, if the *utility* distribution associated with **y** dominates the utility distribution of **x** according to the generalized Lorenz criterion' (Foster and Jin, 1998, p. 270). Explain why the Dalton poverty indices (on which, see exercise 6.3.12, p. 152) are characterized here as 'utility gap measures' and account for Foster and Jin's result.

6.4.3   In Ravallion (1994a, p. 67), three poverty curves are defined: (i) the *poverty incidence curve*, (ii) the *poverty deficit curve* and (iii) the *poverty severity curve*. Explain these curves, and relate dominance of G over F by one of them to the conditions in theorem 6.1, parts (i), (ii) and (iii) respectively.

6.4.4   By consulting Shorrocks (1995), show that the modified Sen index of exercise 6.3.9(a), p. 151, 'has an interesting representation in terms of the area below a curve . . . this interpretation provides a fine analogy with the link between the Gini coefficient and the Lorenz curve' (Foster and Sen, 1997, p. 177).

6.4.5(a)   TIP dominance corresponds to reduced poverty for a somewhat larger class than $\mathbf{P}_{NG}$. Describe this class, for discrete income distributions, referring to Jenkins and Lambert (1998a), especially pp. 43–44.

6.4.5(b)   Explain why, if $H(\mathbf{x}|Z) = H(\mathbf{y}|Z)$, TIP dominance of $\mathbf{y}$ over $\mathbf{x}$ ensures $P^{SEN}(\mathbf{x}|Z) \leq P^{SEN}(\mathbf{y}|Z)$, $P^{KAK}(\mathbf{x}|Z, \kappa) \leq P^{KAK}(\mathbf{y}|Z, \kappa)$ for all $\kappa \geq 1$ and $P^{CHU}(\mathbf{x}|Z, \alpha) \leq P^{CHU}(\mathbf{y}|Z, \alpha)$ for all $\alpha \geq 1$. (Use part (a) of this question and see especially footnote 6 in Jenkins and Lambert, 1998a).[23]

6.4.6   Recall the example on p. 147 in which, with a poverty line of $Z = \$10$, $\mathbf{x} = (\$7, \$8, \$9, \$10, \$20, \$30)$ is transformed into $\mathbf{y} = (\$6, \$8, \$10, \$10, \$20, \$30)$ by means of a transfer of $\$1$ from the person with $\$7$ to the one with $\$9$. We noted that P^{SEN}, P^{KAK} and P^{CHU} all fall as a result of this transfer (because of the reduction in the headcount ratio from $\frac{1}{2}$ to $\frac{1}{3}$), and that P^{CHU2} and P^{CHAK} go up (because basic incomes become more unequal). Confirm now that in fact all indices in $\mathbf{P}_{NG}$ rise as a result of the transfer, by constructing the relevant TIP curves and using theorem 6.3.

6.4.7   Jenkins and Lambert (1998a, p. 55) say, in respect of theorem 6.5, that 'If $H(G|Z_G) > H(F|Z_F)$, then (b) is stronger than (a) in the sense of implying greater scope for ordering-preserving changes in poverty line relativity . . . on the other hand, (a) is easier to check than (b)'. Explain.

6.4.8   'Our conclusions about the increase in UK poverty between 1979 and 1988/89 are robust to whether an absolute or relative poverty line is used, or indeed something in between' (Jenkins and Lambert, 1997, p. 324). Explain how the TIP dominance conditions in theorems 6.3, 6.4 and 6.5 led the authors to this conclusion.

6.4.9   Let $\mathbf{x} = (70, 80, 90, x_4, x_5, \ldots, x_N)$ and $\mathbf{y} = (72, 96, 108, y_4, y_5, \ldots, y_N)$ where $y_i \geq x_i > 120$ for $4 \leq i \leq N$, and suppose that the appropriate poverty lines are $Z_x = 100$ and $Z_y = 120$. Use theorem 6.4 to show that $P(\mathbf{x}|Z_x) \leq P(\mathbf{y}|Z_y)$ for all $P \in \mathbf{P}_{NG}$. Now use theorem 6.5 to show that in fact $P(\mathbf{x}|Z_x) \leq P(\mathbf{y}|Z')$ for all $Z' \in [115, 120]$ and all $P \in \mathbf{P}_{NG}$. Finally use lemma 6.1 to show that, if the poverty line in $\mathbf{y}$ were reduced to 100, indeed if *any* common poverty line were used for both distributions, then the poverty comparison between $\mathbf{x}$ and $\mathbf{y}$ would be thrown into reverse.

6.4.10(a)   'The notion of "poverty aversion" that researchers have in mind means a lot more than just "disliking poverty" . . . "poverty aversion" and distribution-sensitivity may be regarded as the two sides of the same coin and can be used interchangeably' (Zheng, 2000b). Explain why Zheng measures poverty aversion as $s_\theta(x|Z) = -\theta''(x|Z)/\theta'(x|Z)$ for the canonical index $P(F|Z) = \int_0^Z \theta(x|Z)f(x)\,dx$ and describe the dominance criterion for reduced poverty according to the class of 'minimum distribution-sensitive poverty indices' which Zheng derives.

6.4.10(b) Verify that for canonical poverty measures for which $\theta(x|Z) = \Phi(\Gamma(x))$ where $\Phi'(0) > 0$, Zheng's measure at the poverty threshold takes the value $\Phi''(0)/\Phi'(0)$ as in theorem 6.6. Verify that for the increasing transformation of $P^{CHU2}(F|Z, \beta)$ which is in this form, $\Phi''(0)/\Phi'(0) = 1 - \beta$ and that for $P^{WATTS}(F|Z)$, $\Phi''(0)/\Phi'(0) = 1$. Verify that for the FGT family, $s_\theta(x|Z)$ takes the value $(\alpha - 1)$ at $x = 0$ and increases towards infinity as $x \to Z$.

6.4.11　Jenkins and Lambert (1997) compute TIP curves for the UK in 1981 and 1988/89 using a common poverty line equal to one half of 1979 average income. The 1988/89 TIP curve intersects the 1981 TIP curve once from above. The 1981 FGT indices are 0.0192 ($\alpha = 1$) and 0.0096 ($\alpha = 2$), and the 1988/89 FGT indices are 0.0187 ($\alpha = 1$) and 0.0108 ($\alpha = 2$). What does theorem 6.6 tell you happened to poverty in the UK between 1981 and 1988/89, as measured by the indices P^{FGT}, P^{CHU2} and P^{WATTS}? Consult Jenkins and Lambert (1997, p. 325) to check your answers.

6.4.12　'One method [of taking social heterogeneity into account when making poverty comparisons] is to summarize the relative needs of different families by means of a simple parametric equivalence scale . . . An alternative approach, which requires much weaker assumptions, is the sequential dominance approach . . . The goal of this paper is introduce a new method, which is (in simple cases) intermediate between these two approaches' (Bradbury, 1997, pp. 245–246). Describe Bradbury's search methodology for making poverty comparisons with 'bounded equivalence scales'.

6.4.13　In chapter 3 we showed that generalized Lorenz dominance of F over G in the sub-population comprising the j most needy groups corresponds, to $\Sigma_{1 \le i \le j} p_i S_i(x) \ge 0$ for all x where $S_i(x)$ is the S-function for group i (see p. 77). Combine this observation with the result in (6.39) above to account for Bourguignon's (1989, p. 75) assertion, in respect of the sequential generalized Lorenz dominance criterion, that 'a distribution . . . dominates another if the poverty gap is smaller for all "poverty income and size" limits'.

6.5　Sequential poverty dominance criteria

When the population is socially heterogeneous, there is an alternative to equivalizing incomes and applying a uniform poverty threshold Z across the entire population. Using sequential criteria developed by Atkinson (1992), Jenkins and Lambert (1993) and Chambaz and Maurin (1998), the analyst may work instead with money income distributions, having determined a ranking of household types by need and made some judgements about the relative poverty contributions of households of each type at each money income level. This is less restrictive than equivalizing. Even if the equivalization methodology is accepted, this alternative approach avoids doubt or dispute about the appropriate equivalence scale relativities.

As in section 3.6 of chapter 3, let us partition the population into socially homogeneous subgroups, indexed by $i = 1, 2, \ldots, n$, in *descending order of need*. Poverty lines denominated in units of money income must be specified, one for each subgroup, and these should be related systematically with one another. We indicated such a line of analysis earlier in the chapter, using a vector of poverty lines, $\mathbf{Z} = (Z_1, Z_2, \ldots, Z_n)$, and suggesting that

$$Z_1 \geq Z_2 \geq \ldots \geq Z_n \tag{6.53}$$

would be a natural relationship: it says that needier households require more money income than less needy ones to escape poverty. We might want to vary the Z_is in (6.53), one relative to another, to see how poverty is affected under different assumptions about relative needs. An appropriate dominance criterion for this scenario would allow for a range of possible configurations of the subgroup-specific poverty lines Z_i subject to the restriction in (6.53).

Let $F(x)$ and $G(x)$ be two alternative distribution functions for money income across households. Let $F_i(x)$ and $G_i(x)$ be the subgroup distribution functions associated with F and G, and let $f_i(x)$ and $g_i(x)$ be the corresponding density functions, $1 \leq i \leq n$. Let aggregate poverty in F take the form

$$P(F|\mathbf{Z}) = \sum_{1 \leq i \leq n} p_{iF} P_i(F_i|Z_i) \tag{6.2a}$$

where p_{iF} is the proportion of the overall population belonging to subgroup i, with a similar definition for G (and possibly different proportions p_{iG}). Subgroup-specific deprivation functions $\theta_i(x|Z)$ may be used to measure poverty in the subgroups:

$$P_i(F_i|Z_i) = \int_0^{Z_i} \theta_i(x|Z_i) f_i(x) \mathrm{d}x \tag{6.2b}$$

or a common deprivation function $\theta(x|Z)$ could be applied in all groups.

As an example, consider the specification $\theta(x|Z_i) = (Z_i - x)^\alpha$ ($\alpha \geq 1$) for $x \leq Z_i$ and $\theta(x|Z_i) = 0$ for $x \geq Z_i$. According to this, poverty in each subgroup is measured using an absolute version of an index belonging to the FGT family (recall exercise 6.3.10, p. 151). This could be appropriate if the judgement is that absolute shortfalls of money incomes are what matter for the determination of aggregate poverty.[24]

Chambaz and Maurin (1998) suggest a relationship between the poverty contribution functions $\theta_i(x|Z_i)$ for different income unit types which has an intuitively agreeable interpretation and is satisfied, in particular, by the absolute FGT example given above. Let P_{CM} be the class of aggregate poverty measures as in (6.2a)–(6.2b) in which the deprivation functions are twice differentiable everywhere and satisfy these restrictions:

$$\theta_i(x|Z_i) \geq 0 \text{ for } x \in [0, Z_i] \text{ and } \theta_i(x|Z_i) = 0 \text{ for } x > Z_i, 1 \leq i \leq n \qquad (6.54)$$

$$\theta_1'(x|Z_1) \leq \theta_2'(x|Z_2) \leq \ldots \leq \theta_n'(x|Z_n) \leq 0 \text{ for all } x \qquad (6.55)$$

and

$$\theta_1''(x|Z_1) \geq \theta_2''(x|Z_2) \geq \ldots \geq \theta_n''(x|Z_n) \geq 0 \text{ for all } x \qquad (6.56)$$

Can you see how (6.54)–(6.55) force the poverty lines to be related as in (6.53)? You can verify that the absolute FGT example satisfies (6.54)–(6.55), for poverty lines Z related as in (6.53), for all $\alpha \geq 1$ and that it also satisfies (6.56) for all $\alpha \geq 2$.

Poverty measures satisfying (6.54)–(6.55) have the appealing property that, at each income level x, the potential of a \$1 addition to a person or household's income to reduce overall poverty is greatest if the recipient is of the neediest type, less for each successively less needy type and least of all for a recipient of the least needy type (and may, of course, be zero for any type depending whether the chosen income level x exceeds the relevant poverty line or not). The benefit to overall poverty of giving the \$1 to someone having x who is of type i rather than type $i + 1$, which is proportional to $\theta_i'(x|Z_i) - \theta_{i+1}'(x|Z_{i+1})$, is less at higher income levels than lower ones according to (6.56). This is also an appealing property.

The properties defining P_{CM} are very reminiscent of the Atkinson–Bourguignon properties for utility profiles upon which the sequential criterion for welfare superiority rests, and the mathematics for reduced poverty according to all indices in the class P_{CM} goes very similarly. Thus write

$$P(F|Z) - P(G|Z) = \sum_{1 \leq i \leq n} \int_0^{\bar{z}} \theta_i(x|Z_i)[p_{iF} f_i(x) - p_{iG} g_i(x)] \, dx \qquad (6.57)$$

(replacing the top limit of integration in (6.2b) by z, an income equal to or greater than any occurring in either F or G; we may do this because of (6.54)). Now follow the steps that led from (3.29) to (3.34) on pp. 76–78. The result is this:

$$P(F|Z) - P(G|Z) = \sum_{1 \leq j \leq n} E_j(z) T_j^*(z) - \int_0^{\bar{z}} \left\{ \sum_{1 \leq j \leq n} E_j'(x) T_j^*(x) \right\} dx \qquad (6.58)$$

where

$$E_j(x) = \theta_j'(x|Z_j) - \theta_{j+1}'(x|Z_{j+1}) \text{ for } 1 \leq j \leq n-1, \ E_n(x) = \theta_n'(x|Z_n) \qquad (6.59)$$

(analogously to the definition of $D_j(x)$ in (3.35)), and

$$T_j^*(x) = \sum_{1 \le i \le j} \int_0^x [p_{iG} G_i(y) - p_{iF} F_i(y)] \, dy \qquad (3.36a)$$

as before. Now for $P \in \mathbf{P}_{CM}$ we have, for each j,

$$E_j(x) \le 0 \text{ and } E_j'(x) \ge 0 \text{ for all } x \le Z_j, E_j(x) \equiv 0 \text{ for all } x > Z_j \qquad (6.60)$$

This follows from (6.54)–(6.56). The sufficient conditions for reduced poverty according to the class $\mathbf{P}_{CM}$ are transparent from (6.58) and (6.60). Chambaz and Maurin (1998, p. 512) show that these conditions are also necessary.

Theorem 6.7

$P(F|\mathbf{Z}) \le P(G|\mathbf{Z})$ for all $P \in \mathbf{P}_{CM}$ if and only if for each j, $T_j^*(x) \ge 0$ for all $x \le Z_j$.

This sequential test begins with the neediest subgroup ($j = 1$), and requires an inequality condition to be checked for all income levels up to the highest poverty line ($x \le Z_1$). Then the second-neediest group gets added in, and the range of income levels over which the sign condition must be checked is reduced (from $x \le Z_1$ to $x \le Z_2$) – and so on, progressively adding in more groups and reducing the maximum income level at which the test must succeed, until all groups have been included and the maximum income level for the test has been brought down to the lowest poverty line ($x \le Z_n$).

There is a close link between this test and the sequential test for welfare dominance which we developed in chapter 3. Compare the result in theorem 6.7 above with the one in theorem 3.8 on p. 79. There, the condition $T_j^*(x) \ge 0$ for each j and for all x was necessary and sufficient for welfare superiority of F over G; here the inequality condition must be checked only up to $x = Z_j$. It is clear that *welfare superiority of F over G equates to less poverty in F than in G for all configurations of poverty lines $\mathbf{Z}$ satisfying (6.53)*. In the absence of demographic differences (i.e. in the case $p_{iF} = p_{iG}$ for all i), the conditions of theorem 3.8 come down to those of the sequential generalized Lorenz criterion.

Corollary 6.1

In the absence of demographic differences between F and G, sequential generalized Lorenz dominance of F over G is equivalent to less poverty in F than G for all members of the class $\mathbf{P}_{CM}$ whatever the configuration of poverty lines $\mathbf{Z}$ satisfying (6.53).

This is a sequential analogue of lemma 6.1 (p. 160), in which we showed that generalized Lorenz dominance of F over G is equivalent to less poverty in F than G for all common poverty lines Z and all measures in the class $\mathbf{P}_{NG}$. Another result gives a sequential analogue to the finding, in theorem 6.3, that poverty dominance for the line Z and the class $\mathbf{P}_{NG}$ implies the same conclusion for all lower poverty lines $Z' \in (0, Z]$.

Corollary 6.2

If the sequential conditions of theorem 6.7 hold for poverty lines $\mathbf{Z}$ satisfying (6.53), then not only is $P(F|\mathbf{Z}) \leq P(G|\mathbf{Z})$ for all $P \in \mathbf{P}_{CM}$ but also $P(F|\mathbf{Z}') \leq P(G|\mathbf{Z}')$ for all $\mathbf{Z}'$ such that each $Z_i' \leq Z_i$ and $\mathbf{Z}'$ satisfies (6.53).

The proof is rather trivial. Can you construct it formally? Hence the sequential poverty dominance criterion is able to cope with changed relativities between poverty lines, yielding the same poverty conclusion for all subgroup-specific poverty lines which are lower than the ones at which the test is carried out (and in the same needs configuration). An extension of the criterion can also be made to cover cases in which different poverty lines vectors, $\mathbf{Z}_F$ and $\mathbf{Z}_G$, are set in the distributions being compared: see exercise 6.5.1.

Numerical integration techniques are required to compute areas under distribution functions in order to perform the sequential checks of theorem 6.7. A sequential procedure which is easy to carry out visually was initiated in Atkinson (1992) and extended to deal with demographic differences in Jenkins and Lambert (1993). This entails dropping the requirement on second derivatives $\theta_i''(x|Z_i)$ in (6.56), so that a wider class of poverty measures is admitted. This widening makes the distributional conditions for reduced poverty more stringent, of course, but they become easier to implement too. The step-wise procedure that is involved is vividly described in Atkinson (1992, pp. 8–10), and is well illustrated by examples drawing on *Family Expenditure Survey* data for the UK in both papers (see exercise 6.5.2).

If value judgements about the relative severity of poverty in the different needs groups would be expressed at *each fixed poverty gap level*, for the hierarchy of needs groups, rather than at each fixed income level as in (6.54)–(6.56), then a sequential version of TIP dominance would emerge. Zoli (2000) contains some interesting considerations in this direction.

Exercises

6.5.1   'The previous analyses assume that the thresholds below which house-
         holds are considered to be poor remain constant from one period to
         the next. It is possible to extend the sequential comparison principles
         to societies in which the definition of poverty changes over time'
         (Chambaz and Maurin, 1998, p. 503). Explain how Chambaz and
         Maurin modify their procedures to permit different poverty line
         vectors $\mathbf{Z}_F$ and $\mathbf{Z}_G$ to be set in the two distributions being compared.

6.5.2(a) Integrate by parts in (6.58) to show that

$$P(F|\mathbf{Z}) - P(G|\mathbf{Z}) = \int_0^{\bar{z}} \left\{ \sum_{1 \le j \le n} E_j(x) T_j^{*\prime}(x) \right\} dx$$

and conclude that the conditions $T_j^{*\prime}(x) \ge 0$ for all $x \le Z_j$ and all j are necessary and sufficient to ensure less poverty in F than in G for all poverty measures satisfying (6.54)–(6.55).

6.5.2(b) Use exercise 3.6.2(a), p. 80, to deduce that in the absence of demographic differences between F and G, sequential rank dominance of F over G is equivalent to less poverty in F than G for all poverty indices satisfying (6.54)–(6.55) whatever the configuration of poverty lines $\mathbf{Z}$ satisfying (6.53).

6.5.2(c) What could Chambaz and Maurin (1998, p. 505) conclude about changes in French poverty at the household level between 1977 and 1994 using the sequential rank dominance test? What could they conclude for the change that took place between 1989 and 1994?

Notes

1 There is some disagreement over whether an income *at* the poverty line ($x_i = Z$) should count as poor. Sen (1976, pp. 374–375) describes Z as the level of income 'at which poverty begins' and includes incomes equal to Z in his headcount, but elsewhere in his paper he talks of incomes which 'fall below the poverty line' as the poor ones, as do Kakwani, 1986, p. 243, Ravallion, 1994a, p. 45, Johnson, 1996, p. 27 and Foster and Sen, 1997, p. 168, for example. If an income $x_i = Z$ were to count as poor then the headcount ratio would have to be $(Q + K)/N$ where K is the number of incomes equal to Z. For a large population, the difference is surely insignificant. Donaldson and Weymark (1986) consider the distinction carefully in finite populations. The distinction is lost entirely if incomes are assumed to be continuously distributed.

2 Zheng (1997) traces six different names that have been used for the measure $D(F|Z)$, poverty deficit being the one chosen by Atkinson (1987) and income gap ratio being another. Like Zheng, we reserve this latter name exclusively for $I(F|Z)$.

3 This axiom is implicit in Sen (1976) and was later made explicit.

4 Donaldson and Weymark (1986) identified two monotonicity axioms – downward and upward, renamed weak and strong by subsequent authors including Zheng, and four transfer axioms – minimal, weak, regressive and progressive. Much hinges upon what is assumed about the effect of an income increment or transfer which takes an income unit out of poverty (see on). The issue of whether an income of exactly Z is counted as poor also figures.

5 In the equivalent income context, 'poor' and 'even poorer' refer to living standards; the 'income transfer' may be either a hypothetical transfer of equivalent income from one household to another, or a realizable money transfer in case poverty is being measured in the artificial population of equivalent adults (see chapter 3, section 3.4).

6 For more on the approach taken by Lewis and Ulph, including the distinction between policies to alleviate poverty and reduce inequality in this framework, see Beath *et al.* (1988). For more on poverty alleviation policies, see Lipton and Raval-lion (1995) and references therein, also Chakravarty and Mukherjee (1998).

7 See Shorrocks (1995, p. 1228) and Foster and Sen (1997, p. 176) on these aspects. These latter authors call P^* the 'continuous version of P'.

8 See exercise 6.1.1. The quantity g is the jump in indirect utility which comes when an individual gains just enough income to purchase one unit of an indivisible participation good.

9 See Shorrocks (1995) for some other versions of the Sen index, and Zheng (1997, p. 145) for an explanation of the asymptotic equivalence of (6.25a) and (6.7).

10 In continuous terms the formulae would be $[\Gamma^*]^\alpha = \int_0^Z \Gamma(x)^\alpha f(x)\,dx/F(Z)$ and $P^{\mathrm{CHU}}(F|Z) = H(F|Z)\,\Gamma^*$.

11 The normalized poverty gap vectors are $\Gamma_x = (0.3, 0.2, 0.1, 0, 0, 0)$ and $\Gamma_y = (0.4, 0.2, 0, 0, 0, 0)$. For $a \,\varepsilon\, \mathbf{R}$, set $w_a = [1 + 2^a]/[1 + 2^a + 3^a]$. You will find that $P^{\mathrm{KAK}}(\mathbf{x}|Z, \kappa)/P^{\mathrm{KAK}}(\mathbf{y}|Z, \kappa) = \frac{3}{4} w_\kappa/w_{\kappa+1}$ and $P^{\mathrm{CHU}}(\mathbf{x}|Z, \alpha)/P^{\mathrm{CHU}}(\mathbf{y}|Z, \alpha) = [3/2]^{(\alpha-1)/\alpha}/[w_\alpha]^{1/\alpha}$, from which the results follow. See Thon (1983) for other examples.

12 One can, of course, add a constant to a canonical poverty index and still retain additive decomposability; Foster and Shorrocks's characterization allows for this. They associate continuity of the overall index with continuity of $\theta(x|Z)$ at the poverty threshold $x = Z$ (neither is the case for the headcount ratio). In inequality analysis additive decomposability does not demand that the weights be population shares (see p. 111) and a between-groups component also arises.

13 In fact 'lexical combinations' of the headcount ratio and a canonical index are also admissible. in which the headcount ratio provides the first-round criterion for poverty comparisons and a continuous canonical index is used as a tie-breaker. For more details on this, see *ibid.*, pp. 698–700.

14 Ebert and Moyes (2000b) characterize the FGT *poverty orderings* axiomatically. In essence they show that the only poverty ordering which preserves poverty-equivalence for equal additions to all incomes and the poverty line, and also for equal scaling of all incomes and the poverty line, is the FGT poverty ordering, according to which two distributions would be poverty-equivalent if and only if they had the same FGT index for a given α.

15 For empirical studies using country-specific poverty lines, see Blackburn (1994) and Hagenaars *et al.* (1998). Gustafsson and Shi (1998) use different poverty lines for rural and urban sub-populations in China, and *Households Below Average Income* sets different low income cut-offs for the UK in different years. In each of these studies, comparisons based on absolute poverty lines are also undertaken (i.e. lines which are fixed in real terms), often with very different results: see Blackburn (1994, p. 374).

16 For the welfare significance of rank and generalized Lorenz dominance, see exercise 3.2.2(a), p. 56 and theorem 3.2, p. 55. The result connecting welfare and the $\alpha = 2$ version of the FGT index comes from lemma 3.3 and theorem 3.4, pp. 63–64: $W_F \geq W_G$ for all $U \in \mathbf{U}$ if and only if (a) $\mu_F \geq \mu_G$ and (b) $P^{\mathrm{FGT}}(F|Z, 2) \leq P^{\mathrm{FGT}}(G|Z, 2)$ for all possible poverty lines Z. Here, the expression 'for all possible poverty lines' means for all $Z \in [0, z)$ where, as in chapter 3, z is the highest income occurring in either distribution with non-zero frequency density. If the restriction on poverty lines in (b) is replaced by 'for all poverty lines $Z \in [0, \infty)$', the condition

on means in (a) can be dropped, because it is implied (see exercise 3.4.1, p. 68). However, this formulation allows for poverty lines Z to be set which are well in excess of the highest incomes in the distributions being compared.

17 In fact, Atkinson's poverty contribution function $p(x, Z)$ is defined to be *negative* for $x < Z$ (and zero for $x \geq Z$), and he is interested in the class of poverty indices which, for income distribution F, are *decreasing* functions of $\int_0^Z p(x, Z)f(x)\,dx$ (and similarly for G, which he writes as $F^\dagger$). Sufficiency of the cited conditions is quite obvious. Atkinson explains necessity very clearly. Atkinson notes that these conditions correspond to restricted forms of rank and generalized Lorenz dominance, but with the comparisons being made up to a given income level and not a given position.

18 As noted in exercise 6.3.7, an increasing transformation of $P^{\text{CHU2}}(F|Z, \beta)$ also belongs to these classes. For $0 < \beta < 1$ this transformed index was introduced in its own right by Chakravarty (1983b): see exercise 6.3.4 on this.

19 When $\rho = 1$, this is rank dominance, when $\rho = 2$ it is equivalent to generalized Lorenz dominance and when $\rho = 3$ it comes down to the distributional condition given in lemma 3.3, p. 63. For the general case, see Fishburn and Willig (1984).

20 Foster and Shorrocks (1988a) use the continuously distributed formulation for the income variate, as Atkinson (1987) does, and a discrete one in their 1988b paper. The two papers led to work on the 'power' of poverty orderings, see Zheng (1999, 2001) on this. In Zheng (1999), the distributional conditions needed to guarantee a *strict* poverty reduction, $P(F|Z) < P(G|Z)$ rather than $P(F|Z) \leq P(G|Z)$ as in the results described in this chapter, are discussed.

21 It can be shown similarly that generalized Lorenz dominance of F over G when both distributions are censored at an income value $x = Z^+$ is equivalent to TIP dominance of G over F for all common poverty lines $Z \leq Z^+$.

22 You should be able to derive this from the analogue of lemma 3.2, which was stated on p. 160, in much the way that an equivalent property was derived for the function $S(x)$ within the proof of theorem 3.4 on p. 64.

23 See also Zheng (2000a, §III) for orderings in terms of these indices, in which the headcount ratio plays a constitutive role.

24 The familiar (relative) FGT index would arise if $\theta(x|Z_i) = [(Z_i - x)/Z_i]^\alpha$ for $x \leq Z_i$. According to Atkinson (1992, p. 7), 'it is not . . . clear that such a normalization is appropriate. In the case of the poverty gap [*viz.* $\alpha = 1$], it would mean that a poverty deficit of £10 for a single person would be treated as twice as important, as far as aggregate poverty is concerned, as a deficit of £10 for a family with a poverty line twice as high'.

7

The income tax

Income taxation modifies the distribution of income. Unless tax liabilities are proportional to incomes, the relative purchasing powers of different income units are affected by income taxation. Typically, income tax systems are built upon the 'progressive principle'. What justifies progression in the income tax? In this short chapter we shall explore this question, and also consider the extent to which observed income tax systems violate the progressive principle. In chapters 8, 9 and 10 to follow, we consider in detail a number of different facets of progression and properties of observed income tax systems.

7.1 Progression: justifications and objectives

In their extended essay, *The Uneasy Case For Progressive Income Taxation*, Blum and Kalven (1953, p. *v*) wrote: 'Every controversy about changes in income tax rates is to some extent a controversy over the principle of progression itself. With the advent of a new national administration which is heavily committed to significant tax reduction as soon as practicable, it is likely that the principle of progression will once again be exposed to public scrutiny'. This has a familiar ring nearly 50 years on. What justifies progressive income taxation, and why do governments pursue it?

We shall not dwell on the political history of progression here. The interested reader is referred to Blum and Kalven (1953, chapters 1–4). Other sources which consider issues raised by the progressive principle include Blum (1979), Bös and Felderer (1989) and Slemrod (1994). Taking as given that government must raise revenue by taxing incomes, we shall identify here some equity principles which have been put forward to justify progression.

First, we should say clearly what we mean by income tax progression. It is that the average rate of tax faced by an income unit increases with income: a better-off taxpayer not only has a bigger tax liability but also loses a bigger share of his income in tax. Mathematically, if the tax liability of an income unit having income x is written as $t(x)$, so that $t(x)$ is the *income tax schedule*, then the definition is this:

$$t(x) \text{ progressive} \Leftrightarrow \frac{t(x)}{x} \text{ increases with } x \qquad (7.1)$$

The tax is *regressive* if its average rate declines with increases in income x. If $t(x)$ is differentiable, as we shall often assume for analytical convenience, the criterion for *strict* progression can be written as

$$\frac{d[t(x)/x]}{dx} > 0 \qquad \text{for all } x > 0 \qquad (7.2a)$$

and that for (weak) progression as

$$\frac{d[t(x)/x]}{dx} \geq 0 \qquad \text{for all } x > 0 \qquad (7.2b)$$

The latter includes both the case of a proportional or 'flat' tax (when $d[t(x)/x]/dx \equiv 0$ for all x) and also the case in which taxation takes place only on income in excess of a threshold level, x_0 say, and may be strictly progressive thereafter (so that $d[t(x)/x]/dx > 0 \Leftrightarrow x > x_0$).

The principle of *horizontal equity* in taxation requires the 'equal tax treatment of equals': income units in identical circumstances should be taxed the same. As we shall see in section 7.3, this principle typically calls for a more complex form of income tax system than our naive modelling as a schedule $t(x)$ suggests, but if we can interpret 'identical circumstances' as 'identical income levels' then the formula $t(x)$ ensures horizontal equity whether or not the tax is progressive.

Progression arises from principles of *vertical equity*. These call for 'the appropriately unequal tax treatment of unequals'. The *ability-to-pay principle* is one such principle, according to which taxes should be designed to equalize everyone's sacrifice in utility terms. Whether the tax schedule should be progressive or not in order to satisfy this property can be established under appropriate assumptions. If there is a common increasing and concave utility-of-income function for all income units, with a sufficiently declining marginal utility as income rises, then the criterion of *equal utility loss for all* justifies more than proportionate tax increases along the income scale. This result is due to Samuelson (1947, p. 227) and can be seen simply as follows.

Suppose that $U(x)$ is the utility-of-income function. A tax schedule $t(x)$ is called for which will cause an equal absolute reduction u_0 in utility for each income unit. Thus the *equal absolute sacrifice* tax schedule $t(x)$ is defined implicitly by an identity:

$$U(x) - U(x - t(x)) \equiv u_0 \quad \text{for all } x \qquad (7.3)$$

Now differentiate with respect to x and re-arrange, to show that $d[t(x)/x]/dx > 0$ for all $x \Leftrightarrow xU'(x) < (x - t(x))U'(x - t(x))$ for all x. It is immediate that if the elasticity of marginal utility, defined in chapter 4 (p. 95) as $q_U(x) = -xU''(x)/U'(x)$, is big enough then strict progression is called for:

$$q_U(x) > 1 \text{ for all } x > 0 \Rightarrow \frac{\mathrm{d}[t(x)/x]}{\mathrm{d}x} > 0 \text{ for all } x > 0 \tag{7.4}$$

The Samuelson result should not be taken to say that *all* progressive taxes are equal absolute sacrifice taxes, nor that *only* progressive ones are. Ok (1995) and Mitra and Ok (1996, 1997) have studied intensively the question whether a given tax schedule $t(x)$ can be rationalized as an equal absolute sacrifice tax for some plausible (increasing and concave) utility function $U(x)$. They show that tax schedules $t(x)$ satisfying $t'(x) > 0$ and $t''(x) > 0$ for all x are equal absolute sacrifice taxes (Ok, 1995, Theorem 2); that among increasing piece-wise-linear tax schedules, essentially *only* the convex ones are equal absolute sacrifice taxes if the utility function must satisfy a certain differentiability condition (Mitra and Ok, 1996, Corollary 3.10; but see also D'Antoni, 1999, on this); and that more generally some non-convex progressive tax schedules are, and some are not, equal absolute sacrifice taxes (Mitra and Ok, 1997, theorem 1 and examples). Mitra and Ok were able to demonstrate, in particular, that the statutory personal income tax codes in Turkey between 1981 and 1985, and in the USA between 1988 and 1990, though progressive, were not equal absolute sacrifice taxes. Young (1990) models the US statutory income tax code before 1986 as an equal absolute sacrifice tax, using the utility function $U_e(x)$ of theorem 4.2, p. 98, which has constant inequality aversion e, and Gouveia and Strauss (1994) similarly model effective US income taxes in the period 1979–1989 as equal absolute sacrifice taxes. We have already mentioned some of their findings (p. 129). Properties of the equal absolute sacrifice tax schedule for the utility function $U_e(x)$ as e varies have been examined by Buchholtz *et al.* (1988): see exercise 9.2.5, p. 231 for more on this.

Musgrave and Musgrave (1984), in their seminal text *Public Finance in Theory and Practice*, present a neat graphical analysis of equal absolute sacrifice and other possible concepts of equal sacrifice: the reader is directed to their chapter 11, section C. They also point out what can be seen as a failing of the ability-to-pay principle, that it does not relate tax payments to the benefits received by income units from the proceeds of taxation: 'This approach leaves the expenditure side of the public sector dangling . . . Yet, actual tax policy is largely determined independently of the expenditure side and an equity rule is needed to provide guidance. The ability-to-pay principle is widely accepted as this guide' (Musgrave and Musgrave, 1984, p. 228).

The *benefit principle*, in contrast, is an attempt to relate tax burdens directly to the expenditure side of budget. If people would voluntarily give up part of their purchasing power in the form of taxes, in order to benefit from the provision of government goods and services, how much would they give? Can progression be justified on this ground? This is a complex question whose answer plainly depends on the sort of goods and services government is providing.

Lindahl's prescriptive theory of the budget, dating back to 1919 and re-examined in Head (1964),[1] says that for pure public goods: 'expenditure on each . . . should be pushed to the point where, for each individual, the utility to him of the last unit of public good is equal to the sacrifice represented by the tax-price he must pay for that unit' (Head, 1964, p. 423). Pure public goods are goods of which every unit can be enjoyed to the full by all people. It might be argued that law and order and defence are such goods. The question is whether the demand over these goods exerted by upper income units is sufficiently greater than that exerted by lower income units to justify progression.

This question has been examined analytically by Snow and Warren (1983) and a criterion developed in terms of the income elasticity of demand. Let $A(p, x)$ be the amount of a public good a person with income x would demand if the price he had to pay were p. The Lindahl 'tax-price' $p(x)$ appropriate to this person is defined implicitly by an identity:

$$A(p(x), x) \equiv a_0 \text{ for each } x \tag{7.5}$$

where a_0 is an appropriate constant. Under this condition, and only this, every individual demands the same quantity of the good at the price he faces. The tax bill for the individual with income x is

$$t(x) = p(x)a_0 \tag{7.6}$$

Snow and Warren prove that

$$\frac{\mathrm{d}[t(x)/x]}{\mathrm{d}x} > 0 \text{ for all } x \Leftrightarrow -\frac{p}{A}\frac{\partial A}{\partial p} < \frac{x}{A}\frac{\partial A}{\partial x} \text{ for all } x \tag{7.7}$$

Can you verify this by differentiation in (7.5)–(7.6)? The result says that the income elasticity of demand must exceed the (absolute value of the) price elasticity of demand to justify progression. This is intuitive. As we go along the income scale, if and only if the increased demand for the good induced by a rise in income is more than the reduction that would come from a matching proportionate increase in the price should the tax bill rise more-than-proportionately, i.e. progressively, to choke off the extra demand that richer people would otherwise exert over public goods. See Snow and Warren (1983, p. 321) for more detail.

The yield of the income tax is not in practice applied solely to the (optimal) provision of pure public goods. Together with the proceeds of other taxes, it in practice finances cash benefits (transfers) as well providing for other kinds of goods and services, for example sanitation and health, transport and education. As Herber (1983, p. 125) points out: 'the benefit principle is not comprehensive enough in its application to serve as a general benchmark of equity in the distribution of tax burden, though it does merit application where it can be utilized through its application of market principles to the public sector'. We further discuss the attribution or imputation of benefits from government expenditure to income units in chapter 10.

Another rationale for progressive income taxation lies in its stabilizing effect on the macroeconomy. As incomes grow, income tax liabilities increase more than proportionately and therefore so does revenue. Of course, government extracts non-income taxes from individuals and households as well as income taxes (for example: property taxes, value-added tax or VAT, specific duties or excise taxes levied on petroleum products, tobacco, alcohol, etc.). There are also business taxes (e.g. corporation and payroll taxes). Some taxes in the government's portfolio provide roughly proportionate revenue sources when incomes are growing (for example, VAT if expenditure on VAT-rated goods and services grows at the same rate as incomes). Other taxes, notably the specific duties, levied on quantities and not monetary values, may respond only to real and not inflationary income growth: these constitute 'sticky' revenue sources. That progression of the income tax guarantees government an elastic revenue source has been seen by Blum and Kalven both as 'conducive to political irresponsibility' on the one hand, and to provide balance with these other forms of taxation on the other: 'A widely accepted argument for having some degree of progression in the federal income tax today is that it merely compensates for the regression of other taxes in our overall tax system' (Blum and Kalven, 1953, pp. vi, 5).[2]

Income and consumption taxes can be attributed simply to the relevant income units. The latter will not necessarily be progressive. For example, the taxes on beer and cigarettes may fall disproportionately on low incomes and therefore be regressive in their overall incidence. However, the business of attributing other taxes to income units can proceed only on the basis of questionable incidence assumptions. Who in the end pays the corporate profits and payroll taxes? The existence of such taxes may depress wage rates (affecting households directly); part may be passed on in prices (and therefore be attributable to households on the basis of expenditure surveys); part may get reflected in reduced dividends and share values for shareholders (who are also householders). We shall not pursue the issues here, except to note that Musgrave and Musgrave (1984, chapters 10 and 12) offer an attractive introductory analysis.

In the analysis that follows, the tax liability $t(x)$ will, from time to time, be interpreted as total liability from all taxes, but the perspective for most of the analysis in this and the following three chapters is the direct taxation of incomes, progressive or not.

Exercises

7.1.1 'To apply the equal sacrifice principle in a real case, a specific form for the utility function would have to be agreed upon, and as a practical matter the same function would have to be assumed to hold for all tax-payers. These assumptions seem to be completely unwarranted ... the equal sacrifice approach can be justified on entirely different grounds than interpersonal comparisons of utility' (Young, 1988, p. 564). What grounds does Young propose? See also Young (1990) however.

7.1.2 '. . . traditionally, economists have used two different principles for evaluating how the tax burden ought to be allocated: the benefit principle and the ability-to-pay principle . . . the ability to pay principle fails as an operational guide to tax progressivity for the same reasons that the benefit principle fails' Slemrod (1994, page 2). Explain Slemrod's point of view.

7.1.3 Explain Burgat and Jeanrenaud's (1996, p. 160) assertion that: 'a key factor that determines the tax rate structure is not the choice between the two approaches to taxation – benefit or sacrifice – but rather the value assigned to the elasticity of the marginal utility of income'.

7.1.4 '. . . equal sacrifice completely ignores the question of whether or not consumption of publicly provided goods and services is efficient, as well as the question of how these benefits affect the burden imposed by a tax' (Neill, 2000, p. 118). Describe Neill's 'equal benefits paradigm', synthesizing the equal sacrifice and benefit principles of income taxation.

7.1.5 Explain Yaari's (1988, p. 381) proposal to 'use the tax structure to retrieve the policy maker's preferences through the Principle of Equal Sacrifice'. Explain the logic of his apparently absurd conclusion on p. 396: 'To ensure complete equality, institute a poll tax!'

7.1.6 Describe Okun's (1975, chapter 1), concern for 'the transgression of dollars on rights'. See also Tobin (1971). Is there a case to be made for progressive taxation on this account?

7.1.7 What rationale for progressive income taxation do Bös and Tillmann (1985) put forward?

7.1.8 Describe Snyder and Kramer's (1988), Marhuenda and Ortuño-Ortín's (1995) and Roemer's (1999, 2000) use of voting models to rationalize people's choice of progressive income tax schedules over flat or regressive ones.

7.1.9 Describe the various alternative incidence assumptions for non-income taxes which are employed in Pechman and Okner (1974, chapter 3). Now summarize the arguments of Dilnot et al. (1990).

7.2   The typical income tax

The income tax is, in all countries, a major source of revenue for the government. In the UK the personal income tax accounts for about one-quarter of general government receipts. We have seen some of the rationales for making income taxation progressive; in the next chapter we shall discuss ways to summarize, or capture in a single index number, the *progressivity* of a given income tax. Our purpose here is to describe briefly the main features of the typical income tax. This will call into question the assumption, already made in order to define progression and pervading much subsequent analysis, that the income tax liability of an income unit whose income is x can be written simply as $t(x)$, a function only of x.

First, we consider the matter of the tax unit. This is usually one of the following: single adult person; married person filing a separate tax return; head of household. A child with its own income is another possibility. What we have been calling an income unit may thus in practice be regarded as more than one tax unit. In some countries (e.g. France) there is provision for *income splitting*: a household can apportion its income among the household members, each to be taxed separately, in a way that reduces the total liability (see on). Thus the tax liability of an income unit may depend not only upon that unit's income but also upon its composition.

The division of income units into family types for tax purposes permits ability to pay to be recognized in the tax code. In most countries, some recognition is accorded by assigning fixed (but different) *lump-sum tax allowances*, or amounts of tax-free income, to the different income-unit types. However, tax is often levied at common rates on *taxable income*, which is income net of these and, usually, certain other lump-sum allowances and *income-related deductions*. Additional lump-sum allowances may be given for dependent children and to old people and widow(er)s. A proportionate deduction of (earned) income may also be permitted, along with other deductions for items of expenditure such as mortgage interest payments, childcare costs, charitable giving, medical expenses, life assurance premiums. The tax unit may be able to choose between a lump-sum allowance and an income-related deduction; the choice made depends on which option provides the higher tax-free sum. The lump-sum allowances are variously known as *exemptions* or *abatements*, and the income-related deductions as *reliefs*.[3]

Thus, in practice, an income unit's tax liability depends very much on its non-income characteristics as well as on its income. To formalize what typically pertains, let income-unit types be indexed by i, and let a_i be the lump-sum allowance of an income unit of type i. Further, let $d_i(x)$ be the income-(and/or expenditure-) related deduction if the income of that unit is x. Then the unit's taxable income is $y = x - a_i - d_i(x)$. Typically, tax liability is determined by y alone, as $s(y)$ where $s(\ )$ is an appropriate function embodying the *rate structure* – but, as an additional complication, there may be separate rate structures for the different categories of tax unit (as in the USA). The total of all non-negative taxable incomes across income units is known as the *base* of the tax.

The rate schedule $s(y)$ is usually piecewise linear. That is, a sequence of bands of positive taxable income attract fixed and increasing marginal rates of tax. Let

$$0 < m_0 < m_1 < \ldots < m_p \tag{7.8}$$

be the sequence of marginal rates, and

$$0 = \beta_0 < \beta_1 < \ldots < \beta_p \tag{7.9}$$

be the thresholds which specify the bands of taxable income to which the respective rates apply. The lowest rate m_0 is paid on taxable incomes $y \in (0, \beta_1)$ and the highest rate m_p applies only to taxable incomes $y > \beta_p$. Thus, if $\beta_k \le y \le \beta_{k+1}$, the tax liability is

$$s(y) = \sum_{j \le k-1} m_j(\beta_{j+1} - \beta_j) + m_k(y - \beta_j) \qquad (7.10)$$

whilst if $y \le 0$ then $s(y) = 0$ (figure 7.1). However in Germany the rate schedule is piecewise polynomial.

Many countries give tax credits, to be offset against tax liabilities to determine the final amount of tax due. If tax credits are *refundable*, people with zero or low tax liabilities may collect a net cash benefit at the end of the day. Non-refundable credits cannot be redeemed in this way. If c_i is the tax credit due to an income unit of type i, then the final tax liability becomes either

$$s(x - a_i - d_i(x)) - c_i \qquad (7.11a)$$

in the redeemable case, or

$$\max\{0, s(x - a_i - d_i(x)) - c_i\} \qquad (7.11b)$$

in the non-redeemable case; either way, this is a far cry from the naive form $t(x)$ which we used in the previous section of this chapter.[4]

We conclude this brief description of typical income taxes with some remarks about progression. The common or garden piecewise linear income tax schedule as outlined above has two sources of progression built into it, and one mitigating factor.

It is clear that the structure of ascending marginal rates makes the schedule $s(y)$ progressive on taxable income y, at least for taxable incomes above the first threshold β_1: just consider figure 7.1. Only if there is a single rate of tax m_0 (put $p = 0$ and let $\beta_1 \to \infty$ in (7.8)–(7.10)) are liabilities proportional to taxable incomes.

For income units of a given type i, the lump-sum allowance a_i also contributes to overall progression. Even if the schedule $s(y)$ were proportional, progression would be provided by the presence of a lump-sum allowance. Consider, for example, incomes of £10,000 and £10,100 each attracting the same lump-sum allowance of £4,000. If we assume for the moment no income-related deductions, the one income unit has 1 per cent more gross income than the other, but 1.67 per cent more taxable income and therefore a tax liability at least this much more and a higher average rate of tax than the other.

However it cannot be said that, as between different income unit types i, the average tax rate on gross income increases with income level. You can easily construct a hypothetical example where, say, a single person experiences a higher average tax rate than a married household with several dependents and more gross income. Therefore progression is a meaningful feature only for the income tax as restricted to income units all of the same type. When the tax is so restricted, tax liability is a function of income x alone.

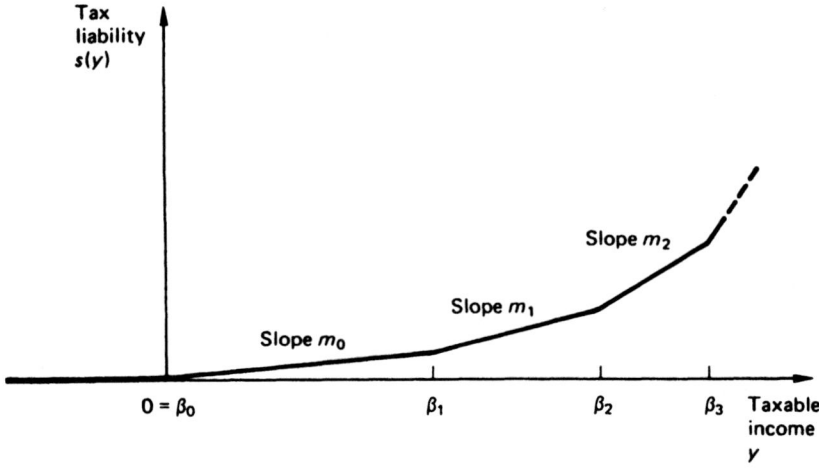

Figure 7.1   The rate schedule $s(y)$ for a typical real-world piecewise-linear income tax

This justifies our writing it as $t(x)$ in the previous section of this chapter, and beyond, for the purposes of analysing the effects of income tax progression.

Income-related deductions also exert an effect upon progression among income units of a given type. Try replacing the £4,000 lump-sum allowance in the example above with a 40 per cent proportionate deduction: what is the differential between taxable incomes in this case? Now replace it with a £3,000 lump-sum allowance plus a 10 per cent deduction. Can you see how the composition of tax-free income affects progression? Certain expenditure-related deductions may rise very rapidly along the income scale, substantially reducing or even reversing the progressive effect of lump-sum components. (Try some figures for the above example: to secure overall regression, you will need to assume that the income elasticity of demand for the appropriate tax expenditure is bigger than one.) Herber (1983, pp. 177–181) calls this effect 'base erosion' and 'dampened progressivity'.

The contribution to overall progression of the structure of allowances and deductions is called the *base effect*, while that of the ascending marginal rate structure is the *rate effect*. We shall consider ways to quantify these two components of income tax progressivity in the next chapter.

Exercises

7.2.1 '. . . the progressive income tax stands alone as a tool for implementing the societal-endorsed, ability-to-pay rule of equity in the distribution of tax burdens. Yet, the actual or effective progressivity of the federal personal income tax is considerably less than its statutory rate structure would suggest . . .' (Herber, 1983, pp. 176–177). Describe the root causes of this phenomenon in the USA, either by reference to Herber's description of the income tax (*ibid.*), or to that of Musgrave and Musgrave (1984, chapters 16 and 17).

7.3   Horizontal and vertical equity

The purpose of the horizontal equity (HE) command generally is to pursue justice and equality and ensure that the law does not serve anybody's self-interest. The purpose of the vertical equity (VE) command is to take appropriately into account different people's relative merits. That word 'appropriately' makes VE a matter of judgement or societal taste, whereas HE can be seen as an absolute. When HE is violated, we say that there is *horizontal inequity*, or HI.

HE in the income tax can be seen as a rule of fairness, offering protection to individuals and families against arbitrary or systematic discrimination and reflecting the basic principle of equal worth. For Pigou (1949, pp. 6, 50), violation of HE by the income tax causes 'a sense of being unfairly treated . . . in itself an evil' and if sanctioned would provide opportunities for 'tyranny, vindictiveness, personal favouritism'. In the UK *Taxpayer's Charter*, it is guaranteed that 'you will be treated in the same way as other taxpayers in similar circumstances'. The purpose is to assure taxpayers that they will neither suffer from capriciousness and error on the part of the taxman nor be subjected to systematic discrimination.

The special income tax schedule for Bantus which used to apply in South Africa during apartheid could be seen as discriminatory, though it was designed to meet their special economic circumstances at the time. The different tax treatment of urban and rural incomes in lesser-developed countries can also be seen as discriminatory (collection difficultues in the rural sector may cause governments simply to impose an agricultural land or head tax). Similarly, taxation that depends on the sources and disposition of people's incomes can cause HI (Gravelle, 1992), as can differences in the way employment and self-employment income are taxed (Freedman and Chamberlain, 1997). HI can also arise when the government grants income tax concessions as an administatively convenient way of encouraging private-sector activities. Many of the deductions described in the last section fall into this category: just consider the reliefs for mortgage interest, childcare costs, charitable giving, medical expenses, life assurance premiums.[5]

How could we detect and quantify the HI in a particular income tax? Should we look for it at the individual or family level? Manser (1979, p. 224) has argued for the family level: 'households who obtain equal utilities in the pre-tax situation should obtain equal utilities after the tax is imposed'. Given a suitable microdata set, we would usually apply an equivalence scale to household money incomes, both before and after tax, and check for cases in which the tax system introduces differences in post-tax living standards where there were none pre-tax. This can happen because of all the factors just mentioned, and it can happen too simply because the income tax is in essence a *money* income tax, not (usually) designed to be consonant with any equivalence scale (though see on for the case of France). HI could also be recorded if the tax designers *did* use an equivalence scale, but not the one selected by the analyst to perform his tests! And of course, if the microdata happens not to contain any pre-tax equals, then no HI can possibly be detected. All of this means that it is not straightforward to measure the HI in an income tax. We consider this issue carefully in chapter 10.

What would a horizontally equitable family income tax with a prescribed degree of vertical equity look like? Why do we not see such taxes in place around the world? In the remainder of the chapter we consider this issue.

Let us assume for ease of presentation and discussion that the only socially relevant differences between households are their pre-tax incomes x and family sizes n, and represent as $\{x_0, n_0\}$ a household with the characteristics $x = x_0$, $n = n_0$. We could be more general than this, with very little pain, by subsuming into n some additional characteristics, making it a vector. For example, to distinguish between the number of adults a and children c in the household, we could replace n by $\mathbf{n} = (a, c)$.

Let the social evaluation function for households be $U(x, n)$. For fixed n, this function, call it $U_n(x)$, may be regarded as defining utility of income. It could satisfy the properties in definition 3.3, p. 75, if increased family size n is judged to connote increased need. (In that case, $U_{n+1}'(x) > U_n'(x) > 0$ and $U_{n+1}''(x) < U_n''(x) < 0$ for all x and all n). But we do not need to make this restriction here.

The starting point for analysis of the equitable income tax is a relation $\sim$ identifying the equals:

$$\{x_1, n_1\} \sim \{x_2, n_2\} \Leftrightarrow U(x_1, n_1) = U(x_2, n_2) \tag{7.12}$$

Any two households with the same pre-tax utility are deemed equals; we do not restrict HE to the equal treatment of *identical* families. To ensure equal treatment of equals we must design a money income tax $t(x, n)$, which takes family size (and any other relevant attributes subsumed in n) into account, such that

$$\{x_1, n_1\} \sim \{x_2, n_2\} \Rightarrow \{x_1 - t(x_1, n_1), n_1\} \sim \{x_2 - t(x_2, n_2), n_2\} \tag{7.13}$$

The way forward is to make the tax $t(x, n)$ act like a tax on utility. Thus we could define $t(x, n)$ implicitly to satisfy an equation

$$U_n(x - t(x, n)) = U_n(x) - \tau(U_n(x)) \tag{7.14}$$

for all x and all n, where $\tau(u)$ is the actual tax on utility.

This construction ensures that (7.13) is satisfied: if two households have equal pre-tax utility levels, they will have equal post-tax utility levels. Hence $t(x, n)$ as in (7.14) is an HE income tax. As for VE, there is scope through the choice of $\tau(\ )$ to design into the tax society's chosen way to tax unequals. For example, the equal sacrifice principle is met by taking $\tau(u) \equiv u_0$ for all u and some constant u_0. The progressive principle would be met in utility terms by making $\tau(u)/u$ an increasing function of u. The restriction $\tau'(u) < 1$ for all u would ensure that post-tax utility is an increasing function of pre-tax utility, which can also be seen as an equity principle (see section 4 in chapter 10 ahead).

If we use an equivalence scale to determine livings standards, the problem of identifying the equals and formulating the equitable income tax becomes a unidimensional one. Let z_n be the equivalence scale deflator for a family of size n. Set $U_n(x) = U(x/z_n)$ for some increasing (and possibly concave) function U. The socially just tax for equivalization follows immediately from (7.14):

$$U_n(x) = U \frac{x}{z_n} \Rightarrow t(x, n) = z_n \, \tau^* \left(\frac{x}{z_n} \right) \tag{7.15}$$

where τ^* is a tax function on living standards which embodies VE.[6] This shows that the socially just money income tax on families should act like a tax on *equivalent income per standard adult*, of whom there are z_n in the household (recall the discussion on p. 71). Vickrey, writing in 1947, forsaw this: 'A more thoroughgoing and equitable procedure [than exemptions and credits] would be to set up some factor indicative of the needs of the entire family, divide the total income by this factor, compute a per capita tax on this 'per capita income', and multiply the tax so computed by the family size factor to obtain the total tax for the family' (Vickrey, 1947, pp. 295–296).

Only in France and Luxembourg has this type of income-splitting been made the basis of the income tax. The rule is known there as the *quotient familial*. The tax function τ^* of (7.15) used in conjunction with this rule is, of course, the schedule which applies directly to the money incomes of single persons. It is progressive in both countries. See Atkinson *et al.* (1987) in respect of France.

Exercises

7.3.1(a) 'In order to better understand how HE and VE fit together, we begin with a consideration of how the court system typically deals with these issues' (Lambert and Yitzhaki, 1995, p. 675). Explain how the search for precedents in determining the punishment to fit a crime is an HE issue, and the application of a tariff or fine system is an expression of VE.

7.3.1(b) What is the distinction raised by Dworkin (1978) between the 'right to equal treatment' and the 'right to treatment as an equal'? Explain how Lambert and Yitzhaki (1995, p. 676) could say in respect of a

US Supreme Court decision that: 'Differentiation between levels of education on wealth grounds was thus seen as a vertical issue and not in conflict with the rights (HE) question'.

7.3.2   'Although many facets of credits and exemptions have been examined in the literature to date ... it has never been thought that, despite the appealing symmetry between the respective implementation procedures – the one correcting income for needs and then taxing, and the other taxing income and then correcting for needs – the one could be equitable and the other *not*' (Lambert and Yitzhaki, 1997, p. 344). Describe the findings of these authors.

7.3.3   Explain Ebert and Moyes' (2000a) use of inequality concepts and equivalizing transformations to identify in a very general context the tax functions for socially heterogeneous populations which are overall inequality-reducing. Assess the validity of their comment, 'the fact that both approaches yield the same factorization is a happy coincidence', in respect of their finding that, for conventional equivalence scales, such a tax function must take the form, that in (7.15), which also derives from horizontal equity considerations.

Notes

1   Snow and Warren (1983) survey the recent literature on benefit (Lindahl) taxes. For reprints of the work of Lindahl, and other early writers in this area, see Musgrave and Peacock (1958) and Musgrave and Shoup (1959).

2   In Lambert (1985c) the argument that progressive income taxation permits a government with 'sticky' revenue sources to maintain a constant share in the economy is found to be unsustainable in a smooth growth model.

3   Steuerle (1983) describes the evolution of allowances and deductions in the USA from 1948 to 1984.

4   In the UK in 1994 the major allowances were restricted so that they became valued at the lowest marginal tax rate for all taxpayers, effectively turning them into non-refundable tax credits. In Germany couples have a choice between allowances and credits. The reader can consult *Inland Revenue Statistics* for the main features of the UK personal income tax and *Statistics of Income: Individual Income Tax Returns* for the US Federal and State income taxes. OECD (1981) contains a comparative survey of income taxes in a number of countries. *Individual Taxes: A Worldwide Summary* gives basic details of income and other individual taxes and tax rates in 117 countries and territories.

5   These implicit forms of government spending have become known as *tax expenditures*. See Willis and Hardwick (1978) for a discussion of this issue with respect to the UK, and OECD (1984) for a wide-ranging review.

6   Write (7.14) as $U_n(x - t(x, n)) = \sigma(U_n(x))$ where $\sigma = \iota - \tau$ and ι is the identity operator. Now let $\sigma^* = U^{-1} \circ \sigma \circ U$. Then $\tau^* = \iota - \sigma^*$.

8

A progressive income tax schedule

We focus in this chapter on the simple model in which the income tax function takes the form $t(x)$, where x is income, keeping in mind the qualifications about relevance raised in the preceding chapter. Since the principal factor affecting allowances and deductions (and sometimes also the rate structure) in real-world income taxes is typically marital status or family size, the reader may think of $t(x)$ as the tax schedule, and $f(x)$ the frequency density function, for a population of single persons, or married couples, or families of a given composition. However, our constructions will apply to any population which is homogeneous in tax-relevant attributes.

As we said in chapter 2 (p. 39), a progressive tax exerts an equalizing effect on the distribution of income, and the tax liabilities themselves are distributed more unequally than the incomes to which they apply (the rich having an even greater share of taxes than of pre-tax income). We shall show in the first section of this chapter that these two properties characterize progressive income taxes. The equalizing property is known as the *redistributive effect* of the tax, and the tax burden property as its *disproportionality* (or *departure* or *deviation from proportionality*). We shall also uncover a welfare recommendation for progression in section 8.1.

In section 8.2, we consider ways to measure the degree of progression along the income scale. Such measures are known as measures of *local* or *structural progression*. The effects of a progressive income tax schedule can also be quantified, once the income distribution to which it will be applied is known, typically by means of index numbers. Such indices are called measures of *effective progression* or *progressivity*.

Progressivity indices encapsulate the entire income tax schedule $t(x)$, and pre-tax income distribution $f(x)$, in a single number. There is not a universally agreed approach to the construction of progressivity indices. Musgrave and Thin (1948, p. 510) advocate basing the index upon redistributive effect: '... effective progression measures the extent to which a given tax structure results in a shift in the distribution of income toward equality', whilst Kakwani (1977b, p. 74) favours disproportionality: '... progressivity ... is supposed to measure the deviation of a tax system from proportionality'. In sections 8.3 and 8.4 we construct some important progressivity indices, based on disproportionality and redistributive effect respectively, which satisfy an important consistency property with the structural measures of section 8.1: given the income distribution, increased structural progression implies increased effective progression (progressivity).

How should progressivity respond if, with the tax schedule fixed, a change in pre-tax income distribution occurs? Musgrave and Thin (1948, p. 510) speculated that '. . . the less equal is the distribution of income before tax, the more potent will be a progressive tax structure in equalizing income', but they did not examine this proposition about redistributive effect analytically. We report on what is known about the effects of pre-tax distributional change on welfare and progressivity at the relevant points in the chapter.

Finally, in section 8.5, we show how the allowances, deductions and marginal rate structure of the typical income tax contribute to structural and effective progression.

8.1   Distributive and welfare effects

The condition for strict progression, in the case of a differentiable tax function $t(x)$, is

$$\frac{d[t(x)/x]}{dx} > 0 \qquad \text{for all } x \tag{8.1}$$

but it is worth making two slight relaxations. One is to allow for points of non-differentiability in $t(x)$, e.g. at the thresholds for the marginal rates in the case of a piecewise linear income tax. In mathematical terms this means that $t(x)$ is differentiable *almost everywhere*, and the distinction between this and full differentiability matters little; (8.1) should apply except at a finite number of points. The second worthwhile relaxation is to weaken (8.1) slightly:

$$\frac{d[t(x)]/x}{dx} \geq 0 \qquad \text{for all } x \tag{8.1a}$$

to admit into the analysis both the case of a tax which is zero below a threshold and that of a flat tax for which $d[t(x)/x]/dx \equiv 0$.

As in chapter 2, pp. 37–38, let $F(x)$ be the pre-tax income distribution function, and $f(x)$ the associated density function. Total income tax revenue is

$$T = N \int t(x) f(x) dx \tag{2.20}$$

and the total tax ratio (or overall average tax rate) is

$$g = \frac{T}{X} = \int \frac{f(x)t(x)dx}{\mu} \tag{2.21}$$

where N is the population size and $X = N\mu$ is the total pre-tax income. We assume $g > 0$ in what follows, thereby excluding from consideration henceforth, for any given tax schedule $t(x)$, income distributions $F(x)$ in which nobody pays tax. (Recall that tax schedules $t(x)$ satisfy

$$0 \le t(x) < x \text{ and } 0 \le t'(x) < 1 \text{ for all } x \qquad (2.19)$$

permitting zero taxation below a positive threshold income level). Since μ is mean pre-tax income, μg is the average tax liability and $\mu(1 - g)$ is the mean post-tax income.

The Lorenz curve for pre-tax income, $L_X(p)$, is defined by

$$p = F(y) \Rightarrow L_X(p) = \int_0^y \frac{xf(x)\,\mathrm{d}x}{\mu} \qquad 0 \le p \le 1 \qquad (2.22)$$

and if L_{X-T} and L_T respectively are the concentration curves for post-tax income and for tax liabilities, then we have

$$p = F(y) \Rightarrow L_{X-T}(p) = \int_0^y \frac{[x - t(x)]f(x)\,\mathrm{d}x}{\mu(1 - g)} \qquad (2.23)$$

and

$$p = F(y) \Rightarrow L_T(p) = \int_0^y \frac{t(x)f(x)\,\mathrm{d}x}{\mu g} \qquad (2.24)$$

Under assumption (2.19) there is no reranking of income units in the transition from pre-tax to post-tax income (because post-tax income $x - t(x)$ is an increasing function of pre-tax income x). This means that the concentration curves L_{X-T} and L_T coincide with the Lorenz curves for post-tax income and tax liabilities respectively (recall the discussion on p. 39).

The relationship between the curves L_X, L_{X-T} and L_T was also established in chapter 2

$$L_X \equiv g L_T + (1 - g) L_{X-T} \qquad (2.25)$$

The Lorenz curve L_X is a weighted average of tax and post-tax income concentration curves. Therefore

$$L_{X-T} \ge L_X \Leftrightarrow L_T \le L_X \qquad (2.26)$$

The income shares of given quantiles in the pre-tax distribution are more equal after tax than before if and only if tax liabilities are distributed more unequally than pre-tax incomes.

When the income tax is progressive, these two equivalent properties can be proven. Moreover, they characterize progressive income taxation. This important result was proved first by Jakobsson (1976) and Fellman (1976); we follow the elegant approach taken by Kakwani (1977a) in the proof given below.

Theorem 8.1

$d[t(x)/x]/dx \geq 0$ for all $x \Leftrightarrow L_{X-T} \geq L_X \geq L_T$ for every pre-tax income distribution $F(x)$.[1]

Proof $\Rightarrow$ Let $F(x)$ be a given pre-tax income distribution function, and define a mapping h: $[0, 1] \to [0, 1]$ from pre-tax Lorenz curve values to tax concentration curve values, as follows:

$$h(L_X(p)) = L_T(p) \qquad (8.2)$$

for $0 \leq p \leq 1$. Because of (2.26) above, it is enough to prove

$$h(q) \leq q \text{ for all } q \in [0,1] \qquad (8.3)$$

Clearly

$$h(0) = 0 \qquad h(1) = 1 \qquad (8.4)$$

Now differentiate with respect to p:

$$h'(L_X(p))L_X'(p) = L_T'(p) \qquad (8.5)$$

This reduces to

$$h'(L_X(p)) = \frac{t(y)}{ty} \qquad (8.6)$$

where $p = F(y)$, from lemma 2.1, p. 32 and exercise 2.5.1(a), p. 41. In particular, since we have excluded negative income taxation from consideration (until chapter 11),

$$h'(q) \geq 0 \text{ for all } q \in [0, 1] \qquad (8.7)$$

The result (8.3) will follow if we can establish convexity of h, i.e. if

$$h''(q) \geq 0 \text{ for all } q \qquad (8.8)$$

(try sketching a graph of $h(q)$ using the information in (8.4), (8.7) and (8.8)). But convexity is immediate because, from (8.6) and by supposition, $h'(L_X(p))$ is increasing in y.

   The $\Leftarrow$ proof needs only a minor additional argument. Suppose, for a contradiction, that $d[t(x)/x]/dx$ is negative on some interval $[x^*, x^{**}]$. Then, for any income distribution whose support is contained within $[x^*, x^{**}]$, taxation according to $t(x)$ is regressive. Therefore, for such a distribution, we have $L_{X-T} \leq L_X \leq L_T$: this follows by changing the inequalities in the $\Rightarrow$ proof, and provides the required contradiction.   QED

   Notice that we have used the non-strict definition of progression in this theorem. The reader can verify that if $d[t(x)/x] dx > 0$ for all x then $L_{X-T}(p)$

$> L_X(p) > L_T(p)$ for all $p \in (0, 1)$, and that only in the case of a proportional tax are L_{X-T}, L_X and L_T coincident.

A progressive income tax is inequality-reducing, but this is not to say that an income tax comprising component schedules which are separately progressive on distinct subgroups (the married and single, say) will necessarily be overall inequality-reducing. It need not be. See exercise 8.1.3, which makes this point quite dramatically.[2]

In what sense can progressive income taxation be seen as 'a good thing'? We know from the Jakobsson–Fellman result that it is inequality-reducing. But this does not imply a welfare improvement. Indeed, positive taxation *per se*, progressive or not, can only reduce social welfare (as long as we do not consider redistribution of the proceeds). Just consider the pre-tax/post-tax generalized Lorenz curve configuration:

$$p = F(y) \Rightarrow GL_{X-T}(p) = \int_0^y [x - t(x)] f(x) \, dx \le \int_0^y x f(x) \, dx = GL_X(p) \qquad (8.9)$$

By the Shorrocks theorem 3.2 (see p. 49), income taxation reduces social welfare according to every individualistic, symmetric, additively separable and inequality-averse social welfare function. Clearly we must look to the other side of the coin, which is the way benefits from government activity are conferred on income units, to find a welfare rationale for income taxation. But progression in the income tax schedule is for sure 'a good thing' compared with another obvious way to raise the same revenue from the same pre-tax income distribution.

Theorem 8.2

Progressive income taxation reduces social welfare by less than an equal-yield flat tax applied to the same pre-tax incomes.

Proof If the income tax were proportional, the Lorenz curve for post-tax income would coincide with that for pre-tax income because the tax would have no effect on relative income differentials. Now consider the generalized Lorenz curve after progressive income taxation. By the Jakobsson–Fellman theorem 8.1, we have

$$GL_{X-T}(p) = \mu(1-g)L_{X-T}(p) \ge \mu(1-g)L_X(p) \qquad (8.10)$$

for all $p \in [0, 1]$. The result follows using the Shorrocks theorem, because $\mu(1-g)L_X(p)$ is the generalized Lorenz curve for income after the flat tax with the same yield.   QED

We do not assert that a change from progressive to proportionate income taxation could be made without affecting the pre-tax income distribution.

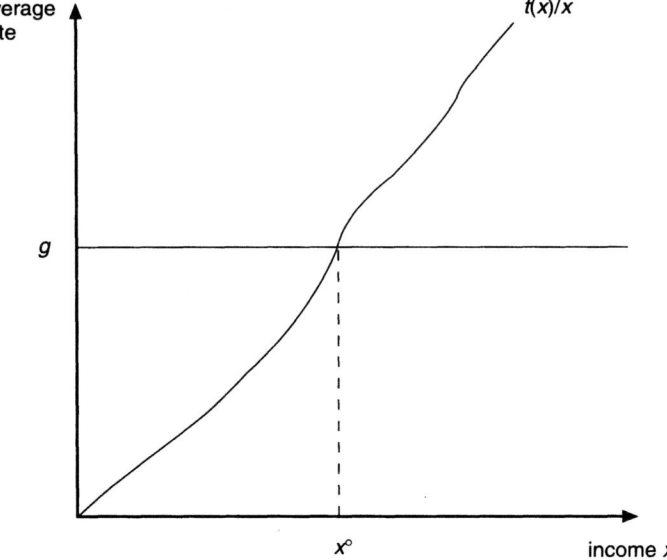

Figure 8.1   Average tax rates for progressive and proportional income taxes

This is unlikely to be the case. Theorem 8.2 provides a rationale for progression *given the pre-tax income distribution*. Put another way, the *impact effect* of progression on a given income distribution is favourable compared with that of proportional taxation.

In fact the result in theorem 8.2 does not depend upon the Jakobsson–Fellman and Shorrocks theorems. Consider figure 8.1, in which the average tax rate is plotted against income for both the progressive tax $t(x)$ and also the equal yield flat tax whose rate is g. One graph is increasing and the other is, literally, 'flat'. The two lines must cross somewhere; let x^n be this point; it defines the 'break-even' income level between those paying less than their proportional share, g, of the total tax burden and those paying more. Plainly, the progressive profile could be achieved by first imposing flat tax at rate g, then taking more income from the rich (those with $x > x^\circ$) and giving some back to the poor (for whom $x < x^\circ$). Since the two taxes raise the same revenue overall by construction, *all of* the extra taken from the rich must be given back to the poor to create the progressive profile. That is, *any progressive income tax can be considered equivalent to a flat tax with the same yield plus appropriate rich-to-poor transfers*. This is precisely why we call a progressive income tax 'redistributive' (recall the discussion on p. 39). Now look again at the wording of theorem 8.2. Since every inequality-averse SWF values rich-to-poor transfers, this result is immediate.

An interesting general question concerns the effect on post-tax social welfare of changes in the pre-tax income distribution. If pre-tax incomes are becoming more equally distributed through time, and the income tax is progressive and fixed, what is happening to social welfare after tax? This question can be addressed very simply if we impose a further restriction on the form of the tax schedule $t(x)$.

Theorem 8.3

If the income tax $t(x)$ is convex, post-tax social welfare is raised by an equalizing shift in the pre-tax income distribution.

Convexity is not a very significant additional restriction to impose. In the non-strict form it admits piecewise linear taxes with lump-sum allowances. Indeed convexity implies progression under a very weak condition (see exercise 8.1.7).

The proof of theorem 8.3 is very simple. Suppose that a change takes place in the pre-tax income distribution causing the Lorenz curve L_x to shift inwards but leaving the mean (or total) income unaffected. Then, by the Atkinson theorem 3.1 (see p. 45), for any concave utility-of-pretax-income function $U(x)$, social welfare $\int U(x)f(x)\,dx$ is increased. Now let $V(x)$ be an arbitrary concave utility-of-*post*-tax-income function, and set $U(x) = V[x - t(x)]$. If $t(x)$ is convex then $U(x)$ is concave. The result follows.

We conclude this section by observing that the defining property of progression, as in (8.1), has an intertemporal implication as well as distributive ones. Progression says not only that the average tax rate increases with income *as between income units*, but also that the average tax rate *experienced by a fixed income unit* increases with growth in that unit's income. Unless the tax schedule is revised between time periods, progression makes individual tax liabilities elastic to any growth which may take place in incomes, and so total revenue is also elastic to income growth through time. Indeed, one perceived problem with the typical income tax is its response to purely inflationary income growth. If the allowances and thresholds for the marginal rates are specified in nominal (cash) terms, then income inflation can push people into higher tax rates despite no underlying change in their real incomes. Indeed, by mid-1977, concern was expressed in the UK House of Commons over its loss of control of the burden of the income tax because of inflation. The Rooker–Wise Amendment to the Finance Act enacted that year required that allowances automatically be indexed to the Retail Price Index (RPI) in future, and subsequent legislation also required the thresholds to be so indexed (from 1981/2). We do not pursue issues of indexation and so-called *fiscal drag* here, but see exercises 8.1.9–8.1.10.[3]

Exercises

8.1.1   Show that $p = F(y) \Rightarrow L_{X-T}(p) - L_X(p) = \int_0^y x[g - t(x)/x] f(x) \, dx/\mu(1 - g)$ and deduce that if $t(x)$ is progressive the derivative with respect to y of this function has a single sign change, being first positive (consider figure 8.1). Use this finding to provide an alternative proof to the one in theorem 8.1 that progression guarantees inequality reduction.

8.1.2   Describe the nature of the extensions made by Eichhorn *et al.* (1984) and Thon (1987) and Arnold (1990) to the Jakobsson–Fellman theorem.

8.1.3   Suppose that single people are taxed progressively and married people are taxed progressively. By determining what obtains in the case of the simple example below, show that the income tax need not be overall inequality-reducing:

Type i	1 = single			2 = married		
Income x	3	4	5	6	7	8
Tax $t(x)$	1	2	3	0	1	2

Now examine Lambert's (1993a) extension of the Jakobsson–Fellman theorem, specifying conditions under which progressive but different tax schedules for the single and the married will act in combination to reduce overall income inequality. Which of Lambert's three conditions is violated by this example? Can you say whether this income tax is welfare superior or inferior to an equal-yield proportional income tax on all income units regardless of marital status?

8.1.4   'From this it can be concluded that if the tax system is progressive, the posttax distribution will be more equally distributed than the pretax income distribution, even if there is tax evasion . . .' (Kakwani, 1980a, p. 237). Describe the model Kakwani uses, and the assumptions which yield this result.

8.1.5   What stronger condition than progression does Mukherjee (1997, pp. 159–161) show is necessary and sufficient to ensure that a tax function $t(x)$ unambiguously reduces relative deprivation at all income levels no matter what the pretax income distribution?

8.1.6   In exercise 3.2.4, p. 56, the absolute Lorenz curve of an income distribution was defined. What property of an income tax schedule $t(x)$ is required to ensure that the post-tax income distribution has a higher absolute Lorenz curve than the pre-tax income distribution? See Moyes (1988).

8.1.7   Suppose that the income tax function $t(x)$ is convex and that $t(0) =$ 0. Prove that $t(x)$ is progressive. *Hint:* For $y > x$, $t(y)/y > t(x)/x \Leftrightarrow$ $[t(y) - t(x)]/(y - x) > [t(x) - t(0)]/(x - 0)$; now use the intermediate value theorem for differentiation (see p. 10).

8.1.8(a) Let $\{y\}$ and $\{z\}$ be two pre-tax income distributions whose generalized Lorenz curves do not cross: $GL_Y \geq GL_Z$. Suppose, further, that a common income tax schedule $t(x)$ applies which is convex. Prove that generalized Lorenz dominance is preserved in the transition to post-tax income: $GL_{Y-T} \geq GL_{Z-T}$. *Hint:* Use the Shorrocks theorem.

8.1.8(b) How is this result strengthened and extended in Moyes (1989)?

8.1.9   Write total income tax revenue T as a function of total pre-tax income X: $T(X) = N\int t(x)f(x)\,dx$. Suppose each income x grows to kx where $k > 1$. Explain why $T(kX) = N\int t(kx)f(x)\,dx$. Now differentiate with respect to k and let $k \to 1$. Hence prove that the elasticity of revenue to equiproportionate growth in incomes, $XT'(X)/T(X)$, exceeds unity for every pre-tax income distribution if and only if $t(x)$ is progressive.

8.1.10   Consider an inflation-indexed income tax $t(x) = Ps(x/P)$, where x is nominal income, P is the price level and $s(z)$ is the fixed real tax on real income $z = x/P$. Letting the total revenue function be $T(X) = PS(X/P)$, differentiate with respect to time to show that the proportionate growth rate of revenue is given by $[T'/T] = ([X'/X] - \pi)e + \pi$, where e is the real revenue elasticity and π is the rate of inflation ($\pi = P'/P$).

8.1.11   Let $x^{(1)}, x^{(2)}, x^{(3)}, \ldots, x^{(n)}$ be the incomes, not all the same, earned by the n members of a certain household in a given tax year. Alternatively, think of the $x^{(i)}$ as a dated stream of incomes accruing to the household in years $i = 1, 2, \ldots, n$. Suppose that the tax schedule is convex. Show that if the income unit could be taxed n times over on the average of its income across components, $x° = \Sigma x^{(i)}/n$, rather than being taxed separately on each component, then the total liability would be reduced. *Hint:* show $t(x°) \leq \Sigma t(x^{(i)})/n$ using Jensen's inequality.[4]

8.1.12(a) Suppose that this period's income y is repeated next period supplemented by interest on savings; $x = y + rS(y)$ will be next period's income where $S(y)$ is the savings function and r is the interest rate. Show that if $S(y)$ is progressive, x will be distributed more unequally than y.

8.1.12(b) Now suppose that there is an income tax $t(\ )$, so that $x = y + rS(y - t(y))$. Sketch Richter's (1984) analysis, which addresses the question 'Will progressive taxation . . . offset the dispersing effect of savings?' (*ibid.*, p. 140) by examining the Lorenz configuration of the distributions of $y - t(y)$ and $x - t(x)$. How was Richter (1984, p. 152) able to show that: '*marginal* tax rates must strictly increase to offset the dispersing effect of progressive Keynesian savings on residual income. Strictly increasing *average* tax rates are not sufficient'?[5]

8.2　The degree of progression

Progression in the income tax schedule introduces disproportionality into the distribution of the tax burden and exerts a redistributive effect on the distribution of income. In order to explore these properties further, we need to be able to measure the degree of income tax progression along the income scale. Such measures are called measures of *structural progression* (sometimes, measures of *local progression*). There is more than one possibility, as we will see. Each such measure will induce a partial ordering on the set of all possible income tax schedules. We could not expect always to be able to rank a schedule $t_2(x)$ unambiguously more, or less, structurally progressive than another schedule $t_1(x)$: we must allow that a schedule could display more progression in one income range and less in another.

Nevertheless, the policymaker and tax practitioner, and indeed the man in the street, would like to be able to say which of any two alternative income tax systems is the more progressive *in its effects*. Is the federal income tax in the USA more redistributive than the personal income tax in Germany? This sort of question will take us, in sections 8.3 and 8.4 ahead, from measures of structural progression to measures of *effective progression*. Measuring effective progression is a matter of reducing a tax schedule and income distribution pair to a scalar index number. The same schedule $t(x)$ could be more progressive *in effect* when applied to distribution A than to distribution B. Trends in effective progression for a given country over time, as well as differences between the income taxes of different countries, can be examined using such index numbers.

Let us begin by defining as $m(x)$ and $a(x)$ respectively the marginal and average rates of tax experienced by an income x:

$$a(x) = \frac{t(x)}{x} \quad \text{and} \quad m(x) = t'(x) \tag{8.11}$$

Since

$$\frac{d[t(x)]/x}{dx} = \frac{xt'(x) - t(x)}{x^2} = \frac{m(x) - a(x)}{x} \tag{8.12}$$

for strict progression it is necessary and sufficient that

$$m(x) > a(x) \text{ for all } x \tag{8.13}$$

The strict inequality rules out the possibility that the tax could be proportional to income in any interval: we may relax it if we wish. Measures of structural progression quantify, in various ways, the excess of the marginal rate $m(x)$ over the average rate $a(x)$ at income level x. We introduce two particularly important measures here.

First, *liability progression* $LP(x)$ is defined at any income level x for which $t(x) > 0$ as the elasticity of tax liability to pre-tax income:

$$LP(x) = e^{t(x), x} = \frac{xt'(x)}{t(x)} = \frac{m(x)}{a(x)} > 1 \qquad (8.14)$$

As we have already noted, for a strictly progressive income tax a 1 per cent increase in pre-tax income x leads to an increase of more than 1 per cent in tax liability. $LP(x)$ measures the actual percentage increase experienced. A change of tax schedule which, for some x_0, causes an increase in $LP(x_0)$ connotes, in an obvious sense, an increase in progression at that income level x_0. If the change in a strictly positive income tax involves an upward shift of the entire function $LP(x)$, then the tax has become everywhere more liability progressive.

Second, *residual progression* $RP(x)$ is defined at all income levels x as the elasticity of post-tax income to pre-tax income:

$$RP(x) = e^{x - t(x), x} = \frac{x[1 - t'(x)]}{x - t(x)} = \frac{1 - m(x)}{1 - a(x)} < 1 \qquad (8.15)$$

The counterpart to the observation above is that a 1 per cent increase in pre-tax income x leads to an increase of less than 1 per cent in post-tax income. $RP(x)$ measures the actual percentage increase in post-tax income. A *reduction* in $RP(x)$ must clearly be interpreted as an *increase in progression*, according to this measure.

These measures were first proposed by Musgrave and Thin (1948). It is inconvenient that $RP(x)$ should decrease when the tax becomes more progressive. We therefore make a minor change of definition in this book, which is not standard in all of the literature, replacing the measure $RP(x)$ by its reciprocal:

$$RP^*(x) = \frac{1}{RP(x)} = \frac{1 - a(x)}{1 - m(x)} > 1 \qquad (8.15a)$$

$RP^*(x)$ can be interpreted as the elasticity of pre-tax income to post-tax income. An increase in $RP^*(x)$ makes the tax more residually progressive at x.

Each of these measures quantifies in its own way the excess of the marginal rate of tax over the average rate of tax at the income level x, and accordingly induces a different partial ordering on the set of all tax schedules (see exercises 8.2.1–8.2.2). Equipped with these measures, we shall, in the next two sections of the chapter, be able to demonstrate that if the income tax becomes structurally more progressive, and the pre-tax income distribution does not change, then this implies enhanced deviation from proportionality (in the case of liability progression) and enhanced redistributive effect (in the case of residual progression).

Exercises

8.2.1   Suppose that taxation is linear above a threshold: $t(x) = \max\ \{0, m(x-a)\}$ where a is a lump-sum allowance and m the marginal rate for taxpayers. Calculate $LP(x)$ for $x > a$ and $RP^*(x)$ for all x. Now suppose that the allowance and marginal rate are subject to change. Show that for taxpayers who remain taxpayers after these changes, the effect on the respective measures of progression is in the same direction as the effect on $\pi_L = a$ and $\pi_R = ma/(1-m)$ respectively. What is the effect on residual progression for someone whose income lies between the old and new values of the allowance a?[6]

8.2.2   Show that for any positive income tax, $LP(x) = RP(x) + [1 - RP(x)]/a(x)$. Conclude that a tax cut of the form: $t_1(x) \rightarrow t_2(x) = t_1(x) - c[x - t_1(x)]$ for all x increases liability progression at every income level while leaving residual progression unaffected. What sort of tax cut leaves liability progression unaffected, and what is the effect of such a cut on residual progression?[7]

8.2.3(a) Let the income tax liability be $t(x) = s(x - d(x)) > 0$, where $d(x)$ is a deduction and $s(y)$ is the schedule defining tax in terms of taxable income $y = x - d(x)$. By proving that $LP_t(x) = LP_s(y)/RP_d^*(x)$, show that progression in the schedule $s(y)$ is not enough to guarantee progression in tax liabilities $t(x)$.

8.2.3(b) How is $RP_d^*(x)$ related to the income elasticity of demand for tax-deductible expenditure items? Under what condition does $d(x)$ dampen progression of the rate structure $s(y)$ to such an extent that the schedule $t(x)$ is actually regressive?

8.2.4   How do Dilnot *et al.* (1984) model mortgage interest relief for the UK income tax? How do they describe the overall UK tax schedule? Defining effective progression as liability or residual progression evaluated at the mean income level in each year, what do Dilnot *et al.* conclude about trends in overall progressivity for the UK income tax since 1948?

8.2.5   Obtain the liability and residual progression measures for a combined income tax $t(x) = t_1(x) + t_2(x)$ in terms of the corresponding measures for its components. Now confirm Ebert and Lambert's (1999) findings that 'overall progression does not demand that each component be progressive *per se*' and (for residual progression) that '$t(x)$ can be more progressive than $t_1(x)$ even when $t_2(x)$ is regressive' (pp. 399–400). What is the significance of the latter finding for the case of the combined British income tax and National Insurance Contribution (which is levied up to a ceiling earnings level)?

8.2.6   Recall Besley and Preston's (1988) concept of μ^*-*inequality equiva-*
lence, where $\mu^* \in [0, \infty)$ is a parameter denominated in units of
income (exercise 5.2.17, p. 120). Describe Besley and Preston's axiom
set for a measure of structural progression, according to which, *inter
alia*, two tax schedules which always yield μ^*-inequality equivalent
distributions of post-tax income should be equally progressive.
Describe the measure of progression which emerges from their
axioms, and show that $t(x)$ is progressive according to this measure
if and only if $d[t(x)/(x + \mu^*)]/dx > 0$ for all x, so that distributional
judgements according to the μ^*-inequality concept can be viewed as
relative inequality judgements on translated distributions.[8]

8.3   Departure from proportionality

As we saw in the last chapter, income tax liabilities depart in a systematic way
from proportionality to pre-tax incomes in the case of a progressive tax. In
the case of a strictly positive income tax, $t(x) > 0$ for all $x > 0$, a formal link
has been established by Jakobsson (1976), and independently by Kakwani
(1977a), between changes in liability progression and changes in the distribution of the tax burden. Their result characterizes the distributive consequence of an increase in liability progression $LP(x)$ at every income level
when the pre-tax income distribution is fixed. The case of an income tax
which is positive only above a threshold income level must be dealt with separately (see on).

Let $t^1(x)$ and $t^2(x)$ be two income tax schedules. Given any particular distribution of pre-tax income, say with distribution function $F(x)$, let L_T^1 and
L_T^2 be the concentration curves for the tax burden induced by the respective
schedules. The Jakobsson–Kakwani result in fact generalizes the result of
Jakobsson (1976) and Fellman (1976) that we gave in theorem 8.1.

Theorem 8.4

For strictly positive taxes $t^1(x)$ and $t^2(x)$, $LP^2(x) \geq LP^1(x)$ for all $x \Leftrightarrow L_T^2 \leq L_T^1$ for every pre-tax income distribution $F(x)$.

Thus, increases in liability progression are associated with enhanced
disproportionality for every pre-tax income distribution. The reader may
confirm that the Jakobsson–Fellman result (theorem 8.1) is recovered by
putting $LP^1(x) \equiv 1$, i.e. making schedule $t^1(x)$ proportional. The proof of the
more general result follows along the same lines as before, and is therefore
only outlined here.

Proof $\Rightarrow$ Define a mapping $h: [0, 1] \to [0, 1]$ from tax concentration curve
values under schedule 1 to those under schedule 2, as follows:

$$h[L_T^1(p)] = L_T^2(p) \qquad 0 \le p \le 1 \tag{8.16}$$

Differentiate with respect to p:

$$h'(L_T^1(p)) = \frac{t^2(y)/\mu g^2}{t^1(y)/\mu g^1} > 0 \tag{8.17}$$

where $p = F(y)$ and g^1 and g^2 are the respective total tax ratios. Now take logarithms and differentiate again. The conclusion is

$$\text{sign } h''(L_T^1(p)) = \text{sign}[LP^2(y) - LP^1(y)] \tag{8.18}$$

So $h(q)$ is increasing and convex under the given assumptions, and of course $h(0) = 0$ and $h(1) = 1$. It follows that $h(q) \le q$ for all q. The proof in the $\Leftarrow$ direction is exactly as in theorem 8.1   QED

   You can confirm that if there is a strict increase in liability progression, $LP^2(x) > LP^1(x)$ for every income x, then the entire concentration curve for tax liabilities is shifted outwards: $L_T^2(p) < L_T^1(p)$ for all $p \in (0, 1)$; and that $L_T^2 \equiv L_T^1$ for every pre-tax income distribution if and only if $LP^2(x) \equiv LP^1(x)$.
   Theorem 8.4 has wider application than its wording may suggest. In the following more general form, it will be useful later.[9]

Lemma 8.1

Let $m(x) > 0$ and $n(x) > 0$ be two attributes of an income or other distributed variate x. The concentration curve for $m(x)$ with respect to x lies nowhere below the concentration curve for $n(x)$ if and only if $e^{m(x),x} \le e^{n(x),x}$ for all x.

   The case of a tax schedule having a threshold income level $a > 0$, below which there is no taxation, is not covered by theorem 8.4. In the proof above, for example, it was vital that $t^1(y) > 0$ and $t^2(y) > 0$ for the establishment of (8.17) and (8.18); did you notice this? Neither Jakobsson (1976) nor Kakwani (1977a) took explicit account of tax thresholds in stating and proving their results, causing Keen *et al.* (2000, pp. 52–53) to comment that 'by [so] restricting attention . . . the literature has immediately removed from consideration – unwittingly it seems – all tax schemes likely to be encountered in practice'. Keen *et al.* went on to provide an extended version of theorem 8.4 which covers this case.

Theorem 8.5

For taxes $t^1(x)$ and $t^2(x)$ with thresholds a^1 and a^2, $L_T^2 \le L_T^1$ for every admissible pre-tax income distribution $F(x)$ if and only if (i) $a^1 \ge a^2$ and (ii) $LP^2(x) \ge LP^1(x)$ for all $x > a^1$.

The new theorem collapses back to the old one in the case that $a^1 = a^2 = 0$. The word 'admissible' in its statement reminds us that, as once before (for theorem 8.1), income distributions must be excluded from consideration in which nobody at all is a taxpayer.

Disproportionality in the distribution of the tax burden is evidenced by the separation of the curves L_X and L_T. The greater this separation, the more pronounced the effect. What can we read into the term $L_X(p) - L_T(p) \geq 0$ which measures the distance apart of L_X and L_T at rank p in the pre-tax income distribution? The lowest-ranked $100p$ per cent of income units receive $100L_X(p)$ per cent of pre-tax income and pay the smaller share $100L_T(p)$ per cent of total tax. What does the difference in percentages tell us? It is more illuminating to think of L_X as the concentration curve for tax liabilities that would obtain under an equal-yield flat tax. *The distance $[L_X(p) - L_T(p)]$ is that fraction of the total tax burden shifted from low incomes (the bottom $100p$ per cent) to high incomes (the top $100(1-p)$ per cent) by the presence of progression in the tax.*

We can define indices of progressivity in terms of the separation of the curves L_X and L_T. Kakwani (1977b) proposed an index which measures (twice) the area between L_X and L_T:

$$\Pi^K = 2\int_0^1 [L_X(p) - L_T(p)]\,\mathrm{d}p \tag{8.19}$$

Recalling the definitions of the Gini coefficient for pre-tax income:

$$G_X = 1 - 2\int_0^1 L_X(p)\,\mathrm{d}p \tag{2.15}$$

and the analogous concentration coefficient for tax liabilities:

$$C_T = 1 - 2\int_0^1 L_T(p)\,\mathrm{d}p \tag{2.32}$$

we see that the Kakwani index can also be written:

$$\Pi^K = C_T - G_X \tag{8.20}$$

This index can be extended, putting a distributional judgement parameter at our disposal. Recall the definition of the extended Gini coefficient given in chapter 5 (p. 115):

$$G_X(v) = 1 - v(v-1)\int_0^1 (1-p)^{v-2} L_X(p)\,\mathrm{d}p \tag{5.19}$$

for $v > 1$. Compare it with (2.15) just above. The analogous extension:

$$\Pi^K(v) = v(v-1)\int_0^1 (1-p)^{v-2}[L_X(p) - L_T(p)]dp = C_T(v) - G_X(v) \qquad (8.21)$$

of the Kakwani index is suggested, where $C_T(v)$ is an extended concentration coefficient for tax liabilities. The analyst must select a value (or range of values) of v for comparisons of effective progression using $\Pi^K(v)$. This index focuses more on disproportionality towards the lower end of the income scale as v is increased (see p. 116). This is a useful feature, not least for analysing regimes in which neither schedule is everywhere structurally more progressive than the other and/or there are differences of income distribution between regimes.

Both Π^K and $\Pi^K(v)$ increase if the liability progression of a strictly positive income tax is increased at every income level, provided that the pre-tax income distribution remains the same. This is because the term $[L_X(p) - L_T(p)]$ in the integrand increases in accordance with theorem 8.4. Hence Π^K and $\Pi^K(v)$ satisfy the consistency property with structural progression we mentioned earlier (p. 188): given the income distribution, increased structural progression implies increased effective progression (progressivity).

A different way of looking at things was proposed by Suits (1977). Independently of Kakwani, but around the same time, Suits set up a framework of analysis in terms of *relative concentration curves*, instead of concentration curves, to examine disproportionality. The idea is to consider the concentration of tax liabilities directly as a function of the concentration of pre-tax incomes. Thus the relative concentration curve for taxes, $R_T(q)$ say, plots cumulated portions of the tax burden falling on various cumulated portions of pre-tax income:

$$q = L_X(p) \Rightarrow R_T(q) = L_T(p) \qquad (8.22)$$

For a flat tax, $R_T(q) = q$; the 45° line provides the reference line for proportional taxation. Moreover $R_T(q)$ is upward-sloping and convex if the tax is progressive (figure 8.2). To see this, just differentiate (8.22) with respect to $p = F(y)$:

$$R_T'(q)L_X'(p) = L_T'(p) \Rightarrow R_T'(q) = \frac{t(y)}{ty} \qquad (8.23)$$

(In fact, $R_T(q)$ is the function $h(q)$ used in the proof of theorem 8.1, p. 190).

Suits defines aggregate disproportionality as twice the area between the relative concentration curve $R_T(q)$ for taxes and the 45° line:

$$\Pi^S = 2\int_0^1 [q - R_T(q)]dq \qquad (8.24)$$

This is the analogue of the Kakwani index Π^K in the other framework.[10] The similarity and the difference between these two indices are evident if we substitute in (8.24) from (8.22)

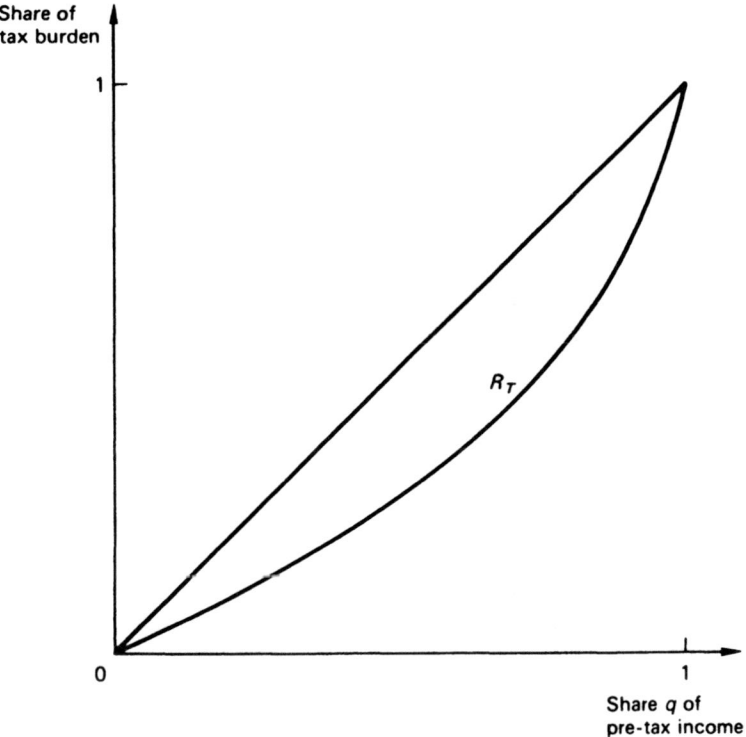

Figure 8.2   The relative concentration curve $R_r(q)$ for taxes

$$\Pi^S = 2\int_0^1 [L_X(p) - L_T(p)]L_X'(p)\,\mathrm{d}p \tag{8.25}$$

and compare with

$$\Pi^K = 2\int_0^1 [L_X(p) - L_T(p)]\,\mathrm{d}p \tag{8.19}$$

The Suits index can be obtained à la Kakwani by attaching a weighting factor $L_X'(p)$ to the distance between ordinary concentration curves at each percentile point p before integrating. The weight is income relative to the mean. Plainly, this weighting procedure yields an index of effective progression which will rank tax schedule and income distribution pairs differently from the Kakwani index. You should consult Formby et al. (1981) for a discussion of this issue.

An attractive property of the Suits index, not shared by the Kakwani index, is that its value lies between $\Pi^S = -1$ and $\Pi^S = +1$, the former being the case

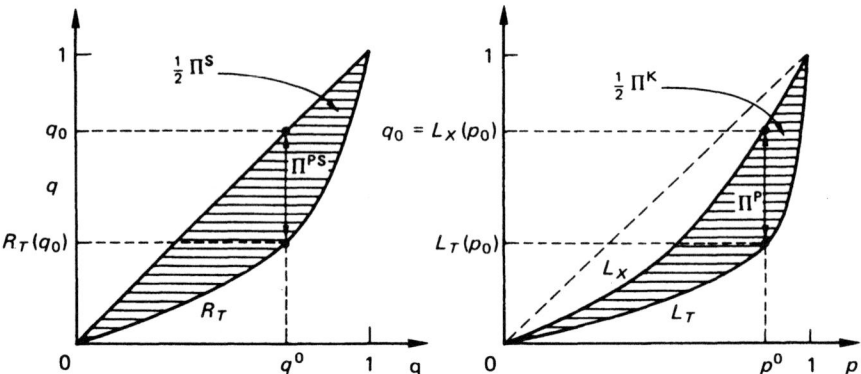

Figure 8.3   The indices Π^K, Π^S and $\Pi^P = \Pi^{PS}$ of departure from proportionality

when the poorest person pays all the tax (extreme regression) and the latter when the richest person does (extreme progression). These are useful benchmarks for appreciation of intervening values. The bounds for the Kakwani index, on the other hand, depend on inequality in the pre-tax income distribution. From (8.20), they are: $-(1 + G_X)$ for maximal regression and $(1 - G_X)$ for maximal progression. Figure 8.3 shows the Kakwani and Suits progressivity indices (along with two other indices, Π^P and Π^{PS}, defined in exercise 8.3.4).

At the beginning of chapter 6, we discussed several rationales for having progression in the income tax. One of these, the benefit principle, is explicitly concerned with the distribution of the tax burden, seeking to relate this with the expenditure side of the government budget. As Pfähler (1988) points out, in choosing to measure progressivity in terms of disproportionality, we secure measures with a particular usefulness: '[This effect] is of primary normative interest if one is concerned with the issue of an equitable distribution of the public good tax burden' (Pfähler, 1988, p. 538).

We conclude our examination of disproportionality at this point (but see exercises 8.3.4–8.3.5 below for further measures). As Pfähler (1988, p. 538) also observes, 'by shifting part of the tax burden from low to high pre-tax income recipients, the progressive tax simultaneously shifts part of the total after-tax income from high to low income recipients'. We turn next to this other feature – the redistributive impact of a progressive income tax. We shall see how the two are related, and later how for a typical income tax schedule the base and rate effects combine to account for overall progressivity.

Exercises

8.3.1   'Does a rise in allowances increase or decrease progressivity? If one assesses progressivity in terms of the distribution of tax payments, the requirement for an unambiguous rise in progressivity . . . [is] that the tax schedule is log concave . . . This property is quite distinct from any existing concept of progressivity, and its potential importance in tax analysis has not been noticed previously' (Keen *et al.*, 2000, p. 65). Give an account of Keen *et al.*'s analysis, and assess the significance of their findings for tax policy.

8.3.2(a) Prove that the Kakwani progressivity index can be expressed in terms of covariances, as $\Pi^K = 2[\text{cov}\{t(x), F(x)\} - g\,\text{cov}\{x, F(x)\}]/\mu g$. *Hint:* consult theorem 2.1(b), p. 33.

8.3.2(b) What corresponding 'easy but accurate way' to calculate the Suits index from microdata does Jenkins (1988a) establish?

8.3.3 If the tax schedule $t(x)$ comprises n components, $t(x) = \Sigma t_i(x)$, show that $g\,L_T \equiv \Sigma g_i\,L_{Ti}$ where g_i is the average rate of the ith tax alone $(1 \leq i \leq n)$ and L_{Ti} is its concentration curve. Conclude that $\Pi^K = \Sigma[g_i/g]\,\Pi_i^K$ where Π_i^K is the Kakwani index of disproportionality for the ith tax.

8.3.4(a) Let Π^P denote the maximum vertical separation between L_X and L_T. Show that $\Pi^P = L_X(p^\circ) - L_T(p^\circ)$ where $p^\circ = F(x^\circ)$ and x° is the breakeven income level depicted in figure 8.1. *Hint:* use lemma 2.1, p. 32, and exercise 2.5.1(a), p. 41, to show that L_X and L_T become parallel at p°.

8.3.4(b) Conclude that Π^P can be interpreted as the proportion of the tax burden shifted up the income scale, from the beneficiaries of progression to the 'losers', as compared with equal-yield flat tax.

8.3.4(c) Let Π^{PS} measure the maximum vertical separation between the relative concentration curve $R_T(q)$ and the 45° line. Prove that for every pre-tax income distribution $\Pi^P = \Pi^{PS}$. *Hint:* use (8.23).[11]

8.3.5(a) Let $k(p)$ be any positive function and let $\Phi = \int_0^1 [L_X(p) - L_T(p)]k(p)\,\mathrm{d}p$. Use integration by parts to demonstrate that Φ can also be expressed as a normalized average deviation of actual taxes from liabilities under an equal yield flat tax: $\Phi = \int(t(x) - gx)W[F(x)]f(x)\,\mathrm{d}x/\mu g$, where $W(\ )$ is a strictly increasing weighting function (compare exercise 5.2.16, p. 119).

8.3.5(b) The measures Φ as above form Pfähler's (1987) class of 'aggregate tax redistribution' (ATR) measures.[12] Explain the relationship between these measures and Mehran's (1976) linear inequality indices. Demonstrate that the ATR indices of effective progression are consistent with liability progression. Show that the Kakwani and Suits indices are ATR measures.

8.3.6(a) Explain how Duclos (1998) derives the Suits index Π^S from a social evaluation function that captures the well-being of economically isolated individuals in society.

8.3.6(b) Explain Duclos' (2000) construction according to which $\Pi^K(v)$ is the difference between the average perceptions of fiscal harshness and relative deprivation in the population. Confirm that all perceptions of fiscal harshness and relative deprivation are given equal weight in the case $v = 2$.

8.3.7   For a strictly positive income tax, let $e_X(p)$ be the elasticity with respect to p of the pre-tax income share $q = L_X(p)$, let $E_C(p)$ be the elasticity with respect to p of the slope of the tax concentration curve $L_T(p)$ and let $E_R(q)$ be the elasticity with respect to q of the slope of the relative concentration curve for taxes $R_T(q)$. Now let $K(p) = [1 - E_R(q) e_X(p)/E_C(p)]^{-1}$. Prove that $K(p)$ measures liability progression at percentile p: if $p = F(y)$, then $K(p) = LP(y)$.[13]

8.3.8(a) Suppose that the tax schedule is convex. Demonstrate, following Lambert and Pfähler (1992), that a small transfer of pre-tax income from a poorer to a richer person reduces the Kawkani index Π^K if the marginal tax rate of the poor person is lower than the average tax rate g and if the rank of the rich person is lower than $(1 + C_T)/2$ where C_T is the concentration index for taxes. Show also that Π^K increases under the reverse conditions.

8.3.8(b) Explain Lambert and Pfähler's (1992, p. 12) finding that 'in order to enhance [or maintain] progressivity, equalizing pre-tax income growth (if such occurs) can be counteracted by a discretionary bolstering of liability progression'.

8.4   Redistributive effect

Another result due to Jakobsson (1976) and Kakwani (1977a) links changes in residual progression with shifts in the concentration curve L_{X-T} of post-tax income when the pre-tax income distribution is fixed. Thus, let $t^1(x)$ and $t^2(x)$ be two income tax schedules. Given any particular distribution of pre-tax income, say with distribution function $F(x)$, let L^1_{X-T} and L^2_{X-T} be the concentration curves for post-tax income induced by the respective schedules. The formal result is as follows.

Theorem 8.6

$RP^{*2}(x) \geq RP^{*1}(x)$ for all $x \Leftrightarrow L^2_{X-T} \geq L^1_{X-T}$ for every pre-tax income distribution $F(x)$.

This theorem does not depend upon taxation being positive, or even non-negative (though negative taxes will be considered separately in chapter 11). For the proof, just use lemma 8.1, p. 200, with $m(x) = x - t^2(x)$ and $n(x) = x - t^1(x)$, both of which are positive for all x under our assumptions about tax schedules. If there is a *strict* increase in residual progression, $RP^{*2}(x) > RP^{*1}(x)$ all x, then the entire concentration curve for post-tax income is shifted upwards: $L^2_{X-T}(p) > L^1_{X-T}(p)$ for all $p \in (0, 1)$. Only if $RP^{*2}(x) \equiv RP^{*1}(x)$ is $L^2_{X-T} \equiv L^1_{X-T}$ for every pre-tax income distribution.

In chapter 9, we shall demonstrate a striking property of income tax schedules ordered by liability or residual progression which is not revealed by the Jakobsson–Kakwani analysis.

Corollary 9.1

Income tax schedules ordered by residual or liability progression cross at most once.

The more residually progressive is the income tax, the greater the separation of the curves L_X and L_{X-T}, and therefore the more pronounced the redistributive effect. What can we read into the term $[L_{X-T}(p) - L_X(p)] \geq 0$, which measures the separation of L_X and L_{X-T} at rank p in the pre-tax income distribution? The lowest-ranked $100p$ per cent of income units receive $100L_X(p)$ per cent of pre-tax income and the larger share $100L_{X-T}(p)$ per cent of post-tax income. What does the difference in percentages tell us? It is better to think of L_X as the concentration curve for post-tax income that would obtain under an equal-yield flat tax. *The distance $[L_{X-T}(p) - L_X(p)]$ is that fraction of total post-tax income shifted from high incomes (the top $100(1 - p)$ per cent) to low incomes (the bottom $100p$ per cent) by the presence of progression in the tax.*

Just as the indices Π^K, $\Pi^K(v)$ for $v > 1$ and Π^S quantify disproportionality of taxes in terms of the separation of the curves L_X and L_T, corresponding indices of redistributive effect can be devised in terms of the separation of the curves L_X and L_{X-T}. Consider therefore

$$\Pi^{RS} = 2\int_0^1 [L_{X-T}(p) - L_X(p)] \, dp = G_X - C_{X-T} \tag{8.26}$$

where C_{X-T} is the concentration coefficient for post-tax income, equal to the Gini coefficient under our assumptions (because L_{X-T} is a Lorenz curve, see p. 39). Π^{RS} thus measures the reduction in the Gini coefficient achieved by the tax. We name it after Reynolds and Smolensky's (1977) application (of a minor variant) to the US tax system.[14] Just as for the Kakwani index Π^K, an extension is available which puts at the disposal of the analyst a distributional judgement parameter. Thus let

$$\Pi^{RS}(v) = v(v - 1)\int_0^1 (1 - p)^{v-2}[L_{X-T}(p) - L_X(p)] \, dp = G_X(v) - C_{X-T}(v) \tag{8.27}$$

for $v > 1$. Under our maintained assumptions $C_{X-T}(v)$ is the extended Gini coefficient for post-tax income.

An index of redistributive effect proposed by Pfähler (1983), Π^{PA} say, differs from Π^{RS} in the same way that the Suits index differs from the Kakwani index,

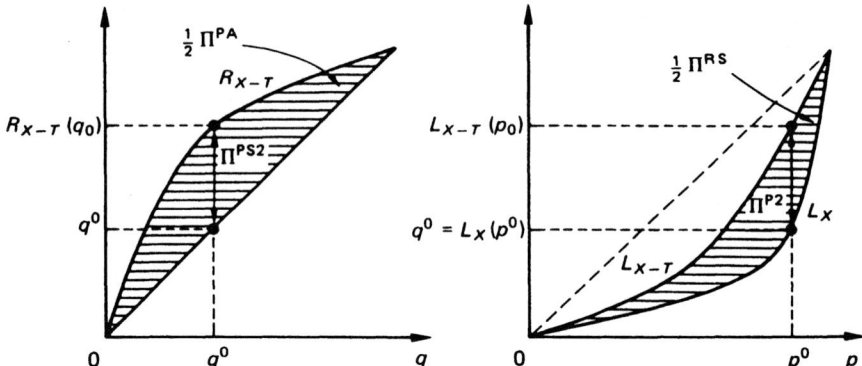

Figure 8.4   The indices Π^{RS}, Π^{PA} and $\Pi^{P2} = \Pi^{PS2}$ of redistributive effect

being defined in terms of the relative concentration curve $R_{X-T}(q)$ for post-tax income:

$$\Pi^{PA} = 2\int_0^1 [R_{X-T}(q) - q]\,dp = 2\int_0^1 [L_{X-T}(p) - L_X(p)]L_X'(p)\,dp \qquad (8.28)$$

(recall (8.24)–(8.25)). Figure 8.4 illustrates the indices Π^{RS} and Π^{PA} (and also shows two other indices, Π^{P2} and Π^{PS2}, defined in exercise 8.4.7).

Disproportionality and redistributive effect are evidently two sides of the same coin. With progressive rather than flat tax, part of the tax burden is shifted up the income distribution; concomitantly some post-tax income is shifted down. Clearly the two effects are closely connected. But how?

Recall the simple relationship between concentration curves:

$$L_X \equiv gL_T + (1-g)L_{X-T} \qquad (2.25)$$

derived on p. 38. This may be re-arranged as $(1-g)[L_{X-T} - L_X] \equiv g[L_X - L_T]$, or

$$L_{X-T} - L_X \equiv \frac{g}{1-g}(L_X - L_T) \qquad (8.29)$$

On the left is the redistributive effect at p, measured as the proportion of total income shifted down the income scale by the presence of progression, and on the right, a term depending on the total tax ratio g, along with disproportionality at p, measured as the proportion of tax shifted up the income scale. Thus redistributive effect is determined by disproportionality and 'tax level', the name sometimes given to $g/(1-g)$. Scaling up the liabilities of an already progressive tax increases its redistributive effect without affecting its disproportionality; changing the tax schedule so that the same revenue is raised more disproportionately increases the redistributive effect.

The same property holds between the indices of redistributive effect and disproportionality which we have developed. Namely, we have

$$\Pi^{RS} = \frac{g}{1-g}\Pi^{K} \tag{8.30}$$

$$\Pi^{RS}(v) = \frac{g}{1-g}\Pi^{K}(v) \tag{8.31}$$

$$\Pi^{PA} = \frac{g}{1-g}\Pi^{S} \tag{8.32}$$

Can you prove these three results using (8.29)? (8.30) was proved by Kakwani (1977b), and (8.32) by Pfähler (1983). Kakwani (1984a, p. 158) clearly did not appreciate that the Suits framework offers the same insight as his own: '... Kakwani's measure has an advantage over that of Suits in one respect: it provides the relationship between measures of progressivity and ... redistributive effect'. (Recall that Kakwani defines progressivity as disproportionality – see the quotation on p. 187.)

The measures we have described can be extended readily from personal income taxes to other income based taxes, provided of course that they satisfy our maintained assumptions (see (2.19), p. 189). In the UK the National Insurance Contribution is an additional tax levied on earnings. It is proportional to earned income between 'floor' and 'ceiling' levels of income, and lump-sum above the ceiling. Its overall progressivity may be negative: see exercise 8.4.2(b). If non-income taxes such as property taxes, the VAT and excise taxes can be attributed to income units as functions $t(x)$ of income x which satisfy our assumptions, then their progressivities can be measured similarly.[15]

Loomis and Revier (1988) point out that if an excise tax, levied on a specific commodity, is attributed to income units as a tax $t(x)$, and an index of disproportionality such as the Suits index is computed, this does *not* quantify disproportionality in the tax burden as experienced by the sub-distribution of those who actually buy the good in question. If $p(x)$ is the proportion of income units having an income of x who buy the commodity, and $a(x)$ is their average propensity to consume it (so that $t(x) = \tau x a(x) p(x)$ for some τ), then clearly the tax will be progressive/regressive in its presumed incidence on the distribution of all incomes if $a(x)p(x)$ increases/decreases with x, but progressive/regressive on buyers' incomes if $a(x)$ increases/decreases with x. Loomis and Revier define a Suits-type buyers index as

$$\Pi^{LR} = 2\int_{0}^{1}[q_b - R_T(q)]\,dq_b \tag{8.33}$$

where $q = L_x(p)$ as in (8.22) and q_b is the cumulative proportion of buyers' income received by buyers in the lowest $100p$ per cent of the gross income distribution. They show that $q_b \gtrless q$ for all q, implying $\Pi^{LR} \gtrless \Pi^{S}$, if $p'(x) \lessgtr 0$

for all x. Hence if buyers are more concentrated in the lower income classes than the overall population, the Suits index Π^S will understate the progressivity of a progressive excise tax and overstate the regressivity of a regressive one.

Another avenue for the measurement of redistributive effect is provided by the Atkinson (1970) index of relative inequality $I(e)$, developed in chapter 5, where e is the inequality aversion parameter. Kiefer (1985) has suggested the index

$$\Pi^{KI}(e) = I_X(e) - I_{X-T}(e) \tag{8.34}$$

which records the reduction in the Atkinson index occasioned by the tax and is thus analogous to Π^{RS} which uses the Gini coefficient. Blackorby and Donaldson (1984a) have proposed

$$\Pi^{BD}(e) = \frac{I_X(e) - I_{X-T}(e)}{1 - I_X(e)} \tag{8.35}$$

which records the percentage increase in equality, where equality is measured as (1 − inequality). There is an important distinction between these two indices. $\Pi^{KI}(e)$ deems two tax regimes equally progressive if they make equal absolute improvements in the Atkinson index, whilst in these circumstances $\Pi^{BD}(e)$ rates as more progressive the regime which effects the given improvement on a more unequal pre-tax income distribution. You can consult Pfähler (1987) for a wide-ranging survey of indices of disproportionality and redistributive effect.[16]

We turn finally to the question of normative significance. In chapter 5 we explored this question for inequality with respect to the Gini coefficient, the extended Gini coefficient and the Atkinson index. What can we say in the case of progressivity? Are the indices we have developed purely statistical/descriptive, or do they have prescriptive/ethical content?

Recall that progressive income taxation reduces social welfare by less than an equal-yield flat tax applied to the same pre-tax income distribution (theorem 8.2, p. 191). Can we say that the more progressive the tax is, the smaller is this reduction? Or that the more progressive it is, the higher is welfare relative to the equal-yield flat tax? The answers are 'yes' in a very special case. If (a) the residual progression $RP^*(x)$ of the income tax schedule is increased at every income level, (b) the pre-tax income distribution remains fixed, and (c) the tax yield is maintained at the existing level, then, by theorem 8.6, the concentration curve for post-tax income shifts inwards, and there is no change in mean post-tax income. Since this concentration curve is also the Lorenz curve for post-tax income, by the Atkinson theorem (theorem 3.1, p. 45) post-tax welfare is increased for every individualistic, symmetric, additively separable and inequality-averse social welfare function.

We cannot expect so robust a welfare recommendation for progression changes which affect the tax yield. This is because the size of the post-tax cake is affected in such cases, as well as the way it is sliced, a situation we shall discuss in some detail in chapter 9. However, all is not lost: we can confer normative significance upon progressivity indices based on the Gini coefficient and Atkinson index by resort to the appropriate abbreviated social welfare functions.

Thus, recall the social evaluation function

$$V(\mu, G) = \mu(1 - kG) \qquad 0 \le k \le 1 \tag{5.25}$$

in respect of the Gini coefficient, derived on pp. 123–125 from non-individualistic welfare formulations involving deprivation and altruism (and, with $k = 1$, from Sen's pairwise maximin criterion). Denote by V_X, V_{X-T} and V_P the welfare values associated with the pre-tax income distribution, post-tax income distribution and distribution of income after the equal-yield proportional income tax:

$$V_X = \mu(1 - kG_X), V_{X-T} = \mu(1 - g)(1 - kG_{X-T}) \text{ and } V_P = \mu(1 - g)(1 - kG_X)$$

$$\tag{8.36}$$

Then we see that

$$V_{X-T} - V_P = \mu(1 - g)k\,\Pi^{RS} \tag{8.37}$$

providing a normative interpretation for the Reynolds–Smolensky index; it is proportional to the so-called *welfare premium from progression*, the superiority of the progressive tax over the equal-yield flat one. Using (8.30) this can also be written as

$$V_{X-T} - V_P = \mu gk\,\Pi^K \tag{8.38}$$

thereby endowing the Kakwani index with similar normative significance (see also exercise 8.4.10). In particular, increased progressivity with no change in yield implies more welfare relative to equal-yield flat tax, equivalently a smaller welfare reduction compared with the no-tax position. If the yield changes, the trade-off with progressivity is explicit.

For the Kiefer and Blackorby–Donaldson indices, the welfare indicator

$$V(\mu, I(e)) = \mu[1 - I(e)] \tag{5.39}$$

can be applied. Normative backing for Π^{KI} is provided in much the same way as for the Reynolds–Smolensky index. Recall that $\mu[1 - I(e)] = \xi$ where ξ is the equally distributed equivalent (EDE) income for the distribution in question (p. 98). Can you detect the normative significance of the Blackorby–Donaldson index Π^{BD}? Consider Blackorby and Donaldson's (1984a, p. 686) statement: 'Our index of relative tax progressivity is constructed by comparing . . . the after tax EDE income with the EDE income that would be achieved by an equal-yield proportional tax', and consult their paper if necessary. See also exercise 8.4.12.

Exercises

8.4.1   Assuming that the pre-tax income distribution is fixed, investigate the redistributive effects of yield-decreasing and yield-increasing changes in disproportionality, as follows. Writing ΔL for the shift in a concentration curve $L(p)$, note that by assumption $\Delta L_X \equiv \Delta[g\ L_T + (1 - g)\ L_{X-T}] \equiv 0$. Now show that (i) $\Delta g > 0$ and $\Delta L_T \leq 0 \Rightarrow \Delta L_{X-T} > 0$ and (ii) $\Delta g < 0$ and $\Delta L_T \geq 0 \Rightarrow \Delta L_{X-T} < 0$, and translate these mathematical statements into the English language.

8.4.2(a) Use the result given in exercise 8.1.1, p. 194, to show that a sufficient condition for L_X and L_{X-T} to intersect is that the lowest and highest incomes x experience average tax rates $t(x)/x$ which are below the overall average tax rate g.

8.4.2(b) What do you conclude about the redistributive effect of the UK National Insurance Contribution, as described in the text?

8.4.3   How can Π^{RS} be expressed in terms of covariances? Consult Jenkins (1988a).

8.4.4   If $t(x) = \Sigma t_i(x)$ as in exercise 8.3.3, p. 205, show that $(1 - g)[L_{X-T} - L_X] \equiv \Sigma(1 - g_i)[L_{X-T_i} - L_X]$ where L_{X-T_i} is the concentration curve for the distribution of income net of the ith tax alone. Conclude that $\Pi^{RS} = \Sigma[(1 - g_i)/(1 - g)]\ \Pi_i^{RS}$ where Π_i^{RS} is the Reynolds–Smolensky index for the ith component tax alone.

8.4.5(a) Show that the maximum value the index Π^{PA} can take is $\Pi_{max}^{PA} = G_X$, which occurs when the tax is perfectly equalizing. *Hint:* Either redraw figure 8.4, or re-examine equation (8.28) setting $R_{X-T}(q) = L_{X-T}(p) = p$.

8.4.5(b) What is the minimum value that Π^{PA} can take? What are the maximum and minimum values of the Reynolds–Smolensky index Π^{RS}? Confirm that $\Pi_{max}^{RS} = \Pi_{max}^{PA}$ and $\Pi_{min}^{RS} = -\Pi_{max}^{K}$.

8.4.6   Let $\Psi = M_X - M_{X-T}$ where M is a member of Mehran's (1976) general class of inequality indices (exercise 5.2.16, p. 119). Show that Ψ is an index of effective progression which is consistent with residual progression and can be written as $\Psi = [g/(1 - g)]\ \Phi$ where Φ is the corresponding member of Pfähler's ATR class (exercise 8.3.5, p. 205). Express Ψ as a normalized average deviation of actual post-tax incomes from those which would obtain under the equal-yield flat tax, and compare with Pfähler's (1987, p. 12) definition of the 'aggregate income redistribution (AIR) class'.

8.4.7(a) Let Π^{P2} be the maximum vertical separation between L_X and L_{X-T}, and let Π^{PS2} be the maximum vertical separation between the relative concentration curve R_{X-T} for post-tax income and the 45° line. Show that these both occur at the same percentile point $p°$ as found in exercise 8.3.4(a) for the corresponding indices of disproportionality, Π^P and Π^{PS}. Prove that $\Pi^{P2} = \Pi^{PS2}$.

8.4.7(b) Conclude that Π^{P2} measures the proportion of total post-tax income shifted down the income scale, to the beneficiaries of progression in the tax schedule from the 'losers', as compared with the equal-yield flat tax. Prove also that $\Pi^{P2} = [g/(1 - g)]\Pi^P$ (consult Pfähler, 1983, if in doubt).

8.4.8 '. . . distributing all but one tax . . . by initial income provides a way to disaggregate the sources of lower . . . [post-tax] Gini coefficients in an additive manner' (Reynolds and Smolensky, 1977, p. 82). Prove this assertion as follows. With Π_i^{RS} as in exercise 8.4.4, let Π_i^* be the Reynolds–Smolensky index of redistributive effect that would obtain if each tax $t_j(x)$, $j \neq i$, were to be replaced by a flat tax $t_j^*(x) = g_j\, x$. Show that $(1 - g)[L_{X-T}^* - L_X] = (1 - g_i)[L_{X-T_i} - L_X]$ where L_{X-T}^* is the concentration curve for post-tax income given this hypothetical configuration of taxes $t_j^*(x)$, $j \neq i$, together with $t_i(x)$. Now use exercise 8.4.4 to conclude that $\Pi^{RS} = \Sigma\Pi_i^*$.

8.4.9 Let $t(x)$ be an income tax whose total tax ratio is g, and let $\tau(x) = ut(x)/\mu g$ be the scaled income tax whose total tax ratio is u. Let $\Pi(u)$ be the redistributive effect of $\tau(x)$. Show that the Kakwani index for the tax $t(x)$ is given by $\Pi^K = \Pi'(0)$.[17]

8.4.10 Use (8.36) and exercise 8.4.5 to show that, when $k = 1$, the loss in abbreviated social welfare caused by progressive income taxation is a decreasing function of the Kakwani index: $V_X - V_{X-T} = \mu g\,[\Pi_{max}^K - \Pi^K]$

8.4.11 Explain Fellman *et al.'s* (1999) use of the extended Gini coefficient to measure the effectiveness of an income tax schedule $t(x)$ as 'the percentage . . . of the maximum reduction in inequality that could have been achieved with the same tax yield' (p. 117).

8.4.12(a) Let ξ_X and ξ_{X-T} be the equally distributed equivalent incomes for the pre- and post-tax income distributions when inequality aversion is e. Show that $\Pi^{BD}(e) = 1 - \xi_{X-T}/[(1 - g)\xi_X]$

8.4.12(b) Whereas g is the rate of the equal-yield flat tax, let γ be the rate of the equal-*welfare* flat tax. Prove that $\gamma < g$ if the tax is progressive and express $\Pi^{BD}(e)$ in terms of g and γ. *Hint:* Show that $(1 - \gamma)\xi_X = \xi_{X-T}$.

8.4.12(c) Duclos' (1995) *performance indicator* τ for an income tax $t(x)$ is the proportion of net income $x - t(x)$ which could be taken away from everybody and still leave the same average utility as after the equal-yield flat alternative. That is, τ is such that the distributions of $(1 - \tau)[x - t(x)]$ and $(1 - g)x$ have the same social welfare. Prove that $\Pi^{BD} = \tau/(1 - \tau)$. *Hint:* Show that $(1 - g)\xi_X = (1 - \tau)\xi_{X-T}$.

8.4.12(d) If residual progression $RP^*(x)$ is increased at all income levels, what happens to τ? If inequality aversion e is increased with the tax schedule fixed, what happens to τ? Consult Duclos (1995) and Duclos (1997) respectively.

8.4.13   Let $e_X(p)$ be defined as in exercise 8.3.7 (p. 206), and correspondingly let $E_{C^*}(p)$ and $E_{R^*}(q)$ be the slope elasticities of $L_{X-T}(p)$ and $R_{X-T}(q)$ respectively. Define $K^*(p) = [1 - E_{R^*}(q)e_X(p)/E_{C^*}(p)]^{-1}$. Prove that $K^*(p)$ measures residual progression at percentile p: if $p = F(y)$, $K^*(p) = RP^*(y)$.[18]

8.4.14(a)   'An understanding of the way the tax schedule and income distribution interact in determining redistributive effect is needed for various purposes' (Lambert and Pfähler, 1992, p. 2). Discuss.

8.4.14(b)   'In Britain in 1985, for example, . . . Musgrave and Thin's speculation [see p. 188] is rejected for transfers from non-taxpayers, and confirmed for transfers from taxpayers into the top 1/3 [of the income distribution]' (ibid., p. 9). Describe the theorem on which this claim is based.

8.4.14(c)   'In order to enhance or maintain redistributive effect, disequalizing pre-tax income growth can be counteracted by a discretionary bolstering of residual progression' (ibid., p. 12). Explain, with particular reference to Dardanoni and Lambert (2001b).

8.4.15   Explain Moyes's (1994, pp. 296–297) finding that 'substituting piecewise isoelastic tax schedules for piecewise linear ones would guarantee that relative inequality after tax decreases as a result of an equalizing growth in incomes'.

8.5   Base and rate effect decompositions

In chapter 7, section 2, we described the typical income tax. For income units of a given type, all attracting the same lump-sum allowance a, the tax liability took the form $t(x) = s(x - a - d(x)) = s(y)$, where y is taxable income, $s(y)$ is the rate schedule and $d(x)$ describes the income/expenditure-related deduction of an income unit with gross income x. As we explained, the lump-sum allowance a and the rate schedule $s(y)$ both contribute positively to progression, while deductions exert a dampening effect, that of base erosion, if they are income-elastic (see also exercise 8.2.3 on p. 198). Can we quantify the contributions to progressivity of the allowances, rate structure and deductions? As shown by Pfähler (1990), the indices Π^K and Π^{RS} can readily be decomposed into components attributable to these features of the income tax code.[19]

Consider first the the allowance a per se, viewed as a subtraction from income. To measure the disproportionality of the allowance using the Kakwani approach, cosmetically all we need do is replace the subscript 'T' by an 'A' in equations (8.19)–(8.20) on p. 201:

$$\Pi_A^K = 2\int_0^1 (L_X - L_A)\,dp = C_A - G_X \tag{8.39}$$

In this, L_A is the concentration curve and C_A the concentration coefficient for the allowance. Since this is a lump sum (equally distributed) quantity, $L_A(p) = p$ for all p and $C_A = 0$; Π_A^K is negative. The redistributive effect of the allowance can be written as

$$\Pi_A^{RS} = 2 \int_0^1 (L_{X-A} - L_X) \, dp = G_X - C_{X-A} \tag{8.40}$$

where L_{X-A} is the concentration curve and C_{X-A} the concentration coefficient for gross income net of the allowance. This is also negative because, as a subtraction from income, the allowance is 'levied' at a declining average rate, a/x, and so is regressive, exerting a disequalizing effect on income distribution (theorem 8.1, p. 190). Let us therefore write

$$-\Pi_A^K = \rho_A^K > 0 \tag{8.41}$$

$$-\Pi_A^{RS} = \rho_A^{RS} > 0 \tag{8.42}$$

so that the positive ρs are the *regressivities* (i.e. the negatives of the progressivities) of the allowance when viewed as a subtraction from income. Finally, if α is the 'average rate' of allowance, $\alpha - a/\mu$, we have

$$\rho_A^{RS} = \frac{\alpha}{1-\alpha} \rho_A^K \tag{8.43}$$

as the decomposition of redistributive effect into level and disproportionality components.

Similar expressions obtain for the disproportionality and redistributive effect of deductions *per se*. To use an obvious notation, we can write

$$\Pi_D^K = 2 \int_0^1 (L_X - L_D) \, dp = C_D - G_X \tag{8.44}$$

$$\Pi_D^{RS} = 2 \int_0^1 (L_{X-D} - L_X) \, dp = G_X - C_{X-D} \tag{8.45}$$

$$\Pi_D^{RS} = \frac{\delta}{1-\delta} \Pi_D^K \tag{8.46}$$

where δ is the average rate of deduction. We cannot sign these terms *a priori*. However, if $d[d(x)/x]/dx > 0$, i.e. if deductions are income-elastic in cross-section, then all terms in (8.44)–(8.46) are positive.

Finally, we come to the progressivity of the rate structure *per se*. The disproportionality and redistributive effect of the tax liability $s(y) = t(x)$ as a function of taxable income $y = x - a - d(x)$ are these:

$$\Pi_R^K = 2 \int_0^1 (L_Y - L_T) \, dp = 2 \int_0^1 (L_{X-A-D} - L_T) \, dp = C_T - C_{X-A-D} \tag{8.47}$$

$$\Pi_R^{RS} = 2\int_0^1 (L_{X-T} - L_{X-A-D})\,\mathrm{d}p = C_{X-A-D} - C_{X-T} \tag{8.48}$$

and they are linked by the equation

$$\Pi_R^{RS} = \frac{g}{1-\alpha-\delta-g}\Pi_R^{K} \tag{8.49}$$

where g is the total tax ratio.

How may we combine the 'A', 'D' and 'R' terms above? A very simple observation provides the key. It is that

$$L_X \equiv \alpha L_A + \delta L_D + (1-\alpha-\delta)L_{X-A-D} \tag{8.50}$$

When multiplied through by mean income μ, this equation says that gross income up to rank p is the sum of allowance, deduction and taxable income up to rank p. As Pfähler (1990) points out, we may re-arrange (8.50) in a most advantageous way:

$$(1-\alpha-\delta)[L_X - L_T] = (1-\alpha-\delta)[L_{X-A-D} - L_T] - \alpha[L_X - L_A] - \delta[L_X - L_D] \tag{8.51}$$

and integrate through with respect to p, to obtain a decomposition of the overall Kakwani index Π^K. Setting $\eta = 1 - \alpha - \delta$ for compactness, we find

$$\Pi^K = \Pi_R^K + \frac{\alpha}{\eta}\rho_A^K - \frac{\delta}{\eta}\Pi_D^K \tag{8.52}$$

As we had expected, the allowance and rates terms contribute positively to Π^K, and the deductions negatively if income-elastic. Finally, combining (8.52) with (8.43), (8.46) and (8.49), we have

$$\Pi^{RS} = \frac{g}{1-g}\left(\frac{\eta-g}{g}\Pi_R^{RS} + \frac{1-\alpha}{\eta}\rho_A^{RS} - \frac{1-\delta}{\eta}\Pi_D^{RS}\right) \tag{8.53}$$

as the corresponding decomposition of the overall Reynolds–Smolensky index.

Exercises

8.5.1 Show that analogous decompositions to (8.52)–(8.53) can be obtained for the progressivity indices Π^S and Π^{PA}, defined in terms of relative concentration curves. *Hint:* Integrate differently throughout (8.51), replacing $\mathrm{d}p$ by $\mathrm{d}q = L_X'(p)\,\mathrm{d}p$ and using (8.24) and (8.28).

8.5.2 Show, more generally, that decompositions into rate, allowance and deduction components can also be obtained for all members of Pfähler's (1987) ATR- and AIR-classes. (See exercises 8.3.5 on p. 205 and 8.4.6 on p. 212.)

Notes

1 Recall the implicit restriction here: distributions in which nobody pays any tax (because all incomes lie below the tax threshold) are excluded. L_T would be undefined for such distributions.

2 Lambert (1988), Arnold (1990) and Dardanoni (1993a) all prove that equality of average tax rates for the married and the single is in fact sufficient to ensure overall inequality reduction from separately progressive taxation of the two groups. Moyes and Shorrocks (1998), on the other hand, prove a striking impossibility result: one cannot design progressive income tax schedules which are different for the married and single with the property that overall income inequality is bound to be reduced by their application. To put this another way, given a partition of the population into subgroups M and S, and two distinct progressive schedules $t_M(x)$ and $t_S(x)$, one can concoct an income distribution across the entire population such that overall inequality is exacerbated by application of the component schedules. Just find an income level y such that $t_M(y) \neq t_S(y)$ and suppose that everybody in each subgroup has y before tax! Ok (1997) shows, on the other hand, that if one limits the choice of income distributions realistically, to exclude equal and 'almost equal' ones, the impossibility result evaporates: distinct and progressive component schedules $t_M(x)$ and $t_S(x)$ can indeed be constructed which are guaranteed to be overall inequality-reducing for all feasible income distributions.

3 An entire chapter is devoted to these issues in the second (1993) edition of this book.

4 This exercise shows that progressive (and convex) tax entails an income loss for households with distinct sources of income that are taxed separately, and for people like authors and artists whose income streams fluctuate through time. Richter and Hampe (1984) have analysed this phenomenon closely. See also pp. 194–196 of the second (1993) edition of this book.

5 Pages 197–198 of the second (1993) edition of this book contain a simplified treatment of Richter's analysis.

6 The indices π_L and π_R were used by Hemming (1980) in an analysis to determine the effects of changes in income tax progression on labour supply.

7 Progression-neutral tax cuts will be considered in more detail in chapter 9.

8 The axiomatic approach for intermediate inequality was originated by Pfingsten (1986a). See also Pfingsten (1987, 1988a, 1988b), Moyes (1992) and an appendix to chapter 6 in the second (1993) edition of this book.

9 For an interesting application in health economics, see Contoyannis and Forster (1999a,b).

10 Pfähler (1985) is a useful source for the analysis of relative concentration curves. In particular, the Suits (1977) index Π^S is traced back to Hainsworth (1964) in this article.

11 The distance measure Π^P corresponds to the Schutz coefficient (p. 33) in the same way that the area measure Π^K corresponds to the Gini. Π^P and Π^{PS} were presented and analysed in Pfähler (1983). Khetan and Podder (1976) defined progressivity in terms of disproportionality as the ratio of the area below L_X to that below L_T: $\Pi^{KP} = [1 - G_X]/[1 - C_T]$. They also proposed a variant based on relative concentration curves, thereby anticipating the Suits framework of analysis.

12 The necessity for an increasing weight $W( )$ in Pfähler's ATR-measures was pointed out by Binh (1991). Both Pfähler and Binh misleadingly specify the weight in the form $W(x)$ rather than $W(F(x))$: in their examples, though, they in fact write $W( )$ as a function of $F(x)$. The equivalence of the two expressions for Φ given in exercise 8.3.5(a) was shown by Pfähler (1991). In Kakwani (1984b, 1986) a family of indices of disproportionality is proposed which closely resembles Pfähler's.

13 This result was proven in Hayes *et al.* (1995). See also exercise 8.4.13 on p. 214.

14 The index Π^{RS} also features in Berglas (1971) and Kakwani (1977b). In fact Reynolds and Smolensky's (1977) proposal was to measure the reduction in the Gini coefficient for income arising from the application of both taxes and government expenditure benefits. They obtained a redistributive effect measure for *all taxes* by (arbitrarily) attributing government expenditure benefits proportionally; just as, for *component taxes*, they also further attributed other taxes proportionally. Their measure of redistributive effect for taxes is, therefore, strictly a Π^*-type measure as defined in exercise 8.4.8 for component taxes.

15 In chapter 10 we show how the indices of this chapter can be adapted for use with taxes which are not income-based and/or induce reranking.

16 Musgrave and Thin (1948) defined effective progression as the ratio $\Pi^{MT} = [1 - G_{X-T}]/[1 - G_X]$, whilst Pechman and Okner's (1974) proposal was $\Pi^{PO} = [G_X - G_{X-T}]/G_X$. A similar distinction to the one between $\Pi^{KI}(e)$ and $\Pi^{BD}(e)$ can be drawn between Π^{RS} and Π^{MT}; the distinction between Π^{RS} and Π^{PO} is just the opposite.

17 Hence $\Pi^{RS} = \Pi(g) = [g/(1 - g)]\Pi'(0)$. Bourguignon and Morrison (1980) prove that Π^{RS} is the only conventional measure of the redistributive effect of an income tax which permits a decomposition of the form $\Pi(g) = f[g, \Pi'(0)]$ where f is a function which may depend on the inequality index used to measure Π (the desideratum being that one should be able to gauge the impact of an income tax by its level and by the inequality impact of an identically-distributed one dollar tax).

18 If a data set contains income units with differing tax treatment (e.g. single and married), then estimates of the functions $K(p)$ and $K^*(p)$ defined in exercise 8.3.7 and here reveal what liability and residual progression respectively *would be* at each percentile point p if, counterfactually, a tax code *had been* in place in which people's liabilities were determined solely by their income levels. In Hayes *et al.* (1995), $K(p)$ and $K^*(p)$ are estimated for the US federal income tax annually during the period 1950–1987 using grouped data, one outcome being a pair of contour plots showing how each has varied across the income distribution and with the passage of time.

19 Loizides (1988) is also relevant.

9

Income tax reform and social welfare

In the UK in the tax year 1976/7, the lowest marginal rate of income tax stood at 35 per cent and the highest at 83 per cent, with eight rates in between. By 1988/9 there were only two rates, 25 per cent and 40 per cent, and allowances had risen in real value by over 30 per cent during the 12-year period. The large tax cuts for upper incomes and smaller reductions for middle-income recipients were accompanied by a fall of more than a million in the number of income units paying tax.

In the USA and also in the Federal Republic of Germany, major income tax reforms have been directed at reducing tax burdens generally and especially for middle income groups. At the same time the fear has been expressed that the revenue forgone may have to be recouped. Future increases in other forms of tax, for example in consumption taxes and/or the corporate income tax, have been suggested. The ultimate pattern of gainers and losers could be complex. It is not impossible that the gains for the middle-income groups may in the end be reversed, or paid for by losses at both ends of the income scale.

Popular analysis begins, and often ends, by identifying the pattern of gainers and losers when taxes are changed. In this chapter, we shall proceed beyond this point in certain special cases by drawing on the material we have developed so far in the book.

We keep to the framework of analysis of the previous chapter, in which income tax liabilities are defined by income levels alone, and taxes do not affect pre-tax incomes. Let the income tax schedule before the tax reform be $t^1(x)$ and afterwards $t^2(x)$, and let the frequency density function for pre-tax income both before and after the reform be $f(x)$. The total tax ratios before and after the reform can be denoted g^1 and g^2:

$$g^i = \int \frac{t^i(x)f(x)\mathrm{d}x}{\mu} \qquad i = 1, 2 \tag{9.1}$$

where μ is mean pre-tax income. The reform will be yield neutral/increasing/decreasing in respect of the distribution $f(x)$ according as g^2 is equal to/greater than/less than g^1.

The first case we consider is the one in which everyone gains or loses by the reform. That is, there is a tax cut or tax increase ('hike') for all. Of course there are many ways to raise or lower all taxes. In section 9.1 we report on some striking results obtained by Pfähler (1984) in the case of progression-neutral tax cuts/hikes for all.

If the tax schedules $t^1(x)$ and $t^2(x)$ cross, they do so at break-even levels of income separating gainers by the reform from losers. The case of a single crossing is considered in section 9.2. Such reform involves redistribution from one end of the post-tax income distribution to the other, and possibly a change in yield also. We uncover social welfare recommendations in support of such reforms in the case that redistribution is from rich to poor. Even cases of increased tax yield can be supported.

In section 9.2 we also analyse composite tax reforms involving a progression-neutral tax cut/hike and redistribution from rich to poor. Some results due to Hemming and Keen (1983) are obtained, which are readily applicable and are also of independent theoretical interest because they throw new light on the Jakobsson–Kakwani theorems given in chapter 8.

The case of a double crossing of tax schedules is our final concern, in section 9.3. Here, the reform involves redistribution from the middle to both ends of the post-tax income distribution or vice versa. We give a social welfare recommendation for such a reform in the former case. Again, even in some cases of an increased tax yield this turns out to be possible.

9.1   A tax cut/hike for everyone

> . . . in the recent (1947) debate on income tax reduction . . . Representatives of the congressional majority and their proponents insisted that to maintain progression it was necessary to reduce rates by an equal fraction of percentage points. (Musgrave and Thin, 1948, p. 512)

If a change in income tax yield is required, there are many ways to secure it. Here we evaluate some ways to do this whilst preserving income tax progression at all points along the income scale.

Let us begin by considering the case of a tax cut, as in the quotation above. If the tax liability on each income is to be cut by the same fraction, so that

$$t^1(x) \rightarrow (1-\lambda)t^1(x) \tag{9.2}$$

for an appropriate $\lambda > 0$, then liability progression (LP) is preserved (you should check this). On the other hand, the tax cut could be designed in such a way that everybody gets the same percentage increase in post-tax income:

$$t^1(x) \rightarrow t^1(x) - \rho[x - t^1(x)] \tag{9.3}$$

for an appropriate $\rho > 0$. This type of tax cut would preserve residual progression (RP), but was apparently not considered in the debate of 1947 in the

US. However, as Pfähler (1984) has shown, it is superior to the other on several counts.

The reforms specified in (9.2)–(9.3) are algebraically the same for a tax hike, the only difference being that the constants λ and ρ are negative.[1] Suppose that the total tax ratio before reform is g^1, and that after reform it will be g^2. You can check by integrating in (9.2)–(9.3) that the constants λ and ρ are determined as

$$\lambda = \frac{g^1 - g^2}{g^1}, \qquad \rho = \frac{g^1 - g^2}{1 - g^1} \tag{9.4}$$

We denote the post-reform schedule by $t^{2L}(x)$ or $t^{2R}(x)$ according as the tax cut/hike is LP-neutral or RP-neutral. The following result applies.

Lemma 9.1

For a tax cut, the schedule $t^{2R}(x)$ is ranked more progressive than $t^{2L}(x)$ according to both liability and residual propgression: $LP^{2R}(x) > LP^{2L}(x)$ and $RP^{*2R}(x) > RP^{*2L}(x)$ for all x. For a tax hike, the opposite is the case.

Proof $LP^{2L}(x) = LP^1(x) = m^1(x)/a^1(x)$ and $LP^{2R}(x) = [m^1(x) - \beta]/[a^1(x) - \beta]$ where $m^1(x)$ and $a^1(x)$ are the marginal and average tax rates on income x before the tax change and $\beta = \rho/(1 + \rho) = \alpha/(1 - g^2)$. The result for liability progression follows. The case of residual progression is left to you.   QED

Given these results, we can draw on material presented earlier in the book to recommend an RP-neutral tax cut or an LP-neutral tax hike:

Theorem 9.1

Post-tax income inequality is less and social welfare higher following the RP-neutral tax cut. For a tax hike, the opposite is the case.

Proof After each reform the Lorenz curves and concentration curves for post-tax income coincide. The first result comes from theorem 8.6, p. 206, and the second follows from theorem 3.1, p. 45.   QED

Thus, RP-neutral tax cuts and LP-neutral tax hikes can be recommended on ethical grounds. Pfähler goes on to examine a remark of Musgrave and Thin (1948, p. 511): 'Let us assume that there is to be a change in the level of yield, and to simplify matters, let the taxpayers be divided into two groups representing the "rich" and the "poor" respectively. Each group will want the change in yield to involve a shift in the burden distribution which is in its own interest'. Pfähler asks: *How would income units vote if they could choose which form of tax cut or hike should be imposed?* The answer turns up another recommendation for an RP-neutral tax cut or LP-neutral tax hike, as we shall see.

Suppose first that the pre-reform income tax schedule $t^1(x)$ is strictly progressive. Then there is a unique benchmark income level x° between those paying less than their proportional share of the total burden and those paying more:

$$x \gtrless x^\circ \Leftrightarrow \frac{t^1(x)}{x} \gtrless g^1 \qquad (9.5)$$

(recall figure 8.1, p. 192). This income level has considerable significance.

Lemma 9.2

(a)   The benchmark income level x° is unaffected by both LP-neutral and RP-neutral tax cuts/hikes.
(b)   Those paying less than their proportional share of the tax burden gain more from an RP-neutral tax cut. For those paying more than their proportional share the opposite is the case.
(c)   Those paying less than their proportional share of the tax burden lose more from an RP-neutral tax hike. For those paying more than their proportional share the opposite is the case.

Proof   Let $\Delta v^L(x)$ and $\Delta v^R(x)$ be the increases in post-tax income after an LP-neutral and RP-neutral tax cut or hike. Then from (9.2)–(9.4),

$$\frac{\Delta v^L(x)}{g^1 - g^2} = \frac{t^1(x)}{g^1} \qquad (9.6)$$

$$\frac{\Delta v^R(x)}{g^1 - g^2} = \frac{x - t^1(x)}{1 - g^1} \qquad (9.7)$$

The new benchmark income remains x° if and only if the tax liability on income x° becomes $g^2 x^\circ$ after the tax cut/hike – that is, if and only if the increase in post-tax income experienced by pre-tax income x° is $\Delta v(x^\circ) = (g^1 - g^2)x^\circ$. From (9.6)–(9.7) this is true of both $\Delta v^L(x)$ and $\Delta v^R(x)$. The results in (b) and (c) follow after a little more manipulation.   QED

If each income unit has one vote, and will vote for the tax cut or hike most favourable to itself, we can see from this lemma exactly who will vote for what. Under quite mild restrictions, the RP-neutral tax cut and LP-neutral tax hike emerge from a majority voting process.

Theorem 9.2

If the tax schedule $t^1(x)$ is strictly convex and the pre-tax income distribution is positively skewed, then more than half the income units would vote for an RP-neutral tax cut or an LP-neutral tax hike.

Proof   By lemma 9.2 the proportion of income units who would vote for an RP-neutral tax cut and an LP-neutral tax hike is $F(x°)$. If the tax schedule $t^1(x)$ is strictly convex, then by Jensen's inequality we have

$$t^1(Ex) < Et^1(x) \tag{9.8}$$

where E is the expectations operator over the pre-tax income distribution. Therefore we can infer as follows:

$$t^1(\mu) < \mu g^1 \Rightarrow \frac{t^1(\mu)}{\mu} < g^1 = \frac{t^1(x°)}{x°} \Rightarrow \mu < x° \tag{9.9}$$

If also the income distribution is positively skewed, so median income x^* is below average, then:

$$\frac{1}{2} = F(x^*) < F(\mu) < F(x°) \tag{9.10}$$

(see figure 2.3, p. 22 and (2.7), p. 23). The result is now immediate.   QED

The relevance of these results lies in the appeal of progression-neutrality as a criterion for 'sharing out' required changes in the income tax yield among income units. Although the results rest on a number of simplifying assumptions, made to get the analysis off the ground, insofar as they are applicable they have considerable relevance and power. As Pfähler (1984, p. 382) says, 'In light of this analysis, the Reagan income tax cut by 25 per cent of the tax liability (during 1981–83) turns out to be preferred by the rich (paying an initial average tax rate greater than the initial total tax ratio), to increase inequality of post-tax income the most, to be the least preferred on social welfare grounds and not to win a majority vote'.[2]

Exercises

9.1.1   Demonstrate that an LP-neutral tax cut increases inequality in post-tax income, and that an LP-neutral tax hike reduces it.

9.1.2(a)   'Treasury representatives and their supporters . . . insisted that, in order to hold progression constant, rates would have to be cut by an equal number of percentage points' (Musgrave and Thin, 1948, p. 512). Suppose that taxes are cut by an equal number of percentage points for everybody: $t^1(x) \rightarrow t^1(x) - \alpha x$ for some $\alpha > 0$. Show that this form of tax cut preserves *average rate progression* defined as $ARP^*(x) = x\, d[t(x)/x]/dx = m(x) - a(x)$ where $m(x)$ and $a(x)$ are the marginal and average rates of tax.

9.1.2(b)   How do the inequality, welfare and voting aspects of an ARP-neutral tax cut/hike compare with those for the RP-neutral and LP-neutral reforms already considered? See Pfähler (1984).[3]

9.2   Single-crossing tax reform

Now we turn to tax reforms designed to benefit some at cost to others – that is, tax reforms which involve transfers of post-tax income between income units. This sort of reform is relevant when government seeks to pursue a redistributive policy, for example one of poverty alleviation, or of redress of perceived disincentives for entrepreneurs, or of easing the tax burden for middle-income groups.

The simplest case of reform involving transfers of post-tax income between income units is when the old and new income tax schedules cross *once*. This occurs, for example, in the case of an income tax which is linear above a threshold when both the threshold and marginal tax rate are increased (figure 9.1). The effect on revenue could be neutral, or not, depending on the pre-tax income distribution. Either way, some income units will gain and others higher up the income scale will lose from this type of reform.

We shall examine here what can be said about single-crossing tax reforms which involve redistribution from rich to poor. The case in which redistribution is from poor to rich will not be pursued. However, in the final section of

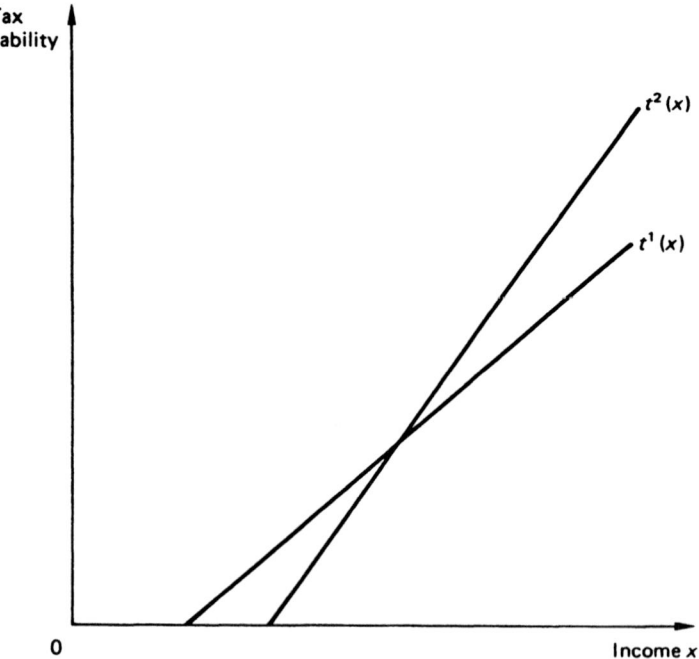

Figure 9.1   Single-crossing tax reform: the case of a tax which is linear above a threshold

the chapter we shall examine reforms where the richest benefit as well as the poorest. Such cases, where middle income recipients are the losers from redistribution to both ends, are also of considerable interest.

We denote by $f(x)$ the frequency density function of pre-tax income, as before, and again write as g^i the total tax ratio of an income tax schedule $t^i(x)$ applied to this pre-tax income distribution. When tax schedules cross once, the effect on generalized Lorenz curves, and thereby on social welfare, is easy to quantify.

Theorem 9.3

If $t^2(x)$ crosses $t^1(x)$ once from below, then

(a) for any pre-tax income distribution such that $g^2 \leq g^1$, $GL^2_{X-T}(p) \geq GL^1_{X-T}(p)$ for all $p \in [0, 1]$;
(b) for any pre-tax income distribution such that $g^2 > g^1$, GL^2_{X-T} crosses GL^1_{X-T} once from above.

Proof If $p = F(y) \in [0, 1]$ then:

$$GL^2_{X-T}(p) - GL^1_{X-T}(p) = \int_0^y [t^1(x) - t^2(x)] f(x) \mathrm{d}x = H(y) \qquad (9.11)$$

say. Now $H(0) = 0$ and $H'(y) \gtrless 0$ when $t^1(y) \gtrless t^2(y)$. Hence $H(y)$ has a single turning point, which is clearly a maximum. As y gets large, $H(y) \rightarrow \mu(g^1 - g^2)$. In case (a) this is a non-negative limiting value, hence $H(y) \geq 0$ for all $y \in [0, 1]$, proving the result. In case (b), the value is negative; therefore $H(y)$ changes sign once.   QED

It is clear from this proof that GL^2_{X-T} and GL^1_{X-T} can only coincide for pre-tax income distributions whose support lies entirely within income ranges on which $t^2(x) \equiv t^1(x)$ (in which case, of course, $g^1 = g^2$). For the reform pictured in figure 9.1, post-tax generalized Lorenz curves would be superimposed up to the percentile point corresponding to the old tax threshold, but so long as somebody paid tax, the curves would necessarily diverge from that point onwards.

In chapter 3 we discussed extensively the links between generalized Lorenz curve configuration and social welfare. Turn back to p. 61 and look at figure 3.6. In the case of generalized Lorenz dominance, the most inequality-averse ranking criterion, Rawlsian leximin, and the least, inequality-neutrality, are in accord. Each prefers the dominating distribution – and, moreover, so do all social welfare functions with intervening inequality attitudes. However when generalized Lorenz curves cross once, and mean incomes are unequal, the two extreme views are in conflict. This is precisely what happens for a single-crossing tax reform involving an increase in yield. Because of the redistribution to the poorest, Rawlsian leximin favours the reform, but because of the reduction in total (or mean) post-tax income, the inequality neutral agent does not. Theorem 3.5, p. 65, is relevant to this case. If the variance in the leximin-superior income distribution is sufficiently less than in the efficiency-superior distribution, then this distribution is favoured by all but the least inequality averse among a restricted class of social welfare functions.

Theorem 9.4

(a)   A yield-neutral or yield-reducing tax change which cuts the liabilities of low incomes, and increases all other liabilities, is favoured by every inequality-averse social welfare function.

(b)   A yield-increasing tax change, which sufficiently reduces the variance of post-tax income, is favoured by all but the least inequality-averse among those social welfare functions which obey the Principle of Diminishing Transfers.

The results in part (a) of the theorem are easy to understand. In the yield-neutral case, the reform amounts to a series of rich-to-poor income transfers. We may call such a reform 'purely redistributive', in contrast to what happens in the yield-reducing case, where in addition there are other net additions to lower incomes. All inequality-averse social welfare functions favour rich-to-poor income transfers, and all Paretian social welfare functions favour net additions to incomes; hence the results.

In case (b) of a yield increase, however, there is a net loss of post-tax income, coming from upper income units. No Paretian social welfare function approves such income reductions *per se*. The increased tax 'take' can be made palatable, however – but not to the least inequality-averse, who, as we have observed, will never approve of any reduction in total disposable income. The way to secure welfare approval is to couple the increased 'take' from the richest with additional transfers from them to the poorest, and at the same time to reduce sufficiently the variance in post-tax income (see exercise 9.2.1).

This welfare rationale for yield-increasing reform is necessarily only partial. However, do not forget that *no* individualistic social welfare recommendation *at all* can be given for either of the tax hikes of the previous section of this chapter – they both make everybody worse off! The LP-neutral tax hike causes a smaller welfare loss, and would be voted for by more than half of the electorate if the choice were restricted to these two reforms and the *status quo* were unavailable, but according to theorem 9.4 an appropriately designed single-crossing reform yielding the required revenue can be seen as an improvement on the *status quo*.

According to the logic of theorem 9.4, yield-neutral welfare-improving redistributive reform could be pursued to the point of perfect equality in post-tax income. What is wrong with this argument? Only that we have assumed a fixed pre-tax distribution of income. The single-crossing result determines the first-round or impact effect of the reform. We cannot expect that pre-tax incomes will, in reality, be invariant during such major redistribution, in view of the disincentives created.

We turn finally, in this section, to a consideration of tax reforms involving a change in yield which are effected by coupling a progression-neutral tax cut/hike with pure redistribution from rich to poor. Of course such reforms will not necessarily involve single crossings of old and new tax schedules, but, as we shall see, much insight and an entire new family of 'single-crossing conditions' will emerge.

Consider, then, the case of a yield change effected by means of an RP-neutral tax cut/hike coupled with transfers from rich to poor. We may view the composite reform as

$$t^1(x) \to t^{2R}(x) \to t^3(x) \tag{9.12}$$

where $t^3(x)$ crosses $t^{2R}(x)$ once from below and $g^3 = g^2$. The effect on the distribution of post-tax income is easy to quantify:

$$L^1_{X-T}(p) = L^{2R}_{X-T}(p) \le L^3_{X-T}(p) \text{ for all } p \in [0,1] \tag{9.13}$$

The equality in (9.13) is because post-tax incomes are scaled in the transition from $t^1(x)$ to $t^{2R}(x)$; the inequality is because the ensuing rich-to-poor income transfers are equalizing.

In the case of an LP-neutral tax cut/hike and pure redistribution, we have

$$t^1(x) \to t^{2L}(x) \to t^3(x) \tag{9.14}$$

where $t^3(x)$ crosses $t^{2L}(x)$ once from below and $g^3 = g^2$. In this case, we can quantify the effect of the composite reform on the concentration of tax liabilities:

$$L^1_T(p) = L^{2L}_T(p) \ge L^3_T(p) \text{ for all } p \in [0,1] \tag{9.15}$$

The equality is because tax liabilities are scaled in the LP-neutral change; the inequality is because, whenever the yield is unaffected as in the transition from $t^{2L}(x)$ to $t^3(x)$, a shift inwards of the Lorenz curve for post-tax income is mirrored by a shift outwards of the tax concentration curve.

We can represent these findings in the following form, in terms of the relationship between $t^3(x)$ and the original pre-reform schedule $t^1(x)$. The result is due to Hemming and Keen (1983), though these authors did not derive it by coupling progression-neutral yield change with pure redistribution as here.

Theorem 9.5

Let $t^1(x)$ and $t^3(x)$ be tax schedules with total tax ratios g^1 and g^3 for a given pre-tax income distribution.

(a) Suppose that $[x - t^3(x)]/[1 - g^3]$ crosses $[x - t^1(x)]/[1 - g^1]$ once from above. Then $L^3_{X-T}(p) \geq L^1_{X-T}(p)$ for all $p \in [0, 1]$.
(b) Suppose that $t^3(x)/g^3$ crosses $t^1(x)/g^1$ once from below. Then $L^3_T(p) \leq L^1_T(p)$ for all $p \in [0, 1]$.

Our own proof is all but complete. We just need the additional observations that

$$t^3(x) \gtrless t^{2R}(x) \Leftrightarrow [x - t^3(x)] \gtrless \frac{1 - g^2}{1 - g^1}[x - t^1(x)] \tag{9.16}$$

and

$$t^3(x) \gtrless t^{2L}(x) \Leftrightarrow t^3(x) \gtrless \frac{g^2}{g^1} t^1(x) \tag{9.17}$$

which follow from the definitions of $t^{2R}(x)$ and $t^{2L}(x)$ in terms of $t^1(x)$ given in (9.2)–(9.3) (note also that $g^3 = g^2$). Direct proof of the theorem is also straightforward. For example, to prove (a), first observe that

$$L^3_{X-T}(p) - L^1_{X-T}(p) = \int_0^y [s^3(x) - s^1(x)] f(x)\,dx = J(y) \tag{9.18}$$

say, where $s^i(x) = [x - t^i(x)]/\mu[1 - g^i]$, then identify the turning point of $J(y)$ as a maximum, and finally infer the sign of $J(y)$ exactly as done for $H(y)$ in the proof of theorem 9.3.

Except in the equal yield case, these single-crossing properties are not determined by the tax schedules $t^1(x)$ and $t^3(x)$ alone. They are crossings of 'normalized' tax and post-tax income schedules, the normalizations depending on the total tax ratios, which in turn depend on the prevailing distribution of pre-tax income. We already know from the Jakobsson–Kakwani theorems that increased residual or liability progression is necessary and sufficient to ensure enhanced redistributive effect or departure from proportionality for all pre-tax income distributions. The contribution of Hemming and Keen's theorem is to secure distribution-dependent crossing properties sufficient to ensure the same outcomes for a given pre-tax income distribution. Following a suggestion of Hemming and Keen, we introduce here some formal definitions that will help clarify the above point.

Definition 9.1

(a) Suppose that the pre-tax income distribution is given. Then:
   (i) $t^3(x)$ is *more R-progressive* with respect to this distribution than $t^1(x) \Leftrightarrow$ for this distribution of pre-tax income, $L^3_{X-T}(p) \geq L^1_{X-T}(p)$ for all $p \in [0, 1]$.

(ii) $t^3(x)$ is *more L-progressive* with respect to this distribution than $t^1(x) \Leftrightarrow$ for this distribution of pre-tax income, $L^3_T(p) \le L^1_T(p)$ for all $p \in [0, 1]$.

(b) $t^3(x)$ is *uniformly more R- or L-progressive* than $t^1(x)$ if it is more R- or L-progressive than $t^1(x)$ with respect to every pre-tax distribution of income.

Thus for a tax schedule to be more R- or L-progressive with respect to a given distribution of pre-tax income means to exhibit more redistributive effect or departure from proportionality for that pre-tax income distribution.[4] To be uniformly more R- or L-progressive means that this must be true for every pre-tax income distribution – namely that, by the Jakobsson–Kakwani theorems, residual or liability progression must be higher all along the income scale. In presenting the Hemming and Keen result as we have, we gain an additional perspective: the sufficient condition for increased R/L-progression with respect to a fixed distribution is that the change in schedule be equivalent to an RP/LP-neutral yield change (if any) coupled with pure redistribution from rich to poor.

In an interesting converse to their result, Hemming and Keen prove that uniformly increased progression is equivalent to the conjunction of the sufficient conditions for increased progression with respect to all pre-tax income distributions.

Theorem 9.6

Let $t^1(x)$ and $t^3(x)$ be two income tax schedules.

(a) $RP^{*3}(x) \ge RP^{*1}(x)$ for all $x \Leftrightarrow$ for each pre-tax income distribution, $[x - t^3(x)]/[1 - g^3]$ crosses $[x - t^1(x)]/[1 - g^1]$ once from above;

(b) $LP^{*3}(x) \ge LP^{*1}(x)$ for all $x \Leftrightarrow$ for each pre-tax income distribution, $t^3(x)/g^3$ crosses $t^1(x)/g^1$ once from below.

Proof The proofs in the $\Leftarrow$ direction are immediate from theorem 9.5 and the Jakobsson–Kakwani theorems. For the proof of (b) in the $\Rightarrow$ direction, note that the normalized schedules $t^3(x)/g^3$ and $t^1(x)/g^1$ each have the same *per capita* yield – mean pre-tax income – and so must cross. We need only show that if $t^3(y)/g^3 = t^1(y)/g^1$ for some income y, then $t^3(z)/g^3 \ge t^1(z)/g^1$ for all $z > y$. Now for any tax schedule $t(x)$, we have

$$LP(x) = \frac{xt'(x)}{t(x)} = \frac{x\,d\{\ln[t(x)]\}}{dx} \tag{9.19}$$

Therefore, in the present case:

$$\int_{y}^{z}[LP^{3}(x) - LP^{1}(x)]x^{-1}\,dx = \{\ln[t^{3}(x)] - \ln[t^{1}(x)]\}_{y}^{z} = \ln\frac{t^{3}(z)/g^{3}}{t^{1}(z)/g^{1}} \qquad (9.20)$$

By assumption, the integral on the left is non-negative. Therefore the argument of the logarithm on the right is greater than or equal to unity. The result follows. The proof of (a) is similar.   QED

One implication of this result is that uniformly increased progression precludes multiple crossing of tax schedules.

Corollary 9.1

Income tax schedules ordered by residual or liability progression cross at most once.

Proof Suppose $t^{1}(x)$ and $t^{3}(x)$ are ordered by residual or liability progression. If they cross, we can construct a hypothetical pre-tax income distribution yielding the same revenue under both schedules. Now apply theorem 9.6: they must cross exactly once.   QED

Notwithstanding the insight the Hemming and Keen single-crossing conditions bring to the Jakobsson–Kakwani theorems, perhaps their most striking feature is their potential for application: 'The single crossing condition described above is exceedingly straightforward. It enables quite powerful statements concerning the distributional implications of different tax systems to be made on the basis of information on tax schedule specifications and total net income alone. It would appear to be particularly valuable when income distribution data are incomplete or of low quality' (Hemming and Keen, 1983, p. 377).

Exercises

9.2.1   Suppose that $t^{2}(x)$ crosses $t^{1}(x)$ once from below and $g^{2} > g^{1}$ as in theorems 9.3(b) and 9.4(b). By substituting the distribution of $x - t^{2}(x)$ for F and the distribution of $x - t^{1}(x)$ for G in theorem 3.5, p. 65, verify that the reform can be recommended on social welfare grounds provided that it reduces the variance of post-tax income by at least $2\mu^{2}[g^{2} - g^{1}][\tau - 1 + \frac{1}{2}(g^{1} + g^{2})]$ where $\tau = [z - t^{1}(z)]/\mu$ and z is the highest income in the pre-tax distribution.

9.2.2   'It must be emphasised that while Jakobsson's condition implies single-crossing, the reverse is not true' (Hemming and Keen, 1983, p. 378). Demonstrate the validity of this assertion.

9.2.3(a) Use equation (9.18) to show that a necessary condition for $t^3(x)$
to be more R-progressive than $t^1(x)$ with respect to a fixed pre-tax
income distribution is that $[x - t^3(x)]/[1 - g^3]$ crosses $[x - t^1(x)]/[1 - g^1]$ an odd number of times, first from above.

9.2.3(b) Show that a necessary condition for L^3_{X-T} to cross L^1_{X-T} once is that
$[x - t^3(x)]/[1 - g^3]$ crosses $[x - t^1(x)]/[1 - g^1]$ an even number of times.
Hint: Sketch the function $J(y)$ defined in (9.18). How many turning
points can it have, and what is their significance?

9.2.4   'Is the current system of income taxation in the UK progressive?
In terms of the standard definition of a progressive tax as one whose
average rate is everywhere increasing the answer is a firm 'No'
. . . the situation is fully described by saying that the UK income
tax is more progressive than proportional taxation given the distribution of pre-tax income in the UK but is not uniformly so'
(Hemming and Keen, 1983, p. 380). Explain the argument underlying this assertion.

9.2.5(a) Let $t(x|U, u_0)$ be the tax schedule satisfying the equal sacrifice
rule $U(x) - U[x - t(x)] \equiv u_0$ (see p. 175). Now suppose $V(x)$ is a more
inequality-averse utility-of-income function than $U(x)$: $q_V(x) \geq q_U(x)$
for all x (p. 95). Prove that if $t(x|V, v_0)$ and $t(x|U, u_0)$ have equal
yields, then post-tax income under schedule $t(x|V, v_0)$ Lorenz
dominates that under schedule $t(x|U, u_0)$. *Hint*: Prove that $W(x)$
$= V(x) - V[x - t(x|U, u_0)]$ slopes downwards. Now show that if
$t(y|V, v_0) \geq t(y|U, u_0)$ then $W(y) \leq v_0$. Deduce that if $t(y|V, v_0) \geq$
$t(y|U, u_0)$ then $t(z|V, v_0) \geq t(z|U, u_0)$ for all $z > y$, whence $t(x|U, u_0)$
and $t(x|V, v_0)$ cross once. Finally, apply theorem 9.3, part (a).

9.2.5(b) Conclude, with Buchholtz *et al.* (1988), that income after any equal
sacrifice tax schedule $t(x|V, v_0)$ for which $V(x)$ is inequality averse is
more equally distributed than income after a yield-equivalent poll
tax. Contrast this result with Yaari's (1988) very different contention
(exercise 7.1.5, p. 179).

9.3   Double-crossing tax reform

'. . . with tax cuts for the top and bottom, it is the middle that is left holding
the bag' (Minarik, 1982, in respect of a proposal to replace the US individual income tax by a flat rate tax with increased low income relief).

Some proposals for income tax reform couple redistribution to the poorest
with redistribution to the richest. If protection of the poorest in tax reform
is a perennial political imperative, redressing disincentives for the entrepreneurs, at the top end of the income distribution, became so in the political
climate of the 1980s. Inevitably middle-income recipients are the losers from
this process. What can we say about such reforms in social welfare terms?

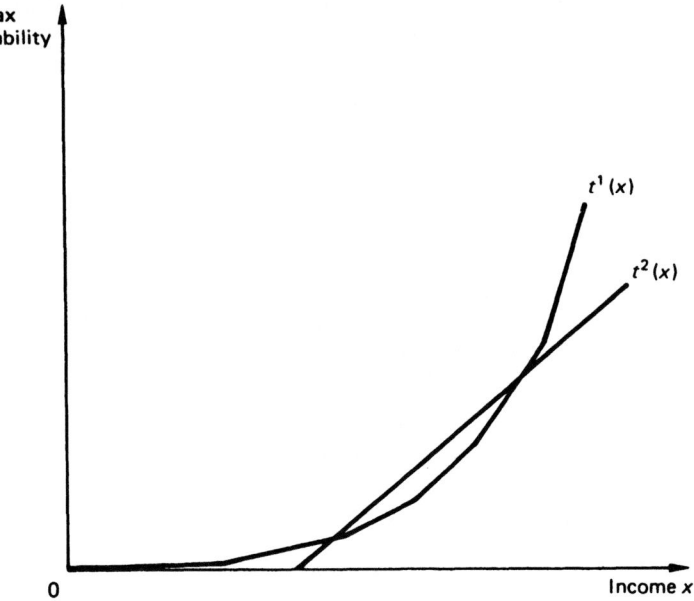

Figure 9.2   Double-crossing tax reform

Simplification of a highly graduated marginal rate structure can work to
the benefit of both ends of the income distribution, as Minarik has pointed
out (see also figure 9.2).[5] A change in the balance of taxation between different components can have the same effect. For example, Creedy (1982) considers proposals to change the balance between the UK personal income tax
and National Insurance Contribution in favour of the latter. The argument
could be one of 'earmarking' taxes to their ultimate purposes or, a less worthy
suggestion, that some forms of tax are less conspicuous than others and the
change of balance might feel like a tax cut to voters. The UK National Insurance Contribution operates between 'floor' and 'ceiling' levels of earned
income (and not at all on unearned income). If its rate were to be increased
to recover revenue returned to taxpayers across a wider income scale, an
additional burden would indeed fall on middle-income units to the benefit of
both ends.[6]

Reform can work in the opposite direction as well. Suppose that income
taxes are to be cut for middle-income recipients, perhaps in fulfilment of a
political commitment. Big tax cuts for middle income units are very expen-
sive, since these incomes are very numerous, and if undertaken the lost
revenue may subsequently have to be recouped by adjustments to other forms
of tax. It is quite conceivable that middle-income units will pay only a part
of the subsequently regained revenue (for example, this would be so if con-

sumption taxes were to be put up). In that case middle-income units still gain ultimately, though not by as much as first thought and at the expense of the two ends of the income distribution.

We must look to the configuration of generalized Lorenz curves in order to analyse the social welfare effects of double-crossing tax reforms. We confine ourselves for the moment to reforms $t^1(x) \rightarrow t^2(x)$ which benefit both ends at the expense of the middle.

Theorem 9.7

If $t^2(x)$ crosses $t^1(x)$ twice, first from below, then for any pre-tax income distribution such that $g^2 \geq g^1$, GL^2_{X-T} crosses GL^1_{X-T} once from above.

Proof As in the proof of theorem 9.3, let

$$GL^2_{X-T}(p) - GL^1_{X-T}(p) = \int_0^y [t^1(x) - t^2(x)] f(x) \mathrm{d}x = H(y) \qquad (9.11)$$

where $p = F(y)$. Then $H(0) = 0$ and $H'(y) \gtrless 0$ when $t^1(y) \gtrless t^2(y)$. $H(y)$ therefore has two turning points, the first being a maximum and the second a minimum. Since $H(y)$ approaches $\mu(g^1 - g^2) \leq 0$ as y becomes large, $H(y)$ must change sign once.   QED

Unhappily, we cannot determine the generalized Lorenz configuration when the tax yield is reduced by a such a reform. (Try to, and you will see the problem.) We defer this case for now. An application of results from chapter 3, namely of theorems 3.4 and 3.5, pp. 64–65, yields the welfare prescriptions we seek.

Theorem 9.8

(a)   A yield-neutral tax reform which cuts the liabilities of low and high incomes and increases all other liabilities, and also reduces the variance of post-tax income, is favoured by every social welfare function which obeys the Principle of Diminishing Transfers.

(b)   A yield-increasing tax reform of this kind, which sufficiently reduces the variance of post-tax income, is favoured by all but the least inequality-averse of the social welfare functions in (a).

In the case of pure redistribution we can gain some understanding of this result as follows. Transfers to the less well off are approved by every inequality-averse social welfare function; transfers to the better off are approved by none. The criterion expressing the balance required for the approval of the restricted class of social welfare functions is variance reduction. Now look at exercise 2.4.9, p. 36. As in the case of single-crossing reform, a double-crossing tax increase can be recommended if the variance of post-tax income is sufficiently reduced (see exercise 9.3.1).

What do these results imply for the particular reforms discussed earlier? First yield-neutral tax simplification, or change of balance, which benefits the richest and poorest income units is welfare improving if variance reducing. Second any move to reduce income tax for middle-income recipients and recover the lost revenue from increased consumption taxes, levied across a wider income spectrum, would be disapproved of if the end result was increased variance in people's disposable incomes. (Since variance *reduction* is sufficient for a welfare *gain*, variance *increase* for the reverse type of reform is sufficient for a welfare *loss*.) Lastly, such an income tax cut for middle incomes only partly recovered from broader-based taxation would be disapproved of by all but the least inequality-averse of social welfare functions if the variance were not sufficiently controlled.

What can we say about social welfare when tax reform benefitting both ends of the distribution involves a yield decrease? In such a case there are net additions to upper and lower incomes in addition to transfers from the middle. The conditions for welfare approval are less stringent in this case. We can regard the reform as taking place in two stages, (i) pure redistribution to both ends of what middle-income units lose, plus (ii) further additions to upper and lower incomes. There is obviously more than one way to make this decomposition, but if a way can be found for which in stage (i) the variance is reduced, then this stage of the reform will be approved by the restricted class of social welfare functions in theorem 9.8. Stage (ii) will be approved by all Paretian social welfare functions. Therefore the composite reform will be approved by the restricted class. In view of exercise 2.4.9, p. 36, the question reduces to this: are there enough gainers at the bottom end of the income distribution who are sufficiently less well off than the losers in the middle? If so, approval is secured.

The nature of the restriction which variance reduction imposes upon tax redesign is a topic which merits further investigation. To check whether variance has been reduced in the *ex post* evaluation of income tax reform is, of course, straightforward given published statistics.[7]

Exercises

9.3.1 Obtain an expression for the degree of variance reduction which is sufficient for the result in theorem 9.8(b). Show that this expression takes exactly the same form as in exercise 9.2.1 on p. 230 except that in this case $\tau = [z - t^2(z)]/\mu$.

9.3.2 Do the single-crossing and double-crossing results of theorems 9.4 and 9.8 afford transitive welfare prescriptions? Suppose that $t^2(x)$ crosses $t^1(x)$ once from below (or twice, first from below) and $t^3(x)$ crosses $t^2(x)$

once from below (or twice, first from below). In what circumstances can a social welfare recommendation be given for $t^3(x)$ over $t^1(x)$?

9.3.3 How did Onrubia *et al.* (2000) combine results on double-crossing reforms, RP-neutral tax cuts and LP-neutral tax hikes to provide a recipe for welfare-improving simplification and decentralization of the Spanish income tax?

9.3.4 What would be the consequences of replacing the French income splitting privileges (*quotient familial*) and income tax rate structure by British-style lump-sum tax allowances and rate structure? Describe the issues, as raised by Atkinson *et al.* (1988), and explain how the sequential generalized Lorenz dominance criterion is brought to bear upon this problem.

9.3.5 Let welfare be the average of an indirect utility function, defined over income and the prices of goods, which is increasing and concave in income. Describe Mayshar and Yitzhaki's (1995) 'concentration dominance' test for identifying opportunities for welfare-improving marginal indirect tax reforms. Sketch the microeconomic assumptions under which it holds. Explain the search procedure which is entailed and depends only on the distributions of disposable income and household expenditures on the goods in question, drawing upon Yitzhaki and Lewis (1996). What is the extension to this test derived in Mayshar and Yitzhaki (1996)?

Notes

1 Note in respect of both cases, however, the theoretical possibility that the marginal or average tax rate faced by an income unit after reform could fall outside the range (0, 1), especially if the supposed change in yield is large. We assume away this possibility in the analysis which follows.

2 For further consideration of the Pfähler (1984) analysis in the American context, see Formby *et al.* (1992).

3 ARP-neutral tax reforms are considered in detail in the second (1993) edition of this book.

4 Necessary conditions for increased R-progression with respect to a fixed pre-tax income distribution are explored by Latham (1988). In the equal-yield case, the condition stated in exercise 9.2.3(a) ahead is obtained (as theorem 2, p. 191). In the two cases $g^3 > g^1$ and $g^3 < g^1$, Latham obtains conditions which follow from the one given in exercise 9.2.3(a) (in his theorems 4 and 5, pp. 193 and 196). The result stated in exercise 9.2.3(b) is obtained by Thistle (1989a) (as Proposition 7, p. 125), where a synthesis of the published results on income tax progression and crossing properties can also be found. See also Latham (1993).

5 Hall and Rabushka (1983) also consider proposals to replace the US individual income tax by a flat rate tax. For a description and evaluation of the major reform of the US income tax which took place in 1986, see Musgrave (1988).

6 In Hutton and Lambert (1983) it is shown that a revenue and revenue elasticity neutral partial switch from the UK personal income tax to the National Insurance Contribution would involve a double crossing of the old and new effective tax schedules.

7 The generalized Lorenz curve and social welfare results for single- and double-crossing tax reform given in sections 9.2 and 9.3 are drawn from Dardanoni and Lambert (1988).

10

Differences in income tax treatment

An income tax system which treats different types of individual or household differently cannot be written in the simple form $t(x)$ where x is pre-tax income. None of the theory developed in the last two chapters can be applied directly to such an income tax. In this chapter we provide a structure within which some of the theory of these preceding chapters can be extended. Some entirely new theory also emerges.

An income tax *not* in the form $t(x)$ may induce horizontal inequity (henceforth HI). In chapter 7, section 7.3, we enumerated many sources of horizontal inequity in the personal income tax. We said there that, in the present chapter, we would look for and quantify the HI in an income tax at the family level. We said we would do this by applying an equivalence scale to household money incomes, both before and after tax, and checking for cases in which the tax system introduces differences in post-tax living standards where there were none pre-tax. This forms our main agenda here.

Hence our starting point is social heterogeneity. We could think of a population in which the households comprise single persons, married couples and families with children. The income tax is typically levied on money incomes, and may or may not take family size into account in some way. Suppose there is a tax function for families of size n, call it $t_n(x)$. All of the theory of chapters 8 and 9 can be applied to the tax function $t_n(x)$ and distribution function $F_n(x)$ (say) of money income among families of size n. However, the *overall* effects of the bundle of schedules $t_n(x)$, $n = 1, 2, 3 \ldots$, cannot be determined from results in chapters 8 and 9. One could do welfare analysis using sequential dominance criteria, drawing upon section 3.6 of chapter 3, retaining money income for the analysis.[1] Or one could equivalize and then determine overall inequality and welfare effects. We follow the latter course of action here.

Let z_n be the equivalence scale deflator for a household of size n. As we saw in chapter 7, p. 185, the equitable income tax must take the form

$$t_n(x) = z_n \tau^* \left(\frac{x}{z_n} \right) \tag{7.15}$$

where $\tau^*(u)$ is the tax function on living standards $u = x/z_n$ which embodies society's chosen degree of vertical equity (VE). Such a tax would act as a tax on *equivalent income per standard adult*, of whom there are z_n in a household of size n. But we do not typically see income taxes like this. Indeed, many income tax systems ignore family size altogether, introducing differential treatments on the basis of factors which could be regarded as socially irrelevant (mortgage interest relief for homeowners could be so regarded). How does the typical income tax, warts and all, measure up against the ideal in (7.15)?

In section 10.1 we review some of the constructions of chapter 8 and assess the extent to which these can be adapted for use in the equivalent income framwork (and also generally when the tax is not of the form $t(x)$ with $0 \le t'(x) < 1$ as assumed before). Differences in the taxes of pre-tax equals provide a major complication, as we could expect, but some results are possible. These show, in particular, that the extent of reranking caused in the transition from pre-tax to post-tax equivalent income distribution is central. It is apparent at this point that we shall need some new constructions to proceed to a thorough analysis.

To assess the degree of HI in an income tax system, we must compare it with an ideal income tax, that of equation (7.15). In section 10.2 we discuss the important question confronting the analyst, *which* idealized tax function on equivalent income should be assumed to represent the vertical stance of a given income tax system? As we shall see, there is more than one possible way to answer this question.

In section 10.3, with the above question assumed resolved, some methodologies to measure the horizontal and vertical contributions to the redistributive effect of the tax system are developed. The relationships between these methodologies and the approaches outlined in section 10.1 are explained.

In section 10.4 we describe a partial ordering of income tax systems by HI which gauges the 'degree of disassociation' induced between people's pre- and post-tax living standards. Whereas the redistributive effect methodologies all rest upon gauging the extent of unequal treatment of equals by the tax system (i.e. upon classical HI), the new approach picks up on a different equity criterion, that of 'no reranking' previously espoused by authors such as Atkinson (1980b) and Plotnick (1981). This approach focuses upon 'procedural unfairness' in the tax system.

10.1   Living standards, inequality and reranking

Suppose now that income tax liability is *not* a function $t(x)$ of money income x, or that, if it is, the assumption $0 \le t'(x) < 1$ is violated. Then the material developed in chapter 8 falls down. However, we can retrieve some interesting results. We will do this first, and afterwards consider what the results mean in the equivalent income context.

There are two problems when tax is not of the form $t(x)$ with $0 \leq t'(x) < 1$ for all x. Both arise because the orderings of income units from poorest to richest by pre-tax incomes and by post-tax incomes can be different. The first problem arises in defining the concentration curves $L_T(p)$ and $L_{X-T}(p)$ in these circumstances; we shall explain this problem in a moment; the second is that, even when these curves have been carefully defined, the latter, L_{X-T}, is not a Lorenz curve (as we saw in chapter 2, see (2.27), p. 40). This means that none of the inequality analysis of chapter 8 goes through.

The problem of definition arises when people with the same pre-tax incomes pay different taxes. Let two persons, i and j, have equal pre-tax incomes but different tax liabilities. How should we define $L_T(p)$ and $L_{X-T}(p)$ at values p such that the group defined as 'the poorest $100p$ per cent of income units before tax' would necessarily have to include one but exclude the other? To take a simple example, suppose the population comprises seven persons, among whom only i and j have equal pre-tax incomes. Suppose further that three persons are poorer than i and j, and two are richer. Then for $4/7 \leq p < 5/7$ only one of the two can be included in 'the poorest $100p$ per cent of persons before tax'. Therefore only one of them can count in the cumulated sums of taxes and post-tax incomes up to percentile p, i.e. in $L_T(p)$ and $L_{X-T}(p)$. Which one should we include?

This sort of problem can be overlooked (and indeed, has been) in studies of redistributive effect and disproportionality which are based on grouped data. Because one is working with aggregates (or averages) of pre-tax income and taxes up to the endpoints x_2 of income ranges $x_1 < x \leq x_2$, differences in the tax payments of pre-tax equals are not evident. Concentration curves get defined only at points of accumulation like x_2 on the pre-tax income range, with interpolation being used in between. In these circumstances, reranking may not be apparent either, though it will typically exist and would be seen in microdata.[2]

We passed over possible difficulties arising from the unequal tax treatment of pre-tax equals when we defined the concentration curves L_T and L_{X-T} in chapter 2 (p. 38). A careful treatment here will expose what is at stake and pave the way for the analysis of section 10.3. Let A and B be any two attributes of income units (for example, their pre- or post-tax income levels, their taxes or, as on p. 28, their expenditures on food). The concentration curve for A with respect to B shows, for each $p \in [0, 1]$, the share in the total of A going to the lowest $100p$ per cent in the distribution of B. As our little example showed, a problem arises whenever two or more income units enjoy a common value, say b_0, of attribute B but *different* values of attribute A, and p is such that some *but not all* of those having b_0 can belong the 'lowest $100p$ per cent' in the distribution of B. There are two quite appealing ways forward. One is to define a lexicographic ordering, in which income units are ordered first by levels of B, from lowest to highest, and second, at any given b_0, by levels of A, again from lowest to highest. Let $C_{A|B}(p)$ be the share in the total of A going to the $100p$ per cent of income units who come first in this lexicographic ordering. Second, if $b_1 < b_2 < b_3 < \ldots b_n$ are the distinct B-values occurring in the population, and if the proportion of income units having less than or equal to b_i is p_i, $1 \leq i \leq n$, we could define $\hat{C}_{A|B}(p_i)$ as the share in the total of A going to those with $b \leq b_i$ and use linear interpolation to define $\hat{C}_{A|B}(p)$ for $p \neq p_i$, $1 \leq i \leq n$. Clearly $\hat{C}_{A|B}(p) \geq C_{A|B}(p)$ for all p, with equality at each p_i. $\hat{C}_{A|B}(p_i)$ is the concentration curve which would obtain if, counterfactually, all those with any given B-value b_0 also had the same A-value, the average of the actual A-values they have; $\hat{C}_{A|B}(p) - C_{A|B}(p)$ measures the *disparity in A given B*.[3]

What is the way forward in respect of our concentration curves L_T and L_{X-T}? With grouped data it hardly matters if there are unequal tax treatments at the microlevel; one cannot detect these; one can only define the curves at points of accumulation p_i and then 'join up'. With microdata, we could use 'joining up', but we also have the option of a lexicographic approach. The natural thing would be to line income units up first by levels of pre-tax income, from lowest to highest, and second, at any given pre-tax income level (i.e. among equals), by levels of post-tax income, again from lowest to highest. If we use this ordering to compute *both* L_{X-T} and L_T, or if we use 'joining up' for both, then the relationship

$$L_X \equiv g L_T + (1-g) L_{X-T} \tag{2.25}$$

derived on p. 38 still holds. This is because, when multiplied through by total pre-tax income, each side of (2.25) expresses the total of all pre-tax income up to the relevant point p in whichever pre-tax income parade has been used to define the curves. Can you see why?[4]

It follows that, as on p. 208, the relationship

$$L_{X-T} - L_X \equiv \frac{g}{1-g} (L_X - L_T) \tag{8.29}$$

also remains true when the curves are carefully defined. However, L_{X-T} is not the Lorenz curve for post-tax income in these circumstances, as we have said. We had better write instead

$$L^* - L_X \equiv \frac{g}{1-g} (L_X - L_T) - (L_{X-T} - L^*) \tag{10.1}$$

where (as in chapter 2, p. 40) L^* is the post-tax Lorenz curve, if we want the left-hand side to capture the inequality effect of the tax system.[5] But now there is an additional negative term on the right-hand side. This is precisely as we anticipated in chapter 2, p. 40: 'the correction factor is a downward shift:

post-tax concentration curve $L_{X-T} \rightarrow$ post-tax Lorenz curve L^*

reflecting the extent of reranking'.

Integrating (10.1), we find that

$$G_X - G_{X-T} = \frac{g}{1-g}(C_T - G_X) - (G_{X-T} - C_{X-T}) \tag{10.2}$$

where the Gs are Gini coefficients and the Cs are concentration coefficients. This is just like (2.33), p. 40. Now the Kakwani index Π^K was originally defined in terms of the concentration of taxes:

$$\Pi^K = C_T - G_X \tag{10.3}$$

whereas the Reynolds–Smolensky index Π^{RS} was designed to capture the inequality impact of the tax system:

$$\Pi^{RS} = G_X - G_{X-T} \tag{10.4}$$

Inserting these into (10.2), along with

$$R = G_{X-T} - C_{X-T} \geq 0 \tag{10.5}$$

as the reranking correction, we have

$$\Pi^{RS} = \frac{g}{1-g}\Pi^K - R \tag{10.6}$$

This generalization of equation (8.30), p. 209, is applicable in the case of any tax system *not* of the form $t(x)$ with $0 \leq t'(x) < 1$. For example, (10.6) is appropriate for differentiated income taxes, and also for non-income taxes where these have been attributed to income units.[6] For such taxes, estimates of $[g/(1-g)]\Pi^K$ derived from grouped data could overstate the true redistributive effect Π^{RS} because of an omitted reranking correction. Kakwani (1984a, p. 165) was the first to raise the reranking issue and derive equation (10.6). See also Kakwani (1986) and Jenkins (1988b). The data may be denominated in either money or equivalent income terms for calculation of the measures Π^{RS}, Π^K and R occurring in (10.6). What about the normative significance of these measures, especially R, in the two cases?

If the population is socially homogeneous, money income analysis is appropriate and the welfare premium $V_{X-T} - V_P$ developed in (8.37)–(8.38), p. 211, on the basis of the social evaluation function

$$V(\mu, G) = \mu(1 - kG) \qquad 0 \leq k \leq 1 \tag{5.25}$$

can be calculated. We find that:

$$V_{X-T} - V_P = \mu(1-g)k[G_X - G_{X-T}] = \mu(1-g)k\,\Pi^{RS}$$
$$= \mu k[g\,\Pi^K - (1-g)R] \tag{10.7}$$

The normative significance of Π^{RS}, Π^K and R is clear. In particular, rerankings detract from the welfare-enhancing property of an otherwise progressive tax system.

If the population is socially heterogeneous, calculation of the terms in (10.6) in the *money* income framework is of course feasible, but the measures derived would be uninteresting. For normatively significant measures, the analysis should be conducted in equivalent income terms when the population is socially heterogeneous.

In the notation of an earlier discussion, let $t_n(x)$ be the money income tax function for families of size n, and z_n the equivalence scale deflator. The question is, whether or not the induced functions $\tau_n(u)$ of pre-tax equivalent income u defined by

$$\tau_n(u) = \frac{t_n(z_n u)}{z_n} \qquad n = 1, 2, 3 \ldots \tag{10.8}$$

are all the same. If they are, so that $\tau_n(u) \equiv \tau(u)$ for all n and some function τ, the question becomes whether $0 \le \tau'(u) < 1$ for all u. If this is so, the results in chapters 8 and 9 can be applied wholesale: just transcribe x into u and $t(\;)$ into $\tau(\;)$ throughout. This is precisely the case identified in (7.15), in which the tax system is equitable and has vertical stance described by τ (we used the symbol τ^* in (7.15)). More likely, the functions $\tau_n(u)$ will differ.

If the tax system induces a non-systematic relationship between pre- and post-tax living standards among households, as when the functions $\tau_n(u)$ described above differ, (10.6) should be applied in equivalent income terms. Normative significance can be gained by using the social evaluation function (5.25) as before, but this time (5.25) must be cast in terms of equivalent incomes. Note that the various rationales for (5.25) all rest, at heart, on pairwise income comparisons. Clearly a process of equivalizing would take place before, say, a single-person household and a family with three children would make such a comparison. Thus (10.7) will again hold, but now μ represents mean pre-tax *equivalent* income and g the fraction of all *equivalent* income taken in tax. The welfare comparison is thus with a flat tax with the same yield *denominated in units of equivalent income*. It is clear that if $R \ge 0$, the welfare premium is less than for an equitable tax with the same yield and the same disproportionality. Some authors argue that rank reversal, if this occurs in the distribution of living standards, is an inequity quite distinct from classical HI (see Atkinson, 1980b, Plotnick, 1981 and Lambert and Yitzhaki, 1995). R measures this inequity. The measurement of classical HI is considered in section 10.3.

Exercises

10.1.1(a) Derive a decomposition $\Pi^{RS}(v) = [g/(1 - g)]\Pi^K(v) - R(v)$ analogous to (10.6). *Hint:* Multiply in (10.1) by $v(v - 1)(1 - p)^{v-2}$ and integrate. Now refer to (8.21), p. 202, and (8.27), p. 207. Write $R(v)$ as an integral.

10.1.1(b) Explain Duclos' (2000, p. 148) result, according to which $R(v)$ can be interpreted as the 'ethically weighted average of ill-fortune in the population' or 'average feeling of resentment towards the arrival of "parvenus" among the rich'.

10.1.1(c) Show that the more general relationship between Pfähler's (1987) AIR measures of redistributive effect and ATR measures of disproportionality is $\Psi = [g/(1 - g)]\,\Phi - R_\Psi$, where $R_\Psi = \int_0^1[L_{X-T}(p) - L^*(p)]k(p)\,dp$ (see exercises 8.3.5(a), p. 205, and 8.4.6, p. 212).[7]

10.1.2   If $t(x) = \Sigma t_i(x)$, the overall redistributive effect is $\Pi^{RS} = \Sigma[(1 - g_i)/(1 - g)]\,\Pi_i^{RS}$ where Π_i^{RS} is the Reynolds–Smolensky index for the ith component tax alone (exercise 8.4.4, p. 212). Suppose now that the overall tax liability is the sum of component taxes which have non-systematic relationships with income. Prove that in this case $\Pi^{RS} = \Sigma[(1 - g_i)/(1 - g)]\,\Pi_i^{RS} - R^*$ where $R^* = R - \Sigma[(1 - g_i)/(1 - g)]\,R_i$, and R and R_i are the measures of reranking for the overall and component taxes respectively. *Hint* Show that $\Pi^{RS} + R = \int_0^1[L_{X-T}(p) - L_X(p)]\,dp$ where L_{X-T} is the overall post-tax concentration curve, and obtain a similar expression for $\Pi_i^{RS} + R_i$ in terms of the concentration curve L_{X-T_i}. Now show that the relationship between these concentration curves which is given in exercise 8.4.4 is still valid.

10.1.3   '. . . the total difference in inequality (0.425 to 0.401) is equal to the *sum* of the reranking and gap-narrowing components . . . Although most of the change . . . came from the gap-narrowing effect, the reranking component amounted to 30 per cent of the total for the standard Gini and 42 per cent . . . for the extended Gini' (Lerman and Yitzhaki, 1995, p. 55, italics added). Explain Lerman and Yitzhaki's approach, according to which the post-tax ranking is the policymaker's desired one, and rerankings contribute *positively* towards redistributive effect Π^{RS} along with reductions in relative income differentials.

10.2   Vertical equity considerations

For the remainder of this chapter we shall work with equivalent incomes, calling these living standards, and with taxes denominated in units of equivalent income. To simplify matters and avoid introducing and maintaining a new notation, *from now on x will stand for pre-tax living standard and T(x) will be tax denominated in units of equivalent income.* We will still speak informally of 'income' and 'tax' in this new situation.

What is meant by the *vertical stance* of an income tax system?

One widely held view is that this is defined by the effect of the tax system *on average* on the relative income differentials of pre-tax unequals. The reference to averaging is necessary because there will typically be many households with a given pre-tax living standard x, and if HI is present then not all of them will have the same post-tax living standard. It is the dispersion of taxes (equivalently, of post-tax living standards) at fixed income levels x, or the unequal tax treatment of equals, which signifies classical HI.

A different line of argument says that vertical equity is about society's choice of post-tax income distribution given the pre-tax income distribution.

The only way inequity can arise is through the *process* of taxation. If there is perfect association between pre-tax and post-tax living standards, then there is no reranking and everything is fine. But if households get reranked in the transition by which society achieves its desired post-tax distribution of living standards, this means disassociation has been introduced, signifying a faulty tax process. Such disassociation is called horizontal inequity by the proponents of the 'no reranking' (henceforth NR) approach, but it is distinct from classical HI.

The classical literature is relatively old: see, for example, Pigou (1949), Johnson and Mayer (1962) and particularly Musgrave's (1990) reconsideration 'Horizontal equity, once more'. The no-reranking literature effectively began with Atkinson (1980b) and Plotnick (1981), and was taken up early-on by King (1983) and then Jenkins (1988c, 1994), *inter alia*. According to the classicists, a 'smoothed' relationship between pre- and post-tax living standards must be calculated to represent the tax system's vertical action, and then HI should be measured locally (at each pre-tax living standard x) by departures from this HI-free counterfactual schedule. The no-reranking approach also begins with the definition of a smooth, HI-free counterfactual relationship to represent the tax system's vertical action. In this case, though, the smooth schedule does not change the *set of* realized post-tax living standards in any way – but it maps each pre-tax living standard differently, namely, to that post-tax living standard whose rank is the same. It thus 'unscrambles' any reranking introduced by the tax system in the passage to the given distribution of post-tax living standards. We focus for the time being upon the classical approach.

Musgrave (1990, p. 118) proposed to measure the vertical performance of the income tax by reference to the hypothetical income distribution 'assuming the actual distribution among but equal division of the burden within each group of equals'. For him, then, the 'smoothing' we spoke of is simple averaging, but this is not the only option. Let $S(x)$ denote the group of households having exactly x before tax: this is the *equals group* located at point x, the basic unit for classical HI analysis.

We introduce two approaches to smoothing here which are representative of recent literature addressing the vertical/horizontal equity question. One attributes to each household in $S(x)$ the mean living standard of the members of the group, which is just as Musgrave suggested; the other attributes the mean welfare level of the group, as judged by an inequality-averse social decision-maker (SDM) with imposed utility-of-equivalent-income function $u_e(v) = v^{1-e}/1 - e$, $0 < e \neq 1$, $u_1(v) = \ln v$, where e is the usual inequality-aversion parameter (and v is post-tax equivalent income).

These two procedures involve hypothetically replacing the dispersed post-tax living standards v within an equals group $S(x)$ by a fixed living standard for everybody, call it $v(x)$, which is in the one case the mean post-tax living standard of the group, call this μ_x, and in the other the equally distributed equivalent living standard, call this ξ_x.[8] Letting x range freely, a hypothetical tax on living standards is traced out,

$$T(x) = x - v(x) \tag{10.9}$$

which represents the vertical effect of the actual tax system (warts and all).
Explicitly, the two 'smoothed' schedules we have just suggested are

$$T_{RN}(x) = x - \mu_x \tag{10.10a}$$

and

$$T_{WN}(x) = x - \xi_x \tag{10.10b}$$

respectively. If applied instead of the actual tax system, these taxes would eliminate HI within every equals group, in the one case without loss of equivalent income to the group (thus raising the same revenue from the group denominated in units of equivalent income), and in the other without loss of social well-being in each equals group. The subscripts 'RN' and 'WN' stand for 'revenue neutral' and 'welfare neutral' respectively for obvious reasons. We will call $T_{RN}(x)$ the *revenue-neutral HE replacement tax* and $T_{WN}(x)$ the *welfare-neutral HE replacement tax*. The function $T_{WN}(x)$ of course depends crucially upon inequality aversion e.

Figure 10.1 shows a simulated scatterplot of post-tax living standards against pre-tax living standards for an income tax with HI. At low levels of

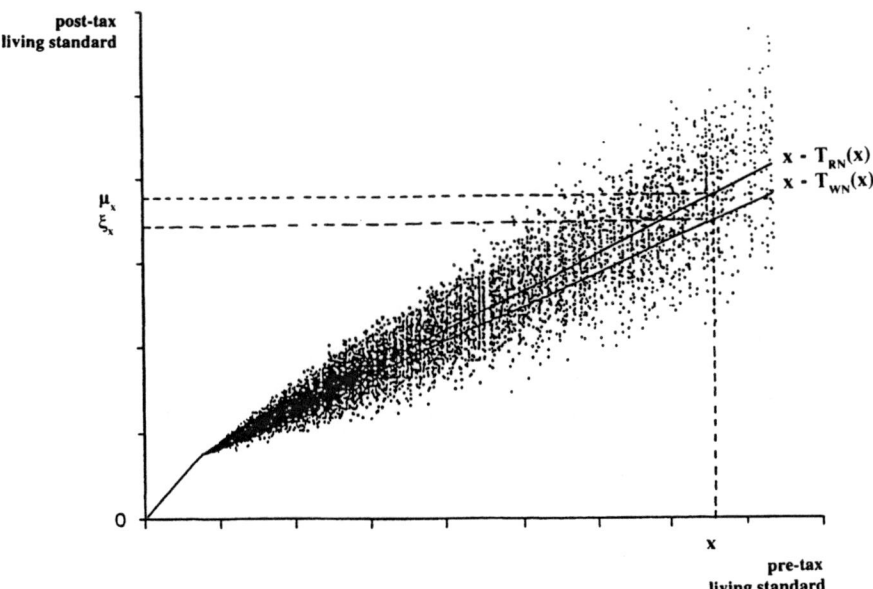

Figure 10.1   A hypothetical income tax with HI

x, where no tax is payable, all points lie along the 45° line. For each set of pre-tax equals who are subject to tax, there is a range of corresponding post-tax living standards. The locus of points (x, μ_x) as x varies traces out the pre-tax/post-tax living standard relationship which would obtain after application of the schedule $T_{RN}(x)$ in (10.10a), and the locus of points (x, ξ_x) traces out that after application of the schedule $T_{WN}(x)$ in (10.10b). At each x, the difference between the amounts of tax levied by these schedules,

$$C_{S(x)} = \mu_x - \xi_x > 0 \tag{10.11}$$

is just the perceived cost of inequality for the sub-population $S(x)$ (recall (4.25), p. 96). This is the maximum amount per capita the SDM would pay (on behalf of the group) to have the inequality within $S(x)$ removed. This amount is positive so long as there is unequal tax treatment. Thus $T_{WN}(x)$ collects more revenue from each equals group than $T_{RN}(x)$.

Comparing the two HI-free replacement schedules $T_{RN}(x)$ and $T_{WN}(x)$, we see that at each pre-tax living standard x the former has a better welfare performance than actual taxes and raises the same revenue,[9] whilst the latter has the same welfare as actual taxes but raises more revenue. These properties will be used in section 10.3.

What sort of tax system could generate a scatter of pre- and post-tax living standards as in figure 10.1? First, the tax code could comprise a bundle of schedules, $\langle t_1(x), t_2(x), \ldots, t_k(x)\rangle$, applying to sub-populations with different tax-relevant attributes. In this case the revenue-neutral replacement schedule would take the form:

$$T(x) = \sum_i \theta_i(x)t_i(x) \tag{10.12}$$

where $\theta_i(x)$ is the proportion of tax units having x in group i. Models like this appear in Hayes et al. (1995) and Kakwani and Lambert (1999) (see exercises 10.2.1 and 10.2.2). Second, the tax liability of a household h with income x could take the form

$$T^h = T(x) + \varepsilon^h(x) \tag{10.13}$$

where $T(x)$ is a progressive schedule and the departures $\varepsilon^h(x)$ from it have zero mean among households h at each pre-tax income level x. Then $T_{RN}(x) \equiv T(x)$ for all x. This model, which is explored in Aronson et al. (1994), could describe random errors in taxation, or a situation in which the ideal tax $T(x)$ is not exactly realized because it is money incomes (rather than equivalent incomes) that are being taxed.

In both (10.12) and (10.13) the tax system is described by a schedule $T(x)$ and departures from it which depend on nonincome factors. (In the one case the departure is $t_i(x) - T(x)$ and in the other $\varepsilon^h(x)$). In both situations, $T(x)$ reveals the underlying vertical stance of the tax system according to the Musgrave averaging criterion. The index Π_T^K thus describes average disproportionality in the tax system, and $[g/(1-g)]\,\Pi_T^K$ measures vertical redistribution (where g is the total tax ratio for both $T(x)$ and the entire tax system). But these measures do *not* feature in (10.6), p. 241, which specifies the overall redistributive effect of the tax system. There, Π^K and $[g/(1-g)]\,\Pi^K$ appear (along with reranking R), and Π^K is the Kakwani index of the *entire tax system*, warts and all (i.e. including the unequal tax treatments). How are the measures Π_T^K and Π^K related? This is one of the matters we will attend to shortly.

We conclude this consideration of vertical equity from the classical perspective with a few words about calculation. How could $T_{RN}(x)$ and $T_{WN}(x)$ be estimated from microdata, especially when, as is often the case, there may be few or even *no* instances of *exact* pre-tax equals in the available sample? Kernel estimation provides the answer (see p. 17). Duclos and Lambert (2000) discuss the statistical and normative issues involved in using kernel smoothing for this purpose. They go on to estimate $T_{RN}(x)$ and $T_{WN}(x)$ for the Canadian tax-benefit system in 1994, in particular displaying $T_{WN}(x)$ for $e = \frac{1}{4}$ and $e = \frac{3}{4}$.[10]

According to the no-reranking approach, vertical equity is about the choice of post-tax income distribution given the pre-tax income distribution. A very different sort of smooth schedule, call it $T_{IN}(x)$, must be constructed to represent the vertical stance of the tax system if this view is accepted. This schedule, which we might call the *inequality-neutral HE replacement tax*, maps existing pre-tax livings standards to existing post-tax living standards, but in a different order (hence, in particular, having no effect on post-tax inequality). $T_{IN}(x)$ is the unique function such that the mapping $x \rightarrow x - T_{IN}(x)$ is monotone increasing and maps the distribution of pre-tax equivalent incomes onto the distribution of post-tax equivalent incomes. It is very easy to calculate $T_{IN}(x)$ from microdata: just sort separately the pre- and post-tax income vectors in the sample, breaking the disassociation which is present, and define $T_{IN}(x)$ as the component-by-component mapping from one sorted vector to the other. Look at figure 10.1 again. Can you see that the mapping $x \rightarrow x - T_{IN}(x)$ would be steeper than either of the two displayed, having a single crossing with each from below? We will have more to say about this mapping in section 10.4.

Exercises

10.2.1   'Discrimination can be interpreted as the loss of vertical equity attributable to group specificity of schedules in the tax code. If the code were to be replaced by the averaged schedule, there would be a welfare increase' (Kakwani and Lambert, 1999, p. 28). Explain the model used by these authors, and describe how they used the equally distributed equivalent income concept to provide measures of vertical equity and discrimination.

10.2.2(a) Explain Hayes *et al.*'s (1995, p. 465) remark in respect of their bundle of tax schedules $\langle t_1(x), t_2(x), \ldots, t_k(x) \rangle$, and effective tax schedule $T(x)$ as in (10.12), that: '... averaging across income ranges overestimates the effective schedule (if this is convex); only if this schedule is perfectly linear does such averaging introduce no error'.

10.2.2(b) Review exercises 8.3.7, p. 206, and 8.4.13, p. 214, in which the liability and residual progression of effective taxes $T(x)$ at percentiles in the pre-tax distribution are computed from elasticities along concentration curves. How could Hayes *et al.* (1995, p. 469) say that 'the profiles $K(p)$ and $K^*(p)$ reveal significantly more about vertical incidence than do the indices Π_T^K and $[g/(1-g)] \Pi_T^K$, which compress the available information until sight is lost of differential effects'?

10.2.3(a) Suppose that the income tax model is that of equation (10.13), with $T(x)$ progressive, but that there is a systematic and positive bias in tax assessments, so that $\varepsilon^h(x)$ has mean $\beta(x) \geq 0$. Show that if the bias is a constant or decreasing fraction of income x, then $[g/(1-g)] \Pi_T^K$ overestimates the amount of vertical redistribution implicit in the tax system (where g is the total tax ratio). *Hint:* Use exercise 8.3.3, p. 205, to show that $g \Pi_{T+\beta}^K = \bar{t} \Pi_T^K + \beta \Pi_\beta^K$ where $\bar{t}$ is the average rate of tax according to the schedule $T(x)$ and β is the average rate of the bias $\beta(x)$ (so that $g = \bar{t} + \beta$). Now compare $[g/(1-g)] \Pi_T^K$ with $[g/(1-g)] \Pi_{T+\beta}^K$.

10.2.3(b) Suppose now that disturbances from $T(x)$ in (10.13) arise from a mortgage interest deduction: $\varepsilon^h(x) = 0$ if h is a non-homeowner and $\varepsilon^h(x) < 0$ if h is a homeowner. Suppose further that the average mortgage interest relief $-\beta(x)$ across *all* households with income x increases with x but less than proportionately. How does this relief contribute to the vertical stance of the tax system?

10.3   Progressivity and classical horizontal inequity

From the classical perspective, one or other of the constructed schedules $T_{RN}(x)$ and $T_{WN}(x)$ delivers the income tax system's vertical performance, and the departures from it within equals groups constitute the local horizontal inequities.

We could measure progressivity in the actual tax system, and in $T_{RN}(x)$ or $T_{WN}(x)$, and compare these. If $T_{RN}(x)$ or $T_{WN}(x)$ is progressive, the vertical stance of the income tax, or its effect on average between equals groups, will be to *reduce inequality*. However, within equal groups, a tax system with HI in fact *introduces new inequality*, where there was none before (pre-tax). So the vertical and horizontal effects of a tax system with HI act in opposition to each other. It is possible to separate out the vertical and horizontal contributions to overall progressivity in certain circumstances. The approaches we describe here are based on the *redistributive effect* and *cost of inequality* concepts.

The redistributive effect of a tax system is measured relative to distributionally neutral taxation with the same yield (see p. 39). Let I be any index of relative inequality. Denote by I_1 the inequality in the distribution of post-tax living standards and by I_0 the inequality after application of an equal-yield flat tax (i.e. pre-tax inequality). Further, let I_S be the inequality that would prevail after application of the income tax function $T_{RN}(x)$ which we take as representing the vertical stance of the tax system in this constant revenue environment. As the identity

$$[I_0 - I_1] \equiv [I_0 - I_S] - [I_1 - I_S] \tag{10.14}$$

shows, a loss of redistributive effect arises from the differences in income tax treatment of pre-tax equals. The redistributive effect would be higher, taking the value $[I_0 - I_S]$, if not for the presence of classical HI. (We know that $I_1 > I_S$ because $T_{RN}(x)$ smooths away the inequality in equals groups: recall exercise 5.2.7, p. 118).

The cost of inequality C measures what the SDM would pay to eliminate the inequality in an income distribution in a constant welfare environment. Denote by C_1 the cost of inequality in the distribution of post-tax living standards, and by C_0 the cost of inequality after application of an equal-*welfare* flat tax. Since the latter does not reduce inequality, whereas the tax system as a whole typically does, we may expect that $C_0 > C_1$. The difference, $[C_0 - C_1]$, is thus the cost saving to the SDM due to the distributive intervention of the tax system; we could call it the *cost effectiveness* of the tax system. Let C_S be the cost of inequality that would prevail after application of the income tax function $T_{WN}(x)$ which we take as representing the vertical stance of the tax system in the constant welfare environment. The identity

$$[C_0 - C_1] \equiv [C_0 - C_S] - [C_1 - C_S] \tag{10.15}$$

shows that the cost effectiveness of the tax system would be higher, taking the value $[C_0 - C_S]$, if not for the presence of classical HI. (The reason we know *a priori* that $C_1 > C_S$ will emerge shortly).

If a generalized entropy index is used to implement identity (10.14), the loss of redistributive effect attributable to classical HI, namely $[I_1 - I_S]$, becomes amenable to decomposition analysis. Look again at (5.11), p. 111. For an additively decomposable inequality index, the overall inequality in post-tax living standards, I_1, can be expressed as a weighted sum of the inequality values calculated for the pre-tax equals groups $S(x)$, call these $I_{S(x)}$, plus a term capturing 'between-group inequality', namely, the inequality that remains when these within-group inequalities have all been smoothed out.

This smoothing out is just what $T_{RN}(x)$ does, and the remaining inequality is I_S! So we have

$$I_1 = \sum_x p_x^{1-c} q_x^c I_{S(x)} + I_S \tag{10.16}$$

In this decomposition, I is one of the generalized entropy indices $E(c)$, $c \in \mathbf{R}$, as defined on p. 112, p_x is the proportion of the overall population who belong to the equals group $S(x)$ and q_x is their share in total post-tax equivalent income.

From (10.16) the loss of redistributive effect attributable to classical HI, call it H, takes the form of a weighted sum of 'local' effects, namely, of the inequalities introduced by the tax system among pre-tax equals at every income level:

$$H = [I_1 - I_S] = \sum_x p_x^{1-c} q_x^c I_{S(x)} \tag{10.17}$$

Only for the two special cases $c = 0, 1$ do the weights for the local horizontal inequities sum to unity, and only in the case of the mean logarithmic deviation (when $c = 0$) are these weights independent of income shares. Precisely in this case, the weights are 'pure', in that the importance attributed to a local HE violation does not depend upon the income level at which it is experienced. Musgrave (1990, pp. 117–118) suggested the business of devising a local measure for HI, and then aggregating into a global index which would be pure in the sense that it would be free of vertical considerations: 'HE measures which are applicable to particular groups do not suffice. To assess the HE quality of the entire system and to permit comparison with other burden distributions, an overall measure of HE is needed. The construction of such an index is awkward . . . an overall picture [must be] given *while inappropriate comparisons between unequals are avoided*' (italics added).

Finally, denoting the redistributive effect of the entire tax system by RE_{sys} and that of $T_{RN}(x)$ by RE_{vert}, we arrive at the vertical-horizontal decomposition we had anticipated earlier:

$$RE_{sys} = RE_{vert} - H \tag{10.18}$$

by substituting terms in (10.14). Any generalized entropy index can be used as the basis of this decomposition, but only for the mean logarithmic deviation does the loss of redistributive effect caused by HI take the form of a global HI index which is pure in the Musgrave sense.[11]

We turn now to the cost of inequality approach. Happily, the cost of inequality measure is additively decomposable in a world of constant welfare (see p. 113), and so a similar form of analysis is possible using this approach. Decomposability yields:

$$C_1 = \sum_x p_x C_{S(x)} + C_S \tag{10.19}$$

in this context (whence in particular $C_1 > C_S$ as claimed earlier). What does this decomposition tell us? C_1 is what the SDM would pay per capita to eliminate the inequality present in the distribution of post-tax livings standards. This inequality could be eliminated in two stages. First, smooth away inequality within the equals groups, at a cost of $C_{S(x)}$ per head in $S(x)$ and $\Sigma_x p_x C_{S(x)}$ per head overall (recall (10.11)); after this smoothing, the distribution of living standards net of $T_{WN}(x)$ is reached; now eliminate the remaining inequality, at a further cost of C_S per head. The two costs add up to the overall cost C_1.

Let us denote by H^* the first-stage cost of eliminating the local horizontal inequities with social indifference:

$$H^* = [C_1 - C_S] = \sum_x p_x C_{S(x)} \qquad (10.20)$$

H^* is also the additional income tax revenue per head collected by $T_{WN}(x)$ over the actual tax system or equal-yield HE replacement tax $T_{RN}(x)$. Can you see why? Look at (10.11) once more. Now denote the cost effectiveness of the entire tax system by CE_{sys} and that of $T_{WN}(x)$ by CE_{vert}. We arrive at the decomposition

$$CE_{sys} = CE_{vert} - H^* \qquad (10.21)$$

by substituting terms into (10.15). This decomposition of cost effectiveness can be compared with the one for redistributive effect given in (10.18).

The index H^* measures the amount by which the presence of classical HI reduces the cost effectiveness of the tax system. Because the weights used to aggregate the local costs $C_{S(x)}$ are the proportions p_x, H^* is a global HI index satisfying Musgrave's purity requirement. H^* is, of course, denominated in units of income; it can be normalized to render it unit-free. The most convenient normalization is by the mean post-tax income:

$$H^{**} = \frac{H^*}{\mu(1-g)} \qquad (10.22)$$

H^{**} is thus the fraction of total post-tax income which can be raised in additional tax revenue by eliminating HI welfare-neutrally in each equals group. H^{**} features in a vertical-horizontal decomposition of tax progressivity. Let Π_{sys}^{BD} and Π_{vert}^{BD} be the Blackorby–Donaldson progressivity indices for actual taxes and $T_{WN}(x)$ respectively (see p. 210 for the definition of a Blackorby–Donaldson index). After a little manipulation, it emerges that

$$\Pi_{sys}^{BD} = \theta \Pi_{vert}^{BD} - H^{**} \qquad (10.23)$$

where $\theta < 1$ is the ratio of mean income after application of $T_{WN}(x)$ to mean post-tax income.[12] Progressivity would be higher if not for the presence of HI. In the absence of HI, the actual tax system and $T_{WN}(x)$ coincide: $\theta = 1$ and $H^{**} = 0$ in (10.23).[13]

What about the Gini coefficient and the Reynolds–Smolensky index Π^{RS}? When we take account of classical HI, an interesting new decomposition of Π^{RS} emerges which extends the one in section 10.1 in which reranking featured alongside the Kakwani index Π^K. Now vertical, horizontal and reranking contributions all feature in the decomposition.

Here is what the identity (10.14) tells us when we implement it using the Gini coefficient:

$$[G_0 - G_1] \equiv [G_0 - G_S] - [G_1 - G_S] \tag{10.14a}$$

This transcribes into

$$\Pi^{RS}_{sys} = \Pi^{RS}_{vert} - [G_1 - G_S] \tag{10.24}$$

to use an obvious extension of previous notation. Following previous procedures, the next step is to decompose the Gini coefficient for post-tax living standards, G_1, across pre-tax equals groups. *But the Gini coefficient fails to decompose into within and between-group components in general.* As we saw in chapter 5 (see pp. 114–115), whenever the subgroup income ranges overlap, one has to add an extra term to make the Gini decomposition work. In the present context, it comes down to this,

$$G_1 = \sum_x p_x q_x G_{S(x)} + G_S + R \tag{10.25}$$

(see (5.17), p. 114), in which the extra term R measures one half of the area between the post-tax Lorenz curve and the post-tax concentration curve – the latter being derived using a lexicographic ordering in which income units are ordered first by levels of pre-tax income, from lowest to highest, and second, at any fixed pre-tax income level x (i.e. within the equals group $S(x)$), by levels of post-tax income, again from lowest to highest. *In other words, R is just $G_{X-T} - C_{X-T}$, the index of reranking defined in (10.5) on p. 241!* Substituting from (10.25) into (10.24), and letting

$$H^{***} = \sum_x p_x q_x G_{S(x)} \tag{10.26}$$

be the obvious index of global HI, we obtain

$$\Pi^{RS}_{sys} = \Pi^{RS}_{vert} - H^{***} - R \tag{10.27}$$

showing how both classical HI and reranking detract from redistributive effect. Note, however, that the index H^{***} does *not* satisfy Musgrave's purity condition; see exercise 10.3.5 on this.

Finally, we can of course write Π^{RS}_{vert} in terms of tax level and the Kawkani index Π^K_T for the schedule $T_{RN}(x)$. This brings us to the decomposition:

$$\Pi_{\text{sys}}^{\text{RS}} = \frac{g}{1-g}\,\Pi_{\text{T}}^{\text{K}} - H^{***} - R \qquad (10.28)$$

which is directly comparable with (10.6) on p. 241:

$$\Pi^{\text{RS}} = \frac{g}{1-g}\,\Pi^{\text{K}} - R \qquad (10.6)$$

What has happened here? The term in (10.6) capturing the disproportionality in actual taxes has been split into two parts in (10.28), one capturing the disproportionality of the revenue-neutral HE replacement tax $T_{\text{RN}}(x)$ and the other the effect of departures from this schedule – i.e. of classical HI. This refined version of (10.6) is applicable whenever one has appropriate microdata.[14]

According to the new classical approaches, one or other of the constructed schedules $T_{\text{RN}}(x)$ and $T_{\text{WN}}(x)$ delivers the income tax system's vertical performance, and the departures from it within equals groups $S(x)$ constitute the local horizontal inequities. As between the two HI-free schedules $T_{\text{RN}}(x)$ and $T_{\text{WN}}(x)$, the former has a better welfare performance than the actual tax system and the same revenue, whilst the latter has the same welfare but raises more revenue. The local horizontal inequities can be summarized in index form either by this welfare-enhancing property, as the additional inequality reduction H or H^{***} that their elimination using $T_{\text{RN}}(x)$ would secure over the actual tax system, or by the per capita revenue increase H^* (H^{**} as a fraction of post-tax income) that would follow upon the adoption of $T_{\text{WN}}(x)$ in place of actual taxes. Of course there would be winners and losers from either of these two hypothetical processes of HI elimination. It is not a policy recommendation that $T_{\text{RN}}(x)$ or $T_{\text{WN}}(x)$ should be substituted for the actual tax system. They serve as yardsticks, against which the social cost of the HE violations in actual taxes can be assessed, much as the 45° line serves as a yardstick for inequality measurement.

Proponents of the no-reranking equity criterion, to which we turn in the next section, have long argued that HI is a feature of the taxation *process* rather than of its *outcome*, as with these classical approaches. Thus Plotnick (1981, p. 283) declared that HI 'addresses the fairness of a *process* of redistribution', whilst Musgrave's (1990, p. 12) view to the contrary was that HE 'enters as an end-state principle'. Among the new classical approaches we have described, based on the generalized entropy indices, the cost of inequality concept and the Gini coefficient, the Gini-based approach is unique in providing measures of *two* inefficiencies stemming from non-HE taxes, the losses of redistributive effect which are down to *both* classical HI *and* reranking. This contribution has clearly gained the approval of Plotnick (1999, p. 555): 'If we agree that procedural fairness matters and that unequal treatment of equals and reranking both qualify as unfair procedures, analysts need to use measures that register both phenomena'.

Exercises

10.3.1(a) 'There are typically few exact equals in sample microdata ... if pre-tax incomes are banded, into "close equals groups", a modified decomposition of redistributive effect can be obtained, into what we may call pseudo-horizontal and pseudo-vertical contributions. For the interpretation of these pseudo-contributions, it is as if horizontally, the tax acts to increase inequality within close equals groups and vertically, it acts to reduce inequality between close equals groups' (Lambert and Ramos, 1997a, p. 29). Explain how these authors could devise a decomposition $RE_{sys} = PVR - PHI$ which approximates to (10.18) and can be computed using sparse microdata.

10.3.1(b) Why would this decomposition 'not work if any other decomposable inequality index than the mean logarithmic deviation were used' (*ibid.*, p. 36)? Explain the role played by Musgrave's purity requirement in obtaining the pseudo-decomposition.

10.3.1(c) By decomposing the cost of inequality measures C_0 and C_1 across close equals groups (before and after tax respectively) and subtracting, show that a decomposition of CE_{sys} into pseudo-vertical and pseudo-horizontal components can be devised which approximates to (10.21).

10.3.2   'An additional, attractive feature of our construction is that, by using the index H^* (or H^{**}), HI can be tracked down to its sources, namely, to particular demographic groups and/or income brackets' (Duclos and Lambert, 2000, p. 94). Explain this remark. Can the same be done for the measure H in equation (10.18)?

10.3.3   'The existence of "fans" and their overlapping provide two conceptually distinct effects stemming from the presence of differences in tax treatment' (Aronson *et al.*, 1994, p. 264). Explain the 'fans diagram' used by Aronson *et al.* (1994) to illustrate their model of the income tax and motivate their Gini-based decomposition analysis.

10.3.4   What value judgements did Johnson and Mayer (1962, p. 461) suggest could be made about the nature and magnitude of a horizontal inequity? What did they see as the implications of the various alternatives they suggested?

10.3.5(a) Show that the welfare premium corresponding to (8.37), p. 211, for a tax system with HI is proportional to $\mu\{g\,\Pi_T^K - (1-g)\,H^{***} - (1-g)\,R\}$.

10.3.5(b) Use (10.26) to show that $\mu(1-g)\,H^{***} = \Sigma_x p_x^2 B_{S(x)}$ where B is the absolute Gini coefficient (see exercise 3.2.4(b), p. 56). Deduce that, even though H^{***} is not a pure HI index in the Musgrave sense, $\mu(1-g)\,H^{***}$ can be regarded as one, by making an appropriate assumption about the nature and magnitude of a horizontal inequity.

10.3.5(c) Show that, although a decomposition for Π^{RS}_{sys} into pseudo-components like the decompositions given in exercise 10.3.1 for RE_{sys} and CE_{sys} is not possible, one can be devised for the welfare premium.[15]

10.3.6(a) Describe the procedure proposed by Wertz (1978) for measuring the 'relative taxation of families', according to which the US individual income tax in 1966 could be characterized as 68.2 per cent progressive, 7.7 per cent proportional and 24 per cent regressive.

10.3.6(b) Explain how Berliant and Strauss (1985) extended Wertz's procedure to include the measurement of horizontal inequity. Explain their finding that the US individual income tax in 1977 was 12 per cent regressive and 82 per cent inequitable.

10.3.6(c) Explain how Aronson et al. (1994, p. 270) could say that 'Berliant and Strauss's procedure . . . is tantamount to drawing up a "fans" diagram for the relationship between pre-tax income and average tax rate, where the "fans" signal horizontal inequity, as ours do, but the overlaps get a vertical interpretation, providing instances of regression'.

10.3.7 Describe Rosen's (1978, p. 314) empirical procedure which, given rich enough microdata, will 'generate two vectors, one of family utilities before tax and one of family utilities after tax'. How did Rosen say that HI should be measured? See also Plotnick (1980).

10.3.8 'Our starting point is the observation that a well-behaved social welfare function need not evaluate "global" (vertical equity) differences in after-tax income using the same weights as it applies to "local" (horizontal equity) differences, even though this constraint has been applied in the past' (Auerbach and Hassett, 2002, p. 1). Describe the approach of these authors, in which different inequality aversion parameters are used for aggregations within and between equals groups. Explain in particular how their aggregate index of HI is related to the indices they obtain within equals groups.

10.3.9 'Real world indirect tax systems are not uniform . . . setting a lower rate for necessities and a higher rate for luxuries . . . differences in tastes will also lead to differences in the amount of taxes paid even for households at the same endowment level' (Decoster et al., 1997, pp. 219–220). Explain how Decoster et al. used results described in this section to evaluate the vertical and horizontal characteristics of Belgian indirect taxes and indirect tax reforms. What normative significance did they say could be attached to their findings?

10.3.10 How did van Doorslaer et al. (1999) investigate the vertical and horizontal equity characteristics of the health care financing systems in OECD countries?

10.4   Horizontal inequity as disassociation

We briefly discussed the *no reranking* equity criterion, henceforth NR, in section 2 of this chapter. Atkinson (1980b) and Plotnick (1981) were the first to propose approaches to the measurement of horizontal inequity based on NR. Violations of NR arise from *procedural unfairness* in the tax system. If family A has a higher living standard than family B before tax, but after tax the reverse is true, then the tax process is faulty. According to NR, the tax system is intended to transform the pre-tax income distribution of living standards into the chosen post-tax one *without creating rank reversals*. The pre- and post-tax equivalent incomes of families should thus enjoy *perfect positive association*. Disassociation, if such exists, is seen as horizontal inequity by the proponents of NR.

The new classical approaches we have described lead to indices of HI which respect Musgrave's purity requirement. A recent approach from the NR perspective also argues for purity in the measurement of HI, in two senses. First the HI in a tax system should be independent of the metric used to measure living standards, and second it should be independent of the tax system's vertical performance. We shall explain these purity requirements shortly, and show how an easily implemented dominance test for HI comparisons derives from them, once a social concern for disassociation is appropriately modelled. As we shall also see, there are links between this dominance test and some constructions in the founding NR contributions of Atkinson and Plotnick.

Let x stand for a household's pre-tax living standard, as before, and now let y be its post-tax living standard. Let $F(x)$ and $G(y)$ be the distribution functions for x and y, and let $K(x, y)$ be the joint distribution function of x and y. According to NR, vertical equity is about the choice of $G(y)$ given $F(x)$, and HI is about the way $G(y)$ is achieved from $F(x)$. As we saw in section 10.2, a unique function $T_{IN}(x)$ can be constructed to represent the vertical stance of the tax system. $T_{IN}(x)$ is in fact defined implicitly by the equation

$$G(x - T_{IN}(x)) = F(x) \tag{10.29}$$

Can you see why? According to NR, HI exists whenever $K(x, y)$ departs from the joint distribution function $K_0(x, y)$ which would obtain if there were perfect association, i.e. if $y \equiv x - T_{IN}(x)$ held:

$$K_0(x, y) = \min\{F(x), G(y)\} \tag{10.30}$$

Can you see why $K_0(x, y)$ takes this form?

If it is accepted that HI is about the taxation process, two riders follow. First, HI should be unaffected if the metric for living standards were changed. Suppose we choose to represent pre- and post-tax living standards by $u(x)$ and $u(y)$, rather than by x and y, where u is a strictly increasing transformation. The same taxation process generates the post-tax $u(y)$s from the pre-tax

$u(x)$s as generates the ys from the xs: the HI should therefore be the same. Second, HI should be free of dependence on the vertical stance of the tax system. Look again at figure 10.1, p. 245. This scatterplot, which represents a joint distribution $K(x, y)$, was actually obtained by first selecting a piecewise linear form for $T_{RN}(x)$, and then simulating a dispersion around it using a random number generator (full details are in Lambert, 1995). The random number generator was thus the 'taxation process'. If this dispersion had been *identically* simulated around a *different* $T(x)$, ought HI to change? The NR view is that it should not.

An HI equivalence relation, call it $\approx_{HI}$, which satisfies these two purity requirements has a very special property. Namely, if $x \to u(x)$ and $y \to v(y)$ are strictly increasing transformations, and if the joint distribution of $u(x)$ and $v(y)$ induced by K is denoted $K^{u,v}$, then for purity $\approx_{HI}$ must satisfy

$$K \approx_{HI} K^{u,v} \text{ for all } K \text{ and all strictly increasing } u \text{ and } v \qquad (10.31)$$

The first purity requirement is that $K \approx_{HI} K^{u,u}$ for all K and all strictly increasing u. The second purity requirement licenses further monotonic transformations in the y-dimension without affecting HI: in particular, it licenses the transformation $u^{-1} \circ v$. Can you see how (10.31) emerges now?

The relation $\approx_{HI}$ enables tax systems to be compared free of the different environments in which they operate. By this we mean that a 'baseline scenario' can be selected within which to make an HI comparison. Suppose that we wanted to compare the UK and US income tax systems. Using (10.31) we can in fact make the comparison *within the UK* – by comparing the actual UK tax system with an artificial one defined such that, if it *were* applied in the UK, it would replicate the UK distribution of post-tax living standards exactly, *but with the degree of association between pre- and post-tax living standards which is found in the US tax system.*

The mechanics of this are as follows. For any given pre- and post-tax US living standards x and y, let t be the pre-tax living standard in the UK which is in the same position in the UK pre-tax parade as x is in the US, and let z be the post-tax living standard in the same position in the UK post-tax parade as y in the US. When the transformations $x \to u(x) = t$ and $y \to v(y) = z$ are made, the US joint distribution function, K_{US} say, changes to $K_{US}^{u,v}$ which we denote K^*. By (10.31), K^* has the US degree of HI:

$$K_{US} \approx_{HI} K^* \qquad (10.32)$$

and by construction it has the UK marginal (pre- and post-tax) distributions. K^* thus represents a tax system that reproduces the UK post-tax living standard distribution from the UK pre-tax one, but with the degree of association that is found in the US. By comparing K_{UK} with the HI-equivalent K^* rather than with K_{US}, the comparison is freed from the different distributional conditions in which the two tax systems operate. In essence, this procedure allows us to 'control for vertical equity' while making the HI comparison.

Hence it is enough to formulate a criterion for comparing the HI in joint distributions K having common pre- and post-tax marginals. To do this, we first define a social decision-maker's utility function $U(x, y)$ over pre- and post-tax living standards, and suppose that the social evaluation function is additive over utilities. The SDMs for whom pre- and post-tax living standards should be positively associated, and the more so the better, are those whose utility functions satisfy

$$\frac{\partial^2 U}{\partial x \partial y} \geq 0 \qquad \text{for all } x \text{ and } y \tag{10.33}$$

(see Epstein and Tanny, 1980).

A very simple theorem links unanimous preference by these SDMs with the configuration of distribution functions having specified marginals. If $K_1(x, y)$ and $K_2(x, y)$ both have the same marginals, then K_2 has more welfare than K_1 according to every SDM whose utility function satisfies (10.33) if and only if $K_1(x, y) \leq K_2(x, y)$ for all x and y.[16] It is natural to say that K_2 has less HI than K_1 in this case, since all disassociation-averse SDMs prefer it. We can write this as

$$K_2 \subseteq_{\text{HI}} K_1 \tag{10.34}$$

The scope of $\subseteq_{\text{HI}}$ can be extended from equal-marginals scenarios to *all* tax systems using $\approx_{\text{HI}}$ and artificial third distributions (to make the marginals the same), just as for our illustrative UK/US example. In that particular case, we have

$$K_{\text{UK}} \subseteq_{\text{HI}} K_{\text{US}} \Leftrightarrow K_{\text{UK}} \subseteq_{\text{HI}} K^* \approx_{\text{HI}} K_{\text{US}} \tag{10.35}$$

but the procedure can of course be applied quite generally.

Finally, if $p = F(x)$ and $q = G(y)$ (where F and G are the marginal distributions of K as before), define the *copula* of K, $C_K(p, q)$, as:

$$C_K(p, q) = K^{F,G}(p, q) \tag{10.36}$$

$C_K(p, q)$ is in fact the cumulated transition matrix for K with quantile margins. See exercise 10.4.1 below for more on this. Drawing upon the mathematical statistics literature, Dardanoni and Lambert (2001a) were able to show that the partial HI ordering $\subseteq_{\text{HI}}$ can be tested directly using copulas, bypassing the construction of artificial third distributions. It comes down to implementing a straightforward *copula dominance* test. In the UK/US case we have been considering, we have

$$K_{\text{UK}} \subseteq_{\text{HI}} K_{\text{US}} \Leftrightarrow C_{\text{UK}}(p, q) \geq C_{\text{US}}(p, q) \qquad \text{for all } p, q \in [0, 1] \tag{10.37}$$

but again the result is general.

The copula dominance test has a strong affinity with previous work in the NR tradition. Transition matrices were advocated by Atkinson (1980b, pp. 8–9) for studying the reranking properties of tax systems, and a dominance test between these in cumulated form was suggested on NR grounds in

Jenkins (1988c, p. 315). Plotnick (1982, p. 378) proposed a similar but stronger partial HI ordering (see exercise 10.4.2).

As Plotnick (1999, p. 555) has suggested, we should all 'agree that procedural fairness matters and that unequal treatment of equals and reranking both qualify as unfair procedures'. Thus *all* of the approaches to the measurement of HI outlined in this chapter, both the classical and the NR, should go into the analyst's toolbag. There is plenty of scope for new work, too. At the time of writing, the new classical approaches still lack dominance criteria, whilst NR awaits the identification of classes of indices to extend $\subseteq_{HI}$ and an accompanying ordering of tax systems by vertical equity.

Exercises

10.4.1 The following table describes tax system 1.

Household	A	B	C	D
Pre-tax living standard	10	15	30	40
Post-tax living standard	9	8	24	22

The transition matrix T_1 and cumulated transition matrix C_1 for this tax system are

$$T_1 = \begin{bmatrix} 0 & 1 & 0 & 0 \\ 1 & 0 & 0 & 0 \\ 0 & 0 & 0 & 1 \\ 0 & 0 & 1 & 0 \end{bmatrix} \qquad C_1 = \begin{bmatrix} 0 & 1 & 1 & 1 \\ 1 & 2 & 2 & 2 \\ 1 & 2 & 2 & 3 \\ 1 & 2 & 3 & 4 \end{bmatrix}$$

Can you see why? (T_1 has a '1' in position (i, j) if the household ranked i before tax is ranked j after tax, and a '0' otherwise; to obtain C_1, just cumulate from the top left entry in T_1, downwards and across.) Tax system 2 differs only slightly from tax system 1:

Household	A	B	C	D
Pre-tax living standard	10	15	30	40
Post-tax living standard	9	8	24	25

Calculate the transition matrix T_2 and cumulated transition matrix C_2. Show that system 1 has more HI than system 2 using the copula dominance test.

10.4.2 Explain the 'marginal preserving swap' concept of Dardanoni and Lambert (2001a). Compare it with Plotnick's (1982, p. 378) swap concept, the 'inequity reducing reversal'. Show that the latter imposes more requirements on mass transfers than the former. Deduce that Plotnick's dominance condition is more restrictive than copula dominance.

10.4.3   'Are classical HI and reranking such very different concepts? If the density function . . . is jointly continuous in x and y, as one finds in very large samples . . . then the one form of HI occurs if and only if the other does' (Dardanoni and Lambert, 2001a). Explain this statement. What properties do Dardanoni and Lambert say would be necessary for a tax system to have (a) reranking but no classical HI, and (b) classical HI but no reranking?

10.4.4   'Do the classical indices tell the same story as the reranking indices and as the composite indices when the tax system changes?' (Lambert and Ramos, 1997b, p. 9). Review the evidence gathered by these authors from their simulation study, and describe their conclusions.

10.4.5   Duclos and Lambert (2000) and Dardanoni and Lambert (2001a) both examine HI in the Canadian tax and benefit system. Describe the change in HI which took place between 1981 and 1990 from classical and NR perspectives.

10.4.6(a) Let x_i and y_i be the pre- and post-tax living standards of household i, where the n households are indexed in such a way that $x_1 < x_2 < x_3 < . . . < x_n$. Let z_k be the post-tax income which would appear in position k if the y_is were listed from smallest to biggest ($1 \leq k \leq n$). King (1983) and Jenkins (1988c, 1994) measure HI in terms of the pairs (y_i, z_i), $1 \leq i \leq n$, in various ways. Explain how and why. Consult also Jenkins and Lambert (1999).

10.4.6(b) What is the relationship between z_i and $x_i - T_{IN}(x_i)$?

10.4.6(c) Suppose that K_0 is a tax regime with no HI, and that K_1 is the regime in part (a) of this exercise. Let K_0^* be the artificial regime derived from K_0 to have the same marginals as K_1 (just as K^* was derived from K_{US} in the text). Show that whereas K_1 consists of the income pairs (x_i, y_i), K_0^* consists of the income pairs (x_i, z_i), $1 \leq i \leq n$.

10.4.7   'The index of overall inequality may be decomposed into its two component parts, the index of horizontal inequity and the index of vertical inequality' (King, 1983, p. 104). Explain King's constructions.

10.4.8   Jenkins (1988c) abstains from making comparisons of income tax effects across different household types using an equivalence scale. How does he instead propose to measure HI in each socially homogeneous sub-population, and then assemble all of the resulting information?

10.4.9   Summarize Kaplow's (1989, 1999) objections to the horizontal equity criterion, which led him to declare that 'there is no normative basis for deeming it to be important and, in fact, it conflicts with the basic foundations of welfare economics. That is, HE stands in opposition to the advancement of human welfare' (Kaplow, 1999, p. 1).

Notes

1 For more on this sort of analysis, the reader may consult Lambert (1993b). See also exercise 9.3.4, p. 235.

2 Lecaillon *et al.* (1984) use grouped data to estimate the disproportionality index Π^K for direct and indirect taxes for nine developing countries together with the USA and Canada (on pp. 162–163). They also analyse contributions to redistributive effect Π^{RS} for several of these countries (on pp. 170–176). They do not take reranking into account.

3 There are, of course, other ways forward too. Any device to order those having exactly b_0 can be the basis of a lexicographic ordering and curve $C_{A|B}$.

4 Joining up does not, of course, have to done linearly; a curve-fitting procedure could be adopted. If non-linear interpolation is used, or if a lexicographic ordering *by taxes* is used to define L_T (as the general procedure we outlined for attributes A and B would suggest), then (2.25) would not hold.

5 The l.h.s. of (8.29) evaluated at p, $L_{X-T}(p) - L_X(p)$, measures the fraction of total income shifted from the top $100(1 - p)$ per cent to the bottom $100p$ per cent by the tax system relative to an equal-yield flat tax (see p. 207). If there is reranking, part of this shifted amount makes some people richer and others poorer in such a way that they switch positions. Income transfers used to induce switches like this have no inequality impact. The inequality impact is $L^*(p) - L_X(p)$.

6 In the case of commodity taxes, we would expect a non-systematic relationship with income due to variations in people's preferences. Recall Loomis and Revier's (1988) construction, described on p. 209.

7 This result is due to Duclos (1993). Duclos also suggested that tax policies be evaluated using the function $\rho.\Psi - (1 - \rho) R_\Psi$ in which $\rho \in [0,1]$ 'indicates the importance of redistribution relative to that of horizontal equity' (p. 355).

8 Equally distributed equivalent incomes were introduced and defined on p. 95.

9 The welfare superiority is because inequality has been eliminated with no change in the mean (theorem 3.1, p. 45).

10 Our treatment of benefits (as negative taxes) in this book is deferred until the next chapter.

11 This result is derived in Lambert and Ramos (1997a). See also exercises 10.3.1(a)–(b). If the Gini coefficient were used to implement (10.14), an additional term representing 'overlap' would appear in (10.18) and the weights would be impure. We come to this shortly. If the Atkinson (1970) index were used in (10.14), the result in exercise 10.2.1, p. 247, would emerge. White and White (1965) first proposed to measure local HI as dispersion of post-tax incomes in 'equal circumstance groups'. They used the coefficient of variation for this purpose. Brennan (1971) considered the standard deviation, coefficient of variation and kurtosis as candidate local measures. Global indices of HI proposed by Habib

(1979) and Berliant and Strauss (1985) use explicitly income-dependent weights for aggregating local inequities. On the latter, see exercise 10.3.6.

12 $\Pi^{BD}_{sys} = [I_0 - I_1]/[1 - I_0]$ and $\Pi^{BD}_{vert} = [I_0 - I_S]/[1 - I_0]$ where I_0, I_1 and I_S are the relevant Atkinson indices. Because all distributions have the same welfare, $C_0 = \mu(1 - \gamma)I_0$ $= \mu(1 - \gamma) - \xi$, $C_1 = \mu(1 - g)I_1 = \mu(1 - g) - \xi$ and $C_S = \mu_S I_S = \mu_S - \xi$, where ξ is the common value of the equally distributed equivalent income, μ_S is mean income after application of $T_{WN}(x)$, and γ is the rate of the equal-welfare flat tax. Using substitutions and (10.20), eliminate ξ and set $\theta = \mu_S/[\mu(1 - g)]$ to derive (10.23).

13 All of the cost of inequality results presented here are derived in Duclos and Lambert (2000).

14 This result in (10.28) was developed by Aronson et al. (1994) using the tax model $T^h = T(x) + \varepsilon^h(x)$ of (10.13), p. 246. Aronson et al. found that, in the UK in the 1980s, vertical redistribution $[g/(1 - g)]\Pi^K_T$ was some 6 per cent higher than actual redistributive effect, with losses of approximately 2 per cent and 4 per cent being attributable to the effects of classical HI and reranking respectively.

15 van de Ven et al. (2001) contains advice about the selection of an appropriate bandwidth.

16 The idea of using the joint distribution function in a partial ordering for positive dependence goes back to Gini (1914). For a proof of the result stated, see Tchen (1980).

11

The net fiscal system

There is strong political interest in measuring the distributional impact of the net fiscal system, and data of sorts is available. Can we say in a simple and direct way how the government operation bites?

Let us rename the income x of an income unit, heretofore called 'pre-tax income', *original income* in recognition that, in the overall scheme of things represented by the net fiscal system, it must be seen as 'pre-tax and pre-benefit', a cumbersome phrase. *Final income* will be income net of tax and including the benefit, somehow attributed and in cash-equivalent terms, that is enjoyed by the income unit from the operation of government. Is the inequality in well-being that is apparent in the distribution of original income moderated in the transition to final income? Can we arrive at a clear picture of how the two sides of the government budget act to determine the distribution of final well-being – or at any rate, in Okun's (1975, p. 65) words (with which we began chapter 2), of the 'box score' that is provided by final income?

If the only government benefits were cash transfers effected by redistributing income tax revenue, the problem could be readily addressed. But in most countries, the income tax and cash benefit systems are separately administered, and the income unit for benefit assessment may be different from the tax unit. Furthermore, government expenditures fund not only low-income support, but also programmes in education, health, defence, justice, diplomacy ... to name some, as well as providing for general administration. Expenditures on some of these operations are poorly measured in available statistics. *A fortiori*, the attribution of benefits to income units is a hazardous business. Indeed, for reasons that will become clear in section 11.1, there is no uncontroversial and operational principle which can guide such an attribution exercise.

Notwithstanding this problem, policymakers and observers want to know about fiscal incidence, and practitioners try to measure it. Just look at de Wulf's (1975) survey, which covers over a hundred fiscal incidence studies carried out for 30 countries. What do such descriptions of net fiscal incidence convey? They cannot possibly tell us about the effect of government on our lives: 'Such a large scale exercise would require tremendous resources, and might not be worthwhile, since such a study implies a comparison of what is with what would have been if what is were not . . . It does not require much thought to see that such a comparison makes little sense' (de Wulf, 1981, p. 59).

At best – and this only if attribution problems can be overcome – we can expect to gain a picture of the *formal incidence* of the existing government operation, as it impinges on a distribution of original income that is itself conditioned by that very fiscal system.

This is no more and no less than we have admitted already in the case of income taxes in chapters 8–10. So let us widen the remit and suppose that the benefits of (at least some part of) the government operation have somehow been attributed to income units. For simplicity, and for consistency with what we assumed for taxes in chapter 8, we begin by assuming that benefits are systematically related to incomes. Then our raw material for analysis consists of two schedules, $t(x)$ for taxes and $b(x)$, say, for attributed benefits. The net tax schedule is

$$t_N(x) = t(x) - b(x) \tag{11.1}$$

How should we measure the progressivity of this net tax with respect to the given distribution of original income?

In section 11.2 we consider how to measure benefit progressivity, or rather benefit *regressivity*. A minor extension of what we have already done for taxes is involved. This is a useful precursor to our treatment of net tax progressivity in section 11.3. As we shall see, under certain assumptions net tax progressivity can be determined from separate estimations of income tax progressivity and benefit regressivity, making it unnecessary for the estimation of net effects that taxes and benefits be jointly assigned to income units in a single dataset. An interesting and politically relevant interaction between taxes and benefits is revealed by this. In section 11.4 we broaden the analysis to include non-income taxes and benefits, thereby bringing horizontal inequity considerations, and material from chapter 10, to bear upon the net fiscal system.

11.1   Attributing benefits to income units

How does government affect people's economic positions? It is clear enough how cash benefits affect people. Their allocation among income units is a matter of record (though a conceptual problem arises in respect of some cash payments by government, as we shall shortly see). The situation is very much less clear when we look at specific government expenditures on goods and services.

Most of the empirical studies which provide the raw material for analysis are studies of *budget incidence*. They 'attempt to identify the users of a service or those on behalf of whom each expenditure was made, and to allocate to such users or intended beneficiaries the value of the resources used in providing the service (i.e. the opportunity cost of the service)' (O'Higgins and Ruggles, 1981, pp. 300–301). In other words, they aim to distribute expenditure totals across income units.

It is not obvious that this is the right raw material for our stated purpose. How do the many types of goods and services provided by government translate into 'effect on people's economic positions'? The case of pure public goods – goods such that every unit can be enjoyed to the full by all people – serves well to illustrate the conceptual difficulties that stand in the way of a satisfactory answer to this question.

At the heart of the difficulty is our use of the income box score. As Brennan (1976, p. 395) argues, 'the authority and significance of the income distribution as a policy-relevant parameter arises because income is the best available index of an individual's economic satisfactions . . . the authority . . . in an all-private goods world presumably derives from the fact that . . . an individual who has twice the income of another has the option to buy exactly twice as much of each good as the other . . . with public goods present . . . it no longer seems quite so clear that the individual with twice the quantity of private goods is twice as well-off'.

How much better-off the person with twice the cash income is, when both consume the same quantity of public goods, can only be reflected in the final income differential between the two if we have correctly valued each's consumption of the public goods. The question is: How should we quantify the benefits of pure public goods provision in income-equivalent terms, to be added to original income at same time that taxes are taken away? As we shall demonstrate by a little formal analysis, it is by no means clear that total benefit should equal the resource cost of production – let alone that a hard-and-fast rule for allocation could be devised.

Suppose that an individual with cash income x demands an amount $A(p, x)$ of a good whose price is p. To specify $A(p, x)$, we need to know the prices of all available goods and the individual's preferences over them. A public good is supplied without price at the point of consumption: taxes have financed its provision for everybody. But what price would the individual have had to face, in order that he would have demanded exactly the amount a_0 provided? The Lindahl price $p(x)$ for a public good tells us this: it is defined by $A(p(x), x) \equiv a_0$ for all x. The Lindahl tax bill is $p(x)a_0$, measuring what in total the individual would have paid (recall (7.6)–(7.7), p. 177).

Is it this 'tax bill' we should seek to calculate and impute to each income unit as an income-equivalent benefit? The informational requirement is formidable but suppose we could surmount it. Suppose, further, that such taxes were actually levied. Then they would exactly cancel the benefits, leaving final incomes equal to original incomes! Would this entitle us to declare the impact of government on the distribution of well-being to be nil? Is there not *still* a benefit from the operation of government that we should seek to capture? Why else would we have government provision?

Arguably this objection is a red herring. For people's actual purchases of private goods, as much as for their notional purchases of public goods, it is the case that price is the marginal valuation put on the last unit purchased. If the price had been higher, less (but presumably still some) would have been demanded. A 'consumer surplus' is enjoyed on all but last unit demanded of any good. Thus the Lindahl tax bill does not measure the full utility benefit, any more than does total expenditure on private goods. Brennan (1976, p. 392) again: 'Neglect of consumer surplus is, however, characteristic of "income-equivalent" measures, and it is such neglect that necessitates discussion of the distribution of income as distinct from, say, the distribution of utilities'.

All of this seems to suggest that, for public goods, the ideal would be somehow to calculate Lindahl prices and attribute Lindahl taxes as benefits. (Actually, Brennan himself is arguing towards a quite different prescription – see exercise 11.1.4 below.) How does the practice of allocating budget outlays to income units measure against this ideal?

For optimal public provision, it should be the case that the last unit of public good produced costs the same as the sum of the Lindahl prices $p(x)$ paid for it by all users. Only if the public good is produced at constant unit cost does this mean that the sum of Lindahl tax bills equals the total production cost. For more on this, see Musgrave and Musgrave (1984, chapter 2) and Aaron and McGuire (1970).

Therefore, for a public good, to distribute the expenditure total by whatever means across income units is unsound as a principle. Insofar as income units' preferences as between public and private goods may also be affected by non-income factors, it is in any case unsound to allocate benefits on the basis of income!

At this point we can take solace in de Wulf (1981, p. 62) – 'many of the issues relating to public goods incidence still inhabit the realm of philosophical inquiry' – and remind ourselves that we are in the business of providing a toolkit for the estimation of fiscal incidence given the raw material that actually exists.

de Wulf (1975) gives a wide-ranging discussion of budgetary outlay incidence studies. However, the problems are not over once it is accepted that the game is to distribute expenditure totals. How should this be done? The case of education serves well to highlight the issues.

One beneficial aspect of the government education service is that it generates incomes for teachers, for others who build schools and so forth. These incomes sum to the expenditure total. Is it the teachers and builders who should be attributed with the expenditures? This is surely unsafe, since we have already counted their incomes in the original income distribution!

To allocate the benefits of public educational provision, we must look not to the people who provide the service but to the recipients of the product disseminated. Is it the students and their families who benefit? Education has both consumption and investment characteristics. There may be negative returns on the investment component: witness the oversupply of graduates in some third-world countries. Does anyone benefit from such overproduction? How should we value the improved economic efficiency which derives from a better-educated workforce, now and in the future? As Pechman (1972, p. 256) points out, the intergenerational aspect may confound the attempt: '. . . there is an understanding that each generation of earners will pay for the higher education of the succeeding generation. There is no practical way of obtaining a distribution of net benefits (or net burdens) by income classes in such a system'.

Another intergenerational difficulty arises with interest payments on, and repayments of, government debt. Should we interpret these cash payments as benefits flowing from the government operation? Incidence studies are not consistent in their treatment of this item of government expenditure. Hammes and Wills (1987) survey the various practices. Their recommendation is that such payments should not be attributed as cash benefits.

By extension, if there is a deficit today, which is financed by borrowing so that benefits today exceed what taxes today can pay for, the future interest payments and repayments that will have to be made on today's borrowing must not be attributed as future benefits. Since the present value of all future repayments equals the amount borrowed, to ignore the advice of Hammes and Wills would amount to counting benefits twice – once today, and again strung out over net fiscal incidence studies into the future.

Should interest payments and repayments of government debt be ignored completely, then? No! They count in the original incomes of the holders of this form of wealth, being conferred as of right by their earlier purchase of debt. Nevertheless, government borrowing clearly has repercussions on the original incomes of all existing holders of wealth; interest rate effects in financial markets ought in principle to be taken into account as costs/benefits.

If deficit financing by borrowing enables benefits unmatched by taxes now, the Hammes and Wills prescription ensures taxes unmatched by benefits in future incidence studies. Suppose that, in contrast, government were to print money to finance today's budget deficit. Can you see how the costs of this would be captured in future incidence studies?

Having noted some of the complexities of benefit attribution, we will proceed. We need to acquire a framework of analysis within which, letting $t(x)$ be the tax paid on an income of x and $b(x)$ the benefit received, we can evaluate the impact of the net tax schedule,

$$t_N(x) = t(x) - b(x) \tag{11.1}$$

on the distribution of original income.

For flexibility of application we should not restrict the sign or magnitude of total net tax. Total benefits could be equal to, less than or greater than total taxes. We should be able to (choose to) take into account in (11.1) either the whole or only part of the net fiscal system; for any given application, coverage will depend on available data. Since attribution problems are the least severe for direct taxes on income and transfer payments under the government's income maintenance programme, presumably these two components of the net fiscal system, at least, will typically be included in the study of fiscal incidence.

Exercises

11.1.1 What proportions of total consumption in the USA in 1972 were accounted for by pure private, pure public and various sorts of mixed goods? See Herber (1983, chapter 2). How can the degree of public-ness of goods be measured? See Dean (1980).

11.1.2 Explain how Philpotts (1986) represents geometrically the problem of attributing income equivalent benefits for public goods in his hypo-thetical two-person economy.

11.1.3 'The welfare interpretation of incidence results obtained by valuing government output at the cost of the inputs used is, at best, uncertain and, at worst, quite useless' (de Wulf, 1975, p. 78). Describe de Wulf's argument.

11.1.4 '. . . this paper is not to be construed as any sort of case for the use of equal allocation of public expenditure between households when mea-sures of the total *utility* gains (or consumer surpluses) for both private and public goods production are possible. It is simply that in most cases informational constraints require the calculation of redistribu-tion through the budget in the more modest terms of income equiva-lents. In these cases, the equal-allocation-per-household rule emerges as, at once, the simplest and most analytically satisfactory means of allocating public goods benefits' (Brennan, 1976, p. 398). Assess Brennan's argument. To do this, you will need also to consult Aaron and McGuire (1970), their Reply to Brennan, which follows his paper, and his Rejoinder to their Reply.

11.1.5 '. . . it is physical level of service that is to be equated in so far as a horizontal equity standard is used for distributing benefits of a gov-ernment service' (Shoup, 1988, p. 1). What specific issues does Shoup raise?

11.2 The regressivity of benefits

Let the benefit enjoyed by an income unit with income x be $b(x)$. We need this assumption to get the analysis off the ground, but it is actually very severe. Cash benefits are not always distributed on the basis of income – for example, child benefit in the UK is not. Since non-income factors may affect preferences over public and private goods, people with identical incomes should not necessarily be attributed identical benefits from public provision. Strictly, therefore, the analysis of this section applies only to an income unit 'type' for which benefits *are* a function of income. This is no more and no less than we assumed for income taxes in chapter 8.

If upper-income units exert sufficiently greater effective demand over pure public goods than lower-income units, these particular benefits will be distributed progressively. This is the basis of the benefit principle for progressive taxation. Snow and Warren (1983) derive an empirically verifiable condition for it, albeit under restrictive assumptions (recall (7.7), p. 177), but conclude: 'one cannot argue that existing evidence strongly supports progression' (Snow and Warren, 1983, p. 324).

In most empirical studies of budgetary outlay incidence, allocations by income class are *regressive*. Thus in O'Higgins and Ruggles (1981) and Ruggles and O'Higgins (1981), for the UK and USA respectively, it is the case that, as income rises, attributed expenditures relative to income fall for all categories considered. Income maintenance is the only government programme more beneficial to low income groups in *absolute* terms in both studies. Education, health and housing benefits are distributed approximately equally across income units.

A good starting point for our analysis is that benefits are distributed regressively:

$$\frac{d[b(x)/x]}{dx} \leq 0 \text{ for all } x \tag{11.2}$$

This need not be so, but it is clear intuitively that if benefits *are* regressively distributed, they will exert an equalizing effect on income distribution. In taking (11.2) as the 'norm', we shall end up with indices of benefit impact which are positive for equalizing benefits and negative for disequalizing ones. We already have this feature for taxes, and it will aid clarity to have it for benefits also when in section 11.3 we combine the tax and benefit systems.

Indeed, because benefit is an addition to income x, whereas tax is a subtraction from it, there is an exact counterpart of the Jakobsson–Fellman theorem 8.1, p. 190, for progressive taxes which confirms the inequality-reducing characteristic of regressive benefits.

We begin with some definitions. First, let $F(x)$ be the distribution function and $f(x)$ the frequency density function for original income. The concentration curves for benefits and for 'post-benefit income' are defined as follows:

$$p = F(y) \Rightarrow L_B(p) = \int_0^y \frac{b(x)f(x)dx}{\mu b} \tag{11.3a}$$

and

$$p = F(y) \Rightarrow L_{X+B}(p) = \int_0^y \frac{[x+b(x)]f(x)\,\mathrm{d}x}{\mu(1+b)} \qquad (11.3b)$$

where b is the average rate of benefit (or total benefits ratio) and μ is the mean original income. Notice immediately from this that

$$L_X \equiv (1+b)L_{X+B} - bL_B \qquad (11.4)$$

which is the equivalent of the relationship $L_X \equiv (1-t)L_{X-T} + tL_T$ that we found for taxes (p. 38).

The extension of the Jakobsson–Fellman theorem is as follows:

Theorem 11.1

$\mathrm{d}[b(x)/x]/\mathrm{d}x \leq 0$ for all $x \Leftrightarrow L_B \geq L_{X+B} \geq L_X$ for every pre-tax income distribution $F(x)$.

This configuration of concentration curves is shown in figure 11.1. The proof of the theorem is almost identical with that for progressive taxes given on p. 190. The only significant difference lies in the observation that, because of (11.4), for each p, $L_{X+B}(p)$ is a weighted average of $L_X(p)$ and $L_B(p)$:

$$L_{X+B}(p) = \frac{1}{1+b}L_X(p) + \frac{b}{1+b}L_B(p) \qquad (11.5)$$

and therefore it is enough for the $\Rightarrow$ direction to prove $L_B(p) \geq L_X(p)$ for all p. The concentration curve L_{X+B} will equal the Lorenz curve for post-benefit income if the benefit schedule satisfies $b'(x) > -1$ for all x. Can you see why? Is this a reasonable assumption?

Benefit regressivity, appropriately measured, will be an input to our consideration of net progressivity. There are two obvious courses to follow: one is disproportionality, and the other is redistributive effect. Let us therefore define two regressivity measures, one of disproportionality modelled on the Kakwani index for taxes,

$$\rho_B^K = 2\int_0^1 [L_B(p) - L_X(p)]\,\mathrm{d}p = G_X - C_B \qquad (11.6)$$

and the other of redistributive effect, modelled on the Reynolds-Smolensky index for taxes,

$$\rho_B^{RS} = 2\int_0^1 [L_{X+B}(p) - L_X(p)]\,\mathrm{d}p = G_X - C_{X+B} \qquad (11.7)$$

Here, C_B and C_{X+B} are the concentration coefficients for benefits and post-benefit income and G_X is the Gini coefficient for original income. Work out for yourself what areas these indices represent in figure 11.1. Note from (11.6) that ρ_B^K is the negative of the Kakwani index of progressivity of a tax equal in value to $b(x)$.

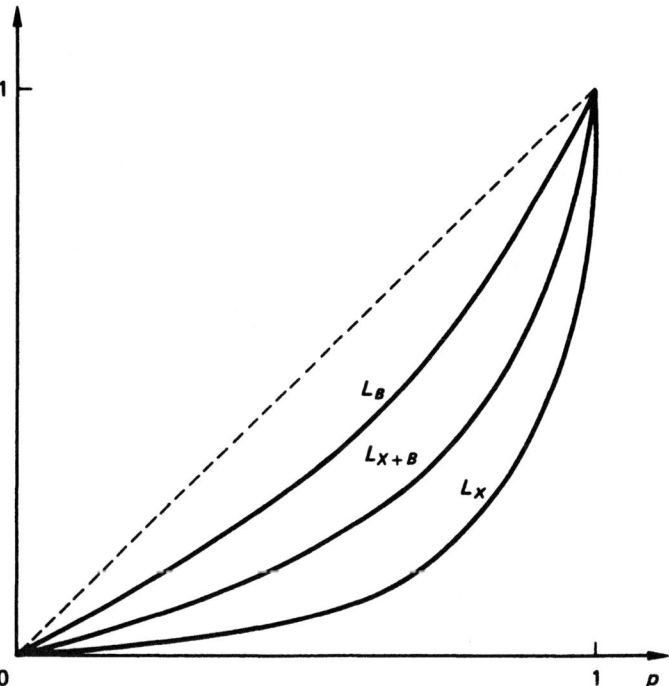

Figure 11.1 Concentration curve configuration in the case of regressive benefits

The redistributive effect for benefits can be decomposed into level and disproportionality components, just as for taxes. This can be seen by re-arranging (11.4) as

$$(1+b)(L_{X+B} - L_X) \equiv b(L_B - L_X) \tag{11.8}$$

and integrating:

$$\rho_B^{RS} = \frac{b}{1+b} \rho_B^K \tag{11.9}$$

Compare this with equation (8.30), p. 209, for taxes. It is clear intuitively, as well as from the equation, that if regressively distributed benefits are scaled up, or if a given total of benefits is rearranged more disproportionately, then the redistributive effect is enhanced.

Generalizations of the indices ρ_B^K and ρ_B^{RS} can be secured, as for taxes, by introducing a distributional judgement parameter v:

$$\rho_B^K(v) = v(v-1)\int_0^1 (1-p)^{v-2}[L_B(p) - L_X(p)]\,dp = G_X(v) - C_B(v) \tag{11.6a}$$

$$\rho_B^{RS}(v) = v(v-1)\int_0^1 (1-p)^{v-2}[L_{X+B}(p) - L_X(p)]\,dp = G_X(v) - C_{X+B}(v) \quad (11.7a)$$

and these satisfy

$$\rho_B^{RS}(v) = \frac{b}{1+b}\rho_B^K(v) \tag{11.9a}$$

because of (11.8).

We can just as readily work in the relative concentration curve framework, described on pp. 202–203 and used to define the Suits and Pfähler indices of tax progressivity. The analogous indices of benefit regressivity are

$$\rho_B^S = 2\int_0^1 [R_B(q) - q]\,dq \tag{11.10}$$

$$\rho_B^{PA} = 2\int_0^1 [R_{X+B}(q) - q]\,dq \tag{11.11}$$

and they enjoy a corresponding relationship

$$\rho_B^{PA} = \frac{b}{1+b}\rho_B^S \tag{11.12}$$

which derives from the identity

$$q \equiv (1+b)R_{X+B}(q) - bR_B(q) \tag{11.13}$$

between the relative concentration curves $R_B(q)$ and $R_{X+B}(q)$ for benefits and post-benefit income.

We now have the ingredients for our study of net progressivity. For taxes, we have two kinds of progressivity index. These are the indices

$$\Pi_T^K, \Pi_T^K(v), \Pi_T^S$$

of disproportionality, and the indices

$$\Pi_T^{RS}, \Pi_T^{RS}(v), \Pi_T^{PA}$$

of redistributive effect. The subscript T, not present in chapter 8, is a helpful addition in the present context. For the regressivity of benefits, we have the indices

$$\rho_B^K, \rho_B^K(v), \rho_B^S$$

measuring disproportionality,[1] and the indices

$$\rho_B^{RS}, \rho_B^{RS}(v), \rho_B^{PA}$$

measuring redistributive effect. The Kiefer and Blackorby-Donaldson indices of tax progressivity Π_T^{KI} and Π_T^{BD} can also be adapted to benefits, but we defer this until later for a reason that will become apparent.

It is worth pausing at this point to consider the rôle of benefit regressivity as an input to the analysis of net fiscal impact. A benefit which is allocated in proportion to income will have nil effect. One might wish to allocate such things as justice, diplomacy and general administration in this way, deliberately to secure a neutral (nil) effect on income distribution. However, other expenditures might give rise to social concern if in reality they were allocated proportionately to incomes. For example, to return to the case of education: 'If it is observed, as is the case, that children from low-income families either do not go to college or go to inferior schools, the system of distributing the benefits of public higher education is inequitable' (Pechman, 1972, p. S257).

A hidden value judgement that inequality is a relative concept underpins the very definitions of progression and regression we have adopted in this book (though see exercise 8.2.6, p. 199). In consequence, we are landed with a concept of distributional neutrality which is less in accord with primitive intuition for benefits than it is for taxes. As Crane (1983, p. 243) remarks of the typical regressive distribution of expenditure benefits: '. . . what this really demonstrates is that the distribution of expenditures is not as skewed toward the upper income brackets as income. In other words, expenditures are pro poor because they are not as pro rich as the distribution of income . . . One could argue that a neutral expenditure pattern would treat all households alike regardless of income'.

Exercises

11.2.1 Devise measures of structural regression for benefits with respect to which the various indices of this section satisfy the consistency condition that regressivity should increase if the distribution of original income stays fixed and the benefit schedule becomes more regressive. *Hint:* Use lemma 8.1, p. 200.

11.2.2 Draw a graph showing the configuration of the relative concentration curves $R_{X+B}(q)$ and $R_B(q)$ in the case of a regressive benefit schedule, and mark on it the indices ρ_B^S and ρ_B^{PA}.

11.2.3 Compare Fellman *et al.'s* (1999) measure of the effectiveness of a benefit schedule with their measure of the effectiveness of a tax schedule (see exercise 8.4.11, p. 213).

11.2.4 Show that, according to the absolute inequality concept, a lump-sum benefit is distributionally neutral and any benefit which gives more to lower incomes ($b'(x) < 0$) is equalizing. Use exercise 8.2.6, p. 199, to show that, according to the intermediate inequality concept of Besley and Preston (1988), an expenditure $b(x)$ is distributionally neutral/equalizing if its level is constant/declining as a fraction of translated income $x + \mu^*$ for some appropriate translation $\mu^* \geq 0$.

11.3 The progressivity of net taxes

It would be convenient if we could use the tax progressivity indices and benefit regressivity indices just listed as inputs to the measurement of net progressivity. This would enable the analyst to 'piece together' the results of separate tax and expenditure incidence studies, where allocations may have have been made across different income groupings. The first attempts to capture the progressivity of the net fiscal system in index form were those of Kienzle (1981, 1982) and Bridges (1984). These authors simply took as their inputs the disproportionality indices Π_T^S and ρ_B^S for taxes and expenditure benefits respectively (see on). For sound measurement, we must clearly base net progressivity on the net tax schedule:

$$t_N(x) = t(x) - b(x) \tag{11.1}$$

Only if it emerges that net progressivity decomposes into separate tax progressivity and expenditure regressivity components is the *desideratum* realized.

Consider first the extension to $t_N(x)$ of the disproportionality approach to progressivity measurement. Since net tax can be negative for some income recipients and positive for others, and may be zero, positive or negative in total, the 'concentration of net tax' is a problematic concept, and measuring disproportionality in it is so *a fortiori*. However, no conceptual problems exist for measuring the concentration of final income. Redistributive effect offers a problem-free basis for the measurement of the progressivity of the net tax schedule $t_N(x)$.

We can see clearly what is involved with the help of some mathematics. Thus let L_{X-T+B} be the concentration curve for final income:

$$p = F(y) \Rightarrow L_{X-T+B}(p) = \int_0^y \frac{[x - t(x) + b(x)]f(x)\,dx}{\mu(1 - g + b)} \tag{11.14}$$

where g is the total tax ratio as in earlier chapters. Assuming $t_N'(x) < 1$ for all x, L_{X-T+B} is the Lorenz curve for final income.[2] It is clear from the definition that

$$(1 - g + b)L_{X-T+B} \equiv L_X - g L_T + b L_B \tag{11.15}$$

Therefore if taxes are progressive and benefits regressive, the net schedule $t_N(x) = t(x) - b(x)$ is equalizing:

$$L_T < L_X \text{ and } L_B > L_X \Rightarrow L_{X-T+B} > L_X \tag{11.16}$$

The Reynolds–Smolensky index of net redistributive effect is

$$\Pi_N^{RS} = 2\int_0^1 [L_{X-T+B}(p) - L_X(p)]\,dp \tag{11.17}$$

The term $[L_{X-T+B}(p) - L_X(p)]$ in the integrand measures that fraction of total final income shifted from high incomes (the top $100(1-p)$ per cent) to low incomes (the bottom $100p$ per cent) by the presence of progression in the net tax schedule. We can re-arrange (11.15) to show how progressive taxes and regressive expenditures both contribute to this income shift:

$$(1-g+b)[L_{X-T+B}-L_X] \equiv g[L_X - L_T] + b[L_B - L_X] \tag{11.18}$$

The terms on the right are departures from proportionality. Therefore let us integrate with respect to p in (11.18), and having done so, divide through by $(1-g+b)$:

$$\Pi_N^{RS} = \frac{g\Pi_T^K + b\rho_B^K}{1-g+b} \tag{11.19}$$

Now substitute from (8.30), p. 209, and (11.9) to obtain an alternative expression for Π_N^{RS}:

$$\Pi_N^{RS} = \frac{(1-g)\Pi_T^{RS} + (1+b)\rho_B^{RS}}{1-g+b} \tag{11.20}$$

Hence net redistributive effect can be computed from the progressivity of taxes and regressivity of benefits, and either the disproportionality indices Π_T^K and ρ_B^K or the redistributive effect indices Π_T^{RS} and ρ_B^{RS} can be used as inputs.[3]

If we try to construct an index of disproportionality for net taxes, à la Kakwani, difficulties immediately become apparent. The first step would be to define the concentration curve for net taxes:

$$p = F(y) \Rightarrow L_{T-B}(p) = \int_0^y \frac{[t(x)-b(x)]f(x)\,\mathrm{d}x}{\mu(g-b)} \tag{11.21}$$

but this curve is undefined if $g = b$. Even when $g \neq b$, it does not have the familiar concentration curve profile.

Figure 11.2 shows what pertains in the case of a net tax schedule $t_N(x)$ which is first negative and then, above some level x_0 of original income, positive. The value x_0 marks the break-even point between those receiving net subsidies $(x < x_0)$ and those paying net taxes $(x > x_0)$. In both parts of the diagram point A locates the break-even percentile $F(x_0)$. When the net tax yield is positive $(g > b)$, the subsidies up to A are just offset by tax payments from income units between A and B; the income units above B account for the whole of the net yield. When the net tax yield is negative $(g < b)$, income units up to C just exhaust this net subsidy; further subsidies to those lying between C and A are exactly offset by the positive tax payments incurred above A. In neither case does L_{T-B} have the usual upward sloping convex shape.

Neglecting this problem, and the consequent irregularity of the curve L_{T-B} in the neighbourhood of $g = b$, and pressing on, our next step is to construct the Kakwani index of net disproportionality:

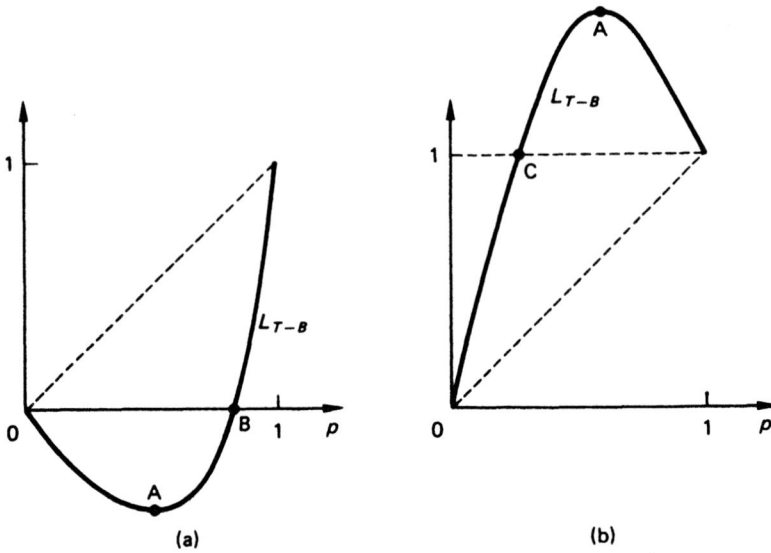

Figure 11.2   The concentration of net tax: (a) $g > b$; (b) $g < b$

$$\Pi_N^K = 2\int_0^1 [L_X(p) - L_{T-B}(p)]\, dp \qquad g \neq b \tag{11.22}$$

Then because of the identity

$$(g-b)L_{T-B} \equiv g L_T - b L_B \tag{11.23}$$

which may be rearranged as

$$(g-b)[L_X - L_{T-B}] \equiv g[L_X - L_T] + b[L_B - L_X] \tag{11.24}$$

and integrated, we have the decomposition

$$\Pi_N^K = \frac{g\Pi_T^K + b\rho_B^K}{g-b} \qquad g \neq b \tag{11.25}$$

of net disproportionality into tax and benefit components.

From (11.19) and (11.25) comes the by now familiar relationship between net disproportionality and net redistributive effect:

$$\Pi_N^{RS} = \frac{g_N}{1-g_N}\Pi_N^K \tag{11.26}$$

where $g_N = g - b \neq 0$. Can you see the problem which arises when g is very close to b? Suppose that the government is operating a balanced budget and statisticians are attempting to allocate all specific expenditure totals across income classes. Suppose, further, that the attempt is not fully successful, so that g_N is small and positive in (11.26). Now, improved techniques make it possible gradually to allocate more and more items. As $g_N \to 0$, the term Π_N^{RS} on the left in (11.26) approaches the true redistributive effect of the fiscal system, finite and positive, shall we say. Then $\Pi_N^K \to \infty$. On the other hand, if it is the incidence of taxes that is incomplete and gradually completed, so that $g_N \to 0$ through negative values, then $\Pi_N^K \to -\infty$! The instability of sign and value of Π_N^K in the neighbourhood of $g_N = 0$ is a most unattractive feature of the disproportionality approach.

We can generalize the indices Π_N^{RS} and Π_N^K by introducing a distributional judgement parameter v, just as we did separately for taxes and benefits. Everything goes through without change:

$$
\begin{aligned}
\Pi_N^{RS}(v) &= \frac{(1-g)\Pi_T^{RS}(v)+(1+b)\rho_B^{RS}(v)}{1-g+b} \\
&= \frac{g\Pi_T^K(v)+b\rho_B^K(v)}{1-g+b} \\
&= \frac{g_N}{1-g_N}\,\Pi_N^K(v)
\end{aligned}
\tag{11.27}
$$

An advantage of this generalization is that the analyst or policymaker can carry out sensitivity analysis on the degree of progressivity of net taxes by calculating the indices for a range of values of v. As $v \to \infty$, the indices should register concern increasingly with the tax and benefit position of the worst-off members of society.

The relative concentration curve framework of analysis also yields indices of net progressivity. Thus, let Π_N^{PA} be the Pfähler index of net redistributive effect and Π_N^S the Suits-type index of net disproportionality when $g \neq b$. This latter index is no less fraught than the Kakwani index, exhibiting similar instability of sign and value in the neighbourhood of a balanced budget allocation. It is left to you to verify that

$$
\begin{aligned}
\Pi_N^{PA} &= \frac{(1-g)\Pi_T^{PA}+(1+b)\rho_B^{PA}}{1-g+b} \\
&= \frac{g\Pi_T^S+b\rho_B^S}{1-g+b} \\
&= \frac{g_N}{1-g_N}\,\Pi_N^S
\end{aligned}
\tag{11.28}
$$

The *ad hoc* combinations of Π_T^S and ρ_B^S used by Kienzle (1981, 1982) and Bridges (1984) avoided the difficulty that occurs with Π_N^S as $g_N \to 0$.[4]

In all these cases, net redistributive effect is a weighted sum of the indices for taxes and benefits when applied separately to original incomes:[5]

$$
\Pi_N = \frac{(1-g)\Pi_T+(1+b)\rho_B}{1-g+b}
\tag{11.29}
$$

Note, though, that Π_N is not a weighted average of Π_T and ρ_B in this formula. The weights sum to more than unity; indeed, the weight on ρ_B is greater than unity. The significance of this observation is considerable. It means that taxes may be regressive in their effect on original income ($\Pi_T < 0$), and yet the net system may exhibit more progressivity than regressive benefits alone ($\Pi_N > \rho_B > 0$). How can this happen?

A moment's thought resolves the apparent conundrum. Suppose that taxes which are regressive on original income are nevertheless progressive with respect to the less unequally distributed post-benefit income. Then clearly they exert an equalizing effect over and above the effect of regressive benefits. A simple example makes the point transparent (see table 11.1). Here, income tax is a declining proportion of original income but an increasing proportion of income including benefit. The net fiscal system is more equalizing than regressive benefits alone, despite regressive taxes. Indeed, in this particular case it is perfectly equalizing! This example is not altogether far-fetched: regressive taxes reinforce the effect of regressive government expenditures in precisely this way for the UK tax and expenditure allocations in O'Higgins and Ruggles (1981) and for the US allocations in Ruggles and O'Higgins (1981).

Table 11.1   Hypothetical example

Original income x	10	20	30	40
Tax liability $t(x)$	6	9	12	15
Benefit level $b(x)$	21	14	7	0
Post-benefit income	31	34	37	40
Final income	25	25	25	25

The inequality that reveals such an interaction of tax progressivity and benefit regressivity is, from (11.29),

$$\Pi_N > \rho_B \Leftrightarrow \Pi_T > -\frac{g}{1-g}\rho_B \qquad (11.30)$$

This simple criterion does not demand that taxes and government expenditure benefits be jointly assigned to income levels to be operational.[6]

The tax progressivity indices $\Pi^{KI}(e)$ and $\Pi^{BD}(e)$, defined on p. 210, can also be extended to net taxes $t_N(x) = t(x) - b(x)$:

$$\Pi_N^{KI}(e) = I_X(e) - I_{X-T+B}(e) \qquad (11.31)$$

$$\Pi_N^{BD} = \frac{I_X(e) - I_{X-T+B}(e)}{1 - I_X(e)} \qquad (11.32)$$

In Blackorby and Donaldson (1984a), it is proposed to evaluate the redistributive effect of benefits by their inequality-reducing impact on post-tax, rather than original, income:

$$\rho_B^{BD}(e) = \frac{I_{X-T}(e) - I_{X-T+B}(e)}{1 - I_{X-T}(e)} \tag{11.33a}$$

By this, a multiplicative decomposition of net progressivity into tax and benefit components is achieved:

$$1 + \Pi_N^{BD}(e) = [1 + \rho_B^{BD}(e)][1 + \Pi_T^{BD}(e)] \tag{11.34a}$$

Estimation of $\Pi_N^{BD}(e)$ requires that taxes and benefits be jointly assigned to levels of original income: can you see why?

This multiplicative decomposition does not make accessible the observation that regressive taxes can reinforce regressive government expenditure benefits. But a variant of it clarifies the situation. Thus, let $\rho_B^{*BD}(e)$ be the regressivity of government expenditure benefits with respect to original income

$$\rho_B^{*BD}(e) = \frac{I_X(e) - I_{X+B}(e)}{1 - I_X(e)} \tag{11.33b}$$

and let Π_T^{*BD} be the progressivity of taxes with respect to post-benefit income

$$\Pi_T^{*BD}(e) = \frac{I_{X+B}(e) - I_{X-T+B}(e)}{1 - I_{X+B}(e)} \tag{11.35}$$

(instead of the other way around). Then a different decomposition of net progressivity Π_N^{BD} emerges:

$$1 + \Pi_N^{BD}(e) = [1 + \rho_B^{*BD}(e)][1 + \Pi_T^{*BD}(e)] \tag{11.34b}$$

Both $\Pi_N^{BD}(e)$ and $\rho_B^{*BD}(e)$ are evaluated with respect to original income. The net redistributive effect exceeds the redistributive effect of benefits alone ($\Pi_N^{BD}(e) > \rho_B^{*BD}(e)$) if taxes which may be regressive on original income ($\Pi_T^{BD}(e) < 0$) are nevertheless progressive on post-benefit income ($\Pi_T^{*BD}(e) > 0$).

Exercises

11.3.1   If the tax and benefit schedules are made up of components, *viz.*
$t(x) = \Sigma t_i(x)$ and $b(x) = \Sigma b_j(x)$, show that net progressivity can be decomposed as $\Pi_N^{RS} = [\Sigma(1 - g_i)\Pi_{Ti}^{RS} - \Sigma(1 - b_j)\rho_{Bj}^{RS}]/(1 - g + b)$. *Hint*: Recall exercise 8.4.4, p. 212.

11.3.2   Suppose that taxes are regressive: $L_T > L_X$. Devise a condition on concentration curves under which the net tax is more redistributive than regressive benefits alone: $L_{X-T+B} > L_{X+B} > L_X$.

11.3.3(a) How do Ebert and Lambert (1999) relate liability and residual progression of the net tax schedule $t_N(x)$ with the corresponding measures of structural progression for taxes and benefits?

11.3.3(b) 'Pfähler (1984) discusses LP-neutral changes on the tax side, and also RP-neutral changes, recommending an LP-neutral tax increase and an RP-neutral tax cut, but he does not take into account the existence of the benefit system, and therefore overlooks the fact that overall progression is affected by these "progression-neutral" changes' (Ebert and Lambert, 1999, p. 402). What are the overall effects, assuming regressive benefits?

11.3.4 Decompose the Kiefer index $\Pi_N^{KI}(e)$ of net progressivity into tax progressivity and benefit regressivity components in two different ways.

11.3.5 Discuss the normative significance and limitations of the net progressivity indices Π_N^{RS}, Π_N^{K}, $\Pi_N^{BD}(e)$ and $\Pi_N^{KI}(e)$. *Hint*: Consult p. 211.

11.4 Net fiscal incidence and horizontal inequity

Taxes are typically *not* a function $t(x)$ of living standard x, as we saw in chapters 7 and 10, and benefit attributions are typically *not* systematically related to living standard by a function $b(x)$ either (though many cash benefits are intended to raise living standards). Our analysis of net taxes must plainly be extended to take horizontal inequity into account.

The measurement theory in section 3 of chapter 10 can be extended straightforwardly to the net fiscal system. All that is needed is to express the analytics of that chapter in terms of the transition from the *original* to the *final* income distribution, rather than from the *pre-tax* to the *post-tax* distribution. This puts at our disposal the following decompositions of net fiscal incidence progressivity into vertical and horizontal components:

$$RE_{sys} = RE_{vert} - H \tag{10.18}$$

for the redistributive effect of the net fiscal system calculated using the mean logarithmic deviation;

$$CE_{sys} = CE_{vert} - H^* \tag{10.21}$$

for the cost effectiveness of the net fiscal system;

$$\Pi_{sys}^{BD} = \theta\Pi_{vert}^{BD} - H^{**} \tag{10.23}$$

for the Blackorby–Donaldson index of net progressivity; and

$$\Pi_{sys}^{RS} = \Pi_{vert}^{RS} - H^{***} - R \tag{10.27}$$

for the Reynolds–Smolensky index.

Duclos and Lambert (2000) estimate the decompositions of *RE*, *CE* and Π^{BD} shown in (10.18), (10.21) and (10.23) for the Canadian income tax and cash benefit system. Including benefits in this sort of analysis means that the HE replacement schedules $T_{WN}(x)$ and $T_{RN}(x)$ underpinning the measurements will typically specify negative averaged taxes for low incomes (i.e. benefits). Duclos and Lambert display the Canadian HE replacement schedules for 1994 in their figure 4 (*ibid.*, p. 100).

The 'pure HI' partial ordering $\subseteq_{HI}$ of section 4 of chapter 10 can also be extended straightforwardly to enable HI comparisons between net fiscal systems. The respective joint distributions of original and final income yield the cumulated transition matrices required for the copula dominance test in this case. Dardanoni and Lambert (2001a) test for copula dominance between the tax and cash benefit systems of the UK, Canada and Israel (and also, within Canada, between the tax and cash benefit systems of 1981 and 1990).

We conclude with some further analysis of the Reynolds–Smolensky index decomposition which will permit us to reconsider the issue of tax and benefit interaction. For systematic taxes and benefits (i.e. those without HI), the Reynolds–Smolensky approach offered an insight into the way taxes and benefits could interact. Specifically, on p. 275 we derived this formula:

$$\Pi_N^{RS} = \frac{(1-g)\Pi_T^{RS} + (1+b)\rho_B^{RS}}{1-g+b} \tag{11.20}$$

decomposing overall redistributive effect into tax and benefit components, and we used it to explain how regressive taxes could reinforce the effect of regressive government expenditures.

For taxes and benefits which are *not* systematically related to income by well-behaved schedules $t(x)$ and $b(x)$, (11.20) is not valid, but a decomposition just like it can be obtained in respect of the schedules representing the vertical stances of the net fiscal system and of taxes and of benefits. If $T_{RN}(x) = n(x)$ is the revenue-neutral HE replacement fiscal system, let us write

$$n(x) = t(x) - b(x) \tag{11.36}$$

where $t(x)$ and $b(x)$ are the revenue-neutral HE replacement tax and benefit component schedules. We can apply (11.20) to these schedules, obtaining

$$\Pi_{n(x)}^{RS} = \frac{(1-g)\Pi_{t(x)}^{RS} + (1+b)\rho_{b(x)}^{RS}}{1-g+b} \tag{11.37}$$

(to use an obvious extension of previous notation). The regressive-taxes-reinforcing-regressive-expenditures feature can be seen in these averaged relationships. Is it still evident that this can happen when horizontal inequity is taken into account?

The way forward is to introduce classical HI and reranking corrections into (11.37) using (10.27) (given above). This involves replacing $\Pi_{n(x)}^{RS}$ (which is of course the term Π_{vert}^{RS} in (10.27)) by $\Pi_{sys}^{RS} + D_N$, and similarly replacing $\Pi_{t(x)}^{RS}$ by $\Pi_T^{RS} + D_T$ and $\Pi_{b(x)}^{RS}$ by $\Pi_B^{RS} + D_B$, where $D_i = H_i^{***} + R_i$ for $i = N, T, B$ (to use obvious notation). Finally, write Π_{sys}^{RS} as Π_N^{RN} and tidy up, to obtain:

$$\Pi_N^{RS} = \frac{(1-g)\Pi_T^{RS} + (1+b)\Pi_B^{RS}}{1-g+b} - E \tag{11.38}$$

where

$$E = D_N - \frac{(1-g)D_T + (1+b)D_B}{1-g+b} \tag{11.39}$$

(11.38) is directly comparable with (11.20). As you can see, however, the final term E in (11.38) stands in the way of a straightforward relationship between overall redistributive effect and the component Reynolds–Smolensky indices. Jenkins (1988b) examined the implications of (11.38)–(11.39) using UK microdata,[7] finding that the regressive-taxes-reinforcing-regressive-expenditures feature present in the O'Higgins and Ruggles (1981) grouped data is also present in the microdata for the same year both before and after reranking is taken into account.

Exercise

11.4.1 'Tax and benefit systems typically contribute to HI in different ranges of income' (Dardanoni and Lambert, 2001a). In which component of the tax and benefit system would you expect HI to be the more pronounced? Review the findings of Dardanoni and Lambert (2001a) and Duclos and Lambert (2000, pp. 106–109) on this question.

Notes

1 The measure ρ_B^S can be attributed to Kienzle (1981), and ρ_B^K to Lecaillon *et al.* (1984), though each called his measure an index of *progressivity*. The misnomer may have arisen because of the association in the tax literature of the word 'progressive' with the word 'equalizing', and has persisted throughout a number of subsequent contributions, for example Blackorby and Donaldson (1984a), Bridges (1984), Layard and Walters (1987, p. 101) and (sadly) Lambert (1985a). However, Reynolds and Smolensky (1977, p. 53) were careful to apply the terms consistently. As we have done here, they called any attribute of income with an increasing average rate *progressive*, and the converse *regressive*. But they recognized the dangers, suggesting instead the nomeclature 'pro-rich' and 'pro-poor', which, though intuitively clear, does not seem to have caught on in the literature.

2 Since $t_N'(x) = t'(x) - b'(x)$, this condition holds automatically if benefits increase with income ($b'(x) > 0$). If $b'(x) < 0$, as for example when $b(x)$ is income support, the condition $t_N'(x) < 1$ requires that the sum of the marginal tax rate and benefit *withdrawal* rate should not exceed unity. If this sum did exceed unity, the tax and benefit system would contain an institutionalized 'trap': people could increase their net incomes by reducing their original incomes.

3 Although the index Π_N^{RS} can be attributed to Reynolds and Smolensky (1977), these authors did not use ρ_B^{RS} to measure benefit regressivity. They obtained an

additive decomposition of the form $\Pi_N^{RS} = \Pi_T^* + \rho_B^*$, as explained in note 14 in chapter 8.

4 Kienzle's (1981) proposal was to measure net fiscal incidence progressivity as $\Pi_N = 1 + \frac{1}{4}[\Pi_T^S + \rho_B^S]$. Bridges (1984) proposed instead $\Pi_N = [g\Pi_T^S + b\rho_B^S]/(g + b)$.

5 The sign properties of the various tax progressivity and benefit regressivity indices featuring here can be summarized as follows, in each case writing $\Pi:(a, b, c)$ to indicate that the value of Π corresponding to maximal regressivity is a, the value corresponding to proportionality is b and the value corresponding to maximal progressivity is c. For taxes, the values are $\Pi_T^K:(-1 - G_X, 0, 1 - G_X)$, $\Pi_T^S:(-1, 0, 1)$, $\Pi_T^{RS}:(-1 + G_X, 0, G_X)$ and $\Pi_T^{PA}:(-1, 0, G_X)$. For benefits, they are $\rho_B^K:(1 + G_X, 0, G_X - 1)$, $\rho_B^S:(1, 0, -1)$, $\rho_B^{RS}:(G_X, 0, G_X - 1)$ and $\rho_B^{PA}:(G_X, 0, -1)$. For net taxes, we have $\Pi_N^{RS}:(-1 + G_X, 0, G_X)$ and $\Pi_N^{PA}:(-1, 0, G_X)$. In all cases, G_X is the Gini coefficient for original income. In the case of the disproportionality indices, maximal progressivity occurs when the richest income unit pays all the tax or takes all the benefit, irrespective of how much or how little this is. For the redistributive effect indices, maximal tax progressivity and benefit regressivity occur when the tax or benefit respectively is perfectly equalizing in its effect on original incomes.

6 Much of the material described in section 11.3 up to this point is drawn from Lambert (1985a) and Lambert and Pfähler (1988).

7 Jenkins did not take classical HI into account in developing the decomposition in (11.38)–(11.39); 'joining up' rather than a lexicographic approach must have been used to compute concentration curves and coefficients (recall the discussion on pp. 239–240). It means that the classical HI components H_i^{***} in the D_i of (11.39) do not appear in Jenkins's decomposition (see his equation (10), p. 69). Duclos (1998) does a similar thing with $\Pi^{RS}(v)$ (recall exercise 10.1.1).

Bibliography

Aaron, H. and M. McGuire (1970). Public goods and income distribution. *Econometrica*, vol. 38, pp. 907–919.

Alexander, S.S. (1974). Social evaluation through notional choice. *Quarterly Journal of Economics*, vol. 88, pp. 597–624. (Followed by R.A. Musgrave and, pp. 633–655, Reply to Alexander and Musgrave by J. Rawls.)

Amiel, Y. and F.A. Cowell (1992). Measurement of income inequality: experimental test by questionnaire. *Journal of Public Economics*, vol. 47, pp. 3–26.

Amiel, Y., J. Creedy and S. Hurn (1999). Measuring attitude towards inequality. *Scandinavian Journal of Economics*, vol. 101, pp. 83–96.

Araar, A. and J.-Y. Duclos (1998). An Atkinson–Gini class of social evaluation functions. CRÉFA Working Paper No. 98-26, Université Laval, Quebec.

Arnold, B.C. (1990). The Lorenz order and the effects of taxation policies. *Bulletin of Economic Research*, vol. 42, pp. 249–264.

Aronson, J.R., P. Johnson and P.J. Lambert (1994). Redistributive effect and unequal income tax treatment. *Economic Journal*, vol. 104, pp. 262–270.

Arrow, K.J. (1963). *Social Choice and Individual Values*. New York: Wiley.

Atkinson, A.B. (1970). On the measurement of inequality. *Journal of Economic Theory*, vol. 2, pp. 244–263.

Atkinson, A.B. (1980a). *Wealth, Income and Inequality*, 2nd edition. Oxford: Oxford University Press.

Atkinson, A.B. (1980b). Horizontal equity and the distribution of the tax burden. In H.J. Aaron and M.J. Boskins (eds) *The Economics of Taxation*. Washington DC: Brookings.

Atkinson, A.B. (1988). On the measurement of poverty. *Econometrica*, vol. 55, pp. 749–764. Reprinted as chapter 2 in Atkinson (1989).

Atkinson, A.B. (1989). *Poverty and Social Security*. Hemel Hempstead: Harvester-Wheatsheaf.

Atkinson, A.B. (1990). Public economics and the economic public. *European Economic Review*, vol. 34, pp. 225–248.

Atkinson, A.B. (1992). Measuring poverty and differences in family composition. *Economica*, vol. 59, pp. 1–16.

Atkinson, A.B. and F. Bourguignon (1982). The comparison of multi-dimensioned distributions of economic status. *Review of Economic Studies*, vol. 49, pp. 183–201.

Atkinson, A.B. and F. Bourguignon (1987). Income distribution and differences in needs. Chapter 12 in G.R. Feiwel (ed.) *Arrow and the Foundations of the Theory of Economic Policy.* London: Macmillan.

Atkinson, A.B., F. Bourguignon and P.A. Chiappori (1987). What do we learn about tax reform from international comparisons? *European Economic Review*, vol. 32, pp. 343–352.

Atkinson, A.B., L. Rainwater and T.M. Smeeding (1995). *Income Distribution in OECD Countries.* Paris: OECD.

Auerbach, A.J. and K.A. Hassett (2002). A new measure of horizontal equity. *American Economic Review*, forthcoming.

Banks, J. and P. Johnson (1994a). Equivalence scale relativities revisited. *Economic Journal*, vol. 104, pp. 883–890.

Banks, J. and P. Johnson (1994b). Equivalence scales and public policy. *Fiscal Studies*, vol. 15, pp. 1–23.

Beardon, A.F. and G.B. Mehta (1994). The utility theorems of Wold, Debreu and Arrow-Hahn. *Econometrica*, vol. 62, pp. 181–186.

Beath, J., G. Lewis and D. Ulph (1988). Policy targeting in a new welfare framework with poverty. In P.G. Hare (ed.) *Surveys in Public Sector Economics.* Oxford and Cambridge, MA: Blackwell.

Benus, J. and J.N. Morgan (1975). Time period, unit of analysis and income concept in the analysis of income distribution, in J.D. Smith (ed.) *The Personal Distribution of Income and Wealth.* NBER Studies in Income and Wealth, vol. 39. New York: Columbia University Press.

Berglas, E. (1971). Income tax and the distribution of income: an international comparison. *Public Finance/Finances Publiques*, vol. 26, pp. 532–545.

Berliant, M.C. and R.P. Strauss (1985). The horizontal and vertical equity characteristics of the federal individual income tax, 1966–1977. In M. David and T. Smeeding (eds) *Horizontal Equity, Uncertainty and Economic Well-Being*, NBER Studies in Income and Wealth, vol. 50, Chicago: Chicago University Press.

Berrebi, Z.M. and J. Silber (1981). Weighting income ranks and levels: a multi-parameter generalisation for absolute and relative inequality indices. *Economics Letters*, vol. 7, pp. 391–397.

Berrebi, Z.M. and J. Silber (1985). Income inequality indices and deprivation: a generalization. *Quarterly Journal of Economics*, vol. 100, pp. 807–810.

Besley, T.J. and I.P. Preston (1988). Invariance and the axiomatics of income tax progression: a comment. *Bulletin of Economic Research*, vol. 40, pp. 159–163.

Bhattacharya, N. and B. Mahalanobis (1967). Regional disparities in household consumption in India. *Journal of the American Statistical Association*, vol. 62, pp. 143–161.

Binh, T.N. (1991). A general class of aggregate progressivity measures revisited. *Public Finance/Finances Publiques*, vol. 46, pp. 157–160.

Bishop, J.A., J.P. Formby and P.D. Thistle (1991). Rank dominance and international comparisons of income distribution. *European Economic Review*, vol. 35, pp. 1399–1409.

Blackburn, M.L. (1994). International comparisons of poverty. *American Economic Review (Papers and Proceedings)*, vol. 84, pp. 371–374.

Blackorby, C. and D. Donaldson (1978). Measures of relative equality and their meaning in terms of social welfare. *Journal of Economic Theory*, vol. 18, pp. 59–80.

Blackorby, C. and D. Donaldson (1980a). A theoretical treatment of indices of absolute inequality. *International Economic Review*, vol. 21, pp. 107–136.

Blackorby, C. and D. Donaldson (1980b). Ethical indices for the measurement of poverty. *Econometrica*, vol. 48, pp. 1053–1060.

Blackorby, C. and D. Donaldson (1984a). Ethical social index numbers and the measurement of effective tax/benefit progressivity. *Canadian Journal of Economics*, vol. 17, pp. 683–694.

Blackorby, C. and D. Donaldson (1984b). Social criteria for evaluating population change. *Journal of Public Economics*, vol. 25, pp. 13–33.

Blackorby, C. and D. Donaldson (1993). Household equivalence scales and welfare comparisons: a comment. *Journal of Public Economics*, vol. 50, pp. 143–146.

Blackorby, C., D. Donaldson and M. Auersperg (1981). A new procedure for the measurement of inequality within and among population subgroups. *Canadian Journal of Economics*, vol. 14, pp. 665–685.

Blum, W.J. (1979). The uneasy case for progressive taxation in 1976. In C.D. Campbell (ed.) *Income Redistribution*. Washington, DC: American Enterprise Institute for Public Policy Research.

Blum, W.J. and H. Kalven (1953). *The Uneasy Case for Progressive Taxation*. Chicago: Chicago University Press.

Boadway, R. and N. Bruce (1984). *Welfare Economics*. Oxford: Blackwell.

Borooah, V.K. and P.M. McKee (1994). Intra-household income transfers and implications for poverty and inequality in the UK, in J. Creedy (ed.) *Taxation, Poverty and Income Distribution*. Aldershot: Edward Elgar.

Bös, D. and B. Felderer (1989). *The Political Economy of Progressive Taxation*. Berlin: Springer-Verlag.

Bös, D. and G. Tillmann (1985). An 'envy tax': theoretical principles and applications to the German surcharge on the rich. *Public Finance/Finances Publiques*, vol. 40, pp. 35–63.

Bossart, W. and A. Pfingsten (1990). Intermediate inequality: concepts indices and welfare implications. *Mathematical Social Sciences*, vol. 19, pp. 117–134.

Bourguignon, F. (1979). Decomposable inequality measures. *Econometrica*, vol. 47, pp. 901–920.

Bourguignon, F. (1989). Family size and social utility: income distribution dominance criteria. *Journal of Econometrics*, vol. 42, pp. 67–80.

Bourguignon, F. and G. Fields (1997). Discontinuous losses from poverty, generalized P_α measures and optimal transfers to the poor. *Journal of Public Economics*, vol. 63, pp. 155–175.

Bourguignon, F. and C. Morrison (1980). Progressivité et incidence de la redistribution des revenus en pays développés. *Revue Économique*, vol. 31, pp. 197–233.

Bradbury, B. (1997). Measuring poverty changes with bounded equivalence scales: Australia in the 1980s. *Economica*, vol. 64, pp. 245–264.

Brennan, G. (1971). Horizontal equity: an extension of an extension. *Public Finance/Finances Publiques*, vol. 26, pp. 437–456.

Brennan, G. (1976). The distributional implications of public goods. *Econometrica*, vol. 44, pp. 391–399.

Bridges, B. (1984). Post-fisc distributions of income: comment. *Public Finance Quarterly*, vol. 12, pp. 231–240.

British Household Panel Survey (annually). University of Essex: ESRC Data Archive.

Broome, J. (1989). What's the good of equality? Chapter 9 in J.D. Hey (ed.) *Current Issues in Microeconomics.* London: Macmillan.

Buchanan, J.M. and R.L. Faith (1980). Subjective elements in Rawlsian contractual agreement on distributional rules. *Economic Inquiry*, vol. 18, pp. 23–38.

Buchholtz, W., W.F. Richter and J. Schwaiger (1988). Distributional implications of equal sacrifice rules. *Social Choice and Welfare*, vol. 5, pp. 223–226. Reprinted in Gaertner, W. and P.K. Pattanaik (eds) *Distributive Justice and Inequality.* Heidelberg: Springer.

Buhmann, B., L. Rainwater, G. Schmauss and T.M. Smeeding (1988). Equivalence scales, well-being, inequality and poverty: sensitivity estimates across 10 countries using the LIS database. *Review of Income and Wealth*, vol. 34, pp. 115–142.

Burgat, P. and C. Jeanrenaud (1996). Do benefit and equal absolute sacrifice rules really lead to different taxation levels? *Public Finance Quarterly*, vol. 24, pp. 148–162.

Burkhauser, R.V., A.D. Crews, M.C. Daly and S.P. Jenkins (1999). Testing the significance of income distribution changes over the 1980s business cycle: a cross-national comparison. *Journal of Applied Econometrics*, vol. 14, pp. 253–272.

Chakravarty, S.R. (1983a). Ethically flexible measures of poverty. *Canadian Journal of Economics*, vol. 16, pp. 74–85.

Chakravarty, S.R. (1983b). A new index of poverty. *Mathematical Social Science*, vol. 6, pp. 307–313.

Chakravarty, S.R. (1988). Extended Gini indices of inequality. *International Economic Review*, vol. 29, pp. 147–156.

Chakravarty, S.R. (1990). *Ethical Social Index Numbers.* New York: Springer Verlag.

Chakravarty, S.R. (1997). On Shorrocks' reinvestigation of the Sen poverty index. *Econometrica*, vol. 65, pp. 1241–1242.

Chakravarty, S.R. and W. Eichhorn (1994). Measurement of income inequality: observed versus true data. Pages 28–32 in W. Eichhorn (ed.) *Models and Measurement of Welfare and Inequality.* Heidelberg: Springer Verlag.

Chakravarty, S.R. and D. Mukherjee (1998). Optimal subsidy for the poor. *Economics Letters*, vol. 61, pp. 313–319.

Chakravarty, S.R. and D. Mukherjee (1999). Measures of deprivation and their meaning in terms of social satisfaction. *Theory and Decision*, vol. 47, pp. 89–100.

Chakravarty, S.R., D. Mukherjee and R.R. Ranade (1998). On the family of subgroup and factor decomposable measures of multidimensional poverty. *Research on Economic Inequality*, vol. 8, pp. 175–194.

Chakravarty, S.R. and S. Tyagarupananda (1998). The subgroup decomposable absolute indices of inequality. Chapter 11 in S.R. Chakravarty, D. Coondoo and R. Mukherjee (eds) *Quantitative Economics: Theory and Practice (Essays in Honour of Professor N. Bhattacharya).* Calcutta: Allied Publishers.

Chakravarty, S.R. and S. Tyagarupananda (1999). The subgroup decomposable indices of intermediate inequality. Mimeo.

Chambaz, C. and E. Maurin (1998). Atkinson and Bourguignon's dominance criteria: extended and applied to the measurement of poverty in France. *Review of Income and Wealth*, vol. 44, pp. 497–513.

Chaubey, P.K. (1993). Gandhian social welfare function: an attempt in characterisation. *Indian Economic Journal*, vol. 40, pp. 66–73.

Clark, S., R. Hemming and D. Ulph (1981). On indices for the measurement of poverty. *Economic Journal*, vol. 91, pp. 515–526.

Conniffe, D. (1992). The non-constancy of equivalence scales. *Review of Income and Wealth*, vol. 38, pp. 429–443.

Contoyannis, P. and M. Forster (1999a). The distribution of health and income: a theoretical framework. *Journal of Health Economics*, vol. 18, pp. 605–622.

Contoyannis, P. and M. Forster (1999b). Our healthier nation? *Health Economics*, vol. 8, pp. 289–296.

Coulter, F., F.A. Cowell and S.P. Jenkins (1992a). Differences in needs and assessment of income distributions. *Bulletin of Economic Research*, vol. 44, pp. 77–124.

Coulter, F., F.A. Cowell and S.P. Jenkins (1992b). Equivalence scale relativities and the extent of inequality and poverty. *Economic Journal*, vol. 102, pp. 1067–1082.

Cowell, F.A. (1980). On the structure of additive inequality measures. *Review of Economic Studies*, vol. 47, pp. 521–531.

Cowell, F.A. (1984). The structure of American income inequality. *Review of Income and Wealth*, vol. 30, pp. 351–375.

Cowell, F.A. (1985a). Measurement of distributional change: an axiomatic approach. *Review of Economic Studies*, vol. 52, pp. 135–151.

Cowell, F.A. (1985b). 'A fair suck of the sauce bottle' or, what do you mean by inequality? *Economic Record*, vol. 61, pp. 567–579.

Cowell, F.A. (1988). Poverty measures, inequality and decomposability. In D. Bös, M. Rose and C. Seidl (eds) *Welfare and Efficiency in Public Economics*. Heidelberg: Springer Verlag.

Cowell, F.A. (1995). *Measuring Inequality*, 2nd edition. Hemel Hempstead: Prentice Hall/Harvester Wheatsheaf.

Cowell, F.A. (2000). Measurement of inequality, in A.B. Atkinson and F. Bourguignon (eds) *Handbook of Income Distribution*. Amsterdam: North-Holland.

Cowell, F.A. and S.P. Jenkins (1994). Parametric equivalence scales and scale relativities. *Economic Journal*, vol. 104, pp. 891–900.

Cowell, F.A. and S.P. Jenkins (1995). How much inequality can we explain? A methodology and an application to the USA. *Economic Journal*, vol. 105, pp. 421–430.

Cowell, F.A., S.P. Jenkins and J. Litchfield (1996). The changing shape of the UK income distribution: kernel density estimates. Pages 49–75 in J. Hills (ed.) *New Inequalities: The Changing Distribution of Income and Wealth in the United Kingdom*. Cambridge: Cambridge University Press.

Cowell, F.A. and K. Kuga (1981). Additivity and the entropy concept: an axiomatic approach to inequality measurement. *Journal of Economic Theory*, vol. 25, pp. 131–143.

Cowell, F.A. and F. Mehta (1982). The estimation and interpolation of inequality measures. *Review of Economic Studies*, vol. 49, pp. 273–290.

Crane, S.E. (1983). Interpreting the distribution of government expenditures in budget incidence studies. *National Tax Journal*, vol. 36, pp. 243–247.

Creedy, J. (1977). The principle of transfers and the variance of logarithms. *Oxford Bulletin of Economics and Statistics*, vol. 39, pp. 153–158.

Creedy, J. (1982). The changing burden of national insurance contributions and income taxation in Britain. *Scottish Journal of Political Economy*, vol. 29, pp. 127–138.

Cutler, D.M. and L. Katz (1992). Rising inequality? Changes in the distribution of income and consumption in the 1980's. *American Economic Review*, vol. 82, pp. 546–551.

Dagum, C. (1997). A new approach to the decomposition of the Gini income inequality ratio. *Empirical Economics*, vol. 22, pp. 515–531.

D'Antoni, M. (1999). Piecewise linear tax functions, progressivity and the principle of equal sacrifice. *Economics Letters*, vol. 65, pp. 191–197.

Dardanoni, V. (1993a). A note on income inequality and progressive taxation. *Rivista di Diritto Finanziario e Scienza delle Finanze*, vol. 12, pp. 40–44.

Dardanoni, V. (1993b). Measuring social mobility. *Journal of Economic Theory*, vol. 61, pp. 372–394.

Dardanoni, V. (1995). On multidimensional inequality measurement. *Research on Economic Inequality*, vol. 6, pp. 201–207.

Dardanoni, V. and P.J. Lambert (1988). Welfare rankings of income distributions: a rôle for the variance and some insights for tax reform. *Social Choice and Welfare*, vol. 5, pp. 1–17.

Dardanoni, V. and P.J. Lambert (2001a). Horizontal inequity comparisons. *Social Choice and Welfare*, forthcoming.

Dardanoni, V. and P.J. Lambert (2001b). Progressivity comparisons. *Journal of Public Economics*, forthcoming.

Dasgupta, P., A. Sen and D. Starrett (1973). Notes on the measurement of inequality. *Journal of Economic Theory*, vol. 6, pp. 180–187.

Davies, J. and M. Hoy (1994). The normative significance of using third-degree stochastic dominance in comparing income distributions. *Journal of Economic Theory*, vol. 64, pp. 520–530.

Davies, J. and M. Hoy (1995). Making inequality comparisons when Lorenz curves intersect. *American Economic Review*, vol. 85, pp. 980–986.

de Wulf, L. (1975). Fiscal incidence studies in developing countries: survey and critique. *International Monetary Fund Staff Papers*, vol. 22, pp. 61–131.

de Wulf, L. (1981). Incidence of budgetary outlays: where do we go from here? *Public Finance/Finances Publiques*, vol. 36, pp. 55–76.

Dean, J.M. (1980). Benefit incidence methodology for mixed goods. *Public Finance Quarterly*, vol. 8, pp. 69–96.

Deaton, A. and J. Muellbauer (1980). *Economics and Consumer Behavior.* Cambridge: Cambridge University Press.

Decoster, A., E. Schokkaert and G. van Camp (1997). Horizontal neutrality and vertical redistribution with indirect taxes. *Research on Economic Inequality*, vol. 7, pp. 219–239.

Del Rio, C. and J. Ruiz-Castillo (2000). Intermediate inequality and welfare. *Social Choice and Welfare*, vol. 17, pp. 223–239.

Dilnot, A.W., J.A. Kay and C.N. Morris (1984). The UK tax system, structure and progressivity, 1948–1982. *Scandinavian Journal of Economics*, vol. 86, pp. 150–165.

Dilnot, A.W., J.A. Kay and M.J. Keen (1990). Allocating taxes to households: a methodology. *Oxford Economic Papers*, vol. 42, pp. 210–230. Reprinted in P.J.N. Sinclair and M.D.E. Slater (eds) *Taxation, Private Information and Capital.* Oxford: Clarendon Press.

Donaldson, D. and J.A. Weymark (1980). A single parameter generalization of the Gini indices of inequality. *Journal of Economic Theory*, vol. 22, pp. 67–86.

Donaldson, D. and J.A. Weymark (1983). Ethically flexible indices for income distributions in the continuum. *Journal of Economic Theory*, vol. 29, pp. 353–358.

Donaldson, D. and J.A. Weymark (1986). Properties of fixed-population poverty indices. *International Economic Review*, vol. 27, pp. 667–688.

Duclos, J.-Y. (1993). Progressivity, redistribution and equity, with application to the British tax and benefit system. *Public Finance/Finances Publiques*, vol. 48, pp. 350–365.

Duclos, J.-Y. (1995). Assessing the performance of an income tax. *Bulletin of Economic Research*, vol. 47, pp. 115–126.

Duclos, J.-Y. (1997). Measuring progressivity and inequality. *Research on Economic Inequality*, vol. 7, pp. 19–38.

Duclos, J.-Y. (1998). Social evaluation functions, economic isolation and the Suits index of progressivity. *Journal of Public Economics*, vol. 69, pp. 103–121.

Duclos, J.-Y. (2000). Gini indices and the redistribution of income. *International Tax and Public Finance*, vol. 7, pp. 141–162.

Duclos, J.-Y. and P.J. Lambert (2000). A normative and statistical approach to measuring classical horizontal inequity. *Canadian Journal of Economics*, vol. 33, pp. 87–113.

Duclos, J.-Y. and M. Mercader-Prats (1999). Household needs and poverty: with application to Spain and the UK. *Review of Income and Wealth*, vol. 45, pp. 77–98.

Dutta, B. and J. Esteban (1992). Social welfare and equality. *Social Choice and Welfare*, vol. 9, pp. 267–276.

Dworkin, R. (1978). *Taking Rights Seriously*. London: Duckworth.

Ebert, U. (1987). Size and distribution of incomes as determinants of social welfare. *Journal of Economic Theory*, vol. 41, pp. 23–33.

Ebert, U. (1995). Income inequality and differences in household size. *Mathematical Social Sciences*, vol. 30, pp. 37–55.

Ebert, U. (1997). Social welfare when needs differ: an axiomatic approach. *Economica*, vol. 64, pp. 233–244.

Ebert, U. (1999a). Using equivalent income of equivalent adults to rank income distributions. *Social Choice and Welfare*, vol. 16, pp. 233–258.

Ebert, U. (1999b). Dual decomposable inequality measures. *Canadian Journal of Economics*, vol. 32, pp. 234–246.

Ebert, U. (2000a). Equivalizing incomes: a normative approach. *International Tax and Public Finance*, vol. 7, pp. 619–640.

Ebert, U. (2000b). Sequential generalized Lorenz dominance and transfer principles. *Bulletin of Economic Research*, vol. 52, pp. 113–122.

Ebert, U. and P.J. Lambert (1999). Combined income taxes and tax-benefit systems. *Economic Record*, vol. 75, pp. 397–404.

Ebert, U. and P. Moyes (2000a). Consistent income tax structures when households are heterogeneous. *Journal of Economic Theory*, vol. 90, pp. 116–150.

Ebert, U. and P. Moyes (2000b). The representative income of the poor is a measure of poverty: a simple axiomatization of the Foster, Greer and Thorbecke poverty orderings. Mimeo, University of Oldenburg.

Economic Trends (monthly). London: Central Statistical Office.

Eichhorn, W. (1988). On a class of inequality measures. *Social Choice and Welfare*, vol. 5, pp. 171–177.

Eichhorn, W., H. Funke and W.F. Richter (1984). Tax progression and inequality of income distribution. *Journal of Mathematical Economics*, vol. 13, pp. 127–131.

Epstein, L.G. and S.M. Tanny (1980). Increasing generalized correlation: a definition and some economic consequences. *Canadian Journal of Economics*, vol. 13, pp. 16–34.

Essama-Nssah, B. (2000). *Inégalité, Pauvreté et Bien-Être Social: Fondements Analytiques et Normatifs*. Bruxelles: De Boeck Université.

Esteban, J.-M. and D. Ray (1994). On the measurement of polarization. *Econometrica*, vol. 62, pp. 819–851.

Fellman, J. (1976). The effect of transformations on Lorenz curves. *Econometrica*, vol. 44, pp. 823–824.

Fellman, J., M. Jäntti and P.J. Lambert (1999). Optimal tax-transfer systems and redistributive policy. *Scandinavian Journal of Economics*, vol. 101, pp. 1–9.

Fields, G.S. and J.C.H. Fei (1978). On inequality comparisons. *Econometrica*, vol. 46, pp. 303–316.

Fishburn, P.C. and R.D. Willig (1984). Transfer principles in income redistribution. *Journal of Public Economics*, vol. 25, pp. 323–328.

Fisher, F.M. (1987). Household equivalence scales and interpersonal comparisons. *Review of Economic Studies*, vol. 54, pp. 519–524.

Fleurbaey, M., C. Hagneré and A. Trannoy (2000). Welfare comparisons with bounded equivalence scales. *Journal of Economic Theory*, forthcoming.

Formby, J.P., T.G. Seaks and W.J. Smith (1981). A comparison of two new measures of tax progressivity. *Economic Journal*, vol. 91, pp. 1015–1019.

Formby, J.P., W.J. Smith and P.D. Thistle (1992). On the definition of tax neutrality: distributional and welfare implications of policy alternatives. *Public Finance Quarterly*, vol. 20, pp. 3–23.

Foster, J.E. (1984). On economic poverty: a survey of aggregate measures, in R. Basmann and G. Rhodes (eds) *Advances in Econometrics* (volume 3). Greenwhich, CT: JAI Press.

Foster, J.E. (1985). Inequality measurement. In H.P. Young (ed.) *Fair Allocation*. American Mathematical Society: Proceedings of Symposia in Applied Mathematics, volume 33.

Foster, J.E. (1998). Absolute versus relative poverty. *American Economic Review (AEA Papers and Proceedings)*, vol. 88, pp. 335–341.

Foster, J., J. Greer and E. Thorbecke (1984). A class of decomposable poverty measures. *Econometrica*, vol. 52, pp. 761–766.

Foster, J. and Y. Jin (1998). Poverty orderings for the Dalton utility-gap measures, in S.P. Jenkins, A. Kapteyn and B.M.S. van Praag (eds) *The Distribution of Household Welfare and Household Production: International Perspectives*. Cambridge: Cambridge University Press.

Foster, J.E. and E.A. Ok (1999). Lorenz dominance and the variance of logarithms. *Econometrica*, vol. 67, pp. 901–907.

Foster, J.E. and A. Sen (1997). On economic inequality after a quarter century, in A. Sen (ed.) *On Economic Inequality* (expanded edition). Oxford: Clarendon Press.

Foster, J.E. and A.A. Shneyerov (1999). A general class of additively decomposable inequality measures. *Economic Theory*, vol. 14, pp. 89–111.

Foster, J.E. and A.A. Shneyerov (2000). Path independent inequality measures. *Journal of Economic Theory*, vol. 91, pp. 199–222.

Foster, J.E. and A.F. Shorrocks (1988a). Poverty orderings. *Econometrica*, vol. 56, pp. 173–177.

Foster, J.E. and A.F. Shorrocks (1988b). Poverty orderings and welfare dominance. *Social Choice and Welfare*, vol. 5, pp. 179–198.

Foster, J.E. and A.F. Shorrocks (1991). Subgroup consistent poverty indices. *Econometrica*, vol. 59, pp. 687–709.

Freedman, J. and E. Chamberlain (1997). Horizontal equity and the taxation of employed and self-employed workers. *Fiscal Studies*, vol. 18, No. 1, pp. 87–118.

Friedman, M. (1947). Lerner on the economics of control. *Journal of Political Economy*, vol. 55, pp. 405–416. Reprinted in M. Friedman (ed.) *Essays in Positive Economics*. Chicago: Chicago University Press.

Friesen, P.H. and D. Miller (1983). Annual inequality and lifetime inequality. *Quarterly Journal of Economics*, vol. 98, pp. 139–155.

Garvy, G. (1952). Inequality of income: causes and measurement, in *Studies in Income and Wealth, Volume 15: Eight Papers on the Size Distribution of Income*. New York: NBER.

Gini, C. (1914). Di una misura della dissomiglianza tra due gruppi di quantita' e delle sue applicazioni allo studio delle relazioni statistiche. *Atti R. I. Veneto*, vol. 74, pp. 185–213.

Glewwe, P. (1991). Household equivalence scales and the measurement of inequality: transfers from the poor to the rich could decrease inequality. *Journal of Public Economics*, vol. 44, pp. 211–216.

Gouveia, M. and R.P. Strauss (1994). Effective federal individual income tax functions: an exploratory empirical analysis. *National Tax Journal*, vol. 47, pp. 317–338.

Gravelle, J.G. (1992). Equity effects of the Tax Reform Act of 1986. *Journal of Economic Perspectives*, vol. 6, No. 1, pp. 27–44.

Gustafsson, B. and L. Shi (1998). The structure of Chinese poverty, 1988. *The Developing Economies*, vol. 36, pp. 387–406.

Habib, J. (1979). Horizontal equity with respect to family size. *Public Finance Quarterly*, vol. 7, pp. 283–302.

Hagenaars, A.J.M. (1987). A class of poverty indices. *International Economic Review*, vol. 28, pp. 583–607.

Hagenaars, A.J.M., K. de Vos and M.A. Zaidi (1998). Patterns of poverty in Europe. Pages 25–49 in S.P. Jenkins, A. Kapteyn and B.M.S. van Praag (eds) *The Distribution of Household Welfare and Household Production: International Perspectives*. Cambridge: University Press.

Hainsworth, G.B. (1964). The Lorenz curve as a general tool of economic analysis. *Economic Record*, vol. 40, pp. 426–441.

Hall, R.E. and A. Rabushka (1983). *Low Tax, Simple Tax, Flat Tax*. New York: McGraw-Hill.

Hammes, D.L. and D.T. Wills (1987). Public debt, interest and fiscal incidence. *Review of Income and Wealth*, vol. 20, pp. 439–442.

Hammond, P.J. (1975). A note on extreme inequality aversion. *Journal of Economic Theory*, vol. 11, pp. 465–467.

Hanoch, G. and H. Levy (1969). The efficiency analysis of choices involving risk. *Review of Economic Studies*, vol. 38, pp. 335–346.

Harrison, A.J. (1981). Earnings by size: a tale of two distributions. *Review of Economic Studies*, vol. 48, pp. 621–631.

Harrison, A.J. and Y.Y. Papageorgiou (1987). Welfare-improving changes in size distributions of income. *Economics Letters*, vol. 23, pp. 23–29.

Harrison, E. and C. Seidl (1994). Perceptional inequality and preferential judgement: an empirical examination of distributional axioms. *Public Choice*, vol. 79, pp. 61–81.

Harsanyi, J.C. (1953). Cardinal utility in welfare economics and theory of risk taking. *Journal of Political Economy*, vol. 61, pp. 434–435.

Harsanyi, J.C. (1955). Cardinal welfare, individualistic ethics, and interpersonal comparisons of utility. *Journal of Political Economy*, vol. 63, pp. 309–321.

Harsanyi, J.C. (1987). Von Neumann-Morgenstern utilities, risk taking and welfare. Chapter 17 in G.R. Feiwel (ed.) *Arrow and the Ascent of Modern Economic Theory.* London: Macmillan.

Hayes, K., P.J. Lambert and D.J. Slottje (1995). Evaluating effective income tax progression. *Journal of Public Economics*, vol. 56, pp. 461–474.

Head, J.G. (1964). Lindahl's theory of the budget. *Finanzarchiv*, vol. 23, pp. 421–454.

Hemming, R. (1980). Income tax progressivity and labour supply. *Journal of Public Economics*, vol. 14, pp. 95–100.

Hemming, R. and M.J. Keen (1983). Single crossing conditions in comparisons of tax progressivity. *Journal of Public Economics*, vol. 20, pp. 373–380.

Herber, B.P. (1983). *Modern Public Finance*, 5th edition. Homewood, Illinois: Irwin.

Hey, J.D. (1984). Decision under uncertainty. Chapter 17 in F. van der Ploeg (ed.) *Mathematical Methods in Economics.* Wiley Interscience: Chichester and New York.

Hey, J.D. and P.J. Lambert (1980). Relative deprivation and the Gini coefficient: comment. *Quarterly Journal of Economics*, vol. 94, pp. 567–573.

Hogg, R.V. and E.A. Tanis (1988). *Probability and Statistical Inference*, 3rd edition. London and New York: Macmillan.

Households Below Average Income: A Statistical Analysis (annually). London: Department of Social Security.

Howes, S. (1996). The influence of aggregation on the ordering of distributions. *Economica*, vol. 63, pp. 253–272.

Hoy, M., J. Livernois, C. McKenna, R. Rees and T. Stengos (1996). *Mathematics for Economics.* Don Mills, Ontario: Addison-Wesley.

Hudson, W.D. (1969) (ed.). *The Is/Ought Question: A Collection of Papers on the Central Problem in Moral Philosophy.* London: Macmillan.

Hume, D. (1990). *Treatise of Human Nature*, 2nd edition. Oxford: Oxford University Press.

Hutton, J.P. and P.J. Lambert (1983). Inequality and revenue elasticity in tax reform. *Scottish Journal of Political Economy*, vol. 30, pp. 221–234.

Individual Taxes: A Worldwide Summary (annually). London and New York: Price Waterhouse.

Inland Revenue Statistics (annually). London: Inland Revenue Statistical Division.

Irvine, I.J. (1981). The use of cross-section microdata in lifecycle models: an application to inequality theory in non-stationary economies. *Quarterly Journal of Economics*, vol. 96, pp. 301–316.

Jakobsson, U. (1976). On the measurement of the degree of progression. *Journal of Public Economics*, vol. 5, pp. 161–168.

Jenkins, S.P. (1988a). Calculating income distribution indices from micro data. *National Tax Journal*, vol. 41, pp. 139–142.

Jenkins, S.P. (1988b). Reranking and the analysis of income redistribution. *Scottish Journal of Political Economy*, vol. 35, pp. 65–76.

Jenkins, S.P. (1988c). Empirical measurement of horizontal inequity. *Journal of Public Economics*, vol. 37, pp. 305–329.

Jenkins, S.P. (1991a). The measurement of income inequality. Chapter 1 in L. Osberg (ed.) *Economic Inequality and Poverty: International Perspectives*. Armonk NY: E. Sharpe.

Jenkins, S.P. (1991b). Poverty measurement and the within-household distribution: agenda for action. *Journal of Social Policy*, vol. 20, pp. 457–483.

Jenkins, S.P. (1991c). Income inequality and living standards: changes in the 1970s and 1980s. *Fiscal Studies*, vol. 12, pp. 1–28.

Jenkins, S.P. (1994). Social welfare function measures of horizontal inequity, in W. Eichhorn (ed.) *Models and Measurement of Welfare and Inequality*. Berlin: Springer Verlag.

Jenkins, S.P. (1995a). Did the middle class shrink during the 1980s? U.K. evidence from kernel density estimates. *Economics Letters*, vol. 49, pp. 407–413.

Jenkins, S.P. (1995b). Accounting for inequality trends: decomposition analyses for the UK, 1971–86. *Economica*, vol. 62, pp. 29–63.

Jenkins, S.P. (1996). Recent trends in the U.K. income distribution: what happened and why. *Oxford Review of Economic Policy*, vol. 12, pp. 29–46.

Jenkins, S.P. (1997). Trends in real income in Britain: a microeconomic analysis. *Empirical Economics*, vol. 22, pp. 483–500. Reprinted in D.J. Slottje and B. Raj (eds) *Income Inequality, Poverty, and Economic Welfare*. Physica-Verlag, Heidelberg, 1998.

Jenkins, S.P. and P.J. Lambert (1993). Ranking income distributions when needs differ. *Review of Income and Wealth*, vol. 39, pp. 337–356.

Jenkins, S.P. and P.J. Lambert (1997). 'Three 'I's of poverty' curves, with an analysis of U.K. poverty trends. *Oxford Economic Papers*, vol. 49, pp. 317–327.

Jenkins, S.P. and P.J. Lambert (1998a). 'Three 'I's of Poverty' curves and poverty dominance: TIPS for poverty analysis. *Research on Economic Inequality*, vol. 8, pp. 39–56.

Jenkins, S.P. and P.J. Lambert (1998b). Ranking poverty gap distributions: further TIPs for poverty analysis. *Research on Economic Inequality*, vol. 8, pp. 31–38.

Jenkins, S.P. and P.J. Lambert (1999). Horizontal inequity measurement: a basic reassessment, in Silber, J. (ed.) *Handbook on Income Inequality Measurement*. Norwell, MA: Kluwer Academic Publishing.

Jenkins, S. and M. O'Higgins (1989). Inequality measurement using 'norm incomes': were Garvy and Paglin onto something after all? *Review of Income and Wealth*, vol. 35, pp. 265–282.

Johnson, D.T. (1996). *Poverty, Inequality and Social Welfare in Australia*. Heidelberg: Physica Verlag.

Johnson, D.T. and P.B. Dixon (1999). Australian poverty quantified by a family-based poverty index. *Economic Record*, vol. 75, pp. 103–114.

Johnson, S. and T. Mayer (1962). An extension of Sidgewick's equity principle. *Quarterly Journal of Economics*, vol. 76, pp. 454–463.

Kakwani, N.C. (1977a). Applications of Lorenz curves in economic analysis. *Econometrica*, vol. 45, pp. 719–727.

Kakwani, N.C. (1977b). Measurement of tax progressivity: an international comparison. *Economic Journal*, vol. 87, pp. 71–80.

Kakwani, N.C. (1980a). *Income, Inequality and Poverty: Methods of Estimation and Policy Applications.* Oxford: Oxford University Press.

Kakwani, N.C. (1980b). On a class of poverty measures. *Econometrica*, vol. 48, pp. 437–446.

Kakwani, N.C. (1984a). On the measurement of tax progressivity and redistributive effect of taxes with applications to horizontal and vertical equity. *Advances in Econometrics*, vol. 3, pp. 149–168.

Kakwani, N.C. (1984b). Welfare ranking of income distributions. *Advances In Econometrics*, vol. 3, pp. 191–213.

Kakwani, N.C. (1986). *Analysing Redistribution Policies: A Study Using Australian Data.* Cambridge: Cambridge University Press.

Kakwani, N.C. (1988). Income inequality, welfare and poverty in a developing economy with applications to Sri Lanka. *Social Choice and Welfare*, vol. 5, pp. 199–222. Reprinted in W. Gaertner and P.K. Pattanaik (eds) *Distributive Justice and Inequality.* Heidelberg: Springer.

Kakwani, N.C. (1999). Inequality, welfare and poverty: three interrelated phenomena, in Silber, J. (ed.) *Handbook of Income Inequality Measurement.* Norwell, MA: Kluwer Academic Publishing.

Kakwani, N.C. and P.J. Lambert (1999). Measuring income tax discrimination. *Review of Economics and Statistics*, vol. 81, pp. 27–31.

Kanbur, S.M.R. and J.-O. Stromberg (1988). Income transitions and income distribution dominance. *Journal of Economic Theory*, vol. 45, pp. 408–416.

Kaplow, L. (1989). Horizontal inequity: measures in search of a principle. *National Tax Journal*, vol. 42, pp. 139–154.

Kaplow, L. (1999). Horizontal equity: new measures, unclear principles. NBER Working Paper No. W7649.

Kay, J.A. and M.A. King (1984). *The British Tax System*, 3rd edition. Oxford: Oxford University Press.

Keen, M., H. Papapanagos and A.F. Shorrocks (2000). Progressivity effects of structural income tax reforms. *Economic Journal*, vol. 110, pp. 1–19.

Kendall, M. and A. Stuart (1977). *The Advanced Theory of Statistics.* London: Griffin.

Khetan, C.P. and S.N. Podder (1976). Measurement of income tax progressivity in a growing economy: the Canadian experience. *Canadian Journal of Economics*, vol. 4, pp. 613–629.

Kiefer, D.W. (1985). Distributional tax progressivity measurement. *National Tax Journal*, vol. 37, pp. 497–513.

Kienzle, E.C. (1981). Measurement of the progressivity of public expenditures and net fiscal incidence. *Southern Economic Journal*, vol. 48, pp. 197–203.

Kienzle, E.C. (1982). Post-fisc distributions of income: measuring progressivity with application to the United States. *Public Finance Quarterly*, vol. 10, pp. 355–368.

King, M.A. (1983). An index of inequality: with applications to horizontal equity and social mobility. *Econometrica*, vol. 51, pp. 99–115.

Kolm, S.-C. (1969). The optimal production of social justice, in J. Margolis and H. Guitton (eds) *Public Economics.* London: Macmillan.

Kolm, S.-C. (1976). Unequal inequalities, I and II. *Journal of Economic Theory*, vol. 12, pp. 416–442 and vol. 13, pp. 82–111.

Kolm, S.-C. (1977). Multidimensional egalitarianism. *Quarterly Journal of Economics*, vol. 91, pp. 1–13.

Kolm, S.-C. (1996). Intermediate measures of inequality: an answer about meaningful properties. Mimeo, revised version forthcoming in *Mathematical Social Sciences*.

Kolm, S.-C. (1999). The rational foundations of income inequality measurement. Pages 19–100 in Silber, J. (ed.) *Handbook on Income Inequality*. Norwood, MA: Kluwer Academic Publishing.

Kondor, Y. (1975). Value judgements implied by the use of various measures of income inequality. *Review of Income and Wealth*, vol. 21, pp. 309–321.

Kuga, K. (1980). Gini index and the generalized entropy class: further results and a vindication. *Economic Studies Quarterly*, vol. 31, pp. 217–228.

Lam, D. (1986a). The dynamics of population growth, differential fertility, and inequality. *American Economic Review*, vol. 76, pp. 1103–1116.

Lam, D. (1986b). Lorenz curves and inequality comparisons under changing population composition. Population Studies Center Research Report No. 86–92, University of Michigan.

Lambert, P.J. (1985a). The redistributive effect of taxes and benefits. *Scottish Journal of Political Economy*, vol. 32, pp. 39–54.

Lambert, P.J. (1985b). Social welfare and the Gini coefficient revisited. *Mathematical Social Sciences*, vol. 9, pp. 19–26.

Lambert, P.J. (1985c). Describing the macroeconomy: the rôle of sticky taxes. *Studies in Economic Analysis*, vol. 9, pp. 17–27.

Lambert, P.J. (1988). Progressive income taxation is inequality-reducing – or is it? Institute for Fiscal Studies Working Paper No. 88/14.

Lambert, P.J. (1993a). Inequality reduction through the income tax. *Economica*, vol. 60, pp. 357–365.

Lambert, P.J. (1993b). Evaluating impact effects of tax reforms. *Journal of Economic Surveys*, vol. 7, pp. 205–242.

Lambert, P.J. (1995). On the measurement of horizontal inequity. Working Paper No. WP/95/135, International Monetary Fund.

Lambert, P.J. and J.R. Aronson (1993). Inequality decomposition analysis and the Gini coefficient revisited. *Economic Journal*, vol. 103, pp. 1221–1227.

Lambert, P.J., D.L. Millimet and D. Slottje (2001). Inequality aversion and the natural rate of subjective inequality. *Journal of Public Economics*, forthcoming.

Lambert, P.J. and W. Pfähler (1988). On aggregate measures of the net redistributive impact of taxation and government expenditure. *Public Finance Quarterly*, vol. 16, pp. 178–202.

Lambert, P.J. and W. Pfähler (1992). Income tax progression and redistributive effect: the influence of changes in pre-tax income distribution. *Public Finance/Finances Publiques*, vol. 47, pp. 1–16.

Lambert, P.J. and X. Ramos (1997a). Vertical redistribution and horizontal inequity. *International Tax and Public Finance*, vol. 4, pp. 25–37.

Lambert, P.J. and X. Ramos (1997b). Horizontal inequity and reranking: a review and simulation study. *Research on Economic Inequality*, vol. 7, pp. 1–18.

Lambert, P.J. and A. Weale (1981). Equality, risk-aversion and contractarian social choice. *Theory and Decision*, vol. 13, pp. 109–127.

Lambert, P.J. and S. Yitzhaki (1995). Equity, equality and welfare. *European Economic Review*, vol. 39, pp. 674–682.

Lambert, P.J. and S. Yitzhaki (1997). Income tax credits and income tax exemptions. *European Journal of Political Economy*, vol. 13, pp. 343–351.

Latham, R. (1988). Lorenz-dominating income tax functions. *International Economic Review*, vol. 29, pp. 185–198.

Latham, R. (1993). A necessary and sufficient condition for greater conditional progressivity. *Canadian Journal of Economics*, vol. 26, pp. 919–932.

Layard, R. (1980). Human satisfactions and public policy. *Economic Journal*, vol. 90, pp. 737–750.

Layard, P.R.G. and A.A. Walters (1987). *Microeconomic Theory*. New York: McGraw-Hill.

Lecaillon, J., F. Paukert, C. Morrison and D. Germidis (1984). *Income Distribution and Economic Development: An Analytical Survey*. Geneva: ILO.

Lerman, R. and S. Yitzhaki (1984). A note on the calculation and interpretation of the Gini coefficient. *Economics Letters*, vol. 15, pp. 363–368.

Lerman, R. and S. Yitzhaki (1985). Income inequality effects by income source: a new approach and application to the U.S., *Review of Economics and Statistics*, vol. 67, pp. 151–156.

Lerman, R. and S. Yitzhaki (1989). Improving the accuracy of estimates of the Gini coefficient. *Journal of Econometrics*, vol. 42, pp. 43–47.

Lerman, R. and S. Yitzhaki (1995). Changing ranks and the inequality impacts of taxes and transfers, *National Tax Journal*, vol. 48, pp. 45–59.

Lerner, A.P. (1944). *The Economics of Control*. London: Macmillan.

Levy, H. (1991). The mean-coefficient-of-variation rule: the lognormal case. *Management Science*, vol. 37, pp. 745–747.

Lewis, G.W. and D.T. Ulph (1988). Poverty, inequality and welfare. *Economic Journal*, vol. 98, Supplement, pp. 117–131.

Lillard, L.A. (1977). Inequality: earnings versus human wealth. *American Economic Review*, vol. 67, pp. 45–53.

Lipton, M. and M. Ravallion (1995). Poverty and policy, in J. Behrman and T.N. Srinivasan (eds) *Handbook of Development Economics*. Amsterdam: Elsevier.

Loizides, I. (1988). The decomposition of progressivity indices with applications to the Greek taxation system. *Public Finance/Finances Publiques*, vol. 43, pp. 236–247.

Loomis, J.B. and C.F. Revier (1988). Measuring regressivity of excise taxes: a buyers index. *Public Finance Quarterly*, vol. 16, pp. 301–314.

Manser, M.E. (1979). Comparing households with different structures: the problem of equity. *American Economic Review*, vol. 69, 222–226.

Marhuenda, F. and I. Ortuño-Ortín (1995). Popular support for progressive taxation. *Economics Letters*, vol. 48, pp. 319–324.

Mas-Colell, A., M.D. Whinston and J.R. Green (1995). *Microeconomic Theory*. New York: Oxford University Press.

Mayshar, J. and S. Yitzhaki (1995). Dalton-improving indirect tax reforms, *American Economic Review*, vol. 85, pp. 793–808.

Mayshar J. and S. Yitzhaki (1996). Dalton-improving tax reform: when households differ in ability and needs. *Journal of Public Economics*, vol. 62, pp. 399–412.

McClements, L.D. (1978). *The Economics of Social Security*. London: Heinemann.

McDonald, J.B. (1984). Some generalized functions for the size distribution of income. *Econometrica*, vol. 52, pp. 647–663.

Mehran, F. (1975). A statistical analysis of income inequality based on a decomposition of the Gini index. *Bulletin of the International Statistical Institute*, vol. 46, pp. 145–150.

Mehran, F. (1976). Linear measures of income inequality. *Econometrica*, vol. 44, pp. 805–809.

Menezes, C., C. Geiss and J. Tressler (1980). Increasing downside risk. *American Economic Review*, vol. 70, pp. 921–932.

Meyer, J. (1975). Increasing risk. *Journal of Economic Theory*, vol. 11, pp. 119–132.

Minarik, J.J. (1982). The future of the individual income tax. *National Tax Journal*, vol. 35, pp. 231–241.

Mitra, T. and E.A. Ok (1996). Personal income taxation and the principle of equal sacrifice revisited. *International Economic Review*, vol. 37, pp. 925–948.

Mitra, T. and E.A. Ok (1997). On the equitability of progressive taxation. *Journal of Economic Theory*, vol. 73, pp. 316–334.

Mondragon-Barreto, E. (2000). Measuring inequality and welfare: methodological issues for the analyst. Mimeo, University of York.

Mookherjee, D. and A.F. Shorrocks (1982). A decomposition analysis of the trend in U.K. income inequality. *Economic Journal*, vol. 92, pp. 886–902.

Moore, R.E. (1996). Ranking income distributions using the geometric mean and a related general measure. *Southern Economic Journal*, vol. 63, pp. 69–75.

Mosler, K. and P. Muliere (1996). Inequality indices and the starshaped principle of transfers. *Statistical Papers*, vol. 37, pp. 343–364.

Moyes, P. (1987). A new concept of Lorenz domination. *Economics Letters*, vol. 23, pp. 203–207.

Moyes, P. (1988). A note on minimally progressive taxation and absolute income inequality. *Social Choice and Welfare*, vol. 5, pp. 227–234.

Moyes, P. (1989). Some classes of function that preserve the inequality and welfare orderings of income distributions. *Journal of Economic Theory*, vol. 49, pp. 347–359.

Moyes, P. (1992). The through-time redistributive effect of income taxation. *Mathematical Social Sciences*, vol. 24, pp. 59–71.

Moyes, P. (1994). Inequality reducing and inequality preserving transformations of incomes: symmetric and individualistic transformations. *Journal of Economic Theory*, vol. 63, pp. 271–298.

Moyes, P. and A.F. Shorrocks (1998). The impossibility of a progressive tax structure. *Journal of Public Economics*, vol. 69, pp. 49–65.

Mukherjee, D. (1997). Deprivation-reducing income tax functions. *Research on Economic Inequality*, vol. 7, pp. 153–163.

Muliere, P. and M. Scarsini (1989). A note on stochastic dominance and inequality measures. *Journal of Economic Theory*, vol. 49, pp. 314–323.

Musgrave, R.A. (1988). Short of euphoria. *Economic Perspectives*, vol. 1, pp. 59–71.

Musgrave, R.A. (1990). Horizontal equity, once more. *National Tax Journal*, vol. 43, pp. 113–122.

Musgrave, R.A. and P.B. Musgrave (1984). *Public Finance in Theory and Practice*, 4th edition. New York: McGraw Hill.

Musgrave, R.A. and A.T. Peacock (eds) (1958). *Classics in the Theory of Public Finance*. New York and London: Macmillan.

Musgrave, R.A. and C.S. Shoup (eds) (1959). *Readings in the Economics of Taxation*. Homewood, Illinois: Irwin.

Musgrave, R.A. and T. Thin (1948). Progressive taxation in an inflationary economy. *Journal of Political Economy*, vol. 56, pp. 498–514.

Neill, J.R. (2000). The benefit and sacrifice principles of taxation: a synthesis. *Social Choice and Welfare*, vol. 17, pp. 117–124.

Newbery, D. (1970). A theorem on the measurement of inequality. *Journal of Economic Theory*, vol. 2, pp. 264–266.

Nygård, F. and A. Sandström (1981). *Measuring Income Inequality*. Stockholm: Almqvist & Wiksell.

OECD (1981). *Income Tax Schedules: Distribution of Taxpayers and Revenues*. Paris: OECD Committee on Fiscal Affairs.

OECD (1984). *Tax Expenditures: A Review of the Issues and Country Practices*. Paris: OECD Committee on Fiscal Affairs.

O'Higgins, M. and P. Ruggles (1981). The distribution of public expenditures and taxes among households in the United Kingdom. *Review of Income and Wealth*, vol. 27, pp. 298–326.

Ok, E.A. (1995). On the principle of equal sacrifice in income taxation. *Journal of Public Economics*, vol. 58, pp. 453–467.

Ok, E.A. (1997). A note on the existence of progressive tax structures. *Social Choice and Welfare*, vol. 14, pp. 527–543.

Ok, E.A. and P.J. Lambert (1999). On evaluating social welfare by sequential generalized Lorenz dominance. *Economics Letters*, vol. 63, pp. 45–53.

Okun, A.M. (1975). *Equality and Efficiency*, Brookings Institution.

Okun, A.M. (1979). Further thoughts on equality and efficiency. In C.D. Campbell (ed.) *Income Redistribution*. Washington, DC: American Enterprise Institute for Public Policy Research.

Onrubia, J., J. Lopez-Laborda and N. Badenes (2000). Simplification and decentralization of the income tax. *Public Finance Review*, forthcoming.

Paglin, M. (1975). The measurement and trend of inequality: a basic revision. *American Economic Review*, vol. 65, pp. 598–609. Comments by E.R. Nelson; W.R. Johnson; S. Danziger, R. Haveman and E. Smolensky; J.J. Minarik; C.J. Kurien; and Reply by Paglin, in *American Economic Review*, vol. 67 (1977), pp. 497–531. Comment by K.L. Wertz in *American Economic Review*, vol. 69 (1979), pp. 670–672.

Parker, S.C. (1999). The beta as a model for the distribution of earnings. *Bulletin of Economic Research*, vol. 51, pp. 243–251.

Pattanaik, P.K. (1968). Risk, impersonality and the social welfare function. *Journal of Political Economy*, vol. 76, pp. 1152–1169.

Paul, S. (1991). An index of relative deprivation. *Economics Letters*, vol. 36, pp. 337–341.

Pechman, J.A. (1972). Note on the intergenerational transfer of public higher-education benefits. *Journal of Political Economy*, vol. 80, pp. S256–S259.

Pechman, J.A. and B. Okner (1974). *Who Bears the Tax Burden?* Washington DC: Brookings Institution.

Petersen, H.-G. (1979). Effect of growing incomes on classified income distributions, the derived Lorenz curves and Gini indices. *Econometrica*, vol. 47, pp. 183–198.

Pfähler, W. (1983). Measuring redistributional effects of tax progressivity by Lorenz curves. *Jahrbücher für Nationalökonomie und Statistik*, vol. 198, pp. 237–249.

Pfähler, W. (1984). 'Linear' income tax cuts: distributional effects, social preferences and revenue elasticities. *Journal of Public Economics*, vol. 24, pp. 381–388.

Pfähler, W. (1985). Relative concentration curve: functional form and measures of non-proportionality. *Bulletin of Economic Research*, vol. 37, pp. 201–211.

Pfähler, W. (1987). Redistributive effects of tax progressivity: evaluating a general class of aggregate measures. *Public Finance/Finances Publiques*, vol. 37, pp. 1–31.

Pfähler, W. (1988). Distributional equity and measurement of tax progressivity, in W. Eichhorn (ed.) *Measurement in Economics: Theory and Applications of Economic Indices*. Heidelberg: Physica-Verlag.

Pfähler, W. (1990). Redistributive effect of income taxation: decomposing tax base and tax rates effects. *Bulletin of Economic Research*, vol. 42, pp. 121–129.

Pfähler, W. (1991). A general class of aggregate progressivity measures revisited: reply. *Public Finance/Finances Publiques*, vol. 46, pp. 161–162.

Pfingsten, A. (1986a). *The Measurement of Tax Progression*. Studies in Contemporary Economics, vol. 20. Berlin: Springer-Verlag.

Pfingsten, A. (1986b). Distributionally-neutral tax changes for different inequality concepts. *Journal of Public Economics*, vol. 30, pp. 385–393.

Pfingsten, A. (1987). Axiomatically-based local measures of tax progression. *Bulletin of Economic Research*, vol. 39, pp. 211–223.

Pfingsten, A. (1988a). Measures of tax progression – an axiomatic approach, in W. Eichhorn (ed.) *Measurement in Economics*. Berlin-Heidelberg: Physica-Verlag.

Pfingsten, A. (1988b). Progressive taxation and redistributive taxation: different labels for the same product? *Social Choice and Welfare*, vol. 5, pp. 235–246.

Philpotts, G. (1986). Public good benefit attribution. *Public Finance Quarterly*, vol. 14, pp. 313–328.

Pigou, A.C. (1949). *A Study In Public Finance*, 3rd edition. London: Macmillan.

Plotnick, R. (1980). A comment on measuring horizontal equity. *Quarterly Journal of Economics*, vol. 94, pp. 383–385.

Plotnick, R. (1981). A measure of horizontal inequity. *Review of Economics and Statistics*, vol. 63, pp. 283–288.

Plotnick, R. (1982). The concept and measurement of horizontal inequity. *Journal of Public Economics*, vol. 17, pp. 373–391.

Plotnick, R. (1999). Comment on horizontal inequity measurement, in Silber, J. (ed.) *Handbook of Income Inequality Measurement*. Norwell, MA: Kluwer Academic Publishing.

Pollak, R. and T. Wales (1979). Welfare comparisons and equivalence scales. *American Economic Review*, vol. 69, pp. 216–221.

Pratt, J.W. (1964). Risk aversion in the small and in the large. *Econometrica*, vol. 32, pp. 122–136.

Pyatt, G. (1976). The interpretation and disaggregation of Gini coefficients. *Economic Journal*, vol. 86, pp. 243–255.

Pyatt, G. (1987). Measuring welfare, poverty and inequality. *Economic Journal*, vol. 97, pp. 459–467.

Pyatt, G. (1990). Social evaluation criteria. In C. Dagum and M. Ziemba (eds) *Income and Wealth Distribution, Inequality and Poverty*. Berlin: Springer Verlag.

Ravallion, M. (1994a). *Poverty Comparisons*. Fundamentals of Pure and Applied Economics, volume 56. Chur, Switzerland: Harwood Academic Publishers.

Ravallion, M. (1994b). Measuring social welfare with and without poverty lines. *American Economic Review (AEA Papers and Proceedings)*, vol. 84, pp. 359–364.

Ravallion, M. (1999). Comment on Kakwani's 'Inequality, welfare and poverty: three interrelated phenomena', in Silber, J. (ed.) *Handbook of Income Inequality Measurement*. Norwell, MA: Kluwer Academic Publishing.

Rawls, J. (1971). *A Theory Of Justice.* Cambridge, MA: Harvard University Press.

Reynolds, M. and E. Smolensky (1977). *Public Expenditures, Taxes, and the Distribution of Income: The United States, 1950, 1961, 1970.* New York: Academic Press.

Richter, W.F. (1984). Saving, taxation and income inequality, in D. Bös, M. Rose and C. Seidl (eds) *Beiträge zur Neueren Steuertheorie.* Studies in Contemporary Economics, volume 7. Berlin: Springer-Verlag.

Richter, W.F. and J.F. Hampe (1984). Measuring the gain from splitting under income taxation. *Methods of Operations Research,* vol. 51, pp. 384–400.

Rietveld, P. (1990). Multi-dimensional inequality comparisons: on aggravation and mitigation of inequalities. *Economics Letters,* vol. 32, pp. 187–192.

Roemer, J.E. (1999). The democratic political economy of progressive taxation. *Econometrica,* vol. 67, pp. 1–19.

Roemer, J.E. (2000). The political economy of income taxation: the infinite dimensional case. Mimeo, University of California at Davis.

Rosen, H.S. (1978). An approach to the study of income, utility and horizontal equity. *Quarterly Journal of Economics,* vol. 92, pp. 307–322.

Rothschild, M. and J.E. Stiglitz (1973). Some further results on the measurement of inequality. *Journal of Economic Theory,* vol. 6, pp. 188–204.

Ruggles, P. and M. O'Higgins (1981). The distribution of public expenditure among households in the United States. *Review of Income and Wealth,* vol. 27, pp. 137–163.

Runciman, W.G. (1966). *Relative Deprivation and Social Justice.* London: Routledge and Kegan Paul/Penguin Books.

Samuelson, P.A. (1947). *Foundations of Economic Analysis.* Cambridge, MA: Harvard University Press.

Saposnik, R. (1981). Rank dominance in income distribution. *Public Choice,* vol. 36, pp. 147–151.

Saposnik, R. (1993). A note on majorization theory and the evaluation of income distributions. *Economics Letters,* vol. 42, pp. 179–183.

Sawyer, M.C. (1976). *Income Distribution in OECD Countries.* Paris: OECD.

Seidl, C. (1988). Poverty measurement: a survey. In D. Bös, M. Rose and C. Seidl (eds) *Welfare and Efficiency in Public Economics.* Heidelberg: Springer Verlag.

Seidl, C. and A. Pfingsten (1997). Ray invariant inequality measures. *Research on Economic Inequality,* vol. 7, pp. 107–129.

Sen, A. (1970a). *Collective Choice and Social Welfare.* San Francisco: Holden-Day.

Sen, A. (1970b). Interpersonal aggregation and partial comparability. *Econometrica,* vol. 40, pp. 393–409. Reprinted as Chapter 9 in Sen (1982).

Sen, A. (1973a). *On Economic Inequality.* Oxford: Clarendon Press.

Sen, A. (1973b). On ignorance and equal distribution. *American Economic Review,* vol. 63, pp. 1022–1024. Reprinted as Chapter 10 in Sen (1982).

Sen, A. (1976). Poverty: an ordinal approach to measurement. *Econometrica,* vol. 44, pp. 219–231. Reprinted as Chapter 17 in Sen (1982).

Sen, A. (1977). On weights and measures: informational constraints in social welfare analysis. *Econometrica,* vol. 45, pp. 1539–1572. Reprinted as Chapter 11 in Sen (1982).

Sen, A. (1978). Ethical measurement of inequality: some difficulties, in W. Krelle and A.F. Shorrocks (eds) *Personal Income Distribution.* Amsterdam: North-Holland. Reprinted as Chapter 19 in Sen (1982).

Sen, A. (1982). *Choice, Welfare and Measurement.* Oxford: Blackwell.

Sen, A. (1983). Poor, relatively speaking. *Oxford Economic Papers*, vol. 35, pp. 153–169.

Sen, A. (1999). Foreword, pages xvii–xxvi in J. Silber (ed.) *Handbook of Income Inequality Measurement*. Norwell, MA: Kluwer Academic Publishing.

Sheshinski, E. (1972). Relation between a social welfare function and the Gini index of income inequality. *Journal of Economic Theory*, vol. 4, pp. 98–100.

Shorrocks, A.F. (1978). Income inequality and income mobility. *Journal of Economic Theory*, vol. 19, pp. 376–393.

Shorrocks, A.F. (1980). The class of additively decomposable inequality measures. *Econometrica*, vol. 48, pp. 613–625.

Shorrocks, A.F. (1982). Inequality decomposition by factor components. *Econometrica*, vol. 50, pp. 193–211.

Shorrocks, A.F. (1983a). Ranking income distributions. *Economica*, vol. 50, pp. 3–17.

Shorrocks, A.F. (1983b). The impact of income components on the distribution of family incomes. *Quarterly Journal of Economics*, vol. 98, pp. 311–326.

Shorrocks, A.F. (1984). Inequality decomposition by population subgroups. *Econometrica*, vol. 52, pp. 1369–1385.

Shorrocks, A.F. (1988). Aggregation issues in inequality measurement. In W. Eichhorn (ed.) *Measurement in Economics: Theory and Applications of Economic Indices*. Heidelberg: Physica-Verlag.

Shorrocks, A.F. (1995). Revisiting the Sen poverty index. *Econometrica*, vol. 63, pp. 1225–1230.

Shorrocks, A.F. (1998). Deprivation profiles and deprivation indices, in S.P. Jenkins, A. Kapteyn and B.M.S. van Praag (eds) *The Distribution of Household Welfare and Household Production: International Perspectives*. Cambridge: Cambridge University Press.

Shorrocks A.F. and J. Foster (1987). Transfer sensitive inequality measures. *Review of Economic Studies*, vol. 54, pp. 485–497.

Shoup, C.S. (1988). Distribution of benefits from government services: horizontal equity. *Public Finance/Finances Publiques*, vol. 43, pp. 1–18.

Silber, J. (1989). Factor components, population subgroups and the computation of the Gini index of inequality. *Review of Economics and Statistics*, vol. 71, pp. 107–115.

Slemrod, J.B. (1994). *Tax Progressivity and Income Inequality*. Cambridge: Cambridge University Press.

Snow, A. and R.S. Warren (1983). Tax progression in Lindahl equilibrium. *Economics Letters*, vol. 12, pp. 319–326.

Snyder, J.M. and G.H. Kramer (1988). Fairness, self-interest, and the politics of the progressive income tax. *Journal of Public Economics*, vol. 36, pp. 197–230.

Spencer, B.D. and S. Fisher (1992). On comparing distributions of poverty gaps. *Sankhyā: The Indian Journal of Statistics*, Series B, vol. 54, pp. 114–126.

Stark, O. and S. Yitzhaki (1988). Merging populations, stochastic dominance and Lorenz curves. *Journal of Population Economics*, vol. 1, pp. 157–161.

Statistics of Income: Individual Income Tax Returns (annually). Washington D.C.: Internal Revenue Service.

Stern, N. (1977). The marginal valuation of income. Pages 209–257 in M.J. Artis and A.R. Nobay (eds) *Essays in Economic Analysis*. Cambridge: Cambridge University Press.

Steuerle, E. (1983). The tax treatment of households of different size, in R.G. Penner (ed.) *Taxing The Family.* Washington DC: American Enterprise Institute.

Strobel, F. (1993). *Upward Dreams, Downward Mobility: the Economic Decline of the American Middle Class.* Maryland: Rowman & Littlefield.

Suits, D. (1977). Measurement of tax progressivity. *American Economic Review,* vol. 67, pp. 747–752.

Survey of Personal Incomes (annual). London: Inland Revenue Statistical Division.

Takayama, N. (1979). Poverty, income inequality and their measures: Professor Sen's axiomatic approach reconsidered. *Econometrica,* vol. 47, pp. 747–759.

Tchen, A.H.T. (1980). Inequalities for distributions with given marginals. *Annals of Probability,* vol. 8, pp. 814–827.

Theil, H. (1967). *Economics and Information Theory.* Amsterdam: North Holland.

Thistle, P.D. (1989a). Uniform progressivity, residual progression and single-crossing. *Journal of Public Economics,* vol. 37, pp. 121–126.

Thistle, P.D. (1989b). Ranking distributions with generalized Lorenz curves. *Southern Economic Journal,* vol. 56, pp. 1–12.

Thistle, P.D. (1994). On Atkinson's index and consensus in rankings of income distributions. Pages 193–208 in W. Eichhorn (ed.) *Models and Measurement of Welfare and Inequality.* Heidelberg: Springer Verlag.

Thistle, P.D. (1997). Generalized probabilistic egalitarianism. Mimeo, University of Nevada at Las Vegas.

Thon, D. (1979). On measuring poverty. *Review of Income and Wealth,* vol. 25, pp. 429–440.

Thon, D. (1983). A note on a troublesome axiom for poverty indices. *Economic Journal,* vol. 93, pp. 199–200.

Thon, D. (1987). Redistributive properties of progressive taxation. *Mathematical Social Sciences,* vol. 14, pp. 185–191.

Tobin, J. (1971). On limiting the domain of inequality. *Journal of Law and Economics,* vol. 13, pp. 263–277.

Townsend, P. (1985). A sociological approach to the measurement of poverty – a rejoinder to Professor Amartya Sen. *Oxford Economic Papers,* vol. 37, pp. 659–668. Reply by Amartya Sen: *ibid.,* pp. 669–676.

Toyoda, T. (1980). Decomposability of inequality measures. *Economic Studies Quarterly,* vol. 31, pp. 207–216.

Tsui, K.-Y. (1995). Multidimensional generalizations of the relative and absolute inequality indices: the Atkinson–Kolm–Sen approach. *Journal of Economic Theory,* vol. 67, pp. 251–265.

Tsui, K.-Y. (1998). Multidimensional inequality and multidimensional generalized entropy measures. *Social Choice and Welfare,* vol. 16, pp. 145–157.

Tsui, K.-Y. (2001). Multidimensional poverty indices. *Social Choice and Welfare,* forthcoming.

van de Ven, J., J. Creedy and P.J. Lambert (1999). Close equals and calculation of the vertical, horizontal and reranking effects of taxation. *Oxford Bulletin of Economics and Statistics,* forthcoming.

van Doorslaer, E. and 23 other authors (1999). The redistributive effect of health care finance in twelve OECD countries. *Journal of Health Economics,* vol. 18, pp. 291–313.

Vaughan, R.N. (1987). Welfare approaches to the measurement of poverty. *Economic Journal*, vol. 97, pp. 160–170.

Vickrey, W.S. (1945). Measuring marginal utility by reaction to risk. *Econometrica*, vol. 13, pp. 319–333.

Vickrey, W.S. (1947). *Agenda for Progressive Taxation*. New York: Ronald Press.

Watts, H. (1968). An economic definition of poverty. In D.P. Moynihan (ed.) *On Understanding Poverty: Perspectives from the Social Sciences*. New York: Basic Books.

Wertz, K.L. (1978). A method for measuring the relative taxation of families. *Review of Economics and Statistics*, vol. 60, pp. 145–150.

Weymark, J.A. (1981). Generalized Gini inequality indices. *Mathematical Social Sciences*, vol. 1, pp. 409–430.

White, M. and A. White (1965). Horizontal inequality in the federal income tax treatment of homeowners and tenants. *National Tax Journal*, vol. 18, pp. 225–239.

Whitmore, G.A. (1970). Third degree stochastic dominance. *American Economic Review*, vol. 24, pp. 617–628.

Wilfling, B. and W. Krämer (1993). The Lorenz-ordering of Singh-Maddala income distributions. *Economics Letters*, vol. 43, pp. 53–57.

Willis, J.R.M. and P.J.W. Hardwick (1978). *Tax Expenditures in the United Kingdom*. London: Heinemann.

Wolfson, M.C. (1994). When inequalities diverge. *American Economic Review (AEA Papers and Proceedings)*, vol. 84, pp. 353–358.

Wolfson, M.C. (1997). Divergent inequalities: theory and empirical results. *Review of Income and Wealth*, vol. 43, pp. 401–421.

Yaari, M.E. (1981). Rawls, Edgeworth, Shapley, Nash: theories of justice re-examined. *Journal of Economic Theory*, vol. 24, pp. 1–39.

Yaari, M.E. (1987). The dual theory of choice under risk. *Econometrica*, vol. 55, pp. 99–115.

Yaari, M.E. (1988). A controversial proposal concerning inequality measurement. *Journal of Economic Theory*, vol. 44, pp. 381–397.

Yitzhaki, S. (1983). On an extension of the Gini index. *International Economic Review*, vol. 24, pp. 617–628.

Yitzhaki, S. (1988). On stratification and inequality in Israel. *Bank of Israel Economic Review*, vol. 63, pp. 36–51.

Yitzhaki, S. (1994a). Economic distance and overlapping of distributions, *Journal of Econometrics*, vol. 61, pp. 147–159.

Yitzhaki, S. (1994b). On the progressivity of commodity taxation. In W. Eichhorn (ed.) *Models and Measurement of Welfare and Inequality*, pp. 448–465. Heidelberg: Springer Verlag.

Yitzhaki, S. (1998). More than a dozen alternative ways of spelling Gini, *Research on Economic Inequality*, vol. 8, pp. 13–30.

Yitzhaki, S. (2001). Do we need a separate poverty measurement? European Journal of Political Economy, forthcoming.

Yitzhaki, S. and R.I. Lerman (1991). Income stratification and income inequality. *Review of Income and Wealth*, vol. 37, pp. 313–329.

Yitzhaki, S. and J. Lewis (1996). Guidelines on searching for Dalton-improving tax reforms: illustrations with data from Indonesia, *The World Bank Economic Review*, vol. 10, pp. 541–562.

Young, H.P. (1988). Equal sacrifice in taxation. In W. Eichhorn (ed.) *Measurement in Economics: Theory and Applications of Economic Indices.* Heidelberg: Physica-Verlag.

Young, H.P. (1990). Progressive taxation and equal sacrifice. *American Economic Review*, vol. 80, pp. 253–266.

Zagier, D. (1983). Inequalities for the Gini coefficient of composite populations. *Journal of Mathematical Economics*, vol. 12, pp. 103–118.

Zheng, B. (1994). Can a poverty index be both relative and absolute? *Econometrica*, vol. 62, pp. 1453–1458.

Zheng, B. (1997). Aggregate poverty measures. *Journal of Economic Surveys*, vol. 11, pp. 123–162.

Zheng, B. (1999). On the power of poverty orderings. *Social Choice and Welfare*, vol. 16, pp. 349–371.

Zheng, B. (2000a). Poverty orderings: a review. *Journal of Economic Surveys*, vol. 14, pp. 427–466.

Zheng, B. (2000b). Minimum distribution-sensitivity, poverty aversion and poverty orderings. *Journal of Economic Theory*, vol. 95, pp. 116–137.

Zheng, B. (2001). Poverty orderings: a graphical illustration. *Social Choice and Welfare*, vol. 18, pp. 165–178.

Zoli, C. (1999a). Intersecting generalized Lorenz curves and the Gini index. *Social Choice and Welfare*, vol. 16, pp. 183–196.

Zoli, C. (1999b). A generalized version of the inequality equivalence criterion: a surplus sharing characterization, complete and partial orderings, in H. de Swart (ed.) *Logic, Game Theory and Social Choice.* Tilburg: Tilburg University Press.

Zoli, C. (2000). Inverse sequential stochastic dominance: rank-dependent welfare, deprivation and poverty measurement. Economics Discussion Paper No. 00/11, University of Nottingham.

Index

CPSIA information can be obtained at www.ICGtesting.com
Printed in the USA
BVOW03s2349140813

328512BV00002B/38/P

9 780719 057328